BRIAN BURRELL

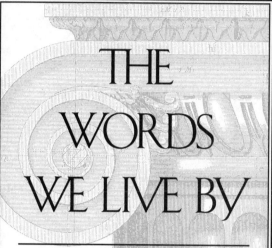

THE
WORDS
WE LIVE BY

THE CREEDS, MOTTOES,

AND PLEDGES THAT HAVE

SHAPED AMERICA

THE FREE PRESS

NEW YORK   LONDON   TORONTO   SYDNEY   SINGAPORE

THE FREE PRESS
A Division of Simon & Schuster Inc.
1230 Avenue of the Americas
New York, NY 10020

THE FREE PRESS and colophon are trademarks of Simon & Schuster
Inc.

Designed by Pei Koay

Manufactured in the United States of America

10   9   8   7   6   5   4   3   2   1

Library of Congress Cataloging-in-Publication Data

Burrell, Brian, 1955–
    The words we live by: the creeds, mottoes, and pledges
    that have shaped America / Brian Burrell.
        p.   cm.
    Includes bibliographical references (p.   ) and index.
    ISBN 0–684–83001–9
    1. National characteristics, American—Quotations, maxims,
etc. 2. Conduct of life—United States—Quotations, maxims,
etc. 3. Social values—United States—quotations, maxims, etc.
I. Title.
E169.1.B948   1997
170'.44—dc21   96–53537
                                                          CIP

Credits are listed on page 369.

FOR MY MOTHER AND FATHER

CONTENTS

PART TWO: THE TEXTS

PREFACE

On a cold, dreary evening in the early spring of 1962 a man parked his rented car near the Robert Taft Memorial in Washington, D.C. Turning to his six-year-old son sitting on the seat beside him, he said, "Wait here, I'll be right back," whereupon he grabbed a notebook and dashed over to the base of the monument. As the young boy patiently waited, his father took out a pen and began to copy down the words inscribed in the stone while shielding the paper from the light rain. When he was finished, he walked back to the car, handed the notebook to his son, and they drove off.

On subsequent business trips over the next decade, often with one child or another in tow, the same scenario was repeated in all kinds of weather and at all times of day or night. Gradually, the father's collection began to fill a folder, and then a large, white loose-leaf binder. In addition to inscriptions from monuments, it included legends and trivia from the place mat menus of roadside diners, mottoes printed on the backs of postcards from historic sites, and newspaper clippings about oaths and pledges. It also contained some outlandish fraternal initiation formulas, codes of ethics of florists and knitted underwear manufacturers, and such esoterica as the statement of purpose of the Barnstable (Mass.) Babe Ruth League.

As the years passed the son would occasionally wander into his father's office at home. The room was not officially off limits, although its somewhat exotic contents made it seem so. In plain view were a few mementos of the Pacific theater—mostly small statues from Korea and Japan. But the desk drawers contained the real treasure—a Distinguished Flying Cross, an Asian-Pacific Campaign Medal, various wings, stars, bars, and a pair of anchor-and-eagle cufflinks. There was also a German Luger and a Zippo lighter with Marine Corps insignia.

While the boy found these things to be interesting, he felt no particular connection to them. Instead, his attention was increasingly drawn to the white loose-leaf binder that sat propped upon a shelf. Taped, typed, and inserted between its covers, a trove of ancient and modern creeds, sacred oaths and pledges, solemn codes, mottoes of great institutions, golden rules of life, and architectural inscriptions from near and far afforded the boy a glimpse into a fantastical world.

The wondrous collection bore the title *The Words People Live By*, and it seemed to encompass the wisdom of the ages, the secrets of the temple, indeed the very fabric of civilization. Within its motley pages the boy discovered the Latin creeds he silently mouthed at church each week, the pledge he recited in school every morning, and the professional codes followed by his doctor and dentist. He came upon the coronation oaths sworn by the kings of England alongside the oath of office of the President of the United States, the Marquess of Queensberry Rules next to Parkinson's Law. He learned that "Wisdom and Knowledge Shall Be the Stability of Thy Times," at least according to an inscription at New York's Rockefeller Center, where his father had once taken him.

After immersing himself in his father's collection he could reel off the motto of the Order of the Garter (*Honi soit qui mal y pense*—Shame to him who thinks evil of it), the inscription over the entrance to the locker room at Notre Dame's football stadium ("Pride, Pride, Pride"), and the cardinal rule of coaching according to John Wooden ("Repetition is the last law of learning").

From time to time he would have occasion to reflect on these words. For example, one night on the village green at Lexington, Massachusetts, the Vietnam Veterans Against the War staged a rally and were arrested along with what seemed like half the town. It all happened across the street from the boy's house, just outside his bedroom window, in what is called the Birthplace of American Liberty. At the edge of the scene, where that night the school buses were lined up waiting to cart away the protesters, there is a rock inscribed with Captain John Parker's order to the Minutemen on April 19, 1775. The boy knew it by heart. "Stand your ground. Don't fire unless fired upon. But if they mean to have a war, let it begin here."

A few years later the boy went off to college. While he was away one president resigned, and another president, who had been sworn in to restore America's faith in the Constitution, came to Lexington to commemorate the bicentennial of the shot heard round the world. He gave a speech at the foot of the Minuteman statue, which just happened to be across the street from the boy's father's office, in which the white binder sat on the bookshelf gathering dust.

THE MARINE CORPS MEDALS and the dog tags are in my desk now, as is the binder. My father turned them over to me some time ago and moved on to other things. He continues to send me clippings in envelopes marked "for the book," because I decided to see if I could finish what he had started.

While growing up I accompanied my father from Plymouth Rock to Cape Canaveral, from the Old North Church to the top of the Empire State Building. Everywhere we went, whether on vacation or on business trips, we had our own business to attend to, even if I didn't always know exactly what it was. As a child I never bothered to ask him why he collected these words. The answer seemed obvious—they fascinated him, so they interested me, and that was that.

But there was more to it. Each week the newspapers seemed to unearth a new controversy that hinged on a few words—an oath of office, a professional code of conduct, a motto, or a mission statement. It might involve a dereliction of duty, a breach of ethics, or a conscientious objection. And each time the writer would stumble over the phrases that defined the issue. Who said them, who wrote them, and how did they come to be used in this way?

In my father's loose-leaf notebook I came up against a great number of questions that I knew I would someday have to answer if I wanted to escape the frustrations of not knowing. What was it that led him to stand in the cold rain at the foot of the Taft Memorial? What *are* the words we live by? Where do they come from? Why do they persist while so many other things fade away? Among the many things he has given me, my father gave me these questions and the need to find their answers. This book describes some of what I found.

INTRODUCTION

We are nothing but ceremony; ceremony carries us away, and we leave the substance of things; we hang onto the branches and abandon the trunk and body.

Michel de Montaigne, Essays, II, 17 "Of Presumption"

In 1966 the Supreme Court ruled that police officers must advise those they arrest of their right to remain silent and of their right to counsel. As a result, the Miranda rights, as they are called, came to be spelled out in words that are by now familiar to just about every American who has ever seen a television crime story.

When Miranda became law, prosecutors and lawmen around the country worried that it would interfere with their ability to obtain confessions. Yet their fears proved groundless. Over time, as it became second nature for a policeman to read a suspect the statement of his Miranda rights, it became just as routine for the suspect to ignore it. One judge concluded that, "when an arresting officer reads from that small card in his hat or pocket, telling a suspect in custody that he has the right to remain silent, that anything he says may be used in evidence against him, and so forth, the officer might as well be reading the batting order of the New York Mets."

And yet the Miranda statement exists for a very important reason—to ensure that the Fifth Amendment to the Constitution (the provision that no one may be forced to incriminate himself) is properly observed. Whether or not an officer reads a suspect his rights is a crucial point, one upon which the admissibility of a confession depends. The actual words, on the other hand, seem almost beside the point.

THE MIRANDA WARNING is typical of the kinds of words that my father used to collect in the scrapbook he labeled "The Words People Live By." Part of what attracted him to such statements was a compelling paradox—that widespread acceptance can lead to a kind of obscurity. What is well-known, it turns out, is not necessarily well understood. For example, the Miranda warning, having lost its urgency through repetition and wide exposure, is now taken for granted; few of us can say precisely what it means or how it came to exist. Like countless other expressions that are spoken daily, referred to frequently, or hidden in plain sight, it remains essentially a mystery to all but a few specialists. The same fate has befallen many other items that found their way into my father's collection. The Nicene Creed and the Pledge of Allegiance, for example, have also become conditioned responses. Their texts come easily to mind—so easily that it does not occur to most people to ask themselves what they are saying, why they are saying it, and in what sense they live by it.

When my father first began collecting expressions such as these in the 1960s, he was inspired by a wonderfully eclectic anthology entitled *A Treasury of the Familiar*, edited by Ralph L. Woods. A collection of poems, speeches, famous letters, and historic documents, the anthology's title evokes "the familiar" in the most familiar sense of the word: well-known from constant association and everyday use. The *Treasury* featured, not surprisingly, some of the best-loved and most inspiring works in the popular canon—poems such as "The Rime of the Ancient Mariner," "Casey at the Bat," "The Wreck of the Hesperus," and "Ozymandias"; speeches such as George Washington's Farewell Address, Lincoln's Gettysburg Address, and Patrick Henry's "Give me liberty or give me death" address; as well as excerpts from the works of Shakespeare, Daniel Webster, and Mark Twain. And yet with the passage of time, as rote memorization has disappeared from public school curricula, treasures such as these become more known *of* than known. At best they are "familiar" in a different sense of the word: possibly known, but imperfectly remembered.

This is what my father was getting at with his own collection—the very things which seem to us to be the most familiar, the most integral to our lives, are by consequence the things we tend to take the most for granted.

THE WORDS WE LIVE BY / 3

Of course he had his eye on something much more specific than did Ralph Woods. While we often turn to poems and stories for inspiration, we "live by" them only in the imagination. They may shape some of our attitudes and even our sense of identity, but this rarely evidences itself in our day-to-day activities. There is, however, a body of literature, to which the Miranda statement belongs, which does more than shape our identity. It defines our sense of duty, determines the scope and substance of many of our activities, and holds together many, if not all, of our institutions.

Woods's *Treasury* contained only a handful of formulas of this type—among them the Boy Scout Oath, the Ten Commandments, the Hippocratic Oath, and the inscription on the New York Post Office. What sets these apart from the rest of Woods's collection is that they do more than inspire; they give direction. They provide a vocabulary of belief, intention, and commitment that we tend to accept more or less unquestioningly. This is what I assumed my father was after: rules of life that are familiar enough to be referred to in general conversation, yet are still prone to frequent misquotation and misapplication. What I would eventually discover as I explored further is that what allows such formulas to sustain a consensus of popular opinion is their inherent vagueness.

Nowhere is this more true than in the United States, where texts as momentous as the Declaration of Independence, as imposing as the inscription above the entrance to the Supreme Court Building ("Equal Justice Under Law"), and as irreverent as Murphy's and Parkinson's laws have become cultural icons. What they have in common is that they provide a shorthand approach to complex ideas and, naturally, not everyone manages to get them right.

For example, the words affixed to the New York Post Office—"Neither snow nor rain nor heat nor gloom of night stays these couriers from the swift completion of their appointed rounds"—are widely believed to be the official motto of the U.S. Postal Service. But this is not their motto at all, or even their unofficial policy. It is merely what one inspired architect thought would be a fitting inscription for the building. Still, the public has come to regard it as a sacred trust. It creates an expectation that is not always lived up to, and can lead to some good-natured chiding when it is not.

Another example, the Hippocratic Oath, is commonly believed to be the binding legal code of the medical profession. Yet it is hardly used anymore at medical school graduation ceremonies. Even at the peak of its popularity it was never anything more than ceremonial. Still, the name alone manages to represent the idea of professional duty.

WHEN I TOOK IT upon myself to expand my father's wide-ranging collection into a book, I set out to find a unifying thesis that would explain why we adopt so many expressions that we do not entirely understand. The most plausible explanation I could find, perhaps not surprisingly, comes from Alexis de Tocqueville's *Democracy in America*, which has the unfortunate distinction of being the most indiscriminately overquoted book ever written on American culture. Yet it is strangely appropriate that Tocqueville should provide the theme of this book, since this very theme explains how he himself, a brilliant social observer, has devolved into little more than a steady source of pithy and ironic epigrams.

What is most remarkable about Tocqueville is that as early as the 1830s he was able to recognize certain defining American traits and tendencies that have remained fairly constant; much of what he wrote seems no less true today. Perhaps only a disinterested foreigner could have seen through to the essence of the American character, and Tocqueville seemed to understand from the outset that a society founded on the principle of equality would produce a citizenry that thinks accordingly, which is to say, differently.

Tocqueville begins the second volume of *Democracy in America* by observing that in order for any society to function, "it is necessary that the minds of all the citizens should be rallied and held together by certain predominant ideas." Unable to prove all things to their own satisfaction, "men will never cease to entertain some opinions on trust and without discussion." Fair enough. We all gravitate towards catch phrases and seize upon general rules that provide ready answers to difficult questions. But to Tocqueville, Americans appeared to present a special and extreme case. In order to establish a common identity with our fellow citizens, he observed, we assent to, cling to, and even fight over beliefs and practices that we do not fully understand.

On his visit to the United States in 1831, Tocqueville noticed that the Americans he encountered tended to exhibit two opposing tendencies: they did not want to be told what to do or think, and yet their collective will could easily be rallied behind certain carefully chosen words, to which he gave a name. "In the United States, Tocqueville concluded, "the majority undertakes to supply a multitude of ready-made opinions for the use of individuals who are thus relieved from having to form opinions of their own."

And what are these ready-made opinions? Tocqueville did not give examples, but my father found plenty. The Pledge of Allegiance, the Golden Rule, "In God We Trust," and any number of expressions that we accept out of convenience, or simply out of habit, certainly seem to qualify. Many of them have wound up as the cornerstones of some of our most revered institutions.

There is probably no more succinct illustration of Tocqueville's ready-made opinions at work than a passage from Sinclair Lewis's *Babbitt*, a novel which chronicles the mid-life crisis of a small city businessman in the 1920s. If I needed any further confirmation that Tocqueville and my father were onto something, this was it. Lewis succeeds brilliantly in capturing the way many of us speak in a kind of code that masks what we really feel. Here, in a thumbnail sketch of the title character, Lewis describes how ready-made opinions permeate one man's life.

> Just as he was an Elk, a Booster, and a member of the Chamber of Commerce, just as the priests of the Presbyterian Church determined his every religious belief and the senators who controlled the Republican Party decided in little smoky rooms what he should think about disarmament, tariff, and Germany, so did large national advertisers fix the surface of his life, fix what he believed to be his individuality. These standard advertised wares . . . were his symbols and proofs of excellence; at first the signs, then the substitutes, for joy and passion and wonder.

George Babbitt's taste in ideas is fixed by the conversations at his barber shop, the editorials in his daily newspaper, and the posturings of his fellow businessmen. But these are not the only opinions to which he subscribes. There are other, far more formal expressions that govern his affairs. Unthinkingly, he assents to the creed of his church, the code of his profession, the oath of his lodge, the rules of his booster club, the vows he swore at his wedding, his fraternity motto, and no doubt the Boy Scout Laws and the Pledge of Allegiance.

Like most of us, George Babbitt proposes to live by a host of opinions that he has never bothered to examine. Formal expressions of principle and purpose have become so finely woven into the fabric of his life that he barely notices them, even though they constrict his every movement. So unthinking is his acceptance of them that he ends up cheating on his wife, breaking several other commandments, and transgressing the few principles his business association bothers to maintain, all without fully comprehending the difference between his actions and his words. He becomes vaguely aware that he has inherited a code that he never asked for. Ironically, this code, which he feels is tearing his life apart, is also what holds it together.

George Babbitt is left exhausted by the contradictions in his life because he fails to comprehend the language that allows his community to function, and he is not alone in his confusion. Can any of us claim to fully understand the words we supposedly live by, or appreciate to what extent we live by them? Obviously not, but my father, for one, wanted to try.

THIS BOOK IS about creeds, oaths, codes of ethics, rules, mottoes, and inscriptions, and the role they play in our lives. That is, it concerns the ready-made opinions we use to profess belief, swear allegiance, and guide actions—words that serve as public expressions of good citizenship, as tests of solidarity, and as the tenets of conventional wisdom. These words, by defining and maintaining our institutions, give a semblance of order, value, and stability to our lives. Many of them have become institutions in themselves.

To what extent does the majority supply these statements (as Tocqueville suggested)? It would be more accurate to say that they are taken up by the majority. As this book sets out to show, the wide variety of formulas that have achieved institutional status in American life were produced by a rather select group. Their usage, however, continues to be shaped by the multitude. Once the words gain a foothold in the public imagination, their meaning can change, often in unpredictable ways.

E Pluribus Unum, for example, a national motto chosen at the time of the country's founding (but not the *official* national motto), means "one from many," being a reference to one nation formed from the union of thirteen individual colonies. In this century the motto has shed this meaning, and it now refers to one nation consisting of many peoples—a multicultural and inclusive idea that would have been lost on the Founding Fathers, who conceived of America as a homogeneous society of transplanted Europeans.

Such expressions are not perfect, but their imperfections are part of their essential American-ness. The Pledge of Allegiance, for example, is less than half as old as the flag itself, and did not assume its current form until the 1950s. It has been used as a political football and as a rigid test of conformity; it has caused much anguish and even incited violence. But having settled into its place in American society, it now serves the purpose which it was created to serve, which is to instill pride and to teach respect for the ideals laid down by the Founders. Ironically, it is because of those very ideals that no one is forced to recite it (although this was not always the case). Yet most people do swear it, everyone manages to live with it, and the country is better for it if only because it serves as a source of discussion, even disagreement, about who we are.

It is one of American society's greatest strengths that it can tolerate many opposing points of view and still sustain a high level of cooperation and community. This is made possible, in part, by the adaptability of expressions such as *E Pluribus Unum* and "In God We Trust." Historian Samuel P. Huntington has pointed out that the American system of government, which relies heavily on written statements of principle and purpose, harbors a natural tension between its institutions and the ideals they were founded to serve. When Americans disagree, he says, it is not over the principles themselves (because almost all Americans assent to the validity of the country's founding principles), but whether those principles are being effectively served. The controversies that have swirled around the Pledge of Allegiance provide one of the more dramatic illustrations of Huntington's contention that "it is the peculiar fate of Americans that the beliefs that unite them as a nation should also divide them as a people."

This is a sobering thought, but one that takes on a much more positive spin when it is flipped around: Americans may be divided on many particulars of belief, but it is their good fortune to be united as a nation behind certain predominant ideas, most of which someone had the good sense to write down.

I HAVE DIVIDED THIS BOOK into two parts. Part I is about the words themselves—who wrote them, how they achieved their place in American culture, and what they have come to mean as opposed to what they actually say. Part II is something closer to what my father originally had in mind. It is an anthology that gives some idea of the variety of institutional expressions in American life. It contains many formulas that are too long or too peripheral to the discussion to be included in Part I. Admittedly, some of them have been included for no other reason than that they appeared in the scrapbook I pored over as a child, and I happened to like them.

I have retained my father's original system of classification in dividing the book into chapters. This approach acknowledges how Western culture has produced certain familiar archetypes—golden rules, creeds, pledges of allegiance and loyalty, initiation oaths, codes of ethics, rules, advice, and mottoes—which have infiltrated the American language. I have also included a chapter devoted to one of my father's favorite sources of words to live by: architectural inscriptions.

Among the chapters some overlap is unavoidable. After all, the line that separates a creed from an oath, code, or motto is not always clearly drawn. The Declaration of Independence, for example, begins as a creed, continues as a kind of code (actually as a list of transgressions against a code of civil government), and ends with a resounding pledge. This mixing of genres is not unusual. What some people refer to as their creed is often more properly their code, or perhaps nothing more than a motto. Many codes of ethics read like oaths; some begin in creedal form with the words "I believe." In Chapter Five the Hippocratic Oath is grouped with codes of professional ethics because it serves as a code even though it reads like an oath. It is printed in its entirety along with other professional codes in Part II.

IN HIS PREFACE TO *Democracy in America*, Tocqueville notes, "I confess that in America I saw more than America; I sought the image of democracy itself, with its inclinations, its character, its prejudices, and its passions, in order to learn what we have to fear or to hope for from its progress." This journey through the landscape of America's ready-made opinions affords a similar prospect. Of course it shows more than America itself. Creeds, codes, oaths, mottoes, and architectural inscriptions were invented by earlier civilizations. But when they were imported to the New World they assumed a distinctively local character. American credos, codes of business practices, patriotic mottoes, rules for success, pledges of allegiance, loyalty oaths, and, of course, stately monuments inscribed with inspiring words— these are the accessories of belief that Americans still acknowledge every day.

The aim of this book is to show how these words quietly influence our attitudes and opinions. At the same time it serves as a collection that tolerates, if not embraces, some odd juxtapositions. What do the Apostles' Creed and the creed of the Elvis Presley Imitators International Association have in common? Or the Mafia initiation oath and the Sunbeam Pledge? Occam's Razor and Murphy's Law? A similarity of form—though just barely. More striking is their similarity of purpose. They reflect an effort to make sense of things, to organize society, and to understand ourselves.

TO THAT END, we begin at the beginning, with what Confucius, some twenty-five hundred years ago, called "a rule of practice for all one's life." This most fundamental of all ethical principles—the Golden Rule—has outlived every great civilization and empire, only to wind up as a historical oddity in American culture, where it lies buried in our overstuffed attic of received ideas. If we can find it, polish it up, and consider it in the light of day, we might better appreciate what we have.

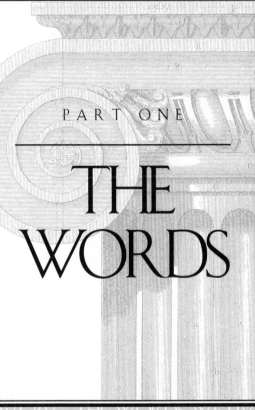

PART ONE

THE
WORDS

DEAL WITH ANOTHER AS YOU'D HAVE
ANOTHER DEAL WITH YOU;
WHAT YOU'RE UNWILLING TO RECEIVE
BE SURE YOU'D NEVER DO.

THE NEW ENGLAND PRIMER

CHAPTER ONE

DO UNTO OTHERS

THE EVOLUTION OF THE GOLDEN RULE

Whatever happened to the Golden Rule? It seems only yesterday it was a figure of everyday speech, an idea so familiar and unassailable that it could confidently be invoked by name alone. In the booming 1920s the Western Implement Dealers Association made "Obey the Golden Rule!" the very first precept of its code of ethics. The Concatenated Order of Hoo-Hoo (also known as the Fraternal Order of Lumbermen) endorsed it as nothing less than "the basic principle of peace and prosperity for the world." Roger Ward Babson, investment wizard and the founder of Babson College, went so far as to claim that "the Golden Rule is founded on the same law of Action and Reaction about which Sir Isaac Newton wrote the *Principia*."

From today's perspective these breathless endorsements seem quaintly naive, if not disingenuous. We still refer to the Golden Rule, but much more tentatively. It seems to have lost its glister, tarnished to no small degree by the cataclysmic events of the twentieth century. Yet even at the height of its popularity it was something of an enigma. It was never entirely clear, even to its staunchest supporters, what was so golden about it.

To many Americans, the very name still sums up the essence of Christian ethics. The Golden Rule epitomizes the Christian virtue of charity in thought and action, which is both an extraordinary reduction and a compelling one. It naturally leads to such questions as: How can anyone be a Christian and a racist at the same time? That is, how can one embrace the Golden Rule and yet hate one's fellow man? The answer, not only for Christians but for people of all faiths (because every religion has its own version of the same golden principle), is that it's impossible—in theory. Yet it is all too common in practice. And this is where the promise held out by the name is not fulfilled.

The Golden Rule, after all, is not a binding law but merely a figure of speech. Its strength lies in its ability to compress all of ethics into one sentence. It principal weakness, not surprisingly, is its generality. How could anything so simple serve as a rule for all men for all time? Yet the fact remains that it has done just that, and apparently continues to do so. Just as the heavens revolve around the polestar, the course of human events seems to swirl around the Golden Rule. But like the polestar, its constancy can only be appreciated through the lens of time—through a consideration of its past. Without some sense of its history, the rule remains unavailable to us.

Is It Just?

In American culture, what goes by the name of the Golden Rule seems on the surface to be a simple proposition: Do as you would be done by. But is it really all that simple? From its apparent beginnings as a Victorian platitude promoted by children's primers, catechisms, and embroidered samplers, this modest proposition somehow acquired the status of a self-evident truth—one of the pillars of the American way of life. When the great Civil War–era statesman Charles Sumner died, the poet John Greenleaf Whittier could write with no irony, "His statecraft was the Golden Rule/ His right of vote a sacred trust/ Clear, over threat and ridicule/ All heard his challenge: 'Is it just?'" Whittier's contemporary, William Dean Howells, in his 1884 novel *The Rise of Silas Lapham*, has one character reprimand another by saying, "In our dealings with each other we should be guided by the Golden Rule."

What Whittier seems to imply is that Sumner always did unto others as he wished to be done unto. But the poet was hardly in a position to know. It seems more likely that Whittier is using the term Golden Rule in a more general way. Charles Sumner apparently lived up to a standard of conduct which clearly distinguished right from wrong. We just don't know what that standard was, and neither did Whittier.

In *Silas Lapham*, on the other hand, Howells's down-on-his-luck character seems to be getting at something else entirely. What he wants, alas, is
a handout—a misreading of the rule which hints at another fundamental
weakness: that the Golden Rule can be construed as a demand to do for
others what you would wish for yourself if you were in the same pitiful
plight. In both instances the rule is invoked in earnest, yet with no apparent insight. It is not at all clear what it means.

Back then it hardly mattered. In Whittier's time, as compared to today,
Americans were less self-conscious, and more apt to speak and believe in
platitudes. To "go by" the Golden Rule or any one of hundreds of old saws
meant to draw from a common fount of received ideas which were not to
be taken too literally. A populace schooled in proverbial wisdom understood in what sense "golden" meant fitting and proper, and they accepted
it. But now, with our sense of disbelief not so easily suspended, we are less
inclined to take things at face value. As a result, we are often left without a
clue as to how some of our culture's most common axioms work. This is
one of the central paradoxes of the words invoked by this book's title: we
have come to accept, and even embrace, a host of expressions we barely
understand. The Golden Rule is perhaps the most glaring case in point.

LIKE ALMOST ALL aphoristic wisdom, the Golden Rule was neither new
nor unique to America. It was part of our inheritance. Long before even
Benjamin Franklin came along someone had already pointed out that time
is money, that people who live in glass houses shouldn't throw stones, and
that God helps those that help themselves. Franklin's unique talent was to
be able to recast these nuggets of age-old wisdom in a distinctly American
voice. Although not one of Poor Richard's concoctions, the Golden Rule
was also reinvented in American culture as a paragon of equity and fairness—a rule so simple that anyone could learn it and profit by it. Naturally,
almost everyone accepted it. But that was part of its problem. What started
out as the gospel truth soon turned into a deceptively solemn piece of
high-minded yet dissembling rhetoric—a symbol of good faith instead of
the real thing. By the 1920s the Golden Rule had become a throwaway
gesture in pretentious codes of ethics, and by the 1950s an obligatory
plank in every politician's political creed.

The Golden Rule's golden age (indeed the golden age of aphorisms) appears to have come and gone. Even politicians now shy away from using it.
As soon as it became an artifact of popular culture, it became all too easy

to write off. One of the Great Ideas that drifted into the mainstream, it has been buffeted about and cast upon the rocks of cynicism and doubt. Which naturally raises the question, is it worth rescuing?

If the name could be jettisoned, this would be a simpler matter. The problem with it, whether most people are aware of it or not (and for the most part they are not), is that it carries a wealth of historical, cultural, and religious associations that make it something more than a generic label. As a matter of historical fact, the name is a relatively recent development. The rule managed to circulate widely across all cultures for well over a thousand years without the benefit of a 10-karat name. Which is to say that what we so blithely call the Golden Rule turns out to be a complex idea with a long history—one that lies behind every philosopher's and theologian's attempt to understand how we should relate to each other. Despite its critics (and there have been many), it still has something useful to say. It is one of those rare artifacts in which the real treasure seems to lie beneath the gliding.

THE LAW AND THE PROPHETS

What exactly is the Golden Rule? Most of us think we know, although the word "exactly" should give us pause, because it implies (correctly) that the question cannot possibly be as simple as it seems.

Properly speaking, the term Golden Rule—capitalized—refers to a passage from the Sermon on the Mount. Of the two versions given in the Gospels of Matthew and Luke, Matthew's is the most widely accepted. Its most canonical English translation is the King James Version of 1611, which reads:

Therefore whatsoever ye would that others should do to you, do ye even so unto them.

Luke is more succinct:

As ye would that men should do to you, do ye also unto them likewise.

But in common parlance the name has become generic, and when not capitalized it can represent any number of seemingly equivalent statements. Those who cannot quote chapter and verse typically resort to such accessible variants as the nonscriptural "Do unto others as you would have others do unto you," or the even more abbreviated "Do as you would be done by." In Victorian America, schoolchildren often learned the Golden Rule in verse. The *New England Primer* rendered it this way:

Deal with another as you'd have
Another deal with you;
What you're unwilling to receive
Be sure you'd never do.

Isaac Watts, the English hymn writer, set the idea to music with this lyric:

Be you to others kind and true,
As you'd have others be to you;
And neither do nor say to men
Whate'er you would not take again.

Although these variations on a theme manage to get the same basic idea across, they should not be considered perfectly interchangeable. This should dispel a common assumption. In searching for connections we often forget how context (or a lack of it) can alter meaning. In the case of the Golden Rule, each rephrasing repackages an old idea, and in some cases the packaging (if not the label) overshadows the content.

To set the record straight, Matthew does not single out any passage from the Sermon on the Mount by giving it a name. In fact nowhere in the Bible does anyone refer to a "golden" rule. Nor did any of the Church fathers, in their lengthy disquisitions and interpretations of Scripture, use such a name. Saints Paul, Augustine, and Aquinas recognized the importance of what we call the Golden Rule within the system of Christian morality. Each of them subjected it to an extended analysis because they knew it required interpretation, but they did not think of it as particularly golden, or as an idea that should stand alone.

In Matthew's account, the maxim comes with this tag-line—"for this is the Law and the Prophets"—which is critical. It establishes the rule as a summary of Old Testament codes given in the biblical books referred to as the Law and the Prophets.* It is meant to be considered as part of a tradition of preexisting laws. When classical scholars refer to the Stoic Maxim, which is yet another version of the same rule stated in negative form ("Do *not* do to others what you do *not* wish them to do to you"), they invoke it

---

*The phrase "the Law and the Prophets" in this context may seem somewhat generic, but it is quite specific. The Law consists of the first five books of the Old Testament, which are also referred to as the Pentateuch or the Torah. The Prophets refers to the next division of scriptures, starting with the books of Joshua, Judges, 1 and 2 Samuel, 1 and 2 Kings, Isaiah, Jeremiah, Ezekiel, and including the twelve minor prophets from Hosea to Malachi. When Jesus and Hillel refer to the Law, they are addressing all of the laws and commandments, including the Ten Commandments, contained in these books.

within the context of Stoic philosophy as a whole. Which is to say that it can only be fully appreciated in context. This is one of the historical facts that the use of the term "golden rule" glosses over. When pious writers invoke the name, most have in mind the passage from Matthew or Luke, in many cases without being aware that the Law and the Prophets come with it, or that the Stoic philosophers promoted it, or that all of the great religions of antiquity acknowledged it, or that great thinkers of all cultures have long debated it. What the name did was to establish a virtual monopoly on the idea. Like a trademark, it legitimized Christianity's sole proprietorship over what would otherwise be in the public domain. The irony of the situation is that the term "golden rule" originally referred to something else entirely.

By the time Isaac Watts began referring to the Golden Rule in the mid-1700s, it was already an established figure of speech, although with two very different meanings. When it was first coined in the late 1500s, the term belonged properly to mathematics. It first shows up around the year 1575 to describe the Rule of Three, an algebraic procedure for solving proportions. A century would go by before anyone thought to use it to describe a type of reciprocity between people rather than numbers. When Watts and other devout writers got hold of it, they managed to wrest it away from mathematics, and solidify the usage that we have today.

Surprisingly, this usage did not take hold outside of the English-speaking world. The Germans, Italians, French, and Spanish have a term that is roughly equivalent to "golden rule," but in those cultures it has retained its primary sense of the mathematical Rule of Three. Only in Anglo-American culture does the name carry any cachet as a moral precept. And while the name made the scriptural maxim easy to refer to, the use of the word *golden* had a curious effect: it both elevated and trivialized the idea it described.

How did the naming come about? No doubt the King James Bible had something to do with it. Although not the first English translation of the Scriptures, the King James was the first one authorized to be read in churches, and thus it circulated widely. Its influence was felt in all of English literature, to the extent that it "established the rhythms of spoken English," as the *Encyclopaedia Britannica* asserts. With the gospels made accessible in the common tongue, isolated passages—many of them from the Sermon on the Mount—became more and more common in everyday speech.

By the mid-1600s the Golden Rule had become a frequently used (although still not named) expression among the scripturally literate, who began to abbreviate it, paraphrase it, and sing its praises. They hailed it, along with its counterpart *love thy neighbor as thyself*, as a new commandment, one that should rightfully stand beside the Ten Commandments as the embodiment of Christian morality. It must have seemed natural to give it a suitably exalted name.

The spirit of the Enlightenment also made a golden rule of morality seem plausible. The Age of Reason raised the possibility of the perfectibility of mankind, and laws of ethics laid out by such thinkers as Spinoza and Hobbes unfolded in empirical fashion much like the axioms of geometry and algebra, with the Golden Rule serving as a fundamental theorem. In those days the leap from mathematics to ethics did not appear to be a particularly dangerous one. Although the comment may now appear to be far-fetched, Roger Babson's comparison of the Golden Rule to Newton's law of actions and reactions was not an isolated crackpot idea, nor a particularly original one. In his Boyle lecture of 1705, the English metaphysician Samuel Clarke had said much the same thing: "Whatever I judge reasonable or unreasonable that another should do for me, that by the same judgment I declare reasonable or unreasonable that I in like case should do for him. And to deny this either in word or action is as if a man should contend that, though two and three are equal to five, yet three and two are not so."

But what is reasonable is not necessarily undeniable. Responding to this line of thinking in the *Encyclopaedia Britannica* almost two centuries later, the English philosopher Henry Sidgwick quipped, "Let us grant that there is as much intellectual absurdity in acting unjustly as in denying that two and two make four; still, if a man has to choose between absurdity and unhappiness, he will naturally prefer the former; and Clarke cannot maintain that such preference is irrational."

BUSINESS IS BUSINESS

Intellectual absurdity has always been the Golden Rule's Achilles heel. Promoted as an invincible moral law, it has one fatal flaw: it is not binding, and can be used for self-serving and deceitful purposes as easily as for good ones. It relies on a mutual desire to do good, and this is not always the case. Sidgwick makes this point as delicately as possible, but other writers have been far less subtle.

In Charles Dickens's *Martin Chuzzlewit*, the title character's sly and con-niving son announces, "Do other men, for they would do you," calling this "the true business precept. All others are counterfeit." Dickens adds, "The father applauded the sentiment to the echo." The wily horse trader David Harum, of Edward Noyes Westcott's 1899 best-selling novel of that name, observed, "'Bus'nis is bus'nis' ain't part of the golden rule, I allow, but the way it gen'ally runs, fur's I've found out, is 'Do unto the other feller the way he'd like to do unto you, an' do it fust.'"

This was hardly a modern discovery. The difference between what is laudable and what is practical or even necessary has long been known. In the fables of Pilpay, which date from the third century B.C., the moral of the story "The King Who Would Be Just" is that "men are used as they use others."

This is one view of reality that the term "golden rule" could not shake as it gained widespread acceptance, and the self-promotion implied by the name prompted a rash of objections and ridicule. Henry David Thoreau, while boating down the Concord and Merrimack rivers, noted in his jour-nal, "Absolutely speaking, Do unto others as you would that they should do unto you, is by no means a golden rule, but the best of current silver. It is golden not to have any rule at all in such a case." George Bernard Shaw (in what was probably a plea in his own behalf) cautioned, "Do not unto others as you would that they should do unto you; their tastes may not be the same." The English poet William Blake went so far as to say, "He has observed the Golden Rule 'til he's become a golden fool."

Most philosophers wisely chose to stay above this unseemly fray by avoiding any mention of the golden name. Thomas Hobbes, John Locke, Jean-Jacques Rousseau, and other enlightened thinkers understood that the term "Golden Rule" referred to a divinely inspired principle and not to something that they could prove like a mathematical theorem. But because they were trying to bring philosophy out of the shadow of religion and es-tablish a rational basis for ethics, they had to find a way to justify the ideal of moral reciprocity without making any reference to God or to gold. None of them could.

A capsule survey can hardly do justice to the depths of philosophical investigation plumbed by these writers, but to be blunt, they managed to bring up to the surface very little of practical use. Their efforts produced some new golden rules, and more questions than answers. The section that follows runs through the high points of their quest, and the impatient reader will lose nothing by skipping it. What it shows is that the Golden Rule sits at the epicenter of any discussion of morals, and justifying it is the key to establishing a coherent and convincing theory of ethics.

CATEGORICAL IMPERATIVES

In *Leviathan*, his groundbreaking analysis of political society written in 1651, Thomas Hobbes set the stage for what is known as modern moral philosophy by justifying the scriptural golden maxim as a rule of necessity dictated by man's essential self-interest. Because the natural state of man is a condition of war, according to Hobbes, in which everyone has the right to every thing, civilized society is only possible when all men mutually lay down their rights and claims. The Golden Rule of the Scriptures (which did not yet go by that name) was nothing more than an easy summation, "intelligible to even the meanest capacity," of the laws of nature which governed survival.

This was not, of course, what the Church wanted to hear. Nor did Hobbes's contemporaries. John Locke tried to claim that moral rules do not spring from political necessity, but instead from intuitive propositions as real and certain as those of mathematics. The French philosopher Jean-Jacques Rousseau sought the basis of the rule in feelings, not reason. He argued that justice comes from God, but it is not recognized equally by everyone, so that, while Hobbesian brutality exists in the world, it is offset by many examples of compassion. "It is this compassion that hurries us without reflection to the relief of those who are in distress," writes Rousseau. But why? Not because of the golden maxim of the Scriptures. A "less perfect, but perhaps more useful" rule, Rousseau admitted, would be: "Do good to yourself with as little evil as possible to others."

The German philosopher Immanuel Kant responded to Hobbes by reinventing the Golden Rule. In his *Groundwork of the Metaphysics of Morals* (1785), he proposed that any action, if it is to be considered moral, must be done out of a sense of duty, and not for selfish reasons or religious scruples. He named his new principle the Categorical Imperative, and stated it this way: "Act as if the maxim of your actions were to become through your will a universal law of nature." In short, think over what you're doing or about to do, and ask yourself if you would want *everyone* to behave that way. In a corollary which he named the Practical Imperative, he declared that people should treat each other "not as means only, but as ends." The

Stoic Maxim, which is how Kant referred to what we call the Golden Rule, is merely a consequence of his more comprehensive imperatives.

The Categorical Imperative has two things working against it as a ready-made opinion. Neither the name nor the rule is catchy enough to survive in the marketplace of popular ideas. Nor did it sway the critics. It advanced the discussion of ethics, and still stands as a milestone on the road to moral enlightenment, but it was not the last word. Kant had set out to establish "the supreme principle of morality," and given the immensity of the task he set himself, he naturally came up short.

AFTER KANT, the Golden Rule still had its defenders among respected thinkers, but they were fighting a losing battle. Prince Kropotkin, the founder of anarchism, referred to it as the fundamental principle of anarchism. "How can anyone manage to believe himself an anarchist unless he practices it?" If this statement seems faintly amusing today it is because of the way anarchy has changed meanings. In its original and benign sense— its forgotten sense—it implies an ungoverned society ordered by free association and communitarian principles. Clearly such a society would need a golden rule if it were to avoid devolving into—there's no other way of putting it—total anarchy.

Another system of ethics that relied heavily upon community interest over self-interest was utilitarianism, which aimed at the greatest good for the greatest number. In presenting this theory, John Stuart Mill endorsed the Golden Rule as "the ideal perfection of utilitarian morality," a seemingly benign remark which merits our attention primarily because of the contempt it aroused in the volcanic Friedrich Nietzsche, who never met a golden rule he didn't despise.

Reading Nietzsche on the Golden Rule is like reading Spiro Agnew on the American press. Whether you agree with him or not, he gets your attention. To Nietzsche, "the rule" (as he calls it) is the very embodiment of the English mentality, and it allows him to set up John Stuart Mill (whom he refers to as "that blockhead") as a stand-in for John Bull. "I abhor his vulgarity, which says: 'What is right for one is fair for another'; 'what you would not, etc., do not unto others'; which wants to establish all human intercourse on the basis of mutual services, so that every action appears as a kind of payment for something done to us."

Nietzsche did not believe in the possibility of equivalence of actions or equality of rights. Reciprocity, he says, "is a piece of gross vulgarity." To him the Golden Rule serves only to insult the superior intellect and to coddle the inferior. Its only value is that it betrays a type of man—"it is the instinct of the herd that finds its formula in this rule."

Kant and the Categorical Imperative came in for the same sort of treatment. "A virtue that is prompted solely by a feeling of respect for the concept of 'virtue,'" as Kant would have it, "is harmful." The struggle to maintain a slavish devotion to unworkable formulas, Nietzsche firmly believed, leads to moral exhaustion. And Kant was paving the way. "The fundamental laws of self-preservation and growth demand the opposite," Nietzsche fumed, "that everyone invent *his own* virtue, *his own* categorical imperative. A people perishes when it confuses *its* duty with duty in general."

Certainly Nietzsche was a difficult character. He rarely bothered to measure his words, many of which could and later did serve to justify the abominable acts of others (Hitler being the most notorious example). Because he tended to write in aphorisms, he is easy to quote out of context, and he left himself open to misinterpretation. Still, he is redeemed somewhat by what could be called a Nietzschean golden rule (although he would have bristled at the label), which demonstrates his sympathy with the ideal of reciprocity. "When the exceptional human being treats the mediocre more tenderly than himself and his peers," Nietzsche wrote, "this is not mere politeness of the heart—it is simply his duty."

THERE ARE NO GOLDEN RULES

Although the Golden Rule has survived in popular parlance, it is no longer taken very seriously. Most uses of the term could properly be classified as "babbittry"—part of the cant of middle-class conformity and materialism. In American culture the name has retained a largely symbolic value. It conveys a vague notion of fairness and generosity, much like two other popular ideals with which it was once frequently linked.

A conscientious citizen, it could once confidently be said, should try to do a Good Turn, offer a Square Deal, and live up to the Golden Rule whenever possible. As part of the Progressive-era rhetoric of the early twentieth century, these three principles derived most of their clout from strong institutional associations. The Good Turn (or Good Deed, as most Americans know it) grew out of the chivalric ethos of Scouting. The Golden

Rule, of course, was lifted from the Gospels according to Matthew and Luke, while the Square Deal *was* the gospel according to Theodore Roosevelt. Like the Golden Rule, the Square Deal was driven by the sheer force of one dominating personality. The phrase seized the public's imagination during Roosevelt's presidency even though no one could say exactly what it meant. When he tried to recapture the nation's highest office in 1912 running on the Progressive Party ticket, his campaign slogan was: A Square Deal All Around.

Just what did it mean? According to the code of ethics of the Fraternal Order of Lumbermen, a Square Deal served "to elevate humanity by charity of action and thought and by justice to all men." They might have said the same of the Golden Rule. Both ideas were sufficiently vague as to appear indisputable—at least while they were in vogue.

But by the late 1950s, when Jimmy Hoffa remarked to reporters (with what would prove to be a terminal sense of irony), "I do unto others what they do unto me, only worse," a new golden rule was born—one that jibed with a more cynical national mood that showed little patience for platitudes. By the 1970s the Golden Rule had all but disappeared, leaving in its wake such piquant observations as: "He who has the gold makes the rules."

This would seem to confirm George Bernard Shaw's conclusion of a century ago that "The Golden Rule is that there are no golden rules." Perhaps what he meant was that there shouldn't be.

RECIPROCITY

The apparent demise of the Golden Rule should not be taken too seriously. It has been around for at least twenty-five hundred years, and the events of the last hundred are not likely to kill it off. Despite all that is said against it—the parodies and the tirades—it embodies nothing more or less than the way civilized people treat each other. It is precisely what any patient parent tries to instill in a misbehaving child. Thoreau would have been correct in saying "better not to have a rule at all in such a case" if the rule were indeed so self-evident that it did not have to be taught. But it does need to be taught, and in this one respect it is not unlike the laws of mathematics or physics.

Putting it into words, of course, is where problems arise. No one is quite content with any one statement of it. Scholars bicker at each other over whose version is best, and there are countless versions to choose from.

With a little digging, the inquiring reader can connect the Sermon on the Mount to a vast body of preexisting literature in which the rule we thought Jesus invented turns up seemingly everywhere. In the fifth century B.C., in what may have been a retelling of an even older story, a young disciple asks the venerable Confucius whether there is one word which might serve as a rule of practice for all one's life. "Is not *reciprocity* such a word?" the Master replies. "What you do not want done to yourself, do not do to others."

A diligent reader will have the satisfaction of encountering this rule again several times in the Analects of Confucius and other Confucian texts, and there are similar satisfactions to be found in the Buddhist Dhammappada, the texts of Taoism, the Hindu Mahabharata, the Jaina Sutras, the Jewish Talmud, and the Koran. Even Aristotle gets into the act, at least according to the sometimes reliable biographer Diogenes Laertes, who quotes him as saying, "We should behave to our friends as we wish our friends should behave to us."

Taking all of these golden rules together, one might be led to think of reciprocity as a rule for all men for all time. The reality is somewhat different: it was not originally meant for all men, and certainly not for women. Throughout antiquity the "others" one should "do unto" hailed from a select group. Aristotle extends the courtesy only to friends—a reading of the rule that allows one to be a Christian, a Stoic, or even an Aristotelian, and yet still be a racist. Confucius simply conceded that social inequality was a fact of life, and broke his rule down into cases: "What a man dislikes in his superiors, let him not display in his treatment of his inferiors." Seneca, the Stoic philosopher and statesman, says much the same thing in addressing the issue of slavery: "As often as you reflect how much power you have over a slave, remember that your master has just as much power over you."

It is here that the Christian Golden Rule gets high marks from some commentators as a more ethical proposal than its predecessors, on two counts in particular. The first is that it is a positive rule—"Do unto others," as opposed to "Do *not* do unto others." The second is that it is a rule for all men (and presumably women). This is the point that Paul, finding the Sermon on the Mount to be too vague, decided to spell out in his letter to the Ephesians. Because everyone stands in the same relation to each other with respect to God, he argues, the good that we do is not to be reciprocated in kind, but in spirit. Whether coming from a servant or a master, "whatsoever good thing any man shall do," Paul wrote, "the same shall he receive from the Lord." This is because "there is no respect of persons with him."

What may seem at first to be an obscure theological point goes a long way to explaining the eventual popularity of the Golden Rule in America. Long before the Golden Rule was golden, it was recognized as a useful expression of what now seems obvious: we should measure our actions by imagining how we would deal with their consequences, not only in this world but in the next. But this idea has not always been so obvious. The assumption that lies behind reciprocity, in its purest sense, is that there is an equality between persons, that the consideration each human being is entitled to is roughly equal. If anything, this is a modern idea, and a distinctively American one. It is a rule that assumes, following Saint Paul and Thomas Jefferson, that all men are equal, not only in the eyes of God but in the eyes of the state. In American culture the Golden Rule became the proof of this—a political tenet of faith.

It is easy to see why. Its strength, aside from its rich scriptural and pan-cultural history, lies in its simplicity. It places every person in a moral relationship to all other people. It demands and at the same time acknowledges everyone's capacity for wisdom, compassion, and good judgment. In one sentence it conveys the ability and the responsibility to do the right thing, and the confidence that one will.

At times this confidence may seem to be misplaced. And yet the golden rule (here uncapitalized to represent a principle that transcends all faiths) can enlighten us if we are willing to wrestle with it. As Confucius said, "A man can enlarge the principles *which he follows;* those principles do not enlarge the man."

IN SO MANY WORDS

There are an uncountable number of ways of expressing the ideal of reciprocity, and since the time of Confucius many people became convinced that they had found its perfect expression. But Confucius himself acknowledged that the ideal of doing unto others could not be adequately expressed in mere words or with simple deeds. What he had written, he conceded, was as unequal to virtue as himself. "To set the example in behaving to a friend as I would require him to behave to me," the Master confessed, "I am not yet able."

Yet the Golden Rule is still an ideal that many try to live up to. Although its name is mired in the past (along with the Square Deal), the rule itself has never really gone away. It continues to show up in a variety of guises that invoke the ideal of reciprocity in ways that people feel comfortable with.

In small-town newspaper profiles and man-on-the-street interviews, when asked to state their personal philosophy, a surprising number of people answer by saying, "To do unto others as I would have them do unto me." This reflects how those of us who have attained a certain level of moral awareness in our day-to-day activities *feel* when given a chance to reflect on the consequences of our actions. We may not always use the term "golden rule" to describe this awareness. Often, we unconsciously act on a concept that since childhood we have found to be easy to grasp and simple to apply.

And the idea is still a viable one; it continues to reveal itself here and there in ways that manage to strike a resonant chord without sounding heavy-handed. In Harper Lee's *To Kill a Mockingbird,* for example, Scout Finch, the narrator, stands on the front porch of her next door neighbor, a reclusive man who has just saved her life. In this final scene, she has an epiphany, and finally understands something her father once told her. "Atticus was right," she says. "One time he said you never really know a man until you stand in his shoes and walk around in them." This, in so many words, is the golden rule.

THE AMERICAN'S CREED (1917)

I BELIEVE IN THE UNITED STATES OF AMERICA AS A GOVERNMENT OF THE PEOPLE, BY THE PEOPLE, FOR THE PEOPLE; WHOSE JUST POWERS ARE DERIVED FROM THE CONSENT OF THE GOVERNED; A DEMOCRACY IN A REPUBLIC; A SOVEREIGN NATION OF MANY SOVEREIGN STATES; A PERFECT UNION, ONE AND INSEPARABLE; ESTABLISHED ON THOSE PRINCIPLES OF FREEDOM, EQUALITY, JUSTICE, AND HUMANITY FOR WHICH AMERICAN PATRIOTS SACRIFICED THEIR LIVES AND FORTUNES. I THEREFORE BELIEVE THAT IT IS MY DUTY TO MY COUNTRY TO LOVE IT; TO SUPPORT ITS CONSTITUTION; TO OBEY ITS LAWS; TO RESPECT ITS FLAG, AND TO DEFEND IT AGAINST ALL ENEMIES.

WILLIAM TYLER PAGE

CHAPTER TWO

WE HOLD THESE TRUTHS

CREEDS AND OTHER PROFESSIONS OF FAITH

THIS I BELIEVE

From 1952 to 1959 one of the most popular features on American radio was a five-minute program entitled *This I Believe*. Hosted by Edward R. Murrow, the country's most respected broadcast journalist, the show featured "the living philosophies of successful men and women from all walks of life." Each week the show featured an invited guest who would read a brief statement of his or her most fundamental beliefs. Murrow, the show's creator, wanted to know what made people tick, what they stood for, and stood up for, as expressed in their own words. "I have never yet heard a man express what he believed," he said, "in a fashion that failed to interest me."

He and the other producers of *This I Believe* were not looking for ready-made opinions or for a rehash of institutional dogmas. What they got was a grab bag of sentiments, ranging from the banal to the poignant, that drew mainly upon stories, upon remembrances of parents, and upon formative influences. The contributors did indeed hail from many walks of life. They included the writers Pearl Buck, Aldous Huxley, Rebecca West, Thomas Mann, Carl Sandburg, and James Michener; politicians and statesmen Adlai Stevenson, Margaret Chase Smith, Bernard Baruch, Herbert Hoover, and Harry S. Truman; athletes Jackie Robinson and Bobby Doerr;

as well as educators, industrialists, actors, musicians, and journalists; a taxi driver, a policeman, and a housewife. Each was allotted three and a half minutes of air time, or about six hundred words, in which to get his or her point across.

What soon became apparent to Murrow and his colleagues is that it is no easy task to come up with a meaningful statement of belief. To ask people to state their creed in their own words is to ask for something intensely personal. In theory, everyone's life builds upon some set of principles or ideals that are at the very core of his or her identity, that underlie every action. But these prove to be so difficult to state that almost everyone chooses to adopt creeds that were written by others.

In retrospect, Murrow seems to have wanted people to explain their personal code of ethics—a different thing altogether. But by asking instead for a *credo* he inadvertently threw down a far greater challenge. What we genuinely believe to be true is not quite as simple as what we merely think *should* be true. If a code is what we bring to the table as we negotiate our way through life, a creed *is* the table; it is there before we arrive. Some people insist on bringing their own table, of course, but it isn't easy. As someone once said, it is easier to believe than to doubt, which is a backhanded way of saying how much more convenient it is to adopt a creed than to invent one. Murrow probably did not intend to have his contributors invent a system of belief, but some of them took it that way, which placed them in rather distinguished company.

THE GREAT AGNOSTIC

At one time, in the not so distant past, a program like *This I Believe* would not have seemed necessary. Prominent citizens who felt secure in their beliefs once made a point of letting those beliefs be known, and they generally found a receptive audience.

The Founding Fathers were consumed by the issue of belief, and with the self-evident truths that would justify their endeavor. Privately, some of them held fast to beliefs that were not quite orthodox. In a letter of 1820 Thomas Jefferson wrote, "I hold the precepts of Jesus, as delivered by himself, to be the most pure, benevolent, and sublime which have ever been preached to man. I adhere to the principles of the first age; and consider all subsequent innovations as corruptions of this religion, having no foundation in what came from him."

Benjamin Franklin also stated a personal religious creed in a letter: "I believe in one God, the creator of the universe. That He governs it by His providence. That He ought to be worshipped. That the most acceptable service that we render to Him is doing good to His other children. That the soul of man is immortal and will be treated with justice in another life respecting its conduct in this." In a purely legalistic sense, such statements are blasphemies because they supersede, if not contradict, the ancient and established Christian creeds.

Yet the rejection of organized religion in favor of a personal conception of God is one of the hallmarks of American thinking. The popular nineteenth-century lawyer and rhetorician Robert G. Ingersoll wrestled with belief throughout his life, only to find that the one thing he could rely on was his own doubt. The Great Agnostic, as Ingersoll was known, was a brilliant public speaker who might well have run for president had he not so strongly insisted upon these doubts. Instead he used the podium and the pulpit to hammer home a personal philosophy of hope. As a result, the Ingersoll Creed became a popular piece of inspirational wisdom that was widely anthologized. It has no definitive version, having been condensed from his writings and speeches, but its most familiar expression is:

> *Justice is the only worship.*
> *Love is the only priest.*
> *Ignorance is the only slavery.*
> *Happiness is the only good.*
> *The time to be happy is now,*
> *The place to be happy is here,*
> *The way to be happy is to make others so.*

Ingersoll's creed, unlike Jefferson's or Franklin's, was a very public pronouncement—a humanist philosophy that he delivered over many years on a national stage. It served as a public act of self-definition, one that reflected a view expressed by the English biologist and evolutionary theorist Thomas Henry Huxley, when he wrote, "The longer I live the more obvious it is to me that the most sacred act of a man's life is to say and feel 'I believe such and such to be true.' All the greatest rewards and the heaviest penalties of existence cling about that act."

Ingersoll (who as a staunch Darwinian himself had much in common with Huxley) was rewarded with the adulation of an adoring public. But he also paid a heavy penalty for his forthrightness. His political career never got off the ground because the Republican Party would not risk supporting Ingersoll for any prominent office or cabinet post. His views were too unorthodox to survive in the political arena.

A CONGREGATION OF ONE

Franklin and Jefferson understood the language of belief well enough to know what sort of confession of faith to make publicly, and which privately. The far less circumspect Tom Paine, like Ingersoll, was far more liberal with his opinions, and it earned him a reputation as an atheist.

In *The Age of Reason* (1794) Paine stated his personal creed in this way: "I believe in one God, and no more; and I hope for happiness beyond this life. I believe in the equality of man; and I believe that religious duties consist in doing justice, loving mercy, and endeavoring to make our fellow-creatures happy. . . . I do not believe in the creed professed by the Jewish church, by the Roman church, by the Greek church, by the Turkish church, by the Protestant church, nor by any church that I know of. My own mind is my church."

Paine's is the creed of an exceptional man, a congregation of one, and he found it to be a lonely and thankless lot. Surprised that his statement of a personal conception of God should lead to a charge of atheism, he betrays an ignorance of the way ready-made opinions work. Which is to say he failed to take into account why a Jewish, Roman Catholic, Greek Orthodox, Islamic, or Protestant creed is necessary. Taking such creeds too literally, seeing them as supposed literal truths instead of statements of affiliation, his own sense of enlightenment led him to condemn those who for convenience or loyalty's sake, or out of a desire to belong, swear the creed of their fathers. By disavowing any creed, he placed himself beyond religion.

Yet there are many good reasons to adopt the creed of one's forefathers. Creeds, after all, are nothing more than stories that try to make sense of the world. They assert certain absolute, unprovable truths which need to be asserted if one is to be free to go about the day-to-day business of getting on in the world. These truths might explain nothing more than a school of thought, or nothing less than the entire universe. They can show where we are coming from, and where we might be heading.

Because his mind was his own church, Paine failed to notice how a church service might provide a place to seek community with others, or that someone might adopt a creed without reading all of the fine print. Nor did he see how a creed might represent nothing more than an occasion to reflect upon one's place in the world, on the value of life, and the reality of death.

These are not simple issues. Any attempt to deal with them must inevitably settle for something arbitrary—which is a characteristic of all creeds.

CONFESSIONS OF FAITH

There are many types of creeds, and not all of them begin with the words "I believe." Many are not even called creeds or used as prayers. But a true creed is more than a simple succession of words. It is an act of faith as well as solidarity. A good one establishes a frame of reference, an identity, an affiliation, a sense of belonging, or a sense of affinity.

This much Paine managed to get right. When he referred to "the creed professed by the Jewish church, by the Roman church, by the Greek church, by the Turkish church, by the Protestant church," he was not referring to specific documents, but to systems of belief. The Jewish church and the Turkish church, as he calls them, do not acknowledge authorized creedal statements like those used in the Catholic, Protestant, or Greek churches, but they do have a creed in the most general sense of the term.

This reflects how the meaning of the word has expanded over time to become interchangeable with the word *faith*, a development that can be credited in part to Anglo-American religious scholars of the late nineteenth and early twentieth centuries, who could understand religions only from a mainstream Christian point of view in terms of creeds. The *Encyclopaedia of Religion and Ethics*, for example, a product of British scholarship of the 1920s, refers to specific texts as Buddhist, Jewish, Muhammedan, and Parsi creeds, a practice which could easily be attributed to religious insensitivity had not these religions themselves taken up the term.

Indeed, Muslims have designated a prayer known as the *Kalima* as the Islamic creed: "I testify that there is no God but Allah, and I testify that Mohammed is the apostle of Allah." In Judaism, the *Shema* ("hear" in Hebrew), the basic Jewish confession of faith, is not considered a creed, although many attempts have been made to formulate one. The most notable are Moses Maimonides' *Thirteen Articles of Faith* and the *Ani Ma'amin* (Hebrew for

"I Believe"), which serves as an inspirational prayer. In the Hindu faith the *Gayatri* is the supreme credo of the Brahmins. In Zoroastrianism, which is the ancient predecessor of the Parsi religion of Northern India, the *Yasna*—the purported words of the prophet Zoroaster—forms the basis of a Zoroastrian creed.

The meaning of the word *creed* also expanded not only across denominational lines, but within Christianity as well. It has become interchangeable with the more specific term *confession*, as in *confession of faith*. Thus the great Protestant confessions, beginning with the ninety-five theses that Martin Luther nailed to the door of the church of Wittenburg, and including the Geneva, Westminster, and Augsburg confessions, come off as creeds in some accounts. In the sense that they clearly distinguish a church's identity, they qualify. But the word initially meant something much more specific and rather exclusive, a point which needs to be explored if modern "creeds," so called, are to make sense.

THE THREE ANCIENT SYMBOLS

Christianity, as it now exists, consists of many denominations and sects, all of which can trace their lineage to a single document (whether they wish to admit it or not), and it is not the New Testament. The Scriptures may have inspired the faith, but it was the first creed that established the Church, and creeds have been the root cause of every division and schism since.

The history of these creeds, of course, is complex. But the idea of a creed and the role it plays in establishing a school of thought is relatively simple (although often misunderstood), and has remained remarkably unchanged through the centuries.

The word "creed" comes from *credo*, or "I believe," the opening word of both the Apostles' and Nicene creeds in Latin. These two creeds, along with the less familiar Athanasian Creed, are the oldest and the most influential doctrinal statements in Christianity, and the paradigms to which anything else called a creed is ultimately compared.

The Apostles' is the oldest of the three, having been written in the third century as a baptismal formula—that is, as a way of initiating new members into the faith. But it is the Nicene Creed that presents the more interesting case because it established the one true Church by defining orthodoxy. Which is to say that in an age in which many different conceptions of God vied for preeminence, the Nicene Creed sifted among a jumble of contending factions and pronounced one faith to be the true faith, condemning all others as heresies, which they remain to this day. Those who recite it each week are probably unaware of how disorderly this process was because they undoubtedly believe that the creeds have existed since the very founding of the Church. But they are not quite that old, nor can any of them be said to be the word of God. They had to be invented, and in the process "the faith" had to be defined and made acceptable to a diverse and rapidly expanding group of followers. And this took many centuries.

Originally, what we refer to as the Apostles' and Nicene creeds were known as "symbols," a term that was first applied to the original Apostles' Creed as the "sign" or "mark" of a Christian. The term "creed" did not come into general use until the tenth century.* The Athanasian Creed, at first known as the "Faith of Saint Athanasius" (or the *Quicunque*, also from its opening word, which means "whomsoever," as in "whomsoever would be saved"), came to be grouped with the Apostles' and Nicene creeds entirely by accident. In the thirteenth century a writer linked them together as the *triplex symbolum* (the three symbols of the faith), and the grouping stuck. They became "the three ancient symbols" or "the ancient creeds," which perpetuated the myth of their authenticity.

Yet the Apostles' Creed, it turns out, was not written by the twelve Apostles, nor the Athanasian Creed by Saint Athanasius (a bishop of Alexandria in the fourth century). The ironies of naming do not end there. The Nicene Creed is not the creed of the bishops who assembled at the Council of Nicea in A.D. 325. But as with the Hippocratic Oath, a historical name, while potentially misleading, can be revealing as well.

The Apostles' Creed, for example, is an expansion of certain scriptural passages. It grew out of the instructional questions that priests posed to initiates for baptism. There were many such formulas in use during the early years of the Church, and from these one version emerged as the official creed after many centuries. The name came later, connecting it to a

---

*The Latin word *symbolum* was first used to describe the baptismal creed in the year 250 by Cyprian, the bishop of Carthage. The Greek root of this word connotes a token, mark, or ticket, in the sense of a talisman that is broken in half, given to two parties, and later matched up in order to establish each party's identity. The word *symbol* as we now use it, in the sense of something that stands for something else, was first used by Edmund Spenser in *The Faerie Queen* in 1590. The first use of the words *credo* and *creed* to refer to any statement of belief (as opposed to the Apostles' Creed specifically) occurred at about the same time.

story in which each of the twelve apostles contributed an article. It may be "a pious fiction," as religious scholar J. N. D. Kelly claims, but not a useless one. It served to connect the faith to the formative years of the Church, and this helped to assure its place.

By contrast, the Nicene Creed, or more properly the Niceno-Constantinopolitan Creed, does have some connection to its namesakes, even if the current version does not accurately reflect the intentions of the two councils for which it was named. From its relatively inauspicious beginnings, it emerged through great turmoil and political maneuvering as the most widely used creed in Christendom. It was forged by a succession of church councils that sought to establish a definitive statement of orthodox belief, and this was not a smooth process.

In other words, the canonical creeds of Christian worship are three out of many hundreds of creeds that circulated in the first few centuries of the Christian Church, and they did not emerge entirely by chance. One grew out of the ceremony of baptism, the other two were carefully constructed and shaped in order to exclude a number of prominent heresies, and all three were made part of liturgical practice, where they have served as prayers for over a thousand years.

Some of the heresies are worth mentioning. For example Nestorius, an archbishop of Constantinople, insinuated the possibility that the humanity of Christ was real and separate in nature from his divinity. Eutyches, archimandrate of Constantinople, stressed the divinity of Christ so much as to deny his humanity. These notions would be put to rest by the Athanasian Creed. But the most persistent heresy, one that is still discussed today, was the belief promoted by Arius, an Alexandrian priest who still has adherents in many parts of the world.

The Arian heresy, as it is now called, was for a time a viable candidate for orthodoxy, which put Arius in line to become one of the Church Fathers. His controversial theory, which he first proposed around the year 323, held that the Son had not always existed (that is, he was not born before all ages), and thus was *not* of the same substance as the Father. The orthodox position held to the unity of the Trinity, and the essential sameness of Father and Son.

Constantine, the Roman emperor who consolidated the East and the West, viewed this situation with alarm, and feared political instability if the Arian issue split the Church. Consequently, in the year 325 he convened a council in what is now northwest Turkey, in the city of Nicea, to settle the matter. With the unbaptized emperor presiding, 220 bishops engaged in what by all accounts was a raucous, almost violent debate. One creed, a compromise between the polarized factions, is said to have been torn to pieces by the assembly merely because the Arians were willing to consider it. In the end Arianism was so thoroughly denounced that the approved creed defined orthodoxy most forcefully in terms of what it was not. This is how those distinctively ecclesiastical terms "anathema" and "anathematization" came into widespread usage. The final passage from the original creed of Nicea illustrates what would become a common feature of subsequent creeds.

> But as for those who say, There was when He was not, and, Before being born He was not, and that He came into existence out of nothing, or who assert that the Son of God is of a different hypostasis or substance or is subject to alteration or change—these the Catholic and apostolic Church anathematizes.

After the Council of Nicea, which Arius was not allowed to attend, Constantine tried to bring the wayward priest back into the fold by urging him to soften his position on the Father and Son. He agreed, to a point, but Athanasius, staunch anti-Arian cleric that he was, insisted that Arius be required to sign the creed of the Nicene Council or face excommunication. (For his hard-line stance on matters of orthodoxy Athanasius wound up with the credit for the creed that was named for him. The scholarly consensus holds that he had nothing to do with it. The Athanasian Creed was written well after his time, and the name came about later still.) In the end Constantine did reunite Arius with the Church, but it hardly mattered. Arianism had never been a cult built around one personality; it had taken on a life of its own quite independent of its unassuming founder. In fact it survives to this day, under different names, in some aspects of Unitarian belief and in the Christology of Jehovah's Witnesses.

Constantine's intervention did not settle the Arian controversy. After his death in 337 the Arian faction gained an upper hand and took control of the Church. But because Arianism was not a unified and coherent theology, many variants of its creed began to circulate. One declared the Son to be "unlike" (anonoios) the Father, another that he was "like" (homoios) him. The orthodox position insisted upon the word homoousios (which became "consubstantial with" or "of the same substance as" in English translations), a nonscriptural term that had made some of the 220 bishops at Nicea uneasy. But this word did at least establish a beachhead against the insinuation of polytheism hinted at by the almost identical term *homoiousios,* which argued for a Son "of a similar substance" as the Father. Such was the substance of the theological differences that threatened to rip the Church apart before it had a chance to establish itself.

To the nonspecialist, all of these early creeds are mostly compelling as stories. Somewhat exotic in their anathematizations (which read like the dire imprecations appended to nineteenth-century Masonic initiation oaths), and to the layman indistinguishable in their theology, they tell a sweeping saga in capsule form about what is sometimes referred to as "the greatest story ever told." It encompasses the creation of the earth, the birth of a Savior, his death and resurrection, and the glory of the world to come. The denunciations (which the Athanasian Creed contains in abundance) may be distracting, but they were perceived as necessary. It is unlikely that the Church would have remained intact without them.

Of course the Church did not remain completely intact. Its first major split, known as the Great Schism, occurred in the eleventh century, leaving the Greek (or Eastern) Orthodox faith irrevocably sundered from the Roman Catholic faith. This was prefigured three centuries earlier when Charlemagne, wishing to establish a uniform creed throughout the Holy Roman Empire, championed a text that had been circulating in Europe for some time. This creed proposed that the Holy Spirit proceeded from the Father *and the Son* (*filioque,* in Latin) rather than "through the Son," as most Greek theologians maintained. Charlemagne did succeed in spreading the *filioque* throughout the West, although Rome did not officially accept it for another two centuries, by which time it had become a central issue dividing the Eastern from the Western church. After the Great Schism the Orthodox church retained the Nicene Creed and still uses it, but without the *filioque.*

IF THE HISTORY of the ancient creeds, turning as it does upon such seemingly indistinguishable but apparently explosive shades of meaning, seems less than sublime, it does at least represent a centuries-long process which had important consequences in Western history. Some observers—including Jefferson, Franklin, Paine, Ingersoll, and Henry David Thoreau (whose backyard was his church)—were not impressed by this history. One of their number, the eighteenth-century poet William Cowper, voiced his disdain in a poem entitled "Hope," which rejects orthodoxy in favor of a not entirely serious personal doxy.

My creed (whatever some creed-makers mean
By Athanasian nonsense, or Nicene)
My creed is—he is safe that does his best,
And death's a doom sufficient for the rest.

Apparently, the tumultuous origins of the ancient creeds has cost them much of their credibility among free thinkers, and this erosion of confidence is likely to continue to prompt many calls for their replacement.

CREEDS AND LOYALTY

To the modern churchgoer, creeds are formulas to be recited by congregations as part of the weekly church service. Through repetition they implant a sequence of key ideas, albeit in a way that discourages any deep reflection about what is being said. That many Catholics can remember reciting the creeds in Latin punctuates this very point: to parishioners, the meaning of the modern creeds resides more in the act of reciting than in the actual words that are spoken. The bishops who assembled at Nicea, for example, knew the distinction between the Greek words *homoousios, homoiousios,* and *homoios,* and must have known as well that this difference would not mean much to their followers. Yet these words, along with the Latin *filioque,* turned out to be the focus of long-standing and bitter feuds over who would get to be keepers of the faith—Arians or the anti-Arians, Eastern Orthodox or Roman.

Was the difference between "and the Son" and "through the Son" so crucial that it should cause the Great Schism that split the Church in two? Probably not. The uproar at the Council of Nicea demonstrated that the creed was indeed a symbol, not so much of fundamental belief as of affiliation. The stronger faction won out by defining orthodoxy through its creed, which it then used to explicitly denounce all heresies. But the importance of this has diminished over time, and those who recite the creed once a week have no idea what Arianism is, nor can they explain what is heretical about it. It now seems entirely beside the point. Congregations are more interested in what the church has to say about abortion, birth control, and euthanasia than what it has to say about the precise relationships between Father, Son, and Holy Spirit. The creeds have settled the matter of the Trinity, allowing churchgoers to dwell on more immediate issues, secure in the consensus of their faith.

There are, of course, some churchgoers who agonize over their inability to accept the facts presented by the creeds as literal historical truths. And there are others who cling passionately to the finer points of orthodoxy. But the vast majority fall somewhere in between. To them, the appeal of a creed is its ability to unite a great number of individual beliefs within an acceptable range of orthodoxy. This is the point of most modern creeds, and it is what makes them so appealing. They allow a congregation to build, not necessarily upon specific beliefs, but upon a general consensus of belief. It is only when a congregation begins to examine a creed too closely that they sometimes find that it fails to say exactly what they want it to. For this reason many denominations, the American Baptists, for example, have rejected the idea of a written creed entirely.

HE'LL DO THAT ONCE TOO OFTEN

There are not only unwritten creeds, but unspoken ones—philosophies of life that exist in a nether world somewhere between actions, thoughts, and words. It was precisely this type of pervasive yet undelineated belief system that inspired the creators of *This I Believe* to explore the phenomenon of collective faith.

While in London in 1940 a young Edward R. Murrow watched with reverent awe as the British people, subjected to nightly bombardment and facing the possibility of subjugation or annihilation, insisted on maintaining a level of business-as-usual that bordered on madness, or so it seemed to the foreign observer. What set of beliefs, he wondered, sustained them? He concluded that their actions were guided by a fundamental conviction that what they were defending was good, that they "had devised a system of regulating the relationship between the individual and the state which was superior to all others." This not only meant defending a way of life, but carrying on with it under duress.

One night Murrow watched as a taxi driver pulled out of the Liverpool Street station just as a couple of bombs whistled down nearby. Both cab and cabbie were rocked by the explosions. Finding himself unhurt and the antique cab intact, the driver slid back his window, and said, "He'll do that once too often, once," whereupon he slid the window shut and drove away. Murrow claimed he had no idea what the cabbie meant (although if that were entirely true he would hardly have bothered to relate the story).

Murrow's take on the story is typically American. He betrays a fascination with unwritten codes of honor and decorum, coming as he did from a culture where few such codes exist. While the British have subsisted for much of their history on unwritten codes that permeate their culture, Americans have tended to gravitate to written statements of belief. The difference between the American and English constitutions, the one written out point by point, the other amorphous and ever-changing, provides a vivid illustration of this phenomenon. The prevalence of written codes of professions and trades in the United States, and their comparative rarity in Great Britain, provides another. It is partly a matter of temperament.

It would sound odd, for example, to hear that an Englishman had taken it upon himself to author a formal document entitled "The English Creed." But the idea is so natural for an American that many American creeds have been written. At one time, in the first half of this century, these proved to be quite popular. But it was precisely this kind of patriotic enthusiasm that Murrow did not want to hear on his show, although many of his contributors could not avoid it.

This is a natural consequence of the American sense of identity. It is perfectly conceivable, for example, for a Frenchman to denounce the French system of government and yet be nonetheless French for it. But in the United States identity is essentially a matter of ideology. What it means to be an American is much different than what it means to be French or any other nationality. It has little to do with where you were born or what your tastes in food or art happen to be. It has almost everything to do with one's sense of civics, which is to say with a belief in liberty, in certain unalienable rights, and in other political ideals expressed in the nation's founding documents. This is why it is natural for an American to try to express his or her identity in the form of a profession of faith.

THE AMERICAN CREED

Since the day the United States of America was founded there has existed a notion that has within the last century come to be known as the American creed. It is not spelled out in any single document, but over time it has evolved into a coherent set of assumptions that most Americans agree upon and admire. These include such abstract ideas as life, liberty, equality, individualism, individual rights, the pursuit of happiness, democracy, and the rule of law and order under a constitution—principles which, in essence, form the national identity.

Something approaching a statement of this creed—not in a single document, but in a collection of them—was once fairly easy to come by. The 1950s instructional pamphlet "How to Become an American Citizen," for example, begins with the texts of "America the Beautiful," the Pledge of Allegiance, and a page-long statement entitled "Bases of Americanism," which lists the precepts of democratic government. In addition to a description of the mechanisms of immigration and naturalization, the pamphlet contains essays on the history and meaning of the flag, some important dates in American history, the text of the Gettysburg Address, and Washington's Farewell Address.

All of these and more can be found in the National Education Association's *American Citizen's Handbook* (1941), which is nothing less than the full statement of the American creed in the form of an anthology. It contains patriotic poems, speeches, hymns, anthems, and stories. As if to emphasize the role belief plays in American culture, it includes, among many other things, a Future Farmers of America Creed, a Country Boy's Creed, a Country Girl's Creed, and something called The American's Creed. It also features the Golden Rule, the Ten Commandments, the Magna Carta (to show how the ideas of rights got its start), and the Mayflower Compact.

In essence, *The American Citizen's Handbook* is to the American way of life what the Book of Common Prayer is to the Church of England, except that is not very easy to find today. This is because the American creed is being pulled in several directions. It still exists, although not in the kinds of simple and direct forms that were once very popular. This is not to say that the reverence accorded the Declaration of Independence, the Constitution, and the Gettysburg Address has diminished. What has diminished is the enthusiasm that once greeted any attempt to state an American creed that might stand as a national prayer.

I BELIEVE IN AMERICA

The mere mention of a patriotic creed brings to mind some of patriotism's more unflattering associations. Dr. Johnson labeled it "the last refuge of a scoundrel." George Jean Nathan, H. L. Mencken's collaborator at *The American Mercury*, called it "an arbitrary veneration of real estate above principles." And H. G. Wells, assessing "The Future of America" in 1920, construed it as "a sentimentality of flag-cheering with no constructive duties." As misused as patriotism may be, it also has its uses, one of which has been to build morale in times of war, which is when patriotism is in greatest demand.

The most successful patriotic American creed (in terms of circulation and exposure) was written in 1917 by William Tyler Page, a longtime clerk of the U.S. House of Representatives. "The American's Creed" consists of a short inventory of principles that ends with an affirmation of the Constitution and the flag. Page's creed was accepted by the House on behalf of the American people at the close of the First World War, and this assured its place in popular anthologies for decades to come. It is periodically dusted off and read into the Congressional Record during commemorative activities on patriotic holidays such as Flag Day.

Wendell Willkie, an industrialist who challenged Franklin D. Roosevelt for the presidency in 1940, contributed another much-anthologized American credo in an essay entitled "Why I Believe in America." Its opening stanza should sound familiar.

> *I believe in America because in it we are free—free to choose our government, to speak our minds, to observe our different religions . . . because we have great dreams—and because we have the opportunity to make those dreams come true.*

Willkie's American Credo may read like just another stump speech, yet it was novel enough in his time to win him much admiration. It served as the epitaph on his grave marker in Rushville, Indiana, and can be found engraved on plaques mounted in public places here and there (such as on the 40th Street boundary wall of the New York Public Library).

In 1946 Francis Cardinal Spellman, after several tours ministering to the spiritual needs of American troops in Europe and Japan, wrote a similar piece entitled "An American Creed." It begins with these words:

> *I believe in America:*
> *In her high destiny under God to stand before the people of the earth as a shining example of unselfish devotion to the ideals that have made us a great nation: the Christian ideal of liberty in harmonious unity, builded of respect for God's image in man and every man's right to life, liberty and happiness.*

These American credos are not highly personal statements. They are patriotic tributes whose purpose is to rally public opinion. Although most of them use the first person singular, they are meant to represent an unshakable collective faith; they depend upon an unqualified conviction that—according to *The American Citizen's Handbook*—"America is great because of the ideals which the pioneers established for its homes, for its schools, and for its democratic community life." This unanimity was strongest during

World War II and its immediate aftermath, as the United States stepped forward to assume the mantle of the world's most powerful nation. At that time the *Handbook*, along with other American credos, served a purpose similar to that of the original creeds—it taught the founding principles to initiates to the faith (new citizens), and renewed this awareness in everyone else. "The future of America depends simply on our being ourselves," states the *Handbook*'s foreword, "on our standing by the ideals that have made us great."

"It is amazing how many interesting books humanistic criticism manages not to notice," writes cultural watchdog Paul Fussell in an essay entitled "The Boy Scout Handbook," in which he praises the best-selling guide for Scouts as a work of "permanent social and psychological consequence." He would certainly have given *The American Citizen's Handbook* the same endorsement. In addition to the Boy Scout Oath and Laws, the Athenian Ephebic Oath, the Oath of Naturalization, it overflows with every type of ready-made opinion for the good citizen. Its method and motivating philosophy come through in the *Handbook*'s foreword, which opens with a code:

> *To be a good father, mother, sister, or friend;*
> *To be a dependable, faithful, and skilled worker in home, school, field, factory, or office;*
> *To be an intelligent, honest, useful, and loyal citizen, with faith in God and love of fellowman;*
> *To recognize the brotherhood of man and to live by the Golden Rule—*
> *These are the aspirations that have brought happiness and achievement to the America we all love.*

In his essay Fussell does not fixate on platitudes as much as practical advice and unassailable ideals, which both the *Scout Handbook* and the *Citizen's Handbook* have in abundance. To its credit, the Scouting hierarchy has updated the language of the guidebook in ways that Fussell finds largely successful. But the *Citizen's Handbook* of 1941 speaks in a remote, almost lost language—the language of good intentions. Most Americans would be hard pressed to disagree with any of its points (except, perhaps, its references to God), but they would be unlikely to accept it as written. It sounds innocent to the point of naiveté.

Fussell concludes his essay by observing, "In the current world of Making It and Getting Away With It, there are not many books devoted to associating happiness with virtue." *The American Citizen's Handbook* is one of them. But he points out that such texts have always provided broad targets for ridicule and parody, usually by those who are the least familiar with their contents. "Anyone who imagines that the scouting movement is either sinister or stupid or funny," he claims, "should spend a few hours with the latest edition of *The Official Boy Scout Handbook*." It might also not be a bad idea to have a glance at *The American Citizen's Handbook*.

THE VOICE OF AMERICA

There is little doubt that *The American Citizen's Handbook* overflows with what Edward R. Murrow and his colleagues dismissed as "uplift," and which they specifically asked the contributors to *This I Believe* to refrain from using. They did not want to hear patriotic credos or testimonials to "the American way of life, or democracy, or free enterprise." But not all of the contributors seemed capable of this.

"I believe in a moral code based on the Ten Commandments and in . . . the Sermon on the Mount," offered Harry Truman. "What do I believe?" asked Adlai Stevenson. "As an American I believe in generosity, in liberty, in the rights of man." Carl Sandburg simply owned up that, "I believe in platitudes." And that hit the nail on the head. What seems trite in one context may possess a magical hold on the imagination in another. What Murrow may have wanted to hear was not necessarily what his audience responded to.

Many Murrow contributors found it easiest to explain their beliefs through stories. Others expressed a faith in "people" or "humanity," in the essential goodness of human nature, in the triumph of good over evil, in the possibility of a better world through the inculcation of virtues. The Golden Rule, the Commandments, and such standards as St. Paul's admonition to fight the good fight, stay the course, and keep the faith made several appearances on the show. But few were completely satisfied with what they had written, and perhaps Murrow felt the same. Yet audiences still loved it.

This I Believe succeeded for a while in creating a national dialogue. It was carried over 196 U.S. radio stations each week, and in 97 foreign countries. It was translated into six languages by the Voice of America, and syndicated in 85 newspapers. It also spawned two books and a successful record album. More than two hundred schools nationwide turned it into a curriculum, with students writing their own six-hundred-word essays. In 1954 the *Cleveland Press* sponsored an essay contest, and two of the winners, a student and a housewife, were invited onto the show. But many of the celebrity invitees demurred. One of them, novelist Kathleen Norris, wrote back saying, "it's either a mawkish sermon, or it's indecent exposure." Indeed, General Lucius D. Clay, who accepted the invitation, compared the experience to getting undressed in public.

"We have discovered," wrote Murrow, "that most people have never attempted to reduce to writing what they believe and why. Almost without exception they have told us that this is the most difficult piece of composition they have undertaken." Murrow himself followed an unwritten set of standards. He understood right from wrong instinctively, and he acted accordingly. He regarded religion, which his mother had wanted him to pursue as a career, as "more ethics than faith," but it was beyond his capacity to put those ethics into words, and it is telling that he never contributed an essay to his own program.

And yet as astonishingly successful as the show became (at the top of its popularity, it may have reached about fifty million readers and listeners each week), it is equally remarkable for its sudden disappearance. The network seemed to lose interest, and Murrow himself paid to have the remaining segments aired out of loyalty to the contributors whose carefully worded beliefs had not yet been used.

The show's demise would not have surprised at least one contemporary observer. In 1952 Roland Sawyer, a reviewer for the *Christian Science Monitor*, noted, "One of the most popular programs ever put on radio . . . these little journeys into philosophy . . . will not have a very long life." While applauding the idea and its inspiration, Sawyer saw it ultimately as little more than a celebrity showcase. He added, "it is difficult to get beyond the good-over-evil formula in six hundred words."

The demise of *This I Believe* coincided with what is perceived to be the decline of authority in America. Murrow and company could speak with assurance to a generation of war veterans, but to the first members of the baby-boom generation they seemed out of touch. The good-over-evil formula sounded more convincing when good and evil were clearly defined. But as Murrow prepared to leave his career as a reporter in order to take over the United States Information Agency under John F. Kennedy, he could see that this distinction was becoming blurred.

AN ECUMENICAL CREED

In the 1960s, traditional creeds began a downhill slide. By the time of the student demonstrations against the Vietnam War, the country was polarized between establishment figures and the voices of the counterculture, who rejected the authority implied by creeds. As flags and draft cards burned, few people had time to concern themselves with beliefs that would seem to have failed. Disbelief, or at least an assault on long-held beliefs, was the new order of the day.

It was not just the American creed that came under attack. As symbols of authority fell, organized religion also suffered. With membership decreasing and alternative forms of worship on the rise, the mainstream churches made an attempt to reach out to popular tastes. Traditional hymns played on the organ gave way to folk songs accompanied by guitar. In the place of creeds that served as strict tests of faith, more inclusive creeds sprung up. The 1950s witnessed the beginnings of the ecumenical movement, which attempted to produce a consensus of religious belief that transcended all faiths. This brought forth a rash of new creeds—personal religious statements of faith that might also (the authors hoped) be taken up by congregations. As theologian Avery Dulles noted in the *Expository Times* (July 1980), many such personal creeds appeared during this period of social upheaval, and while acknowledging the ancient creeds they asserted their individuality by using new words to "escape from the domination of the past."

The Catholic Church did not replace or rewrite its creeds. Instead it translated them, which amounted to much the same thing. In the early 1960s the reforms of Vatican II, undoubtedly with the intention of making the mass more "relevant," declared that the creeds, indeed the entire mass, would no longer be recited in Latin, as it had been for centuries. Once the creeds appeared in English, they lost some of their mystique. Many of the Protestant denominations also sought to free themselves of tradition, but having always spoken the ancient creeds in English, their only option was to replace them.

In 1983 a committee of the Presbyterian Church (U.S.A) produced the *Presbyterian Brief Statement of Faith* to mark the reuniting of the two largest U.S. Presbyterian Churches. The *Brief Statement* was written as a substitute for the Apostles' Creed. Brief enough for worship, but deep enough to reflect the Reformed tradition and the distinctiveness of Presbyterianism, it was designed to be used in the liturgy as an alternative not only to the ancient formulas, but to the lengthy Protestant confessions of faith. But the Presbyterians' General Assembly, unlike the Vatican, did not issue a binding edict, leaving the choice to its congregations. Many elected to stick with the old creed.

The democratic approach has proven more successful within smaller constituencies. The Moss Side Baptist Church in Manchester, England, for example, produced a charming confession of faith by asking its members to respond to the question: "What is God like?" The most common elements of their answers were then arranged into a creed which pleased the entire congregation. It is reprinted in Part Two (p. 247).

CONCLUSION

Why do creeds matter? Before there were any creeds people managed to get along very well without them. Many cultures still adhere to unspoken principles that are sustained by customs or rituals. But Western culture, and the United States in particular, perhaps because of Aristotle's insistence that all human activity should be grounded on first principles, has continually strived to produce documents that clearly state such principles, whether in the form of religious creeds, declarations of independence, or bills of rights.

Creeds are statements of original intent. More than any other forms of expression, they serve as points of departure from which an individual or an organization may wander, but to which they must eventually return. And because these documents play such an instrumental role in establishing the institutions that shape our lives, we naturally gravitate to them as familiar, comforting, and even inspiring texts. Their utility as instructions for the conduct of life is somewhat beside the point. What matters more is their ability to establish a common identity and a common purpose.

I PLEDGE ALLEGIANCE TO MY FLAG AND THE REPUBLIC
FOR WHICH IT STANDS: ONE NATION, INDIVISIBLE,
WITH LIBERTY AND JUSTICE FOR ALL.

THE *YOUTH'S COMPANION* FLAG PLEDGE,
FIRST RECITED ON OCTOBER 19, 1892

CHAPTER THREE

SO HELP ME GOD

LOYALTY OATHS AND PLEDGES OF ALLEGIANCE

INTEGRITY

Sir Thomas More, one-time Lord Chancellor under Henry VIII, was tried, convicted, and beheaded on July 6, 1535, for refusing to swear an oath recognizing the King as the supreme head of the Church of England. For this act of conscience, More would be canonized as a saint.

In 1961 the playwright Robert Bolt chose the story of More's trial and execution as the subject for his play *A Man for All Seasons*. A study in loyalty, or loyalties, the play shows More as a man committed to many constituencies—his wife, his family, his friends, the English people, the King, the Church, and God. As the action of the play unfolds, these interests gradually come into conflict, and he tries to balance them. In the end More is forced to declare his highest duty.

The words that lead to More's undoing are those of the Act of Succession, which acknowledged Henry VIII as the head of the Church of England, allowing him to bypass the Pope's refusal to sanction his divorce from Catherine of Aragon and his marriage to Anne Boleyn. The act was secured by means of an oath—not simply a loyalty oath, to which More would have had no objection, but a test oath, which would have required him to deny the supremacy of Rome. Because a test oath applies to thoughts rather than actions, it comes down hardest on those who insist upon the sanctity of words. Thomas More died for refusing to compromise his beliefs. In passing the ultimate test put to his conscience on his own terms, he remained true to his faith and forfeited his life. He was not the first to do so, nor would he be the last.

In the play, when More is asked why he will not capitulate and simply assent to the words and trust God to know his heart, he replies, "What is an oath but words we say to God?" Yet More's wife, his daughter, and his friends wish to keep the man and damn the words. Could he not just as well abide by his vows to his wife—his promise to honor her, keep her, and guard her? And what of his obligation to his friends?

But More knew too well that even if an oath is no more than words we say to each other, it is through such words that one's integrity is fixed. And integrity consists in knowing which words take precedence over others. Someone's "word," as in the expression "a man is only as good as his word," is a testament to his good faith. This is why people of the highest integrity—those whose faith is well-defined—take oaths very seriously.

An oath, writes Bolt in his introduction to the play, anchors a man to his most fundamental beliefs, to what he considers right and wrong, and to how he defines himself relative to those beliefs. Thus a perjurer—one who forswears himself—"has no self to commit," in the sense that he forfeits the idea of self and is set morally adrift. For such a man, the line that fixes what "we cannot bring ourselves to do" falls further and further back. More was undoubtedly aware of the words of Saint Augustine, who wrote, "if you are compelled to swear, know that it comes of a necessity arising from the infirmity of those whom you are trying to persuade of something, which is certainly an evil from which we daily pray to be delivered."

In his final answer to his accusers, Bolt's Thomas More says: "What you have hunted me for is not my actions, but the thoughts of my heart. It is a long road you have opened. For first men will disclaim their hearts and presently they will have no hearts. God help the people whose Statesmen walk your road."

NOT ALL OATHS COMPEL PEOPLE to compromise their beliefs. More, for example, lived in one of the most oath-bound societies ever known, one in which he would have routinely sworn professional oaths (as a lawyer), oaths of office, oaths of attainment and affiliation, as well as his wedding vows. He would have found in these, for the most part, a satisfying way of establishing and maintaining social and professional responsibilities, and of instilling a common method, philosophy, and purpose to his activities.

But sometimes a purpose can be poorly served by an oath. This has proven to be the case with loyalty oaths, many of which, because they were motivated out of fear, ultimately undermined the very principles they were designed to protect. Yet oaths can also serve as focal points of satisfying rituals that reinforce the most noble aspects of loyalty and duty. The ancient Greeks, like the medieval English, used oaths extensively, and two of these—the Hippocratic Oath of medicine and the Ephebic Oath of citizenship—remain in use to this day because they continue to satisfy a need for ceremony.

THIS CHAPTER EXAMINES the uses and misuses of loyalty and test oaths from the time of Henry VIII to the present. It also shows how one loyalty oath in particular—the Pledge of Allegiance—took shape over a half-century, withstood many challenges, and settled into the daily routine of Americans as proof and reminder that liberty can tolerate and even profit by dissent.

The next chapter will show how oaths can serve as voluntary, meaningful, and satisfying acts—willingly entered into, in the case of wedding vows; purposefully undertaken, in the case of oaths of office and citizenship; secretly contracted, as are most initiation oaths; or hopefully proposed, in the case of temperance pledges.

LOYALTY

A Man for All Seasons proved to be the hit of the 1962 Broadway season. The reason is not hard to find. Not only is it a tightly crafted drama, but it was a timely one. Just ten years before its premiere, Senator Joseph McCarthy had set off a national witch hunt for Communists and their sympathizers, a mania which resulted in the institution of many loyalty and test oaths. Rather than seeking actual threats to national security, McCarthyism evolved into a purge of those who might in any way have appeared to be "un-American." Unfortunately, this term came to apply to anyone who did not share the senator's patriotic enthusiasm, and whose belief in freedom, free expression, honor, and even the right to remain silent could be used to prove unreliability, and to condemn them. A decade before McCarthy,

Adolph Hitler had engaged in an even more sweeping purge, one which had encouraged citizens to betray their friends and neighbors to the state. In both instances, test oaths proved to be useful tools with which to coerce men to "disclaim their hearts."

The idea of a legislated test oath first occurred to Henry VIII, who found it to be an effective means of identifying and eliminating possible enemies. What ensued cannot be called a glorious history. In addition to More, some fifty of the king's servants lost their heads over this one oath. Its single positive effect, at least as Anglicans see it, was the establishment of the Church of England. But historically, the ruthless imposition of test oaths has proven to be a costly enterprise. Hitler drove many of the most loyal citizens and best minds out of Germany, or to their graves. McCarthyism started to do the same in the United States. While not everyone was innocent, the test oath machinery did not discriminate. Its most prominent victim was J. Robert Oppenheimer, the director of the Manhattan Project, whose security clearance was revoked because of his personal loyalty to a friend, and because he questioned the morality of further nuclear bomb research.

The recurrent use of test oaths shows that there will always be those who seek to advance their own interests by exacting not simply loyalty, but rigid conformity. This can create a compelling dramatic premise, but it does not argue against the utility of *all* oaths, or against the swearing of oaths. For just as an oath can be an insidious device, it can also serve as a badge of responsibility and a reminder of a sacred trust. A pledge of good faith and service, for example, when it is part of a well-designed ritual, can inspire loyalty and dedication. The Pledge of Allegiance, even though it has not always been purely voluntary, is a good example, as is the Boy Scout Oath.

It is, of course, of great interest how some loyalties play off against others. How does a man like Thomas More reconcile the loyalty he has sworn to his wife with his duties as an official of the state, his obedience to the king, and his faith in God? This is not an easy question, but any attempt to answer it must begin with the words themselves. "An oath," says More, "is *made* of words." But what do the words say? Where do they come from, and how do they work? After all, it falls to such words to establish and maintain loyalties that come into conflict—that join people in a common purpose, or cause them to be cast out of society.

THE ORIGINS OF TEST OATHS

When they are finally examined in the light of day, the words that Thomas More refused to swear have surprisingly little dramatic weight. At first glance it is difficult to see what he objected to. The oath would have required him to "bear faith, truth, and obedience only to the King's Majesty and to his heirs of his body and of his . . . lawful wife Queen Anne . . . according to the limitation in the Statute made for the surety of his succession . . . and that . . . you shall observe, keep, maintain and defend the said Act of Succession and the whole effects and contents thereof."

More would gladly have acknowledged the legitimacy of the divorce, the remarriage, and even the revised line of succession to the crown. There was one point, however, which did not escape his legal acumen. To accept the Act of Succession would be to deny the spiritual supremacy of the Pope. That this conclusion is not obvious from a first reading attests to the king's skill in implementing changes—profound changes—in English society by parliamentary means. Through a succession of statutes, Henry VIII gradually effected a revolution—one that drove the Catholic Church out of England and instituted a state religion. More could see exactly what the king was trying to do, and he would have no part of it.

Such an ambitious plan, it can be argued, required the ruthless elimination of possible dissenters if it was to succeed. This explains the rise of loyalty and test oaths in England, and their subsequent expanded use in later crises. By enacting four loyalty oaths during his tenure, each longer and more restrictive than its predecessor, Henry VIII sought to secure support for the many lines of succession that came about through his marriages, and to keep the power of the Church of Rome in check. His successors perpetuated this policy through a series of new oaths of supremacy (which acknowledge the supremacy of the king in spiritual affairs, and thus renounce the authority of the Pope), abjuration (of any support for pretenders to the throne), allegiance, and obedience.

After three centuries of this type of maneuvering the English ended their use of test oaths through the Parliamentary Oaths Act of 1868, which substituted a simple loyalty oath and extended the right of affirmation— essentially the replacement of the word "swear" with "affirm."

In this respect Americans had taken the lead on their former countrymen. In the United States oaths are required for local, state, and federal office, for induction into the military, for naturalization, and for passport applications. But oaths of government office must be carefully worded to avoid compromising the convictions of Quakers, Mennonites, atheists, or any other group that either respects the scriptural admonition to "swear no oaths," or does not feel bound by a sacred oath. Article Six of the United States Constitution declares that all state and federal representatives, executive and judicial officers, "shall be bound by Oath or Affirmation to support this Constitution." But it adds that "no religious Test shall ever be required as a Qualification to any Office or public Trust under the United States."

THE HISTORY OF ENGLISH test oaths does have a parallel in the United States, however, where insecurity at the highest levels of government gave rise to suspicion and paranoia, and inspired the use of restrictive and often counterproductive oaths. During the Civil War the loyalty issue was particularly acute, and it divided Unionists over the conditions of amnesty for Confederates who defected during the war, and for repatriated secessionists afterward. Abraham Lincoln (and Andrew Johnson afterward) inclined towards leniency, but Congress did not. Their restrictive "ironclad oath of loyalty" loomed as a major obstacle on the road to reconstruction. By disqualifying anyone who had served the Confederacy from holding local government office, the oath effectively barred all potential candidates in some parts of the South, and many offices went unfilled.

The ironclad oath succumbed to a constitutional challenge in 1867 when it was declared a law *ex post facto* (imposing a penalty for an act which was not punishable when it was done). Interestingly enough, with the test clause removed it survives as the oath of office used to swear in members of Congress.

IT IS NOT UNUSUAL for test oaths to outlive the fear that inspired them. They usually succumb to constitutional challenges because they violate the very rights they propose to protect. No exception to this rule was McCarthyism, which gave the term "loyalty oath" an especially negative connotation. As Supreme Court Justice William O. Douglas commented, "Test oaths are notorious tools of tyranny." Yet many of them, like the ironclad oath, remain in use today, albeit with certain controversial passages removed.

THE MOST DANGEROUS ENEMY THEY CAN FIND

In 1961, the year of *A Man for All Seasons*, Rod Serling, creator of *The Twilight Zone*, wrote a short story entitled "The Monsters Are Due on Maple Street." On the surface a simple tale of everyday horror, the story is far more interesting for what lurks beneath the surface, in the depths of Serling's allegorically driven mind. Although today the plot reads like an episode of *The Simpsons*, when Serling wrote it the American public felt far too threatened to see any humor in it.

IT IS AN IDYLLIC Indian summer weekend afternoon in suburban America. Children are playing, men are washing their cars and mowing their lawns. The Good Humor man stops by and waits for the neighborhood children to beg nickels from their parents. The Ohio State–SMU football game can be heard on someone's radio. Suddenly there is a bright flash across the sky, and everything stops—cars refuse to start, electricity and water cease to flow, even portable radios fall silent.

As the neighbors gather around to figure out what's going on, a small boy makes a startling announcement: this is what happens, he says, when the aliens come. There is probably even an alien among them already, he adds, at least according to the comic books he reads. This announcement sets off a chain reaction: suspicions grow, fingers are pointed, tempers flare, and by nightfall the neighbors have become an unruly mob turning on itself in search of the alien in their midst.

The next morning no sign of life remains on the street. Homes have been burned and bodies lie about. From a nearby hillside two aliens survey the carnage.

> "Understand the procedure now?" the first figure said. "Just stop a few of their machines and radios and telephones and lawn mowers. Throw them into darkness for a few hours and watch the pattern unfold."
>
> "And this pattern is always the same?" the second figure asked.
>
> "With few variations," came the answer. "They pick the most dangerous enemy they can find and it's themselves. All we need to do is sit back and watch."
>
> "Then I take it," the second figure said, "this place, this Maple Street, is not unique?"

Figure one shook his head and laughed. "By no means. Their world is full of Maple Streets . . . "

The subtext of the story may seem transparent, even simplistic. But it does set the tone of the era. A few years earlier—on October 4, 1957, to be precise—the Soviet satellite Sputnik I streaked across the autumn sky, sending shock waves across every Maple Street in America. Coming at a time when the Cold War had increased fears and heightened paranoia, the Sputnik launch initiated a panicked reaction on several fronts.

The most frequently cited response was NASA's accelerated commitment to the space program, which led to the moon landing in 1969. But more immediate was the passage in 1958 of the Eisenhower administration's National Defense Education Act (NDEA), authorizing a seven-year, $1 billion loan program for students at colleges and universities across the country. This was the first federal student loan program—a measure designed to insure America's technological superiority. But there was a catch. In the spirit of the day, Congress attached a requirement in the form of a test oath to the application. The first part of the oath was uncontroversial. It covered the same points as the naturalization oath and most civil service oaths—a promise to bear true faith and allegiance to the country and to the Constitution. The second part of the oath went further, however, by requiring the applicant to swear that:

I do not advocate, nor am I a member of, any party or organization, political or otherwise, that now advocates the overthrow of the United States or (this state) by force or violence or any other unlawful means; that within five years preceding the taking of this oath I have not become a member of any such party or organization . . .

The obvious defense of such an oath, which was put forth at the time and repeatedly made, is that any good citizen should have no trouble swearing it—that it merely reiterates an assent to the American way of life. Senator Strom Thurmond remarked, "If a person does not love his country, and if he is not willing to take an oath that he will support the Constitution, I say he has no business getting a loan from the Government." But of course the oath asked far more than that.

The obvious objection to the oath, also put forth at the time and repeatedly made, is that it served no useful purpose. It could hardly weed out Communists or other subversives, because such people would have no qualms about swearing it. Both of these arguments miss the real issue.

A test oath is not intended to weed out subversives. It is intended to identify those who do not possess the requisite enthusiasm for weeding out subversives—those who may be loyal, but cannot be counted on to un-hesitatingly betray all other loyalties. Its operative principle, ironically, is summed up by Eldridge Cleaver's popular maxim of the 1960s: If you're not part of the solution, you're part of the problem.

What proponents of test oaths usually overlook, however, is that the na-tion was founded by subversives, and that the Founding Fathers made a point of stating in the Declaration of Independence that when a regime becomes oppressive, the people have a legitimate right to overthrow it. In a sense, then, the test clause of the NDEA oath, like most test oaths, is as un-American as the beliefs it supposedly targets. It is an insult to people of conscience, and it denies freedom of thought, of association, and of ex-pression. As such, most test oaths have managed to backfire, ultimately un-dermining the very principles they were designed to protect. Yet when faced with a crisis, a majority of Americans have unhesitatingly supported them, and only in rare instances have they come to realize just how costly such a reaction has been.

The NDEA oath did not go unchallenged. It immediately encountered a boycott by thirty-two U.S. colleges and universities, including many in the Ivy League and Big Ten, who refused to accept any loan money offered under such conditions. Sixty-four other schools voiced their protests, al-though they continued to accept NDEA applicants.

In 1959 Senator John F. Kennedy tried to abolish the test oath through Congress, citing its futility as well as its implicit assumption that students and teachers are second-class citizens. But it is easy to see why students and teachers were singled out. Loyalty is a quality of citizenship that is the province of the schools. Through the Pledge of Allegiance, civics classes, and American history texts, teachers are entrusted with the task of instill-ing a sense of national pride and unity in the nation's children. Thus they are the first ones that politicians suspect in times of greatest national inse-curity.

If Kennedy needed any ammunition against the test oath, he did not have to look very far. In the late 1940s, at the outset of the Cold War, the regents of the University of California instituted an oath with a test clause similar to that of the NDEA oath, and required every staff employee and faculty member to sign it. Resistance was immediate, but initially ineffec-tive. After a year of bitter internal dispute, during which the trustees in-sisted on administering the oath regardless of the consequences, more than a hundred scholars resigned from the university, were fired, or were simply not reappointed. Many were among the top researchers in their fields. The university was forced to drop fifty-five courses from its curriculum, and many departments suffered badly. In the final analysis, the reputation and the research capability of the entire university had been compromised, and it took a decade to rebuild. For all their efforts, the regents could boast of having identified just two Communists: a piano accompanist employed in dance classes and a part-time graduate teaching assistant.

The regents' oath gave way the next year to the Levering Oath, a similar state-wide test oath designed to keep Communists out of state jobs. Instigated by then-governor Earl Warren, this oath also proved to be unconstitutional and counterproductive.* But once instituted, it was very difficult to get rid of, which has proven to be the case with most test oaths.

The University of California regents' oath is one of the darker episodes in American higher education. Many careers were needlessly destroyed, and the goals of education, if not the ideals of freedom, were poorly served. This single oath did more to undermine the American system of education than any subversive could possibly have done. Yet in spite of this example, the NDEA program went through, the Kennedy challenge failed, and the test oath lived out its natural life. When signing it into law, President Eisenhower had declared it to be "an emergency undertaking to be terminated after four years." What saved it was its built-in obsolescence. Before any other legal challenges could be mounted, the program came to a close.

THE LAST RECOURSE OF LIARS

This journey into the Twilight Zone of loyalty and test oaths had a moral and an ending. The moral is that the golden mean of eternal vigilance is indeed the price of liberty, yet the extremes of excessive paranoia and complete indifference exact a heavy toll. The lesson was slow to sink in. A few test oaths survived the 1960s, only to be struck down by the courts in the 1970s. But their spirit still remains. Loyalty oaths (not test oaths) are still a common requirement for state workers. The state of Vermont even requires a loyalty oath for voter registration.

*In what he later admitted to be a mistake, Warren also supported the internment of Japanese-Americans during World War II.

Other nations tend not to drag their citizens through such chicaneries. Although historically many countries have employed loyalty oaths, the United States is one of the few that have made them part of the fabric of everyday life. Loyalty oaths, pledges of allegiance, and even naturalization oaths are not seen as necessary or even desirable in the countries of the European Union. Perhaps this is because the American idea of citizenship is grounded in ideology more than cultural identity, and consequently there is a greater desire to legitimize it with words and gestures.

One irony of the test oath controversies is that the most conservative voices in these debates would have found very little sympathy for their cause among the Founding Fathers, whose original intent was to keep the nation as oath-free as possible. Even when faced with the issue of British loyalists who remained in America after the Revolution, patriot leaders did not resort to purges. Although some states did require the swearing of loyalty and test oaths during the war, this fervor did not carry over to the pursuit and punishment of loyalists afterwards. Many loyalists were hounded out of the country in the immediate aftermath of the war, but this vindictiveness soon dissipated, and they were welcomed back into society.

Besides, oaths were not trusted. This reflected a residual resentment Americans held against British rule, which had since the time of Henry VIII mandated oaths of loyalty and initiation in all walks of life. Where oaths had become so overused, they were considered meaningless at best, and offensive at worst. Benjamin Franklin, echoing Samuel Johnson, wrote, "I have never regarded [oaths] otherwise than as the last recourse of liars." In particular, Franklin believed that there should be no reliance placed on the promises of loyalists who after the war would swear to be good Americans.

On the other side of the Atlantic, British officials found loyalty oaths, which many of their spies had sworn on both sides, to be undependable predictors of future service, and looked to past actions as indicators of future reliability. But neither side tried to institute test oaths in an exclusionary or punitive way. George Washington, in fact, had no qualms about employing former loyalists in his administration.

What seems to be an instance of noble high-mindedness on the part of the Founding Fathers should be weighed against the fact that after the Revolutionary War, loyalists were not considered much of a threat. In drafting the Constitution, the Founders saw fit to include a succinct presidential oath of office, and although they suggested an oath for government service, they did not bother to write one. They saw no need for a loyalty test oath for citizens, nor for a pledge of allegiance. To their credit, most of the Founders believed that a sound system of government had no need for mandated oaths. In James Madison's notes taken at the Constitutional Convention, James Wilson of Pennsylvania is on record as saying he was never fond of oaths, considering them as "left-handed security only. A good government did not need them, and a bad government could not or ought not be supported."

Looking back on the process of drafting the Constitution, one can see how unlikely it would have been for states' rights advocates to have accepted a constitutionally mandated pledge of any kind. They would have preferred to leave it to the states themselves. In time, this is how such oaths were instituted—most of the states drafted their own loyalty oaths for their civil servants. One by one, they would also mandate a pledge of allegiance for all schoolchildren. But this did not occur until the country was well beyond its hundredth birthday.

THE OLD MAN

On June 14—Flag Day—in 1972, the United States House of Representatives convened at noon with more than a quorum in eager attendance. The session began with a recess called for the purpose of observing and commemorating the day.

With all due ceremony, the Joint Chiefs of Staff, the Commandant of the Coast Guard, and the Leaders of the Military Women filed in and took their seats near the rostrum. The United States Air Force Band played "This Is My Country," and when the Doorkeeper announced the arrival of the Flag of the United States borne by a color bearer and guard, they launched into "Americans We."

Mr. Nichols, the distinguished gentleman from Alabama, then took the floor to introduce the day's honored guest, the television comedian Red Skelton, who at that time hosted the most popular variety show on television. Skelton had been invited to Congress to recreate a dramatic reading of the Pledge of Allegiance which he had first performed on his television show in 1969. In that year—a particularly tumultuous one for the nation—Skelton had drawn upon his experience entertaining troops in Korea to deliver a dose of rousing old-fashioned patriotism on his show.

The reaction to this telecast was instantaneous. CBS was flooded with requests for transcripts, and sent out over two hundred thousand copies. Skelton recorded the piece, and the record became a best-seller that year.

The wave of enthusiasm carried Skelton all the way to the United States Capitol, where on that special day he stood before the House and once again assumed the manner of one of his most popular and familiar characters, the Old Man. This is what he said:

One of the greatest speeches I think I have ever heard was when I was a small boy, and we boys and girls had just finished reciting the Pledge of Allegiance, and our teacher called us together and said, "Boys and girls, I have been listening to you recite the Pledge of Allegiance all semester, and it appears to me it has become monotonous to you, or could it be that you do not know the meaning of those words? If I may I would like to recite the Pledge of Allegiance and give you a definition for each word.

I—me, an individual, a committee of one.

Pledge—dedicate all of my worldly goods to give without self-pity.

Allegiance—my love and my devotion.

To the Flag—our standard, Old Glory, a symbol of freedom. Wherever she waves, there is respect because your loyalty has given her a dignity that shouts freedom is everybody's job.

Of the United—that means we have all come together.

States—individual communities that have united into 48 great states, 48 individual communities with pride and dignity and purpose, all divided with imaginary boundaries, yet entitled to a common purpose, and that's love for country.

Of America.

And to the Republic—a state in which sovereign power is invested in representatives chosen by the people to govern. And government is the people and it's from the people to the leaders, not from the leaders to the people.

For which it stands.

One nation—meaning, so blessed by God.

Indivisible—incapable of being divided.

With liberty—which is freedom and the right of power to live one's own life without threats or fear or some sort of retaliation.

And justice—the principle or quality of dealing fairly with others.

For all—which means 'it's as much your country as it is mine.'

Since I was a small boy, two states have been added to our country and two words have been added to the Pledge of Allegiance—'Under God.' Wouldn't it be a pity if someone said, 'That's a prayer,' and that would be eliminated from schools too?"

After the applause in the chamber died down, Skelton led the assembly in the Pledge, the Air Force Singing Sergeants presented "I Am an American," someone read William Tyler Page's "American's Creed," the national anthem was sung, the colors were retired from the chamber, and with that the ceremony concluded.

SUCH OCCASIONS LEAVE no room for dissenting opinions or opposing views, but there were many opposing views and disgruntled voices across the nation at the time. While Skelton's performance was reassuring to many, it undoubtedly grated on some people, although it shouldn't have.

What the Flag Day ceremonies of 1972 implied, but never uttered, is that the Pledge, the flag, the national anthem, and the nation itself, can accommodate a wide range of opinions—diametrically opposed opinions—without shattering, or being in any way diminished. That is their essential strength. The Pledge is not perfect, even in its annotated form. Each phrase that Skelton so reverently explained has at one time or another been the source of conflict, controversy, anguish, and confusion. Yet it has held together and come through the decades remarkably well. What follows is its story, in which a series of phrases took shape over a period of sixty years and came to serve as a ritual that unites all Americans—even those who refuse to recite it.

RUSSO V. CENTRAL SCHOOL DISTRICT

In the fall of 1969 on yet another of the country's Maple Streets, a young art teacher named Susan Russo began a three-year probationary appointment at a Rochester, New York, high school. On her first day, she discovered that the Pledge of Allegiance would be recited each morning in every homeroom. Although she had never encountered this practice before, it was standard in many school systems. In fact, it was mandated by law in the state of New York.

Back in 1943 the Supreme Court had declared that a student could decline to recite the Pledge for reasons of conscience, but it did not extend this privilege to teachers who had to lead the exercise. Susan Russo did not have to lead her homeroom in the Pledge; it was broadcast over the school's PA system. But she found that even though she had never been a dissident, a protester, or any kind of activist, and while she had never acted

out in any way in her own school years, she could not bring herself to recite the Pledge with the class. The words "with liberty and justice for all"
struck her as particularly hollow. So she stood with the others, her hands
at her sides, and said nothing.

Russo's quiet defiance went unnoticed for a while, but eventually came
to the attention of the school's principal, who visited her homeroom one
morning in order to observe. When he saw that his new teacher did not
speak the words of the Pledge or place her right hand over her heart, he
summoned her to his office.

The confrontation between teacher and principal would eventually
lead to the nonrenewal of her contract at the end of the school year, and
that would lead the parties involved to the state court, and eventually to
the Supreme Court as *Russo v. Central School District*. Years later, when all
was said and done, Susan Russo was exonerated and reinstated. But by answering the dictates of her conscience, all the while fighting to prevent
her cause from being taken up by others who might use it to advance their
own agendas, she incurred the enmity of the entire community, and was
treated as a pariah. In the end, she grew to respect the position of the
principal and the superintendent who had rescinded her appointment.
She realized that they were just as sure of their position, in their own
good conscience, as she was of her own. What she learned went beyond
any court decision.

It is no surprise that court battles over the reciting of the Pledge have
been waged with regularity over the last fifty years. What is surprising is
that the Pledge itself, which now seems sacrosanct, is less than half as old
as the flag it sanctifies, and has been subjected to almost as many alterations in its brief career. To say the least, its history is short, and has been
anything but smooth.

THE YOUTH'S COMPANION FLAG PLEDGE

The original Pledge of Allegiance was written by an ordained Baptist minister named Francis M. Bellamy, although some controversy surrounds this
attribution. Bellamy worked as a staff writer for *The Youth's Companion* in the
1890s, where his boss was James Upton, the magazine's publisher. Exactly
who came up with the idea for a flag pledge is not clear. Some people believe Upton dictated the pledge to Bellamy, others that Upton merely directed Bellamy to come up with something suitable. In the 1950s the

Library of Congress investigated and handed down a verdict in favor of Bellamy's sole authorship. That seemed to settle the matter.

In retrospect the need for such a pledge cannot be denied. The only existing pledge of that era, a verse written by Colonel George T. Balch, was hardly the stuff of which national symbols are made. The now deservedly forgotten tribute reads:

We give our Heads! and our Hearts! to Our Country!
One Country! One Language! One Flag!

Upton and Bellamy had a better idea. In order to counteract the rampant commercialization of the flag, as well as the lack of any federal or state guidelines as to where, when, and how the national symbol should be displayed, they proposed that a flag should be flown at every school house, and that students should recite a pledge to it each day.

"The Youth's Companion Flag Pledge" was the centerpiece of their vision. To inaugurate it, they lobbied to have it recited across the country on the opening day of the World's Columbian Exposition—October 19, 1892—which also happened to be the first celebration of Columbus Day (yet another part of the *Youth's Companion's* ambitious plan). Their efforts were fully rewarded. On that day, in schools across the land, teachers read a proclamation from President McKinley, after which the nation's schoolchildren saluted the flag with their right hands placed over their hearts, palms facing down, while they repeated the words:

I pledge allegiance to my flag and the Republic for which it stands: one nation, indivisible, with liberty and justice for all.

ONE NATION, UNDER GOD

Bellamy's pledge was an immediate success. New York stepped forward as the first state to require its recitation in the schools, enacting this into law the day after the outbreak of the Spanish–American War in 1898. The practice was informally followed elsewhere, buoyed by the Pledge's popularity, and gradually became law in more and more states.

In 1923 a National Flag Code Committee was formed to determine the proper etiquette for displaying and handling the American flag. The committee recommended that the Pledge should be made part of the flag code, and that the words "the flag of the United States" should replace "my flag," so that immigrants would have no doubt as to whose flag they would be saluting. The following year the committee went even further, adding the words "of America," so as to eliminate the remote possibility that some other union of states—Brazil or Mexico, perhaps—might be an unintended beneficiary of someone's allegiance.

The present version of the Pledge of Allegiance swept in on the same wave of patriotic enthusiasm that anointed "In God We Trust" as the national motto. In April 1953, Representative Louis Rabaut of Michigan, reacting to the suggestion of a constituent, drafted a House resolution proposing that the words "under God" should be added to the Pledge, apparently citing the use of that phrase in the Gettysburg Address as source and justification. Credit for the addition of the phrase is often given to the pastor of President Eisenhower's Presbyterian church in Washington. The Reverend George M. Docherty's remarks to his congregation are often quoted as the impetus for the change. "There [is] something missing in the Pledge," Docherty is reported to have said, "[something that is] the characteristic and definitive factor in the American way of life. Indeed, apart from the mention of the phrase 'the United States of America,' it could be the pledge of any republic. In fact, I could hear little Muscovites repeat a similar pledge to their hammer-and-sickle flag in Moscow."

If Docherty deserves any credit, it is for confirming that the inclusion of the words "under God" was entirely a political act, and not a religious one. In the mid-1950s it was all too easy to play upon Cold War fears, and those who objected to the phrase by insisting upon the separation of church and state had no chance against the religious patriotism of the era. President Eisenhower signed a bill into law on June 14, 1954, establishing the first Flag Day, and making official the amended Pledge. He marked the occasion, and perhaps his own ambivalence, by stating, "Our form of government has no sense unless it is founded on a deeply felt religious belief—and I don't care what it is."

This addition, the reference to God, naturally caused problems and brought court challenges. In the spirit of the worst test oaths, it seemed to dare anyone to object to it, knowing that people would, and that by doing so they would immediately call into question their own patriotism. But the most important challenges to the Pledge predated this change, and centered on the compulsory flag salute itself.

WITH LIBERTY AND JUSTICE FOR ALL

In 1940, two Jehovah's Witness children refused to stand and pledge allegiance to the flag in their Pennsylvania classroom, as required by a state law. They had been taught a very literal obedience to biblical injunctions, especially those forbidding the worshipping of graven images. The flag, in the context of the pledging ceremony, appeared to be just such an image. For their actions the children were expelled. When the case reached the Supreme Court, the school's position was affirmed as correct, and thus the *Gobitis* case went into the law as a setback for the freedom of religion.

Three years later a similar case in West Virginia again pitted Jehovah's Witness children against a state law, but this time the Supreme Court had a change of heart. In *West Virginia State Board of Education v. Barnett*, the majority opinion sidestepped the precedent the court had set in *Gobitis*, citing the refusal to recite the Pledge not as an instance of religious expression, but as one of free speech. In language that parallels a scene from *A Man for All Seasons*, the Court ruled that remaining silent was an acknowledged form of expression—in this case a protected one. Justice Robert Jackson, in his famous opinion, added that "compulsory unification of opinion achieves only the unanimity of the graveyard."

Many observers saw this reversal of opinion, in the midst of a world war, as a result of the growing awareness of Nazi totalitarianism and methods of indoctrination. The issue was thrown into high relief by the children's flag salute of that era, which had evolved from the original gesture in which the right hand was placed over the heart with the palm facing down, into a more dramatic procedure in which the students would shoot out their right arms in something like a Nazi salute. In 1942 Congress hastily revised this ritual, substituting the placing of the right hand flat over the heart. In *Barnett*, the Supreme Court also seemed to want to distance itself from excesses committed in the name of German nationalism.

RICHARD STANDS

Much fun has been made of children's interpretations of the Pledge. Art Linkletter, a daytime television fixture in the 1960s, got a lot of mileage out of such innocent readings as: "the republic for Richard Stands" and "one nation under guard."

Surprisingly, the reference to God has proven less controversial than the Pledge's unmistakable beginning and ending. "I pledge allegiance to the flag" and "with liberty and justice for all" are its most resonant phrases, and the ones that have caused the most trouble. The first, because it connotes the worshipping of images, inspired the Supreme Court cases of the 1940s. It was the second phrase, however, that stirred up a tempest in the 1960s and '70s, as the American military became further and further mired in Vietnam. At home, as cities began to smolder under the resentment of civil rights abuses, more and more students began to see "with liberty and justice for all" as a sham, and they refused to stand for it.

Susan Russo did not fall into the category of peace activist. She would probably have more closely identified with Red Skelton's audience. In objecting to the confident self-assurance of the Pledge she did not wish to make a highly visible statement, so she stood—silently and respectfully, but not worshipfully. Her silence on something she had not been aware was the law constituted what she thought was a protected form of expression.

Her principal, along with school administrators around the country facing similar protests, argued that "liberty and justice for all" represents an ideal worth working towards, not a statement of fact. No one disputed the point, but the idea of requiring everyone to pledge upset those who saw a lack of commitment to this ideal on the part of political and business leaders.

When the Supreme Court sided with Russo in 1972, it extended the right it had established in 1943 with *Barnett*. Acts of conscience, so long as they did not infringe on the rights of others, were protected in the schools, and this applied to teachers as well as students. As a result of this decision, schoolchildren still learn patriotism, but they also learn to tolerate—even appreciate—other points of view, including the refusal to recite the Pledge.

By making the Pledge voluntary, the Court enlarged, rather than diminished, the principles of liberty and justice for all. Their point of view fell into step with Red Skelton's own teacher's interpretation. Liberty is the "freedom and the right of power to live one's own life without threats or fear or some sort of retaliation." And justice is "the principle or quality of dealing fairly with others." The *Barnett* and *Russo* decisions vindicated these very points.

As for Skelton's concern that the Pledge would be declared a prayer, the Supreme Court also went out of its way to interpret it as a nonreligious statement, thus sparing the words "under God" from any further assaults. This has not prevented politicians from using the Pledge as though it were a sacred text—a creed that glorifies the nation as a promised land brought into existence under the watchful eye of providence. Although it sounds a bit high-flown, no politician has ever prospered by underestimating the power of this vision.

BUSH, DUKAKIS, POLITICS, AND PATRIOTISM

To Massachusetts Governor Michael Dukakis, looking over a mandatory Pledge law that came across his desk in 1977, it seemed perfectly reasonable to seek a legal opinion from the Massachusetts Supreme Judicial Court. This was standard practice. Looking back on *Barnett* and *Russo*, the Court advised the governor that such a law would not withstand a constitutional challenge. So it then seemed equally reasonable for the governor to veto the bill, which he did, having no way of knowing how it would come back to haunt him.

Ten years later Dukakis found himself in the fight of his life as the Democratic Party candidate for president, trying to end the Republican hold on the White House. His adversary, George Bush, as all political candidates do, examined his opponent's record closely, and noticed the veto of the Pledge bill. It was then that Dukakis, holding a slight lead in the polls, found his patriotism being questioned. "What is it about the Pledge of Allegiance that upsets him so much?" asked Bush, as he draped himself in the flag and went about the country leading recitals of the Pledge at every photo opportunity.

Dukakis took this as an attack on his loyalty, which missed the point. By way of rebuttal, he wondered how anyone could support a candidate who knew a law was unconstitutional, but signed it anyway. This also missed the point.

Bush was questioning the Massachusetts governor's willingness to stand up for national pride even at the cost of being legally incorrect. The fact is (and was) that such laws exist in many states, and have gone unchallenged. Ironically, the Massachusetts legislature overrode Dukakis's veto in 1977, and the law is still on the books. This is because the day it went into effect, the state attorney general pronounced it unenforceable, and since no one has tried to enforce it, no one has had to contest it. This is the way such laws work in most places, and it is one of those rare instances in American law in which both sides get their way.

Because of his rather technical frame of mind, Michael Dukakis failed to recognize that an unconstitutional law could safely go into effect where no one would be likely to try to enforce it. Having vetoed the law, he found himself in a legally correct, but politically vulnerable position. He could have fallen back upon the basic American freedoms of expression, religion, and the idea of individualism. Instead, he argued legalistically, and suffered in the polls. He never recovered.

It is probably true, as George Bush stated in his attack, that the Founding Fathers, including Samuel Adams, John Hancock, and John Adams, would not have objected to "teachers leading students in the Pledge of Allegiance to the flag of the United States." It is far less certain that they would have stood for the mandating of this practice by state or federal law. Hancock and the Adamses, after all, were from Massachusetts as well, and they had a fine appreciation of individual liberty and a keen resentment of the imposition of duties, monetary or otherwise.

The majority of Americans, Michael Dukakis included, support the reciting of the Pledge. Although most adults have not had occasion to recite it since high school, they can still conjure up the words, which flow forth in a familiar cadence that resurrects fond memories of school days. Not everything about school days is quite so innocent, but the Pledge, especially as it appears to immigrants and second-generation Americans, constitutes a fixed point of identity—something of almost religious significance. Yet the ritual seems to be strong enough to accommodate those who do not agree and would prefer to sit it out. The same is true for the national anthem, which has been trampled upon and compromised far more than the Pledge, but remains one of the most welcome rituals in American life. Everyone, from the bleachers to the sky boxes, gladly stands for it.

WOMAN'S CHRISTIAN TEMPERANCE

UNION PLEDGE (1874)

I HEREBY SOLEMNLY PROMISE, GOD HELPING ME, TO ABSTAIN
FROM ALL DISTILLED, FERMENTED AND MALT LIQUORS, IN-
CLUDING WINE, BEER AND CIDER, AND TO EMPLOY ALL
PROPER MEANS TO DISCOURAGE THE USE AND TRAFFIC IN
THE SAME.

FRANCES E. WILLARD, PRESIDENT

CHAPTER FOUR

'TIL DEATH DO US PART

OATHS OF CITIZENSHIP, RITES OF SECRET INITIATION, TEMPERANCE PLEDGES, AND WEDDING VOWS

INAUGURATION

In a special midnight ceremony in the wee hours of January 1, 1934, Fiorello LaGuardia swore the oath of office of the mayor of New York City. Later that day he made the first of many radio addresses to his constituency, and to the entire nation, thanks to the NBC radio network. Among other things, he talked of reforming Tammany Hall politics, eliminating waste in government, supporting the president, and bolstering the spirit of a citizenry that was reeling from a national depression.

LaGuardia's first-day promises would sound familiar to any modern-day political observer. The mayor spoke of his intention to redesign government, clean up the slums, balance the budget, and restore confidence in government. At the close of his address, however, he diverged from the expected. With great solemnity he made a personal commitment in the form of a public pledge—specifically, the "oath of the young men of Athens."

Although it is no longer very well known, this oath would have been recognized by many who heard it that day. And it would find a very sympathetic hearing today among those who desire a return to community values and civic virtue. These are the words the mayor recited:

We will never bring disgrace to this, our city, by any act of dishonesty or cowardice, nor ever desert our suffering comrades in the ranks. We will fight for the ideals and sacred things of the city, both alone and with many. We will revere and obey the city's laws and do our best to incite a like respect in those about us who are prone to annul them and set them at naught. We will strive unceasingly to quicken the public sense of civic duty. Thus in all these ways we will transmit this city not only not less, but far greater and more beautiful than it was transmitted to us.

The Athenian Oath of Fealty, also known as the Athenian Ephebic Oath, turns out to be as old as old as the venerable Hippocratic Oath of medicine. It was the oath sworn by Athenian youths when they entered the Ephebic College, which trained them as citizen-soldiers. Unlike Henry VIII's Oath of Supremacy, the Ephebic Oath is not a test oath, but an act of commitment to an ideal of community service. It has served as such, on and off, for almost 2500 years, and although rarely heard of today, it is still very much in use.

INITIATION

The Mafioso live by a code they refer to as *omerta*—a code of silence which has, at least until recent years, been their great source of strength. It not only anchors their oath of initiation, but shields it from the prying eyes of the outside world. As a result, the oath has become a kind of chimera. For years the FBI had tried to tape a Mafia initiation ceremony in order to prove conclusively that the organization exists, and that it is a real conspiracy rather than a screenwriter's fiction. In 1989 they succeeded. A bug planted in the Medford, Massachusetts, headquarters of the Patriarca crime family picked up the following ceremony:

> *I, ————, want to enter into this organization to protect my family and to protect all of my friends. I swear not to divulge this secret and to obey with love and omerta. [The inductee's trigger finger is then pricked and the blood is smeared on the image of the patron saint of the sponsoring family. The card is then burned in the hands of the inductee, who swears:] As burns this saint so will burn my soul. I want to enter alive into this organization and I will have to get out dead.*

As part of the code of *omerta*, members accept plea bargains whenever a prosecutor's case would divulge the family's secrets. In this way they keep their rituals off the record. The Patriarca case proved to be no different. Although portions of the tapes were played in court cases in Hartford and Boston in 1991 and 1992, the brothers eventually pleaded guilty, and the tapes which the FBI had hoped to release to the press sunk out of public view. Reporters filed Freedom of Information suits, hoping to obtain the entire initiation ritual, but to no avail. The chimera had escaped.

The Mafia oath has everything one could hope for: it invokes the strong bond of family, it ties into a long-standing tradition, it requires the drawing of blood, it makes use of a sacred relic, and of course it carries a portentous and dire threat. It is clearly an oath that changes the swearer for life. It cannot be entered into lightly, and once taken, it cannot be undone. Moreover, the FBI believed that the very existence of the Mafia could not be proven without it.

Yet as serious as it may seem to federal agents, it cannot be denied that there is something very juvenile about the entire enterprise. The Mafia oath, in fact, differs hardly at all in style and substance from the oath that Tom Sawyer proposes to Huck Finn as a suitable initiation for Tom Sawyer's Gang:

> It's to swear to stand by one another, and never tell the gang's secrets, even if you're chopped to flinders, and kill anybody and all his family that hurts one of the gang. . . .
> An' all that swearing's got to be done at midnight, in the lonesomest, awfulest place you can find—a haunted house is the best, but they're all ripped up now. . . .
> And you've got to swear on a coffin and sign it with blood.

This is not to suggest that founders of the Mafia consulted the final chapter of *The Adventures of Tom Sawyer* when they designed their ritual. Instead, they simply dipped into the extensive lore of secret initiation—which is more or less what Tom Sawyer was doing.

MOST OATHS ARE DESIGNED to mark rites of passage. They signify a change of status that is willingly entered into, but cannot easily be reversed. Sworn during ceremonies that are often very elaborate and laden with symbolism, they constitute the dramatic climax precisely because they represent the point of no return. If the words are sometimes overwhelmed by the ceremony, they clearly are important. Whether one is entering into a profession, a secret society, or a lifelong partnership, the right words should set the tone.

The purpose of this chapter is to explore some of the most compelling such words, a few of which are of great antiquity, but all of which are born of the same idea. They show that a good oath, or at least a memorable one, is an essential element of a truly satisfying ritual.

THE ATHENIAN EPHEBIC OATH

In the United States, loyalty is expressed in a variety of ways. The Pledge of Allegiance is one of the more obvious of them, but from time to time there have been other attempts to inspire civic responsibility and pride of an even more idealistic sort. One of the most popular pledges of this type flourished in early-twentieth-century America, some 2300 years after it was written. An oath of ancient Greece, it has enjoyed several revivals, mostly because of its evocation of admirable ideals. In particular, to some civic leaders in America, it made a connection between the American republic and the great civilizations of antiquity, of which Athens seemed to be the epitome. It is still used today, here and there, in much the same spirit.

The Athenian Ephebic Oath originated as a citizenship oath sworn by all native-born citizens of Athens. It acquired its middle name when it became the oath of the *ephebi*, the young men between eighteen and twenty years of age who underwent training in citizenship and arms at the Ephebic College, which was established in 335 B.C. The Ephebic Oath would now be merely a historic artifact known only to a handful of specialists but for one remarkable fact: it was revived by American classicists early in the twentieth century to serve as a graduation oath at many colleges, universities, and secondary schools. Although the modern heyday of the oath was brief—about half a century—it still lives, and it lingers in the memories of many who swore it and recall it as a fine enumeration of civic ideals.

The practice seems to have begun in 1913, when the College of New York City (now City College of New York) administered an ancient oath to the members of its graduating class. Why this oath was chosen is not entirely clear, but the college's president, Dr. John H. Finley, may have been the moving force, for it was he who translated and adapted it to suit the occasion. The oath of 1913 reads much like the oath that Fiorello La-Guardia recited at his inauguration twenty years later, with fairly minor changes.

Perhaps because it satisfied a taste for classicism while conveying a sense of institutional pride lacking in most graduation ceremonies, the oath caught on elsewhere. Brooklyn College soon adopted it as their graduation pledge, as did every senior high school in the Los Angeles system. (In fact, an Ephebian Society was formed in Los Angeles in 1918 as a civic betterment association.) The University of Washington also used it at their freshman convocation ceremony.

The wording of the oath was taken from a variety of Greek texts, from which a consensus version had been pieced together—not a definitive text, but one that served as an adequate jumping-off point for schools that wished to adapt it to their tastes. However, in 1932, classical scholars were excited to hear of a French expedition which had made a remarkable discovery in the ancient Athenian township of Acharnae. There, on a large stone tablet, in well preserved letters, archaeologists found the engraved text of the original oath. The head of the tablet carried the unmistakable title "Traditional Oath of the Ephebi Which They Are Obliged to Swear." Almost to the word, it confirmed the validity of the modern oath then in use, and further spread its renown.

By the 1930s the Ephebic Oath, sometimes titled the Athenian Oath of Citizenship, had become a popular inspirational piece. It achieved that crowning measure of acceptance in American culture: it was widely anthologized in speakers' manuals, commonplace books, civics texts, and even the Boy Scout Handbook. Thus when Fiorello LaGuardia used it as the conclusion of his first broadcast to the citizens of New York City, it was well-known to a good portion of his audience.

The appeal of the Ephebic Oath, aside from its association with the height of Athenian culture, is its unique capacity to serve as a universal oath of citizenship and loyalty to a city or a school community. It is more proactive than most U.S. loyalty oaths and oaths of office. It inspires the swearer not merely to uphold the ideals of the city, but to promote a similar respect in others. It issues a challenge to make the community better and more beautiful through one's lifelong efforts.

It is somewhat surprising, and thus all the more gratifying, that the City College of New York and Brooklyn College have retained this oath in their commencement ceremonies. Although rarely encountered elsewhere today, the oath seems remarkably appropriate to a reborn sense of community and of civic virtue, and could well be revived yet again as a voluntary rite of passage for young citizens.

INITIATION AND MANHOOD

In the 1870s, at the same time that Mark Twain was at work on *Tom Sawyer*, a single-minded investigator by the name of Ezra Cook of the National

Christian Association was devoting his energies to finding and exposing the elaborate initiation rituals of the Masonic lodges in order to reveal them as blasphemous and insidious threats to society. Freemasonry both occupied men's thoughts and shaped their respective literary endeavors. Twain had joined a Masonic lodge a decade earlier, at a time when fraternalism was coming into its own as a dominant cultural phenomenon. Having seen the elaborate and sinister initiation firsthand, Twain could perceive its comic possibilities. But Ezra Cook found nothing amusing in what he considered to be the outbreak of a moral crisis.

Unlike the FBI in their attempts to track down the Mafia initiation oath, Cook easily found what he was looking for and published it. But his exposés of fraternal rituals succeeded for the wrong reasons. So elaborate were the lodge rituals that members who took part had difficulty remembering their lines. Cook's exposés, against all of his intentions, were the perfect remedy. After his death, E. A. Cook Publishing became the official publishing arm of the Masonic lodges, and Ezra Cook undoubtedly turned over in his grave (probably at midnight).

If Cook had been as attuned to the popular culture of his day as Twain was, he might have seen the flaw in his plan. He was convinced that if people had had any idea what went on behind the closed doors of these mysterious lodges, they would have been shocked, outraged, and moved to storm the gates of the temple. Instead they wanted to hear more, drawn in by such dire imprecations as:

> All this I most solemnly promise and swear, binding myself under no less a penalty than that of having my thumbs cut off, my eyes put out, my body bound in chains of brass and carried away to a strange and distant land, should I in the least violate this my Super-Excellent Master's obligation. So help me God and keep me steadfast in the due performance of the same.

This oath, and many others like it, are contained in Cook's *Revised Knight Templarism Illustrated* (Chicago, 1879), which lays bare the secrets of the Masonic orders of the York Rite. Although some readers may have been shocked, devotees of popular fiction and theater would have bought right into it. At the height of fraternalism's popularity the theme of secret initiation buoyed the sales of best-selling novels and popular plays. In fact *The Adventures of Tom Sawyer* can only be fully understood in the context of Twain's own Masonic initiation. Even though Twain became disillusioned with Freemasonry, he recognized the Masonic ritual as the most finely crafted secret ceremony ever devised. Its success not only attracted millions of members, but inspired countless spin-offs whose plot lines and symbolism are not accidental.

IN HIS BOOK, *Secret Ritual and Manhood in Victorian America* (1989), Mark Carnes argues that secret ritual provided solace and psychological guidance for young men coming into manhood in Victorian America. It helped them cast off the maternal bond and enter into the society of men. Fascination with ritual was not restricted to the lodges alone, however. All manner of organizations were founded upon or adapted to ritualistic practice. Carnes remarks that the meteoric rise of Joseph Smith's Mormon Church, fraternal temperance societies, the Know-Nothing Party, the Grange, mutual insurance societies (such as the Royal Arcanum), and the Knights of Labor, owed not so much to their espoused beliefs, financial benefits, or stated purposes, but to the aura of ritual they adopted. Thus any society which cloaked its true purpose in the trappings of secrecy, mystery, and initiation tended to flourish.

The Copperhead societies of Northerners sympathetic to the South during the Civil War are said to have attracted much of their membership with their rituals rather than their politics. The same can be said of the original Ku Klux Klan of the 1870s. Anything that promised access to the mysteries of the ancients or of natural religions, according to Carnes, succeeded if the rituals were carefully designed and managed.

Yet for all their grandiosity, these rituals did not possess any claim to archeological authenticity. Instead, they were composed by clever and sometimes eccentric men devoted to the business of selling their own peculiar version of the lost wisdom of extinct cultures. Through trial, error, and imitation, they cobbled together a dizzying variety of themes, featuring Red Men, Odd Fellows, Woodsmen, and Elks. The rituals that succeeded did so by adhering closely to a common plot line, which Carnes summarizes as follows: "(1) an initiate at the outset of his task was portrayed as immature or unmasculine, (2) he overcame obstacles as he embarked on a difficult journey through the stages of childhood and adolescence, (3) this journey or ordeal reached a climax when he was killed (or nearly killed) by angry fathers, (4) he was reborn as a man into a new family of approving brethren and patriarchs."

This story played out night after night not just in the lodges, but also in the theater in the form of pilgrimage dramas. In fiction, as Carnes points out, this framework supplied the plots of some of the most popular books of the day. The typical Horatio Alger novel follows a young man through such a journey, as does *Tom Sawyer*, Stephen Crane's *Red Badge of Courage*, and Lew Wallace's *Ben-Hur*. In fact Wallace, in the wake of the runaway success of his novel, was asked to write the rituals for a new order to be called the Knights of Ben Hur. He agreed after asking that Knights be changed to Tribe, insisting that knights did not exist in the biblical time of Ben Hur. The order became an immediate success.

The vicarious initiatory coming-of-age tale was not simply a passing fad. In its most successful modern incarnation, it reappears in an intergalactic setting, but the plot elements are identical: a young, orphaned hero sets out to find himself, stumbles upon a dangerous but important mission, is befriended by one father figure with mystical powers, nearly dies at the hands of another father figure, and ultimately proves himself, thereby earning the highest honors, which are bestowed in a lavish public ceremony. The resemblance of *Star Wars* to fraternal initiation is no accident. George Lucas may not have been aware of this connection, but he understood the ingredients of a successful adventure story, and he knew that they could work their magic even in a galaxy far, far away.

SECRET INITIATION has persisted through the ages because it satisfies some innate need, particularly for young men. It is, after all, a man's ritual, marking the rite of passage into a brotherhood. In American culture, by far the most influential secret societies, even to this day, are the fraternal orders such as the Masons, Shriners, Elks, Odd Fellows, and Moose. Yet they have little left in the way of secrets to keep. At the height of their popularity, these fellowships were almost completely occupied with the enactment of rituals—every night of the week they conducted initiation ceremonies and awarded higher degrees of attainment, to the exclusion of any other activity. But such theatrics stopped attracting new members around the time of the Great Depression. To be sure, many lodges still exist and try their best to maintain the old practices, but they have a difficult time appealing to youth. Still, there is a diverse culture supporting secret ritual. Not only the Mafia, but college fraternities, inner-city gangs, and even athletic teams and clubs provide this type of bonding experience, although in a comparatively undeveloped way.

SECRET SOCIETIES

Secrecy has proven to be both the greatest strength and the greatest weakness of covert societies. It adds a mystical element to their ceremonies, but the fear it incites in outsiders can easily be used against the society itself. In 1307 Jacques de Molay, the Grand Master of the Knights Templars, the order founded to escort pilgrims to the Holy Lands, stood accused of blasphemy and indecent acts committed at the Templars' initiation ceremonies. King Philip IV of France, intent on bringing down the wealthy knights, took advantage of the order's secrecy to discredit them in the eyes of the Pope, and to seize their great wealth and vast holdings. Caught in a political bind, Molay and the Templars confessed under torture, then retracted their confessions. The Church ultimately condemned Molay to burn at the stake in 1314, and the knights were effectively disbanded.

Ezra Cook tried to use the secrecy of latter-day Templars in a similar way, just as the FBI hoped to do with the Mafia, yet neither succeeded. Strange as it may seem, Masonry, which modeled itself on Molay and the Templars, was a product of the Enlightenment, and started out as a surprisingly democratic venture—secret, but with much to admire. It elaborated on a remote connection to the old Masonic trade guilds by appropriating some of their signs and symbols, but it was remarkably open-minded.

Freemasonry in England owed its initial success largely to its philosophy—a combination of rationalism and egalitarianism. In an age permeated with caste barriers in every aspect of social life, Freemasonry united aristocrats and craftsmen in the pursuit of a perfect society. Celebrated Masons such as Mozart, George Washington, and Benjamin Franklin did much to advertise and popularize this brand of comradeship, and they personify the intellectual and aristocratic appeal that caused the movement to spread rapidly throughout Europe and the English colonies. But Masonic practice of the Colonial era had more to do with conviviality than secrecy.

In the 1820s, however, the Masons were rocked by a scandal that threatened to bring down the entire American branch of the order. In 1826 William Morgan, a disgruntled Mason who had made known his intention of publishing the order's secret rituals, disappeared, and the suspicion of murder came to rest upon members of the organization. A few political opportunists fueled the ensuing public outrage and exploited it by forming an Anti-Masonic party, which tried to unseat Masons who held key positions in the government. Their efforts culminated in an attempt to defeat Andrew Jackson in 1828. Although the party's agenda ultimately devolved into anti-Jacksonianism more than anti-Masonry (most anti-Masons were absorbed into the newly formed Whig party in 1836), Masons were forced underground for a decade or two, so virulent was the crusade waged against them. Yet Masonic fraternalism would reemerge by 1850 in the forefront of what become a national preoccupation with ritual-based camaraderie. By century's end, this would come to be known as the golden age of fraternity.

In Europe, Freemasonry was associated with other types of secret societies, mostly Irish, French, and Italian groups that were motivated by religious beliefs to oppose monarchies and the perpetuation of monarchical oppression. Opposition societies usually formed in defense of the status quo. This was especially true in Northern Ireland, where the issues are still not resolved, and where these societies continue to clash to this day. In retrospect, to cast these as exclusively political societies is misleading; many were formed for political purposes, yet imitated fraternal orders, divided along religious lines, and functioned as social clubs. Most of them arose in response to oppression, and formed secretly because they had no other choice. In Ireland, Roman Catholic societies took shape in the wake of the subjugation of Ireland and the suppression of the Catholic Church begun by Henry VIII. In Italy, a variety of secret societies with ties to Freemasonry (and thus Protestantism) came to be known under the blanket term of the Carbonari. In France, secret societies intent on overthrowing the monarchy flourished after the abdication of Napoleon. All of them used secret initiations involving solemn oaths.

A strong opposition (or oppressor) is the tie that binds secret political societies and maintains their internal cohesion. In the absence of a common enemy, they either dissolve from within or, vulnerable because of their secrecy, are easy prey to divisive forces from without. They derive much of their power from the principle of exclusion or exclusivity. But a Tom Sawyer's Gang can only last for so long before its entire reason for being becomes the enactment of rituals that have no meaning. Some men will always search for such meaning, and will continue to swear secret oaths in the hope of finding it. For better or worse, it constitutes one of their greatest preoccupations.

Not all initiations are secret, of course. The remaining sections of this chapter explore two very public initiations, in which oaths serve as statements of commitment designed to ensure the stability and continuity of civil society.

TAKING THE PLEDGE

The temperance question is undoubtedly as old as the production and distribution of alcoholic beverages. Yet the advent of distilled, as opposed to fermented, spirits marked a change from the public perception of a drinking problem (which had been acknowledged in almost all cultures of antiquity) to the certainty of a drinking crisis by the 1800s. In the seventeenth and eighteenth centuries the popularization of whiskey and gin created a major social dilemma that inspired many local attempts at reform. But the problem overwhelmed all such efforts until they became effectively organized under the rubric of "temperance."

Temperance, strictly speaking, means moderation. One of the four classical virtues promoted by Aristotle (the others being prudence, fortitude, and justice), it is an age-old idea roughly expressed by the golden mean, which is the avoidance of excess in either direction—whether through overindulgence or underindulgence. But in Victorian America, temperance gradually acquired a quite different meaning. Through the phenomenon of the Temperance Movement, the idea changed from careful moderation in the use of alcohol, to complete abstention, and ultimately to prohibition of all intoxicating drink. The rallying cry of this movement was the pledge— a token of initiation into the ranks of the saved.

The Temperance Movement refers to the proliferation of anti-drinking societies which spread through the United States, Canada, and Great Britain during the nineteenth century. At first a local phenomenon, it gained momentum through charismatic leaders and became a national movement by mid-century, and an international movement shortly thereafter. Ironically, some organizations in the vanguard of the movement styled themselves along the ritual-based lines of the fraternal lodges, many of which constituted a major source of the perception of a national drinking problem.

The first temperance society was founded in Saratoga, New York, in 1808. By 1833, there were six thousand local societies in the United States, but as yet no national organization. In retrospect, the early societies could be called "moderation" societies because of their goals of restraint with drink, and abstinence only from distilled spirits (except for "medicinal purposes"—a phrase that would find its way onto the labels of many highly potent magic elixirs and snake oils). As the movement grew, the concept of temperance narrowed. In 1826 temperance leaders called for abstinence only from distilled spirits; by 1836, from *all* spirits; and in 1842 the Sons of Temperance called for an additional pledge to fight all trafficking in liquor.

Divisions within the Temperance Movement yielded eventually to the hard line. Moderation gave way to abstinence. Fermented spirits were grouped with hard liquors. Personal abstinence was extended to include abstaining from offering liquor to others. (This last measure, called the "long pledge," was aimed at bartenders and distributors who gladly took the "short pledge" of personal abstinence to appease the crusaders.) By mid-century the movement was clearly headed in the direction of prohibition.

The first international temperance organization, the Order of Good Templars, was founded in 1851 as a fraternal society. Many more temperance lodges would follow, each instituting an elaborate array of insignia, ceremonies, secret signs, codes, and oaths. Noting the trend, and growing increasingly conscious of their image, many of the established fraternal orders, which were mainly interested in initiation ceremonies anyway, instituted bans on drinking at all lodge functions. (It was partly in reaction to this that some disgruntled Masons formed the Nobles of the Mystic Shrine—the Shriners—who quickly developed a reputation for inebriety.)

The evangelical aspect of the Temperance Movement and its resemblance in some particulars to the fraternal movement reflects an early stage of its history. But as a men's movement temperance could not compete with fraternalism. It failed to provide a sufficiently satisfying rite of passage, and it is doubtful that the millions who took the pledge in the Chataqua-like atmosphere of the traveling temperance crusades meant what they said or took any long-term satisfaction from the ritual. The pledge acted as a badge of conformity and a token of affiliation, but little more. The ceremony surrounding it often overshadowed its meaning and true purpose.

Temperance took a more serious turn, however, with the founding of the Woman's Christian Temperance Union in 1875. This organization rallied a large segment of the population—women—around an unambiguous motive—prohibition. Eschewing ceremony and ritual, the WCTU grew under the leadership of president Frances Willard into a world-wide organization of considerable political clout. Along with the Anti-Saloon

League (founded in 1893), the WCTU carried the prohibition movement into the twentieth century, and its success culminated in the passage of the Eighteenth Amendment to the Constitution in 1919.

It is a curious fact that the nineteenth-century idea of temperance in America should have evolved into the exact opposite of the classical virtue, which is as opposed to total abstinence and self-denial as it is to wretched excess. But temperance crusaders found that they could not afford to compromise if they were to succeed in overcoming the social evils brought about by drink. Temperance was primarily a women's movement which, in collaboration with Protestant ministries, sought to establish some control over male behavior. Their use of a pledge was not unlike the use of loyalty and test oaths by anti-Communists. The Temperance Movement needed to demonize liquor in order to succeed, and they used the pledge as a tool to gain unanimity on this point, and to ferret out those who showed inadequate enthusiasm for their cause.

For a while, saloon keepers could circumvent the movement by taking the short pledge of personal abstinence, which allowed them to stay in business. They had no need to be convinced of the dangers of drink; they could see the results for themselves on any given day. Nor was a pledge necessary to convince them that they themselves should avoid drink, which would have been a professional liability anyway. So the point of the pledge was not to suppress behavior, but to coerce a total group commitment, extending beyond actions to attitudes. As with a test oath, solidarity was the point.

Unlike loyalty or fortitude or even temperance proper, abstinence is not a virtue. To deny people their vices is to deny human nature; it simply leads to greater evils. In the case of Prohibition, the spillover took the form of organized crime, black markets, and speakeasies, with hardly a dent in the drinking problem. The temperance pledge proved to be a highly effective organizational tool, but it did not sustain the movement because it did not effect a true change in people's behavior. After the repeal of Prohibition in 1933, the movement was quickly relegated to history, although it left behind an expression which embodies its goals and methods. It can still be found in the language of self-help and recovery: to take the pledge.

WEDDING VOWS

The modern Christian wedding ceremony is one of the oldest rituals still performed virtually unchanged since it came into its present form sometime in the 1400s. The dramatic high point of the ceremony is the troth-plight, or exchange of vows—a poignant yet compelling recitation of comfortingly familiar words that happen to constitute one of the most frequently broken public promises. But if the institution of marriage were not anchored by such a revered tradition, more marriages would undoubtedly fail. For despite its age and seeming irrelevance to the nuclear era, the classic wedding vow retains a significance that transcends everyday concerns and imparts to the union of two people a satisfying resonance. If the words seem timeless, it is because for all intents and purposes, they are.

Marriage is perhaps the most important of all social rituals. It is little wonder, then, that such a carefully crafted ceremony has grown up around it. What is most remarkable about the marriage ceremony is its uniformity across cultures and religions, and its staying power. Its essential structure in the Christian religions is the same as that of the Jewish ceremony, and both mirror the practices of ancient Rome. Even the familiar words of the Christian rite have remained nearly intact for the last five hundred years. The pledge to "love, honor, and obey, in sickness and in health, 'til death do us part," for example, would have been as familiar to an English peasant couple of the 1400s as it is today. In fact the origins of this poetic exchange can be traced as far back as the eleventh century. The wedding ceremony itself contains elements that are even older. Many of the ceremonial trappings of modern weddings have been carried on for more than two thousand years; the classic wedding vows for perhaps a thousand.

WHEN A YOUNG COUPLE sits down with a priest or minister to discuss the details of their wedding, they have very little pertinent literature at their disposal. Missals and prayer books sketch the rudiments of the ceremony, but not its historical development. Surprisingly, the history of wedding rites is not well documented. There is little commentary on the ceremony of marriage in the Bible, for example. This is because marriage was a secular ritual in most ancient cultures. In turning it into a religious celebration the early Roman church adopted (or adapted) many of the pagan rituals of imperial Rome. Some of these rituals survive: the sharing of the cake (originally an offering to Jupiter), the veiling of the bride, the giving of a ring (as a pledge to fulfill the contract), the throwing of rice and other grains (as a symbol of fertility), and carrying the bride over the threshold (although it is not clear whether this was done by the groom or by a group of boys who escorted the bride to her new home).

In the earliest written accounts, the wedding ritual consisted of two distinct and separate ceremonies: the *sponsalia* or betrothal (which included vows and the giving of a ring—originally an iron band), and the *nuptiae*, or nuptials (the marriage ceremony proper). Neither ceremony was religious or sacramental, at least until the Middle Ages, when the Church converted them into a liturgy by merging the betrothal and nuptials, which were sometimes separated by as much as a year, and adding the priestly benediction and ring blessing.

Knowing the history of this ceremony and the evolution of the vows might not change the way modern couples live their married lives, but it could change the way they design their own weddings. The 1960s witnessed the rejection of many received notions, including the traditional wedding, but this is one tradition that keeps coming back, and if the classic vows were more widely circulated they would undoubtedly be more widely used.

IN HIS BOOK *Nuptial Blessing* (1982), Kenneth Stevenson outlines the history of Christian marriage rites by tracing the development of the priestly blessing. He also surveys historical documents which show how that other crucial ritual element, the marriage vow, developed out of the rite of betrothal and the early consent formulas administered by priests. Because matrimony was not recognized as a sacrament in the Roman Church until the Council of Trent in 1563, there is little uniformity to be found in the liturgies of marriage services of the Middle Ages. But as Stevenson demonstrates, between the eleventh and sixteenth centuries, as the wedding ceremony evolved, certain now-familiar phrases began to appear more frequently. This process culminates in the ceremony from the Sarum Missal of the fifteenth century, and in Thomas Cranmer's service for the First English Prayer Book of 1549, both of which remain the standard of almost all Christian services (although there are currently an uncountable number of variations).

There has never been true uniformity in the Christian marriage service, but the ceremony has proven to be remarkably durable without the need for the establishment of uniform standards. Protestant churches, for example, do not recognize matrimony as a sacrament, and have never followed • a central liturgical authority. The Anglican and Episcopal churches, while they insist on using the text for weddings provided in the Book of Common Prayer (which grew out of the First English Prayer Book), do allow couples to rewrite their betrothal vows—within reason. Even Catholic parishes in the wake of Vatican II regained the authority to compose their own wedding rites. And yet most couples choose to follow tradition in this particular rite of passage, and if they do not use traditional vows, they at least retain some of the familiar language of the medieval rites.

FOR BETTER, FOR WORSE

The earliest reference to a matrimonial promise in a wedding service, according to Stevenson, occurs in the Lanalet Pontifical, a tenth-century collection of Anglo-Norman prayers and services. The nature of the promise is unknown, but early ceremonies are known to have limited couples to responses rather than declarations.

But in the twelfth century, Pope Alexander III altered the Church's theory of marriage in a way that would have profound effects, some of which he may not have anticipated. The most immediate effect was an elaboration of the formula of consent. Prior to this time, many marriages were arranged, thus requiring the permission, if not participation, of the parents. But Alexander's papal decree removed this barrier, setting the stage for an expanded ceremony, one which involved a more elaborate declaration by the young couple. The Church would now recognize as valid any marriage between a man and woman of the proper age who were not already married, and had freely and willingly declared their consent. As an unintended consequence, many couples seized the opportunity to marry without their parents' permission, something the Pope frowned upon but had to accept.

Thus the wedding ceremony grew with the institution of marriage itself; with the Pope's decree, parents lost control over their children's futures in a way that still causes them untold anguish. Their authority was usurped by the Church, and the permission which they once assumed was theirs alone to give, was turned over to their children in the ceremonial form of the consent formula.

IN AN ENGLISH manuscript written in Bury St. Edmunds around the year 1125, the outline of the modern ceremony first appears. "The man is asked by the priest if he wishes to have her as his lawful wife. The same question is asked of the woman." The ring formula is even more familiar. The bridegroom says, "With this ring I thee wed, this gold and silver I give thee, with my body I thee honor, with this dowry I thee endow."

The betrothal rite, which today begins with a private negotiation of engagement, occasionally took liturgical form in the Middle Ages, primarily in French rites. But its importance as a public ceremony was supplanted when the rite of consent became part of the nuptial mass. This first took the form of questions posed to the couple by the priest. The Magdalen Pontifical, an English rite of the twelfth century, contains the beginning of a recognizable formula:

"N, do you want this woman," and if he answers yes, "do you wish to serve her in the faith of God as your own, in health and infirmity, as a Christian man should serve his wife?"

The Roman rite of the first half of the thirteenth century has the priest ask:

Do you want this woman as your wife, to guard her in health and sickness, as long as she lives . . . ?

The service of St. Maur-des-Fosses, a French ritual of the second half of the thirteenth century, inserts the phrase "for better or for worse."

FROM THE TENTH to the thirteenth century the wedding service developed locally throughout Western Europe by building upon a basic plan. This consisted of an opening address, followed by the consent formula, the vows, ratification by the priest, the blessing of rings and other blessings, and finally a nuptial mass. All but the last of these usually took place at the church door.

The role of the priest remained dominant in these proceedings until sometime in the fourteenth century when a major change took place. Where initially the couple's role consisted of responding to questions posed to them (in what is known as the consent formula), in the 1300s a ceremony emerged in which the bride and groom declared their own intentions in full by speaking their vows. This ceremony is remarkably close to the ceremony still used today. Although not the product of a single author, it is credited to one place and one time—to a text known as the Sarum rite.

A LITURGICAL ROLLS-ROYCE

The Sarum Missal contains the liturgy of the cathedral and Diocese of Salisbury, England. The wedding rite that it introduced, according to Stevenson, is not only the definitive northern European medieval marriage service, but it "contains the richest expression of marriage in vernacular devotion, for it not only develops the consent and the ring-giving formulas, but produces that masterpiece of medieval vernacular liturgy, the marriage vow."

The Sarum earns Stevenson's admiration for its poetic vitality and range of expression. "To have and to hold" comes from early Anglo-Saxon poetry (where it was used, in "Beowulf" for example, to refer to property and weaponry). "For better for worse, for richer for poorer, [for fairer for fouler], in sickness and in health, 'til death us depart" exhibits the vow's distinctive rhythmic and alliterative qualities. The woman's promise "to be bonowre and buxom in bedde and at borde" (which meant to be meek and obedient) was dropped from the English Prayer Book of 1549, although the concomitant promise to "obey" survived in some ceremonies into the twentieth century.

The Sarum rite acquired some alterations during the Reformation. Martin Luther and John Calvin each made changes, but the most notable contribution was made by Thomas Cranmer, the Archbishop of Canterbury, who undertook the composition of the First English Prayer Book after Henry VIII's death in 1547. Cranmer's form for the Solemnization of Matrimony is essentially that of the Sarum and York Cathedral Manuals. He retained the consent and vows with few changes, but backed off from the explicitness of references to bed and board. Other familiar elements—the call for impediments (which are invoked by Shakespeare in Sonnet 116: "Let me not to the marriage of true minds / admit impediments . . ."), the ring-giving formula, and the final scriptural quotation from Matthew ("those whom God hath joined together . . .")—existed in prior settings, but Cranmer wove them into a ceremony that is still considered the definitive service. Other Protestant denominations originated their own services, but Cranmer's has had the greatest cultural impact in England and America. Stevenson calls it a "liturgical Rolls-Royce."

Like other early English Church texts, the Sarum is noteworthy for its use of English in spoken exchanges involving the couple, following the Church of England's long-standing practice of providing basic formulas of worship in the vernacular. The First Prayer Book, of course, did away with the Latin entirely.

I AM THE MELODY AND YOU ARE THE WORDS

In place of the traditional church ceremony many couples now opt for an alternative service, often writing their own vows. Many of these vows are modeled after those of the Book of Common Prayer or are loosely constructed around passages from the Bible. The most popular such passage is undoubtedly the expression of devotion from the Book of Ruth (1:16–17).

> *For whither thou goest, I will go; and where thou lodgest, I will lodge: Thy people shall be my people, and thy God my God. If thou diest, I will die, and there will I be buried: the Lord do so to me, and more also, if aught but death part thee and me.*

Another popular quotation comes from the Hindu Rig-Veda (10:85), a collection of Sanskrit hymns of the tenth or eleventh centuries B.C. The wedding ritual includes the lines, "I take hold of your hand for good fortune, so that with me, the husband, you may attain to old age. . . . I am the words and you are the melody; I am the melody and you are the words."

Part of what makes these ancient texts so emotionally satisfying, besides their poetic beauty, is the simple fact of their age and endurance. Although many couples look to modern sources to supply readings for their weddings, others find that something old is better than something new.

There is, it should be noted, ample historical precedent for creating personal vows, just as there is for choosing civil and common law marriages. But it is the traditional vows that dominate the modern conception of the wedding ceremony. In fact if the long history of the traditional vows was more widely known, it would undoubtedly create an increased interest in historical accuracy. Through the exchange of centuries-old formulas, the bride and groom participate in a long-standing ritual whose reassuring predictability and permanence lend emotional resonance to a ceremony which is often the most memorable moment of the couple's lives.

WE BELIEVE IN ICE CREAM, AND IN THE GREAT FUTURE THAT
LIES BEFORE THE INDUSTRY, BECAUSE ICE CREAM IS THE ONE
PRODUCT WHICH CONTAINS ALL OF THE LIFE GIVING, BODY
BUILDING PROPERTIES PECULIAR TO MILK, COMBINED WITH A
VARIETY AND PALATABILITY FOUND IN NO OTHER MILK
PRODUCT.

WE BELIEVE THAT ALL LEGITIMATE BUSINESS MUST REST
UPON THE SECURE FOUNDATION OF A FAIR REWARD FOR
HONEST SERVICE.

WE PLEDGE OURSELVES: TO CONDUCT OUR BUSINESSES UPON
THE BASIS OF SERVICE AND SQUARE DEALING TO THE PUBLIC,
AND TO THE INDUSTRY OF WHICH WE ARE A PART;

TO PROMOTE, IN OUR RELATIONS WITH OUR COMPETITORS,
A SPIRIT OF FAIRNESS AND TOLERANCE;

TO OURSELVES REFRAIN, AND TO DISCOURAGE OTHERS,
FROM ANY AND ALL PRACTICES WHICH WOULD BE
DETRIMENTAL TO THE INTEREST OF THE PUBLIC, OR OF
THE INDUSTRY;

AND TO CO-OPERATE IN EVERY PRACTICABLE WAY
TOWARD A FULLER APPRECIATION OF ICE CREAM AS
WHOLESOME, ALL-YEAR-ROUND FOOD.

PACIFIC ICE CREAM MANUFACTURERS'
ASSOCIATION (1922)

CHAPTER FIVE

ON MY HONOR I WILL DO MY BEST

CODES OF ETHICS AND CONDUCT

The Electrical Supply Jobbers' Association, now known by the less color-ful name of the National Association of Electrical Distributors, at one time maintained an elaborately decorated code of ethics as a token of their good will. The code's preamble, set in oversized gothic letters, acknowl-edged the complexity of the business world and the need for a system of basic principles of action, presumably written so that anyone could follow them. On the lower part of the page, in smaller gothic type, an attempt at such a system was laid out in the form of six precepts, the first of which gives some idea of the code's accessibility, or lack of it. It reads: "It is the function of a jobber to provide the most efficient yet economical means for offsetting the natural obstacles which oppose direct communication be-tween the producer and consumer of electrical materials." The code closes with a seventy-seven-word version the Golden Rule.

The supply jobbers' code can be found, along with almost two hundred other codes representing a wide range of business and professional associ-ations, in a book assembled by Edgar Laing Heermance in 1924, and pub-lished under the name of *Codes of Ethics: A Handbook.* Heermance's volume is both enlightening and entertaining, not merely for throwing open a win-dow onto a world of well-intentioned boosterism, but also for showing the variety of business enterprises that once existed, and the even wider range of associations that formed to represent them.

The book contains one code each for the Associated Office Furniture Manufacturers, the National Association of Upholstered Furniture Manufacturers, and the National Retail Furniture Association. It lists three associations of ice cream manufacturers, two ice manufacturers, a national association of hat manufacturers, as well as a national association of men's *straw hat* manufacturers. Each has its own distinct code.

There is a National Knitted Outerwear Association, whose code begins with a ringing endorsement of the Golden Rule, and another association for knitted *underwear* manufacturers, whose code opens with a plug for the "square deal." Trade associations are not the only occupations represented. *Codes of Ethics* also contains the standards of practice of the most respected professions: The American Medical Association, American Dental Association, American Bar Association, and the American Institute of Architects, along with national societies of teachers, engineers, chemists, and veterinarians. All are represented by well-meaning one- or two-page codes.

THE SIMILARITIES AMONG many of these documents are striking. Of the 198 codes Heermance includes, forty mention the Golden Rule, while twenty-one invoke the Rooseveltian Square Deal; thirty-six pay homage to the idea of service, eighteen to public welfare, and eighty-one condemn the practice of slandering a competitor and his goods.

There are other popular themes. The American Bottlers of Carbonated Beverages, for example, wanted to stress the importance of public image. The first precept of their code is typical. It reads: "I shall at all times conduct my business in such a manner as to reflect credit unto myself and the bottled carbonated beverage industry." The implication of such a rule is that every bottler instinctively knew how to maintain "such a manner," and that prior to the code a few bottlers may have gone against this instinct, which was indeed the case. In fact the reputation of business at the turn of the century was so bad that the federal government had to step in to regulate it.

Some of the trades tried to do it themselves. The Intermountain States Truckmen and Auto Carriers Association led off its code with the warning—"Don't act repulsive to an officer of the law, he is carrying out the will of the people." Their jarring grammar at first obscures a fundamentally sound and laudable principle: that the public welfare should be protected, and that it is in the interest of truckers to maintain good relations with those who are empowered to protect it. Whether the code ushered in a new era of cordial relations between teamsters and the highway patrol is not known.

Heermance, to his credit, betrays little irony and not a shred of cynicism about all of this. He was convinced that his book was part of a serious mission, that it would facilitate the drafting of new codes which were much needed, and that it would also present "a fair picture of American ethics, as embodied in contemporary standards." He was clearly caught up in the spirit of the newly emerging field of social science, which at that time proposed that laws of ethics not only exist, but operate in the same way as those of physics.

Coming upon Heermance's *Codes of Ethics* seventy years after its publication is like opening a time capsule that was sealed during an age of idealism and innocence. Hailing from a time when a standard greeting was "How's business?", codes of ethics, especially those that Heermance reproduces in their original typographical splendor, appear to be a quaint throwback, a nostalgic gesture that was once considered obligatory in every waiting room, outer office, and workshop. In the modern corporate world, where efficiency and profit have established their priority over loyalty to customers and employees, there would seem to be little interest in decorous codes. Even business schools make little attempt to work ethics into their curricula. Which makes it all the more surprising to come across a document such as the vision statement of a prominent publishing company, circa 1995, listing the firm's four basic motivating principles, two of which would not be out of place in Heermance's handbook:

> We will treat each other, our authors, customers and business partners with care, integrity and respect.
> We will face reality and embrace change in all aspects of our business life.

In the vernacular of Total Quality Management, one of the more recent wrinkles in management philosophy, this is called a mission statement rather than a code of ethics, although the content and purpose are essentially the same. To the cynic, the content is nothing but platitudes and the purpose merely to put a good face on things. To proponents of TQM, however, it is not about ethics or public relations, but about efficiency and morale. And it is regarded, as it was in the 1920s, as an essential exercise in self-definition. Who we are, it seems to say, is defined by our mission, and by the way we agree to go about achieving it. Whether we succeed depends on how well we stick to our program.

While Edgar Heermance's *Codes of Ethics* raises the question of why codes loomed so large in the 1920s—specifically: what brought about the ethics-in-business movement that produced so many of them?—the phenomenon of the mission statement spreads the net even wider. What is it about the very idea of a code of ethics or a mission statement that is so appealing and that seems so necessary, especially in American culture (which seems to hold a monopoly on the practice)?

The answers have little to do with ancient tradition. The term "code of ethics," it turns out, is less than two hundred years old. Nor is the code of ethics a uniquely American invention. It is an import, although one that built its reputation on these shores. The stereotype of the framed business ethics code grew out of a short but intense period of post-war economic expansion in the United States—a period that Heermance's book documents. Of the 198 codes he collected (and he left out hundreds), all but five had been written within the previous ten years, and the vast majority had appeared within the previous five. They were written over such a short span in response to specific events, a fact that is reflected by the wordings of many of them.

Heermance did not delve into these motivations, perhaps because he thought it would detract from the overall moral tenor of the movement. Nor did he comment on the title of his book, and the extent to which the codes he collected were actually ethical. (He left this discussion to a follow-up volume entitled *The Ethics of Business* [1926], which assesses the effectiveness of codes and the prospects for the future, but again falls short of explaining what, if anything, was specifically ethical about them.)

Still, Heermance's choice of title must have seemed a natural one. By far, the majority of the documents he collected were christened Code of Ethics. Other titles were common, including: Rules of Professional Conduct, Standards of Practice, Declaration of Principles, and Aims and Ideals. In many ways these are more accurate, or at least more appropriate, names. But by the 1920s the term "code of ethics" had acquired a special connotation. The average citizen understood what it meant and could relate to it, and this alone accounted for much of its appeal.

The stock market crash of 1929, and the depression that followed, put a dent in the reputation of one-page codes, but it did not diminish the professional and corporate sector's enthusiasm for them. The stereotypical code still symbolizes an approach to doing business and a way of organizing society that Americans find comforting. This feeling often has as much to do with the way the code looks or with who wrote it as with what it actually says. The text is not irrelevant, but what matters more is the perception of trust that lurks behind it. Without some degree of public confidence, a code is hardly worth the sheepskin on which it is printed.

THE GREAT CODE

What is a code of ethics? Although the image of a framed set of business commandments comes immediately to most people's minds, the answer is not quite that simple. A code is, in essence, a list of rules or principles, and there are many kinds. The ancient Babylonian Code of Hammurabi, for example, lists a set of prohibitions and the specific punishments they carry. It is one of the earliest examples of a written code of law.

Another is the Ten Commandments, which is still considered by some to be the highest code—the Great Code that was handed down from the mountain to help guide an entire people. Also known as the Decalogue (from the Greek meaning "ten words"), the commandments remain one of the most influential of all codes, and a model for business and professional codes of the modern era. It has inspired countless sets of rules grouped in tens, as well as such new commandments as Jesus' admonition that "ye love one another as I have loved you." It has also inspired some dubious precepts of practical necessity known as eleventh commandments.

The Ten Commandments have exercised a greater influence on moral and religious life in the West than perhaps any other written words. They are the summary of the Jewish law and the source of all subsequent commandments, of which there are many. Yet all commandments stand in relation to the ten. They remain an icon etched in stone—literally "written with the finger of God."

There are, of course, many other codes of antiquity, including legal statutes, standards of trade, building codes, and procedural rules such as those that govern the technical aspects of occupations. Codes of etiquette, which establish social conventions, have also existed since ancient times. But as compelling as these ancient codes and commandments are, none of them has much to do with ethics. They are primarily concerned with distinguishing right from wrong in a rigidly technical sense—where someone has decided what must be done, what must not be done, and what punishments will be meted out. And this is not what ethics is properly about.

To be considered "ethical," say ethicists, a code must address questions involving moral choice—what people *ought* to do, as opposed to what they are required to do. Any set of rules that is made mandatory, therefore, cannot be about ethics. This is the paradox that lies at the heart of discussions of binding written rules. It would seem that a code or commandment cannot properly be about ethics unless it restricts its scope to ideals, suggestions, goals, and general principles.

If this seems confusing, it might help to consider a simple model in which what is ethical is clearly and easily distinguishable from what is merely required, and what can be stated in a written code is easy to distinguish from what cannot. Such a code is the one that governs the game of professional baseball.

THE CODE OF BASEBALL

In major league baseball there are two governing bodies—the American League and the National League. Each has a constitution (or code of law) that lays down the rules of the game. These rules, at the simplest level, determine how the game is played, and they are rigorously enforced. Among other things, they establish the fact that there are three outs in each half inning, that a designated batter is allowed in the American League, and that in the National League a pitcher must bat for himself if he is to remain in the game. Each league also has a constitution which governs the business aspects of the game, determining how owners can sell their corporate image, how they may go about drafting and signing players, and when a player can become a free agent. These could be called professional baseball's standards of practice.

There is another tier of rules implied in the league constitutions, and it covers players, coaches, and, to some extent, owners, both on and off the field. It has to do with etiquette or decorum. Anything "calculated to bring disrepute upon the league or the game of professional baseball" is punishable by a fine or suspension. These rules forbid using drugs, betting on sports, or being rude to fans. In recent years violations of this code have taken up almost as much space in the sports pages as accounts of the games themselves. At the close of the 1996 season, for example, when Baltimore

Oriole second baseman Roberto Alomar spat in the face of an umpire, the incident dominated the sports pages to the point of overshadowing the first round of the playoffs. It made sadly evident major league baseball's lack of a true code of conduct, or awareness of ethics, a commissioner who could deal with such incidents swiftly and unambiguously.

What makes this important, and more than simply a game, is the fact that sports has always served as a teaching laboratory for ethics. As children play and emulate their sports heroes they absorb lessons that reflect the unwritten rules of the game, which constitute baseball's, or any sport's, true code of ethics. This is the code that coaches and veteran players pass along to rookies. It covers such matters as pitching inside, running out pop flies, and the decorum of the home run trot. It covers not only what Roberto Alomar should not have done in the first place, but also what he should have done to try to atone for it. It also covers the way his coaches and teammates should have reacted to it (much of which, of course, takes place out of view of the fans). That is, baseball's code of ethics covers the choices a player *can* make and *has to* make for himself because they are not (and cannot be) written down.

Many people argue that baseball, and in fact all of sports, was once far more gentlemanly than it is today (yet another example of how the idea of chivalry, in every age, has been thought to be in decline). Still, there is a code of ethics and honor in major league baseball, and players have a way of enforcing it. The penalties may not be specified, and can vary from player to player and team to team, but they exist. Deion Sanders, as a rookie, encountered this code when he declined to run out an infield pop-up. Out of indignation, the opposing catcher—the venerable Carlton Fisk—almost took Sanders apart. None of Sanders's teammates came to his defense.

A true ethical code, like the code of baseball ethics, is an unspoken arrangement that loses its moral foundation as soon as someone tries to turn it into a set of laws. Instead, it reveals itself in the course of "playing the game" (which is itself an expression that connotes living up to a high standard of behavior). When fans see the written regulations of the game enforced they are not seeing ethics at work. When they see major league players observing the rules of the game, the terms of their contracts, and the etiquette laid down the by league constitutions, they are not witnessing moral choices. Yet moral choices must still be made. Should a manager allow his team to run up the score in a lopsided game? Should a hitting champ sit out the last game of the season to protect his batting average? Should a league commissioner immediately suspend a player who flouts the authority of an umpire and brings disgrace upon the game? The range of situations addressed by these questions cannot be entirely anticipated and codified. Yet it is through these choices that athletes (if not also managers, owners, and commissioners) demonstrate their character, or what is sometimes called their heart.

The example of baseball also shows that a written code can only approximate what an unwritten code can do. Because an unwritten code functions within a consensus of understanding, it represents a shared imperative to uphold certain agreed-upon standards. Where there is no such consensus, where some individuals feel that they are above the code, or where there are simply too many individuals who are oblivious to the difference between right and wrong, a written code is the only alternative.

CRICKET

The sports analogy yields up a few other instances in which "playing by the rules" comes to mean much more than studying the rule book. For example, the English game of cricket, baseball's distinct cousin, has become a synonym for fair play. The sport has a long tradition of decorum, which has led to the use of the term *cricket* to refer to what is ethical, upright, or sportsmanlike with respect to a set of agreed-upon rules. By the late 1800s this usage became common even outside of the game. When someone's actions were deemed "not cricket," it implied that they fell short of common expectations of decency, honor, or fairness.

A similar usage also emerged out of the sport of boxing. In the mid 1800s prize fighting had degenerated to a point where it reflected badly upon the gentlemen who patronized it. John Graham Chambers, a member of the British Amateur Athletic Club, took it upon himself to devise a set of rules which would serve to civilize the sport. They were published in 1867 under the sponsorship of Sir John Sholto Douglas, the ninth Marquess of Queensberry, which explains how they came to be known as the Marquess of Queensberry Rules.

Chambers's rules were so effective that they remain essentially the rules of boxing in use today. He established the size of the ring, the length of rounds, and the ten count. But more importantly, because Douglas's rules civilized a brutal sport in an era that emphasized courtesy and fair play, the term "Queensberry rules" took on an expanded sense, conveying the idea of fairness, of playing by the rules. Like the word "cricket," it invokes a code of proper behavior without formally stating it.

In other arenas—the workplace, for example—ethical choices must also be made within a structure of formal and informal "rules of the game" that manage to elude written expression. Yet written codes purporting to be about ethics do get written out, and therefore must serve a useful purpose. In theory, they simply cannot work; a written code of ethics is a contradiction in terms. But this technicality is lost on most people. The gesture alone does seem to matter. The use of the word "ethics" creates the impression that honor is at stake, that what is not cricket will be discouraged, and that Queensberry Rules will apply.

Thus any organization that maintains a code of ethics, whatever it says, is thought to be accountable to a higher standard, and it can expect itself to be measured by that standard. Although it has never been legally binding, the Hippocratic Oath has played this role in the profession of medicine for centuries. Even though it is hardly used in ceremonies anymore, and most people have only a vague idea of its contents, doctors find that the name alone erects a standard they are expected to meet, one that defines a heightened sense of responsibility without being too specific.

CODES AND PROFESSIONS

The first modern code of ethics, which is to say the very first document to be referred to by that name, was written in 1793 by Thomas Percival, a physician and advisor to the Manchester Infirmary in England. To the dismay of most medical historians, Percival decided upon the title *Medical Ethics*, even though his code is properly one of etiquette—it addressed the interactions of physicians and surgeons in a hospital setting. What makes this dismay particularly acute is that the title would lead to the idea that ethics consists of nothing more than a set of specific rules of behavior, that ethics can be imposed on a group of people by posting a notice on a bulletin board, and that the lack of a code can indicate a lack of moral values.

This small controversy should not diminish Percival's achievement. His *Medical Ethics* not only defined the practice of medicine as a modern profession, but served as the model for the fledgling American Medical Association's Code of Ethics of 1847. Although this immediately led to an explosion of well-intentioned imitations that would come to adorn many office walls, one can hardly blame Percival. He may have unwittingly unleashed a stereotype about what a code of ethics is, but he did manage to assure that medicine would be the first field to have one. And his code also succeeded in improving professional behavior in medicine, which alone would seem to justify his use of the term "ethics." Through his code Percival helped to define a professional as an ethically motivated practitioner, which was a new idea in the eighteenth century.

AT ONE TIME there were three professions—medicine, the law, and the clergy. (The military is also thought to constitute a profession, but is usually left out of discussions of professional ethics, perhaps because it is seen to be entirely concerned with honor and etiquette rather than ethics.) The "professions" are so designated because those who become members do so by "professing"—by making a public promise to serve others in a specialized capacity that constitutes a trust. (The Greek root of profession is *prophaino*, which means "to declare publicly." The Latin noun *professio* describes a public statement much like an oath of office.)

Each of the original professions grew out of the order of priests, whose responsibility was to preside over specialized learning. In the early Middle Ages it was typical for a doctor, lawyer, or scholar to be a clergyman, whose professed loyalty was to the Church. It was only when the Church's authority began to wane that the separate professions began to emerge as autonomous organizations.

Physicians, in particular, sought to establish their own authority and a monopoly on their field by first establishing guilds, and then by inventing the professional association. The words *professional* and *professionalism* in their modern sense began to appear in the late eighteenth and early nineteenth centuries when a number of learned and professional societies took shape in England, following the example of medicine. These were formed partly to fill the void of leadership created by the decline of the guilds, but also to advance research and create cooperation. By the seventeenth century other occupations were casting off the restrictions of the old hierarchical guild system and forming new associations to protect their interests. The trade guilds re-emerged after a few centuries as business associations; the craft guilds as professional societies.

THE EQUATION THAT allows professional associations to control the practice of a certain skill is simply this: in return for the authority that professionals enjoy through their monopoly over specialized services, they must agree, if only ceremonially, to abide not only by the rules of professional conduct, but by some code of honor. The function of the association is to ensure that the code is enforced. In addition, in the ethical conception of a profession, the privilege of authority must be balanced by a devotion to service. It makes little sense to impose a code on a mature industry in the hope that it will suddenly become more "ethical."

It was by cultivating trust through its code that medicine rose to its current preeminence, and this explains why medicine was the model for modern professionalism. It is the most organized profession, and its path to success, its rise to respectability, much like that of Horatio Alger's heroes, was guided by a set of precepts.

THE STATE OF MEDICINE

In eighteenth-century England, four groups of medical practitioners coexisted under an elaborate yet informal system of etiquette. Three of them were organized into recognized guilds, which allowed them to set their own standards of practice. These were the physicians, the surgeons, and the apothecaries. A fourth group, midwives, had no organizational power, and were bound principally by an oath required by the state that served as their code of conduct.

Physicians stood at the top of this pecking order. They were, in theory, the most educated, the best organized, and the most respected. Under Henry VIII, the Royal College of Physicians received its charter in 1517, and was given the right to control licensing and to punish charlatans. This effectively established the physicians as a guild, and gave them wide-ranging powers of self-regulation. Surgeons sought to attain a similar level of respect, but they were burdened by a long-standing association with barbers. Because barbers had traditionally performed minor surgery as well as bloodletting (which explains the bloody symbolism of the barber pole), the two trades were incorporated together as the Barber-Surgeons Guild in 1512. In 1540 a statute decreed that from then on surgeons would refrain from barbery and barbers would refrain from all but minor surgery, such as pulling teeth. It was not until 1745, however, that barbers and surgeons were at last separated into two distinct corporations.

Before 1543 apothecaries went by the title of "irregular practitioners," and when first recognized as a guild, they were merged with grocers. In 1703 they earned the right, legally, to prescribe and dispense medicine, something they had traditionally done anyway. Apothecaries were, in effect, physicians to the poor. Generally the first to be called upon to deal with an illness, they yielded to physicians only in serious cases.

With so many undifferentiated practitioners of medicine, the enforcement of standards of practice was mostly local. The three guilds viewed each other with suspicion, and got along by an informal arrangement. The Royal College of Physicians, in the mid-1500s, did issue a set of *Statuta Moralia*, or moral statutes, which had nothing to do with morality and everything to do with the business of medicine. But these did not go beyond interactions between physicians, or between physician and patient. The College had no power to ensure that physicians outside its domain were properly trained or that they followed the statutes, and consequently the profession had its share of illiterates and fakes.

This was the situation in English medicine until the eighteenth century, although it would soon change forever with the drafting of the first medical code of ethics—the invention of a modest physician whose influence would spread far beyond his original intentions, if not his wildest dreams.

THOMAS PERCIVAL'S CODE

In 1780 Thomas Percival, the most highly respected physician on the staff of the Manchester Infirmary in England, resigned after serving only two years. At the age of forty, poor health kept him from performing up to his own standards, and he decided he could better serve his profession by studying it, rather than practicing it. Having already published a respected body of scientific papers, and having successfully lobbied for reforms in public health and hygiene, as well as in public health education, Percival could leave medical practice knowing that he would still be able to work for the welfare of his fellow citizens.

Percival had become a doctor against long odds. He was not of the gentry, and this social liability had disqualified him from admission to the Royal College of Physicians. He was not an Anglican, and this had barred him from admission to Oxford or Cambridge. To make matters worse, he suffered from acute astigmatism and was prone to severe headaches. Yet his progress through life distinguishes him as a man spurred on by obstacles rather than deterred by them. He attended college at Edinburgh, where his earliest scientific papers earned him the distinction of becoming the youngest man ever to be made a Fellow of the Royal Society. He went on to study medicine at Leyden, and soon thereafter set up practice in Manchester, a textile manufacturing community.

Percival managed to amass an impressive record as a scientific researcher, public health advocate, and public intellectual. His numerous medical and philosophical essays attracted wide attention, and led to correspondences with such luminaries as Benjamin Franklin, Denis Diderot, D'Alembert, and Voltaire. In these letters he comes across as a man of courtesy, dignity, and humor—in short, a gentleman whose intellectual accomplishments allowed him to rise above the pettiness and squabbling that infected much of the medical profession of his day.

THE IDEA OF professionalism in Percival's day was very different from what it is today mostly because the idea of a "code of ethics" did not yet exist; the phrase had not yet been coined. Physicians had, since antiquity, acknowledged the Hippocratic Oath as an inspirational guide to their craft, but the ancient oath was neither mandatory nor very specific. The Royal College of Physicians' "moral statutes" suggested the idea of moral obligation, but in name only. They treated the physician primarily as someone who provides a service, as opposed to someone who represents a calling. Also, the Royal College had a very limited sphere of influence that did not extend to surgeons. This left the practice of medicine in England in a precarious state, with hardly any protocol to use in the event of a crisis, which was bound to occur.

In 1789, a typhus epidemic broke out among the textile workers of Manchester, and the infirmary found itself overwhelmed. The trustees responded by immediately doubling the size of the staff, a move that did not sit well with many of its longtime physicians and surgeons, who saw it as a vote of no confidence. Several among them, including two of Percival's closest friends, resigned in protest. Besieged from within and without, the trustees agreed that they needed a code of hospital etiquette, something that had not existed up to that point, and they turned to Percival, who seemed to be the only person with the knowledge and standing to make it work.

Once the project was underway, its scope quickly expanded. Percival saw it as an opportunity to lay down a set of rules for all of medical practice, and not merely for the interaction of guilds within a hospital setting. His original title, *Of Professional Conduct Relative to Hospitals*, soon gave way to the more comprehensive label *Medical Ethics, or a Code of Institutes and Precepts Adapted to the Professional Conduct of Physicians and Surgeons.* Setting aside the question of whether "ethics" belongs in the title, Percival's code initiated the idea of a unified profession in which physicians and surgeons work together, pursuing the same ideals, and sharing the same status. It gave concrete form to a way of attending to the sick that had previously been sustained by unwritten agreements, but never consistently, and never universally. The code left medical practitioners wondering how they ever got along without it.

TENDERNESS AND STEADINESS, CONDESCENSION AND AUTHORITY

Ethicists may argue that Percival's *Medical Ethics* is little more than a code of etiquette that anticipates jurisdictional disputes and settles them. But it goes far beyond that in one important respect. Percival saw the physician as a gentleman, with all of the chivalric baggage that term entails. The most quoted part of his code is its preamble, in which he says, "Physicians should study . . . in their deportment, so as to unite *tenderness* with *steadiness* and *condescension* with *authority*, as to inspire the minds of their patients with gratitude, respect, and confidence."

It has been pointed out by many commentators that this attitude (highlighted by Percival's own italics) reeks of self-importance and lacks any regard for the interest or rights of patients—that at best it could be called a code of courtesy. How this comes across now matters little. At the time, the Manchester Infirmary embraced Percival's code and prospered. And the code also served a larger purpose. By borrowing from and adapting some of the Royal College's statues (which had gone mostly unchanged since the 1600s), it carried the guild practice of medicine into the modern era, helping to define medicine as the first truly modern profession.

By today's standards, a profession is a specialized occupation controlled by a central organization. Its practitioners undergo extensive training, apprenticeship, and certification, and they adhere to an ideology or group philosophy that defines their mission, their duties to society and to each other. In the field of medicine the process that led to this concept began with the Hippocratic Oath, was clarified by the formation of the Royal College of Physicians, and was brought into focus by Percival's code. It is beside the point whether Percival's *Medical Ethics* is really about ethics. The name, it turns out, was accidental. Percival intended to call it *Medial*

Jurisprudence, but some friends objected. So he chose *Medical Ethics* instead.

Percival's code successfully stated what needed stating: that the posses-sion of specialized knowledge and the authority to use it comes with an obligation to use it wisely (a point which is sometimes lost on individuals who take up a profession for other reasons). Thus the code of any modern profession, whether it exists or not as a physical document, stands in the public's mind as the embodiment of this obligation. This was Percival's contribution—formalizing the idea that a profession's reason for being is grounded in a shared sense of purpose. The written code may not state the mission very effectively, or to everyone's satisfaction, but the fact that a code exists within a profession is often enough to legitimize it.

Medical Ethics also managed to fill an immense void. Local medical soci-eties in the United States adopted large portions of it, and not surprisingly, when the newly founded American Medical Association met in 1847 for the express purpose of drafting a code, they adopted Percival's text almost verbatim, calling it, officially, their "Code of Ethics."

AS PROFESSIONAL SOCIETIES sprouted throughout the United States in the late nineteenth century, the AMA stood out as the model to be emu-lated. Within the space of thirty years the association took a disorganized and not entirely respectable occupation, and transformed it into the well-regulated and highly exclusive profession that it remains today, mostly by writing and enforcing a code of ethics.

Other modern professions also took shape during the nineteenth cen-tury, following the lead established in England, where the Institute of Civil Engineers was founded in 1818, the Royal Institute of British Architects in 1834, and the Pharmaceutical Society in 1841. In America, the American Society of Civil Engineers was founded in 1852, the American Institute of Architects in 1857, and the American Chemical Society in 1876.

But unlike their British counterparts, the American societies did not draw their membership solely from the ranks of gentlemen. Therefore, al-though the British could operate under unwritten codes of gentlemanly conduct that were ingrained into the upper reaches of society, Americans had no such tradition to draw upon, and naturally turned to written codes. Beginning with the AMA, American professional societies carefully drafted their standards of conduct, and most followed the AMA's lead in giving them the title "Code of Ethics."

Thus did this quaint phrase come into general use, and although its originator has gone largely unacknowledged, it makes Percival, if not the Father of Modern Medicine, at least the Father of Modern Professionalism.

THE HIPPOCRATIC OATH

Like Newton, Thomas Percival succeeded as an innovator by standing on the shoulders of giants. In particular, his claim to the title of "father of *modern* medicine" acknowledges a great debt to Hippocrates, the ancient Greek physician and still undisputed Father of Medicine. The Hippocratic Oath, the original code of medical ethics, is his legacy, and it has ruled over medicine and shaped the public image of the physician for over two thousand years. Oddly, very few people know what it actually says.

OF ALL PROFESSIONAL oaths, the Hippocratic is the best known and the most misunderstood. It has come to represent the ruling ethos of Western medicine even though the code of conduct it contains is in direct opposition to many contemporary medical practices. Most medical schools had dropped it from their graduation ceremonies by the 1970s, yet the Oath is still revered and respected for what it represents—a solemn contract that sanctifies the doctor–patient relationship, establishes the physician's devotion to the profession, and declares the physician's first principle: above all else, do no harm. (*Primum non nocere*, the Latin version of this precept, is not stated verbatim in the Oath. It comes from Book One of the *Epidemics*, a text attributed to Hippocrates, in which he writes: "As to diseases, make a habit of two things—to help, or at least to do no harm." This idea is echoed in two places in the Oath.)

Today the Oath is championed by opponents of abortion and doctor-assisted suicide (two practices that the Oath specifically forbids). It is a convenient banner to wave at those who would dare to question conservative traditions. But the text of the Oath is not so simple that it can be reduced to a few simple prescriptions, nor can it be said to represent any widespread tradition of medical practice in Greek society or in any subsequent culture that adopted it.

Despite its outdated preamble—"I swear by Apollo the Physician, and Aesculapius and Hygieia and Panacea, and all the Gods and Goddesses"— its arcane prohibitions, and its great antiquity, the Hippocratic Oath achieved its greatest influence in late-nineteenth and early-twentieth-century America. Its insistence on the distinction between physicians and surgeons—a distinction that persisted through the Middle Ages (when barbers were actually barber-surgeons)—did not deter the American Medical Association from sanctioning it in the mid 1800s, even though they were striving to establish uniform ethical standards for both physicians *and* surgeons. Indeed, as the United States emerged as the world leader in medical education, research, and practice, the Hippocratic Oath also emerged as the ethical symbol of modern medicine.

As medical ethicists like to point out, there are many misconceptions about the Oath. To begin with, it is no longer believed to have been written by Hippocrates, a fifth-century B.C. Greek physician who may or may not have existed. Name recognition came late to him, first through the *Corpus Hippocraticum*, a collection of over fifty medical treatises, of which only a few are thought to be his work, and then through the famous Oath, which takes its name from the *Corpus*.

Although it enjoyed great popularity and widespread use in the medical schools of Europe as well as those founded in the United States, by 1960 only seven U.S. medical schools were using it, and after the 1970s its ceremonial use had practically disappeared. Today it is used here and there, typically in a revised form made palatable to a modern audience.

This contradicts the popular conception of the Oath, which presumes that every medical student is required to swear it upon entering the profession, and that it is somehow legally binding. It still is not unusual for lawyers, both on television and in real life, to try to bully a testifying physician by reminding him or her of the sacred oath he or she once swore. The problem with this scenario is that the physician is probably as ignorant of the content and meaning of the Oath as the lawyer. Its use has never been a standard practice, it has never been enforced, and its text is not closely read by most medical students.

The rejection of the Oath began early. The 1717 commencement program of the medical school of the College of Philadelphia (now the University of Pennsylvania) notes that the Oath "prescribed by Hippocrates to his Disciples [and] generally adopted in Universities and Schools of Physic on like occasions," would be replaced by a promise to stand by the "ties of Honour and Gratitude," and to "consult the safety of their Patients, the good of the community, and the dignity of their Profession." Over the next two centuries the practice of replacing the Oath with something more suitable would continue. As conscientious members of the profession began to object to the Oath's outdatedness, many medical schools turned to formulas, such as the World Medical Association's 1948 Declaration of Geneva (a version of the Hippocratic Oath that reflects an awareness of, if not a reaction to, atrocities committed by Nazi doctors) and the Prayer of Maimonides (thought to be composed by the medieval Jewish philosopher, but actually written by a German doctor in the 1700s).

By the mid 1960s, less than a tenth of America's eighty-six medical schools were using the original Oath at commencement, and by the 1980s its ceremonial use had declined even more. Yet its reputation has survived undiminished. Commentators and even many doctors invoke it routinely in ignorance of what it actually says. Ironically, it appears likely that the Oath was irrelevant to the very age that produced it.

SCHOLARS EXAMINING THE Hippocratic Oath have managed to dispel many of the myths that surround it. Textual evidence, for example, places the document late in the fourth century B.C. (ruling out the authorship of Hippocrates, who would have lived a century earlier, if he lived at all). Its principles of medical ethics—to refrain from assisting attempts at suicide or performing abortions, and to refrain from the surgical removal of stones—are those of the Pythagorean School, although some writers attribute them to the Asclepiads, a cult that worshipped Apollo. Which is to say that while the oath has traditionally been regarded as a message of timeless validity, under close examination it is revealed to represent a minority of Greek opinion, both popular and professional.

The renown of the Oath, in fact, has little to do with its role in classical antiquity. Its current reputation owes instead to the efforts of Church Fathers who rewrote the text in suitably Christian language and preserved it as the code of medical education. The championing of the Oath was undoubtedly due to its insistence on preserving life—especially that of the fetus. Thus it should be regarded as a Church document as much as a Greek text. Not only does it fail to reflect the views or practices of Greek physicians of the Hippocratic era, or any other era, but it has never been enforced by law, or mandated by any known school of medicine in ancient times. Through its affiliation with the Church, however, its use as a profession of duty was perpetuated by the universities of Europe, and this is how it made its way to American professional schools, which in the 1800s sought to adopt many of the trappings of European academicism. In this sense the Oath represents yet another vestige of America's Christian heritage.

THE LASAGNA OATH

With the advance of medical technology raising moral questions that could not have been imagined even a few decades ago, it becomes increasingly difficult to expect a short statement of principles to encompass a single ethic for an entire profession. Yet when medical schools in the 1970s began searching for alternatives to the Hippocratic Oath, they may have been unaware of what it was they were trying to replace.

In a 1964 article for the *New York Times Magazine*, Dr. Louis Lasagna, at that time a professor at the Johns Hopkins Medical School, reflected on the gradual abandonment of the ancient pledge, and on the need for a new declaration of ethics. In proposing a new oath (one which was later adopted at many schools), he acknowledged that what made the ancient oath so special, more than the message it conveyed, was the tradition it represented. Recalling how he swore it at his own medical school graduation, Lasagna wrote, "It was, for me, a thrilling experience. The words were less important than the spirit of the moment. I still believe that some such ceremony should occur at every medical school commencement." What he does not address is how a new oath, a modern oath, could be expected to elicit the same sensation.

What finally brought about the Hippocratic Oath's demise as a ceremonial pledge was not its injunctions but its lack of political correctness—its paternalistic tone, its implicit exclusion of women from the profession, its reference to slaves, and its invocation of the Greek gods. Now that it is hardly ever used in ceremonies (at least in its original form), its influence might be considered at an end. But an increasing number of medical ethicists are coming to its defense. If the Hippocratic Oath did no more than inspire a romantic vision of medicine's long history at the expense of reasoned debate of current medical issues, they say, then it would have outlived its usefulness. Many think it has. But its defenders argue that this misses its larger significance. For one thing, they say, the Oath serves to focus public attention on the constantly changing field of medical ethics. For another, it solidifies in the popular consciousness the idea of a public trust that binds the physician to the profession, and at the same time to the best interest of the patient.

In other words the Hippocratic Oath has become a constructive ready-made opinion whose political shortcomings are more than compensated for by its power of suggestion. Having been in continuous use for two and a half millennia, the Oath could hardly be expected to disappear overnight, nor should it.

As for the Lasagna Oath, the graduating class still swears it occasionally at Tufts Medical School, where Dr. Lasagna himself went on to teach (and where students vote each year on what pledge they would like to recite). This practice is becoming more popular at other schools, where students are choosing to carry on the tradition. In this way the Hippocratic Oath (often in name only) continues to define the duty of the physician while other oaths are recited in its place. As Lasagna himself admitted, the words are subsumed by the spirit of the moment—a fact that confronts anyone who is faced with making a commencement address. No one listens all that closely.

WE BELIEVE IN ICE CREAM

In the early 1920s the Pacific Ice Cream Manufacturers Association, like many American trade associations of that era, collected its standards of practice in an impressively designed and ornately lettered Declaration of Principles. Technically a code of ethics, the Declaration took the combined form of a creed, a code, and a pledge, and it began with this pronouncement:

> *We Believe in ice cream, and in the great future that lies before the industry, because ice cream is the one product which contains all of the life giving, body building properties peculiar to milk, combined with a variety and palatability found in no other milk product.*

The statement goes on to denounce certain practices that to the unsuspecting consumer raise troubling questions about the palatability of the ice cream business as a whole. With its vague prohibitions, it sounds less like guidance and more like a reassuring advertisement, which to a large extent it really is.

At the turn of the century many business leaders looked with envy upon the monopoly over professionalism enjoyed by the well-established and highly skilled occupations. They wanted in. The American Medical Association had blazed a trail, and many business and trade associations were determined to set out upon it. One of the ways they sought to gain respect was by the drafting of codes of ethics, as if by doing so they might join the ranks of the professional elite. But this does not entirely account for the magnitude of the ethical movement that Edgar Heermance and others saw fit to document. After all, could peanut butter or ice cream manufacturers expect to enjoy the same level of respect as the American Bar Association and the American Medical Association simply by drafting a code? Clearly, other factors were at work.

Boosters like Heermance would have preferred to let stand the idea that the ethics in business movement was entirely self-motivated. The reality is that the federal government stepped in to force the hand of the business associations, primarily by passing the Clayton Anti-Trust Act of 1914, and by forming the Federal Trade Commission the following year. Codes of ethics, although they existed well before the 1920s, emerged as a cultural phenomenon during that decade. This had more to do with the First World War and the rapid economic growth and opportunism that accompanied it, than with self-motivated moral crusading. In this respect the trades differed from the professions. Less specialized and far less organized, they became ethics-minded only when they had to.

ANTI-TRUST

At the turn of the century public opinion of big business turned increasingly hostile. Price fixing, cutthroat competition, collusion, unsafe working conditions, and charges of hypocrisy were a few of the growing number of complaints about the way businesses operated.

The curtain began to fall on the "golden age" of American business with the revelations of the muckraking journalists of the early 1900s, and with an increasing number of highly publicized atrocities culminating in New York's Triangle Shirtwaist Factory fire of 1911. (With its fire doors barred to keep the sweatshop workers inside, the building burned to the ground, killing 146 women.) In the ensuing public outrage, big business finally began to get the message that change would have to come from within if they were to avoid the imposition of reforms from without. Already, labor laws were being overhauled and security codes tightened. When business leaders did not act quickly enough on their own, the Federal Trade Commission stepped in.

In 1918 the FTC asked representatives from the business and trade associations to submit lists of what they considered to be unfair practices. Officially, this was known as a trade practice submittal. It was, in essence, a clever way of getting each industry to take responsibility for its own transgressions.

As the trade practice submittals came in, ethical codes quickly followed. Not surprisingly, many of them were dominated by lists of trade practices to be avoided, hinting at the unsavory nature of business tactics that had made the codes necessary at all. The National Ice Cream Manufacturers Association's code lists sixteen types of unfair competition, including the introduction of foreign substances into a competitor's product, bribing competitors' employees, publicly attacking a competitor's reputation, making threats, infringing on trademarks, bidding up the price of raw materials, and selling below cost. The National School Supply Association Code of Business Practices lists a dozen cautions in a similar vein, including, "Do not harass competitors by fake requests for estimates on bills of goods, for catalogs, etc.," "Do not make false or disparaging statements respecting a competitor's products, his business, financial credit, etc."

Such abuses did not prevail in every industry. In the retail trade, visionary businessmen such as A. T. Stewart of New York ended the ordeal of haggling with aggressive salesmen (the accepted practice in retail stores until the mid 1800s), by clearly marking the price of each item and by selling only good quality merchandise. Stewart, a pious man, sought to graft his religious principles onto his business practices. His competitors thought such honesty suicidal, until they saw customers coming from miles around just to shop at Stewart's. His successors Marshall Field of Chicago, Edward Filene of Boston, and John Wanamaker of Philadelphia, further revolutionized retail practices by establishing uniform pricing, accepting returned merchandise for a full refund, and assuming responsibility for working conditions by instituting employee codes of conduct.

Elsewhere, a clear lack of discipline among the growing number of trade associations in the booming post–World War I American economy set off an alarm. The Federal Trade Commission began breathing down the necks of various trades. Better Business Bureaus formed in the larger cities, and tried to help local associations regulate themselves. But only one organization possessed enough clout to make ethics the nation's business. Their intervention turned business reform into a national movement, and by extension, the framed business code of ethics into an American business icon. And as often turns out to be the case, there was one man in that organization who got the ball rolling, and thereby changed the face of working America.

THE ROTARY CAMPAIGN

Rotary International, or the Rotary Club, as it was originally called, had been founded in 1905 in Chicago as a businessmen's society. Its name derives from the early practice of rotating meetings between members' places of business. With the decline of the fraternal lodges as a popular social activity, business clubs such as the Lions and Kiwanis emerged in early twentieth-century America as a major social force, and Rotary served as the model. These clubs did not at first aspire to a leadership role predicated on the public interest. They formed as means of establishing contacts between local businessmen and professionals—a premise of mutual patronage that would soon prove awkward. After the First World War the business clubs faced strong criticism because of what were perceived as selfish motives.

Recognizing the need to serve a higher purpose, the clubs soon found one that would ensure their survival. After the war, they regrouped around the banner of community service, and emerged as "service" clubs dedicated to community spirit and good works. (In the 1920s, the decade in which Sinclair Lewis's *Babbitt* is set, the clubs were known as booster clubs for the way they zealously promoted their communities.)

By the 1920s the big three—Rotary, Lions, and Kiwanis—had grown into international organizations with influential governing bodies and millions of members representing every profession and proprietary trade in the country. Not only did they promote their own codes of ethics, but they were in a natural position to take the lead in reforming business practices.

In May of 1922, in a special issue of the *Annals* of the American Academy of Political and Social Science devoted to business and professional ethics, Guy Gundaker, a successful Philadelphia restaurateur and chairman of Rotary's Committee on Business Methods and soon to be the organization's president, introduced a campaign "for an intensive drive on the writing of codes of standards of correct practice in all crafts corresponding with the businesses or professions represented in Rotary." Gundaker was a code man. He had taken it upon himself to write the rather lengthy code of the National Restaurant Association, which Rotary used as its model of effective code-writing. He also knew too well that many existing codes were couched in high-sounding phrases and platitudes that "are so indefinite and general that they have no practical significance." Yet he also believed that codes had great potential to smooth the businessman's relations with other businessmen, with organized labor, with the public, and especially with the government.

Within a year of Gundaker's challenge Rotarians around the country came through with thousands of new codes, representing occupations as diverse as shoe retailers, implement dealers, truck drivers, and morticians. Edgar Heermance himself, it should be noted, was a staunch Rotarian whose efforts to collect and analyze the codes was an extension of Gundaker's campaign. He hoped his collection would serve as a textbook for the establishment of proper standards of practice.

In the early 1920s, which might be called the decade of the business and trade association, a wide range of codes flourished—some in earnest, some clearly dubious. Many, as Gundaker well knew, were little more than window dressing. With the intervention of Rotary, however, these codes gained a measure of legitimacy and assumed a proud place on the walls of waiting rooms, newsrooms, automotive repair shops, photographic studios, barber shops, and factories all across America.

After Black Friday in 1929, the religious fervor of big business subsided, as did the moral posturing that went with it. But most of the codes remained in place, even though the movement that inspired them had given way to more immediate concerns. Most of the associations that survived stuck with their codes, and new codes continued to be churned out.

In the early 1960s Commerce Secretary Luther Hodges revived the ethics-in-business movement when he issued a challenge reminiscent of Gundaker's. After a notorious antitrust case involving the electrical industry, public confidence in business eroded yet again, and Hodges proposed to issue a departmental code of ethics for American business. He called it "A Statement of Business Ethics and a Call for Action." A year later, in 1963, his book *The Business Conscience* came out. Together these two documents brought about a new interest in code writing. This time around its chronicler was Jane Clapp, who in 1974 published a far more comprehensive volume than Heermance's, entitled *Professional Ethics and Insignia.* It contains hundreds of codes, creeds, pledges, mottoes, and insignia from the entire range of professional and trade organizations.

The most up-to-date source book on the current state of professional and business ethics is Rena Gorlin's *Codes of Professional Responsibility* (Bureau of National Affairs, 1994). It is the most comprehensive collection of codes yet, and also is the first collection to avoid invoking ethics in its title, surely a conscious and wise decision on the part of the editor.

PERSONAL CODES OF ETHICS

Robert Louis Stevenson, in addition to his popular novels and memorable verses, once composed a personal philosophy of life which is often quoted. The great American sculptor Augustus Saint-Gaudens chose it for the inscription to accompany his bas-relief portrait of the poet. The words help to give some measure of the man:

> *To be honest, to be kind—to earn a little and spend a little less, to make upon the whole a family happier for his presence, to renounce when that shall be necessary and not to be embittered, to keep a few friends, but these without capitulation—above all, on the same grim condition, to keep friends with himself—here is a task for all that a man has of fortitude and delicacy.*

Not content to live by someone else's code, a select group of self-appointed moralists in each generation choose to write their own codes of life. It is an interesting exercise in self-definition. The line dividing such a code from a personal credo or motto is a thin one. It usually depends on what the author chooses to call it. Prior to the emergence of professional and business codes of ethics, popular titles ranged from "A Rule of Life" to "My Credo" to the title Stevenson chose: "Philosophy of Life." Yet as professional codes caught on, philosophies like Stevenson's increasingly carried the title of "code of ethics" or "code of life."

The public is always on the lookout for words of wisdom by any title—but codes of life have a special appeal. In the 1960s a code in the form of a prose poem turned up in an Anglican church in Baltimore. It began with the words: "Go placidly amid the noise and the haste, and remember what peace may be in silence." The poem—"Desiderata"—was at first thought to be an ancient prayer written in 1692, but turned out to have been written in 1927 by the poet Max Ehrmann. It had gone unnoticed until the story of its great antiquity became folklore and the poem became a national sensation. Ehrmann, who died in 1954, did not live to enjoy his poem's popularity or notoriety. He once said: "I would rather write one beautiful thing that might abide in the perpetual flux around us and live and die poor than to be the author of forty commercial novels." He seems to have gotten his wish.

There are many other endearing personal codes of ethics, a few of which seized the public's imagination shortly after the authors' deaths. The poet William Henry Channing, a good friend to Henry David Thoreau, wrote a letter to a friend in 1841 which was later excerpted as a stand-alone piece in his biography, and given the title "My Symphony." It begins with Channing's intention "to be a working man, poor, humble . . . to live content with small means; to seek elegance rather than luxury, and refinement rather than fashion; to be worthy, not respectable; and wealthy, not rich; to study hard, think quietly, act frankly . . ." Channing's wish became a popular and much anthologized piece.

Some personalities loom so large during their lifetime that the pronouncement of a personal code becomes an event, one which is often repeated, refined, and embellished through countless lectures. Such a case is Robert G. Ingersoll, one of the most celebrated orators of the nineteenth century, who framed a code in terms similar to Channing's: "To love justice, to long for the right, to love mercy, to pity the suffering, to assist the weak, to forget wrongs and remember benefits—to love the truth, to be sincere, to utter honest words, to love liberty, to wage relentless war against slavery in all its forms . . ."

The renowned physician and teacher Sir William Osler offered another code of the public man at a farewell dinner in 1905. He entitled his talk "L'Envoi" (the send-off), and in it he said, in part: "I have had three personal ideals. One is to do the day's work well and not bother about tomorrow. . . . The second ideal has been to act the Golden Rule. . . . And the third has been to cultivate such a measure of equanimity as would enable me to bear success with humility, the affection of my friends without pride, and to be ready when the day of sorrow and grief came to meet it with the courage befitting a man."

AT ONE TIME these personal codes constituted a small but popular literary genre, one that no longer commands much attention. For a while, they created an expectation that great men and women would bestow upon the public brief, trenchant expositions of the most useful and universal aspects of their personal philosophy. Like personal creeds, which flourished during the same period, these codes played up notions of honor and self-sacrifice by using the language of chivalry. At the turn of the century, the ideals of Arthurian legend sustained a movement known as muscular Christianity, and the organizations it inspired, such as the Boy Scouts, couched their rituals in a lofty language that the public accepted uncritically. But the language of good intentions and idealism had to change with the times.

By the end of the 1920s many codes were beginning to acquire an edge, reflecting an urban mentality that was taking hold of the country. Their tone became less self-important, less idealistic. A good example is "Testament of a Critic," by George Jean Nathan, H. L. Mencken's collaborator at the *American Mercury*. It begins: "My code of life and conduct is simply this: work hard, play to the allowable limit, disregard equally the good and the bad opinion of others, never do a friend a dirty trick, eat and drink whatever you feel like when you feel like, never grow indignant over anything, trust to tobacco for calm and serenity, bathe twice a day. . . ."

A wake-up call at the end of the 1920s found the nation in bad shape, and sorely in need of a new approach to life. Nathan's idea of self-indulgence turned into overindulgence for too many people, and the Depression put an end to rampant idealism. The code that best represents the 1930s offered something of a corrective, and it became the prototype for a number of codes that would be written to deal with addiction. It went by the name of the Twelve Steps of Alcoholics Anonymous.

The year was 1938 when Bill W., a struggling alcoholic, wrote out the principles that had turned his life around. Many of these had come from the Oxford Group, a pioneering treatment center, and also from William James's *Varieties of Religious Experience*. The Twelve Steps is more than a personal code of ethics. It has become the basis of the entire recovery movement. Yet unlike most institutionalized codes, it is still a highly personal statement.

The most successful recent incarnation of the genre of personal codes is the Fulghum Credo, from Robert Fulghum's *All I Really Need to Know I Learned in Kindergarten* (1988). An unpretentious bouquet of the simple lessons children are plied with every day ("Share everything, play fair, don't hit people, put things back where you found them . . ."), it indicates how the appeal of the high-blown and sometimes pompous philosophies of orators and statesmen have given way to simpler, more innocent, and less demanding counsels of soft-spoken sages.

CONCLUSION

"The great multitude of men everywhere and always have demanded detailed codes of ethics," wrote Walter Lippmann in his *Essays in the Public Philosophy*. "They are necessary to their comfort, their convenience and their peace of mind." But the heart of a code is not in the details. Its mere existence, the very name itself, serves to remind us of the values and ideals we admire. The codes we live by grew out of notions of chivalry and honor that were born on medieval battlefields and refined by Renaissance courtiers. Resurrected in the modern era by dedicated professionals, they were finally mass produced for the general public by business and trade associations. Their popularity might appear to have run its course, but it has not.

The ideal of personal honor within a principled society is nowhere better represented than by the Boy Scout Laws, which comprise perhaps the best-known codes of ethics. They were written by Sir Robert Baden-Powell, who founded the Scouts in 1907 in the midst of the muscular Christianity movement—a revival of chivalric idealism in the spirit of Sir Walter Scott. Along with the Boy Scout Oath ("On my honor I will do my best to do my duty to God and my country, and to obey the Scout Law . . ."), the Boy Scout Laws constitute a code which for many people epitomizes the highest ideals of citizenship. All subsequent codes benefit simply by association.

A charming story, by way of illustration, if not conclusion, is related by Ronald Berenbeim in his book *Corporate Ethics* (1987), where he recounts the origin of a particular corporate code. The story illustrates the importance and pervasiveness of the Scout ideal, and how it has worked its way up from the pup tent to the corporate boardroom.

> One CEO commented that the idea for a code grew out of his experience with the Boy Scouts of America. He formed a task force, gave the members a copy of the Scout oath and law, and said, "Start with this. I don't want our code to look like the Boy Scout oath and law, but I want all the points covered there to be in our code."

It would not be fair to dismiss this story as a case of misplaced nostalgia or preciousness. It deserves to be read against the full Scout oath (see p. 264) and laws (see p. 279), which suffer in some quarters from a reputation that they do not deserve. No one could argue with the principles they put forth. They are the very preconditions of civility, of good citizenship. Scouting may seem anachronistic, as is the very idea of a code, but its ideals are timeless, which explains why they are continually being reformulated.

THE TEN COMMANDMENTS OF SUCCESS

I. WORK HARD. HARD WORK IS THE BEST INVESTMENT
A MAN CAN MAKE.

II. STUDY HARD. KNOWLEDGE ENABLES A MAN TO WORK
MORE INTELLIGENTLY AND EFFECTIVELY.

III. HAVE INITIATIVE. RUTS OFTEN DEEPEN INTO GRAVES.

IV. LOVE YOUR WORK. THEN YOU WILL FIND PLEASURE
IN MASTERING IT.

V. BE EXACT. SLIPSHOD METHODS BRING SLIPSHOD RESULTS.

VI. HAVE THE SPIRIT OF CONQUEST. THUS YOU CAN
SUCCESSFULLY BATTLE AND OVERCOME DIFFICULTIES.

VII. CULTIVATE PERSONALITY. PERSONALITY IS TO THE MAN
WHAT PERFUME IS TO THE FLOWER.

VIII. HELP AND SHARE WITH OTHERS. THE REAL TEST OF BUSI-
NESS GREATNESS LIES IN GIVING OPPORTUNITY TO OTHERS.

IX. BE DEMOCRATIC. UNLESS YOU FEEL RIGHT TOWARDS
YOUR FELLOW MEN YOU CAN NEVER BE A SUCCESSFUL
LEADER OF MEN.

X. IN ALL THINGS DO YOUR BEST. THE MAN WHO HAS DONE
HIS BEST HAS DONE EVERYTHING. THE MAN WHO HAS DONE
LESS THAN HIS BEST HAS DONE NOTHING.

CHARLES M. SCHWAB (1862 – 1939)

CHAPTER SIX

TO THINE OWN SELF BE TRUE

THE SECRETS OF SUCCESS, ADVICE FROM PARENTS, AND THE
GOSPEL ACCORDING TO MURPHY, PARKINSON, AND OTHERS

SUCCESS

At the age of twenty-five Niccolò Machiavelli entered public life, and for the next fourteen years navigated the turbulent waters of Italian politics, serving as a military officer, ambassador, secretary, courier, and confidant to the ruler of the republic of Florence. But with the rise to power of the Medici family in 1512, he found himself banished to his farm and removed from the urgencies of statecraft that had once made his blood stir. Consigned to spend his days in various pastoral pursuits—snaring thrushes, clearing trees, and selling wood—he grew restless.

Each afternoon he would repair to his aviary with copies of Dante, Ovid, and Petrarch, read of their "tender passions and their loves," while remembering his own, and "enjoy [him]self for a while in that sort of dreaming." From these reveries his daily routine would take him to the local inn, where he would inquire of the news from other villages, and of the "tastes and different fancies of men." He would play at tavern games, sink into vulgarity, and inevitably be drawn into "a thousand disputes and countless insults with offensive words," which he imagined could be heard as far away as the next village. "So, mixed up with these lice," he wrote, "I keep my brain from growing moldy, and satisfy the malice of this fate of mine."

In the evening, upon returning home, Machiavelli would remove his dusty clothes and exchange them for his court robes. Thus attired, he would sit at his desk for the next four hours, and in the calm isolation of his farmhouse, he produced the work that would forever assure his fame, or infamy.

THE STORY IS TOLD by Machiavelli himself in a letter of 1513, which is referred to wherever it is reprinted as the most famous letter in Italian literature. It is not, of course, famous in America, although the story it tells of the humble roots of success is a familiar theme in American culture. The success, in this case, is not merely Machiavelli's reentry into the world of politics, but an even greater splash in cultural history. To read his letter today is to discover how one man achieved immortality, and this accounts for the letter's fame. It is one of the earliest success epics.

In later versions it would be replayed by Elbert Hubbard, a former soap salesman, who repaired to his study one evening after a lively debate with his son, and dashed off an essay about it for his magazine, *The Philistine*. The result, a short tract on the work ethic entitled "A Message to Garcia," went on to sell over fifty million copies worldwide, making Hubbard a fabulously rich man, and for a short time providing him with the kind of circulation enjoyed by Machiavelli's *Prince*. It no longer sells, but Hubbard's saga, including his ultimate demise on the *Lusitania*, is still compelling.

Then there is Dale Carnegie, a child of hardship driven by his admiration of oratorial skill, who clawed his way to modest success teaching public speaking at a New York City YMCA. The book culled from his lecture notes and christened with the catchy, self-explanatory title *How to Win Friends and Influence People*, launched Carnegie into superstardom, making his name a synonym for success. Sales of his book so overshadowed those of ordinary best-sellers that it inspired comparisons to the Bible.

WHAT MACHIAVELLI, Elbert Hubbard, and Dale Carnegie had to sell was advice, and in some sense, themselves. Each succeeded in reducing a law of human nature to its essence, thereby helping others to make sense of the world, or to understand how to succeed in it. At the very least, they showed how they had done it. They proposed how to live, and the public listened. Through accidents of time and idiosyncrasies of style—which is

THE WORDS WE LIVE BY / 125

almost to say, by pure dumb luck—each man entered the language as a symbol of perseverance. But the public perception is nowhere near as complex as the men and their works.

The author of *The Prince* inspired the word *Machiavellian,* which describes a particularly ruthless or clever way of getting to the top and staying there. Hubbard, like Machiavelli, wrote volumes of poetry and prose, and believed that there was much to be learned by examining the lives of famous men. But he too is remembered (by an ever diminishing minority) by a single phrase: find me the man who can carry the message to Garcia. Dale Carnegie created an industry around the art of public speaking, yet he is remembered primarily for the title of his best-selling work.

Each of these men teaches the same lesson about ready-made opinions: there has always been money to be made from giving advice, but it has never been a sure thing. The public, whether in the form of one's contemporaries, or in the larger sense known as "posterity," is fickle, and often gets things wrong. The history of advice and advice givers is a litany of misunderstandings, out of which comes one simple fact: people take what they want and use it as they please. As Baltasar Gracian, the author of *The Art of Worldly Wisdom* and a popular giver of advice himself, observed, "What the multitude thinks, is so, or soon will be."

By a consensus of opinion, Horace Greeley is the first to have said, "Go West, young man!" Jimmy Durante said, "Be nice to people on your way up, because you're going to meet them again on your way back down." P. T. Barnum said, "There's a sucker born every minute." And Vince Lombardi hammered home the creed, "Winning isn't everything; it's the only thing." None of these attributions is entirely accurate, and Barnum, for one, would not have wished to be remembered by that motto. But facts rarely get in the way of a useful myth.

The advice that people take to heart is usually sustained by legends. For the most part, an isolated piece of advice, unattributed and of unknown origin, has no credibility, however pithy it might be. If advice is to succeed, to make an impression, it needs to have a story behind it or a name attached to it—something to give it momentum, and thereby justify why anyone should pay attention to it.

The perfect marriage of such words and reputations is to be found in advice books, which constitute one of the oldest known literary genres. There are many types to choose from: the book of advice to a child, the book of conduct for gentleman, the book of etiquette, and, of course, the book of how to succeed at life, love, or business. In some instances a single work has made a deep impression on a generation, enough in some cases to keep the author's name alive in succeeding generations. In this way certain pieces of advice, and the names of those who give it, become part of popular culture, in many cases enjoying (or suffering) reputations that are way out of proportion with what was actually said (or meant). They have the dubious distinction of being referred to rather than read. The result is a curious disparity between popular opinions and the words that sustain them.

THE ART OF WORLDLY WISDOM

Although advice is supposedly free, fortunes have been made by dispensing it, by giving it away. Of course it is never given freely. The advice giver may profit financially or by acquiring fame. Machiavelli, in his forced retirement, wanted to be a player in the world of political intrigue that he had once engineered so skillfully from behind the scenes. By writing *The Prince*, which took the form of a deferential letter to Lorenzo de Medici (the man who swept into power in Florence and brought the Renaissance with him), Machiavelli eclipsed the fame of his patron, and emerged as perhaps the most celebrated, if not notorious, personality of the era.

Yet Machiavelli could not control his place in history. His book, which does not contain numbered rules, has been reduced by quotation dictionaries to a set of maxims, most of which reveal what the author conceded was the unseemly but necessary aspect of maintaining power—that because the course of history is controlled by fortune as much as by virtue, the prince has no choice but to eliminate possible sources of bad luck. "You have to destroy those who can or might hurt you," he wrote.

Traditionally, advice and conduct books have stressed either good morals or good manners (or both) as being good in themselves. But to Machiavelli, manners, morals, words, and deeds are good only insofar as they help the prince to acquire and maintain power. "It is good to appear merciful, truthful, humane, sincere, and religious," he writes, adding, "it is good to be so in reality. But you must keep your mind so disposed that, in case of need, you can turn to the exact contrary."

THE PRINCE did not turn out to be the font from which all subsequent advice and conduct books would flow. It was influential, to be sure, but few subsequent writers were willing to endure the criticism it brought upon itself and its author. The genre would instead produce guides for the conduct of a gentleman (Baldassare Castiglione's 1528 *The Courtier* is the most important work of this type), and guides for the successful would-be political flunky (the anonymous and misleadingly named *Walsingham's Manual* is the most notorious example). Advice on the proper education of children would result in several best-sellers from such luminaries as Sir Walter Raleigh, William Penn, and Lord Chesterfield. And the book of prudential and witty maxims would also enjoy an enduring popularity. In 1993 Gracian's *The Art of Worldly Wisdom* (a guide to the conduct of life originally titled the *Oráculo Manual,* or The Oracle) was reissued as a gift book and became a best-seller yet again over three hundred years after the Spanish Jesuit wrote it.

Most advice addresses specific situations or circumstances, but it can easily be appropriated and put to uses for which it was never intended, which, in a strange way, is many an advice giver's wildest dream. Everyone has an opinion, but some people's two cents worth goes further than others, and can sometimes buy fame, fortune, or notoriety. This is how advice giving turns into myth making, and a name like Machiavelli's becomes a Rorschach test for a single idea, one which cancels out everything else the author ever did. Horatio Alger presents a similar conundrum. He wrote over a hundred novels, but none that precisely fits the rags-to-riches formula with which his name is indelibly associated.

It would be impossible to do justice to the entire genre of advice in a single chapter. As a source of ready-made opinions, advice has produced a few definitive works that show how Americans have seized upon certain expressions and turned them into cultural milestones.

This chapter examines some of these milestones. It begins with the story of a man who could not follow his own advice, which is not an uncommon problem among advisors. The do-as-I-say-not-as-I-do school of thought is further explored in a section on advice to children. Rules and advice are also considered in the context of success literature in America through an examination of the Horatio Alger myth and the career of Dale Carnegie. The chapter ends with an exposé of advice as theory, in which social scientists propose to explain the working world through Murphy's, Parkinson's, and Peter's laws and principles, and end up getting it all wrong.

BY GOD HE WAS RICH

The Ten Commandments of Success was industrialist Charles M. Schwab's contribution to the genre of advice. It was never famous or influential, and it is not even a particularly original piece of writing. What makes it worth mentioning at all is that it is written by everyone's favorite millionaire, whose final gesture to the world proved that success should not be equated with riches alone.

To the American business community, if not to the nation as a whole, Charlie Schwab, the first president of U.S. Steel, embodied the American dream. Like Willie Loman's brother Ben in Arthur Miller's *Death of a Salesman*, Schwab was utterly certain of his destiny. While in his twenties he walked into the jungle of the Carnegie steel works, quelled the Homestead riot, brokered the formation of the country's largest steel company, and when he walked out a few years later, "By God he was rich."

Charles Schwab, like Ben Loman, started from nothing. But by his mid thirties he was rubbing elbows with the captains of industry, principally because, as he himself admitted, he was so good with people. Dale Carnegie (no relation to Andrew Carnegie, the tycoon who hired Schwab and gave him control of his steel company) quoted Schwab as saying that his smile had been worth a million dollars—his salary in the year 1900. A year later it would be worth two million. Later, as head of Bethlehem Steel, Schwab commanded an income that in today's dollars would eclipse the bloated paychecks of the most overpaid CEOs. His single greatest regret, in all his years of deal making, was passing on the chance to finance the Wright brothers. He dismissed their experiments as "a harum-scarum stunt," even though the brothers possessed the very entrepreneurial qualities he admired.

Work hard, study hard, have initiative, love your work, be exact, have the spirit of conquest, cultivate personality, help and share with others, be democratic, in all things do your best. These suggestions framed the gospel according to Schwab. He was the world's best salesman: a man who took huge risks and always came out ahead. Unlike Donald Trump, Schwab was not only respected, but admired and well-liked. A master of business diplomacy, he rode the crest of high esteem until the day he died. But not unlike Trump, he had some shortcomings, and these tend to get lost in the hagiography.

According to *Time* magazine, the man who bought Bethlehem Steel and built its assets from $15 million to $720 million "left no more to his heirs than if he had kept working at the $1-a-day job in which he entered the steel business in 1881." Schwab died bankrupt. And to make matters worse, he left his neighbor and alma mater, St. Francis College, holding the bag on a $25,000 loan instead of the $2,000,000 endowment he had been promising them for years. Evidently, he should have listened more closely to the Wright brothers.

"IF A MAN love to give advice," wrote Lord Halifax, himself an unrepentant advice giver, "it is a sure sign that he himself wanteth it." It is also said that to profit from good advice requires more wisdom than to give it, and that success tends to make a fool seem wise. This helps to explain how a Donald Trump can write a fantastically successful book on the art of the deal, and shortly thereafter just barely escape the embarrassment of total ruin. Yet Americans love a comeback kid. They are quick to forgive the occasional setback because a favorite subplot of the American success saga is to make a huge fortune, lose it, and then make it all back again.

Charles Schwab, hero to Dale Carnegie (if not Andrew Carnegie), and to millions of Americans a real-life incarnation of the mustachioed and monocled tycoon of the game of Monopoly, didn't leave himself enough time to make a comeback. But the scandal of his bankruptcy passed. It merited no more than a few paragraphs in *Time*, and it ended well. St. Francis College wound up with Schwab's estate for a pittance, and Schwab remains a business legend. It is as though he took to heart Andrew Carnegie's belief that, "He who dies rich dies disgraced." The value of his stock as a giver of advice never fell.

Schwab was in a good position to give advice without heeding it. He instinctively knew how to succeed, and gave advice only because it was expected of him, and not because he felt he could do justice to his own methods with mere words. He may have died a bankrupt, but he always lived the good life, never forgoing any of its pleasures. It hardly mattered to him whether the world took his advice, it was not very specific anyway—merely an assortment of generalities of the kind that were expected in that era. It was not meant to be followed as much as admired, along with the man himself.

ADVICE TO SONS

In their own modest way, most parents try to give the kind of advice to their children that they feel is expected of them. It is, after all, a parent's job to instill life's lessons and share the fruits of experience. The difficulty, if not impossibility, of this task is underscored by the failure of many brilliant minds to make any headway with their own children. The genre of advice to children has spawned many memorable works, which have, paradoxically, made their greatest impression on an audience of adults. For all of the wisdom that has been directed their way, it would seem that children remain essentially immune to good counsel.

Although some of the most celebrated works of antiquity anticipate the genre of fatherly advice (Ciceros' De Officiis is perhaps the best example), the modern concept of paternal benevolence begins properly with Shakespeare. What is usually overlooked is that the playwright did not invent the genre. He was merely playing around with it.

In Act One of Hamlet, as young Laertes prepares to set out for Paris, his father takes the boy aside and as a parting gift offers him some worldly advice.

> Yet here, Laertes! aboard, aboard, for shame!
> The wind sits in the shoulder of your sail,
> And you are stay'd for. There, my blessing with thee!
> And these few precepts in thy memory
> Look thou character. Give thy thoughts no tongue,
> Nor any unproportioned thought his act.
> Be thou familiar, but by no means vulgar.
> Those friends thou hast, and their adoption tried,
> Grapple them unto thy soul with hoops of steel;
> But do not dull thy palm with entertainment
> Of each new-hatched, unfledged comrade. Beware
> Of entrance to a quarrel. But, being in,
> Bear't that th'opposed may be aware of thee.
> Give every man thine ear, but few thy voice;
> Take each man's censure, but reserve thy judgement.
> Costly thy habit as thy purse can buy,
> But not expressed in fancy; rich, not gaudy;
> For the apparel oft proclaims the man,

And they in France of the best rank and station
Are of a most select and generous chief in that.
Neither a borrower nor a lender be,
For loan oft loses both itself and friend,
And borrowing dulleth edge of husbandry.
This above all: to thine own self be true,
And it must follow, as the night the day,
Thou canst not then be false to any man.
Farewell. My blessing season this in thee!

This passage is the best-known piece of fatherly wisdom ever given, and it is likely to remain so. It has survived numerous attempts at debunking, and can weather one more: this touching scene is actually a parody intended to show up the father as a self-serving hypocrite who would have his son be the same.

Ambiguity, one of Shakespeare's most endearing qualities, is well represented in the character of Polonius, who might seem to be deserving of the undignified death that awaits him were he not such an apparently loving father. His advice is problematic. It is so beautifully composed that its literal message melts down and congeals into a Hallmark sentiment. What the father is really saying is that you must pay attention to appearances, and consider how any word or act will make you look. He is entirely concerned with superficialities rather than principles of character. Yet this is overthrown by his final thought, the words that linger in the listener's mind and drown out all the rest: to thine own self be true.

Shakespearean scholars point to several possible sources of inspiration for this scene. In Elizabethan times, and for some time after, the advice book, and especially the book of advice to a son, was a best-selling genre. As Shakespearean scholar G. B. Harrison notes in his introduction to Henry Percy's book of 1609, *Advice to His Sons*, "It is as natural and seemly for old men to give good counsel to younger as it is natural and reprehensible for younger men to neglect it."

Prior to the Elizabethan era, advice had mostly been given piecemeal, but it soon began to fill advice books such as Percy's. Although addressed to one person, most parental advice books were written with a larger audience in mind. King James wrote the *Basilikon Doron* (or Kingly Gift) in 1599 for the education of his four-year-old son, Prince Henry, and also for immediate publication. Sir Walter Raleigh penned *Instructions to His Son and to*

Posterity in 1616 while he was in prison, as a public statement. Both books went through many printings and countless editions. But these works come after *Hamlet*. For his inspiration, Shakespeare could have turned to Thomas Elyot's *Book Named the Governor* (1531), a popular and early example of a guide to the proper education of youth. A better bet, however, is a book by William Cecil entitled *Certain Precepts for the Well Ordering of a Man's Life*, which presents orthodox Shakespearean scholars with a small problem.

William Cecil, also known as Lord Burghley (or Burleigh), was Queen Elizabeth's private secretary, and thus a man belonging to the innermost circle of the royal court. When he wrote his ten precepts in 1584, they circulated among a select group of intimates. This had led most scholars to argue that Shakespeare never saw it; it would not be formally published until two years after the playwright's death. But the similarities are tantalizing. Burghley would appear to be the very model for the character of Polonius, and his advice echoes the playwright's famous verses. As G. B. Harrison puts it, "the parallel is close; it leaves the disquieting suspicion that Shakespeare had seen a copy of Burleigh's *Advice*." Disquieting because of the nagging authorship question—a controversy that many Shakespearean scholars wish would go away.

The Burghley connection, along with many other awkward facts of Shakespearean biography, plays into the hands of those who champion Edward de Vere, the Earl of Oxford, as the real author of the plays. Vere was Burghley's son-in-law, an intimate of the court of Elizabeth, and thus a very Hamlet-like figure. He would have read his father-in-law's advice book, and would have been as contemptuous of it as he was of both the author and the intended recipient. Thus the means and a motive for the parody can be easily established.

This is merely the tip of the iceberg in a discussion whose scope widens with each passing year. Who wrote Shakespeare's plays? It is not entirely clear, but it raises the intriguing possibility that Shakespeare's fatherly advice is not only misunderstood, but misattributed, which is not unusual in the genre of advice.

LORD CHESTERFIELD

William Cecil, Lord Burghley, had two sons and composed advice for each one. His first son, Thomas, bitterly disappointed his father, and it was with some relief that Burghley turned to the education of his second son, Robert, who served the family name more honorably, and for whom the *Ten Precepts* were written.

Like Burghley, Philip Dormer Stanhope, the Earl of Chesterfield, also had two sons to whom he wrote endearing letters of fatherly advice. In fact his collected correspondence is thought to be the high point of the genre. But as with Burghley, the advice, most of which was composed for the first son, made the greatest impression on an audience for whom it was never intended.

Chesterfield's eldest son Philip was born out of wedlock to his French mistress. Lest this should seem unduly hypocritical in a man who preached the salutary effects of good character, it should be noted that in Chesterfield's social circle, a mistress was considered neither particularly secret not scandalous. The liaison occurred before Chesterfield married, and although he soon took a wife, he retained a strong attachment to his first boy, and expended a great deal of effort toward his moral education.

The son in this case turned out to be a disappointment in spite of the more than four hundred letters that his father addressed to him—a prolific output for which he became the very model of paternal benevolence. Unlike Burghley, Raleigh, or King James, Chesterfield did not write his fatherly advice for publication or for fame. One of the most admired and respected men of his era, he was also one of its greatest prose stylists. In taking an interest in his son's development, he emulated his own grandfather, Lord Halifax, whose letters to Chesterfield's mother had circulated in the form of a book entitled *Advice to a Daughter*. Both grandfather and grandson were civil servants of the highest scruples, and both lived by strict personal codes of conduct that prevented them from accepting bribes (a standard practice of the day) or engaging in any form of Machiavellian underhandedness. Not that Chesterfield downplayed the role of diplomacy and the importance of appearances. His advice to his son, in addition to lessons on character, contains valuable insights into the means of advancing oneself in life, and especially in politics.

Fortunately, what Chesterfield failed to get through to an unappreciative boy would not go unheeded or unappreciated by posterity. When the letters were published soon after his death in 1773, the unexpurgated version turned out to contain a few surprises, in addition to the expected endorsements of character and virtue. These included tips on choosing the proper mistress, a disparaging assessment of the intellectual capacity of women, and advice on how to make your way in genteel circles by affecting certain poses.

Yet the volume proved popular from the start: it went through twenty editions in its first twenty-five years. Its unselfconscious reflections on the necessities and the realities of life made it quite popular with the French, although American sensibilities were at first offended. However, with careful editing, an abridged version proved to be very popular and influential in the United States as well.

A FLAVOR OF Chesterfield's style and message, and especially his insistence on the importance of character, comes through clearly in this letter to his godson, written in 1766.

> *Do you be sure never to speak of yourself, nor against yourself, but let your character speak for you. Whatever that says will be believed, but whatever you say of it, will not, and only make you odious or ridiculous.*

This was a theme that Chesterfield reworked many times. He also promoted the same values of diligence and attentiveness that would preoccupy Benjamin Franklin. "Whatever is worth doing at all," he wrote, "is worth doing well." And, "Never think any portion of time whatsoever too short to be employed."

From the very beginning, Chesterfield was realistic about his chances of success, and his earliest correspondence with his son seems to anticipate the futility of the exercise. One of these letters, written to Philip when the boy was fourteen years old, conjures an image of a father setting aside a demanding schedule to engage in a time-consuming commitment which he acknowledges is very one-sided.

> *Dear Boy,*
>
> *Though I employ so much of my time in writing to you, I confess I have often my doubts whether it is to any purpose. I know how unwelcome advice generally is; I know that those who want it most like it and follow it least; and I know too that the advice of parents, more particularly, is ascribed to the moroseness, the imperiousness, or the garrulity of old age. But then, on the other hand, I flatter myself that as your own reason, though too young as yet to suggest much to you of itself, is however strong enough to enable you both to judge of and receive plain truths.*

That such a commanding writer as Chesterfield had stayed the course and still failed may have discouraged fathers of later generations from continuing the practice. How could anyone hope to do better? There is little that has been written after *Letters to His Son* that can compete with it. Collections of letters from parents to children have been published since, but none has had a very great cultural impact, and the genre seems to be temporarily on hold. Fathers and mothers continue to give advice, but few do so with an eye toward eventual publication.

FEAR TASTES LIKE A RUSTY KNIFE

During a televised interview in 1957 on Edward R. Murrow's *Person to Person*, Harry S. Truman confessed that, "I have found the best way to give advice to your children is to find out what they want and advise them to do it." He was probably not the first father to come to this conclusion. Lord Chesterfield and William Cecil had watched their eldest sons seek their own ruin despite all their best counsels. Supreme Court Justice Oliver Wendell Holmes once wrote of his father, "I feel a humorous filial piety, and, by the way, chuckle to come on a letter from his father to him at school inculcating some virtue in the same dull terms that he passed it on to me. If I had a son I wonder if I should yield to the temptation to twaddle in my turn."

Children may yearn to read stories about inspiring role models, about virtuous heroes and victors over adversity, as long as they do not involve their own parents. Familiarity breeds, if not contempt, then at least a dose of intolerance. A true appreciation of parents comes later in life (if at all), when age and experience strip a child of his sense of immortality, allowing him to see his parents' flaws and limitations in light of his own. It is then that the temptation to twaddle sets in.

This is nicely illustrated in the final and most poignant scene of John Cheever's *The Wapshot Chronicle*. After the funeral of his father, a man comes across a note entitled "Advice to My Sons" intended to be found after the father's death. The son is heir to the legacy of the Wapshots, a New England family that came to the New World in the 1600s, and whose story has been recorded in his father's journal. The page of advice serves as the father's final say. Far from dull, and not intended for a child, it is hard-boiled, wistful, and unvarnished.

Never put whiskey into a hot water bottle crossing border of dry states or countries. Rubber will spoil taste. Never make love with pants on. Beer on whiskey, very risky. Whiskey on beer, never fear. Never eat apples, peaches, pears, etc. while drinking whiskey except long French-style dinners, terminating with fruit. Other viands have mollifying effect. Never sleep in moonlight. Known by scientists to induce madness. Should bed stand beside window on clear night draw shades before retiring. Never hold cigar at right-angles to fingers. Hayseed. Hold cigar at diagonal. Remove band or not as you prefer. Never wear red necktie. Provide light snorts for ladies if entertaining. Effects of harder stuff on frail sex sometimes disastrous. Bathe in cold water every morning. Painful but exhilarating. Also reduces horniness. Have a haircut once a week. Wear dark clothes after 6 P.M. Eat fresh fish for breakfast when available. Avoid kneeling in unheated stone churches. Ecclesiastical dampness causes prematurely gray hair. Fear tastes like a rusty knife and do not let her into your house. Courage tastes of blood. Stand up straight. Admire the world. Relish the love of a gentle woman. Trust in the Lord.

Leander Wapshot placed his advice to his sons in a volume of Shakespeare that had belonged to his own father. Having made his wife promise, years earlier, to have Shakespeare read at his burial, he knew that his son would find the page. And the way his message was discovered would add weight to his words by placing them in a special context.

Wapshot understood that advice needs to be suitably framed, that the words alone, as charming as they might be, cannot by themselves hope to compete with the many distractions of modern life. Perhaps, in what are always referred to as simpler times, it was easier to get people's attention. But in the twentieth century, the audience for advice is different; it has become more jaded, more skeptical. Oddly, this is the kind of audience that Shakespeare probably thought he deserved—one that would understand parody when they saw it.

THE PURITAN'S PROGRESS

From time to time social scientists manage to come up with interesting, sometimes useful, and perhaps even definitive names for cultural trends. On occasion, a clever name will by itself cause people to take notice of what otherwise would have passed them by. In 1951 David Riesman, a sociologist, wrote a book entitled *The Lonely Crowd*, whose title captured the atmosphere of post-war America. It sold enormously well to the suburban middle class because it was all about them—their lives, their work, their homes, their habits, their attitudes, and most of all, their essential loneliness. The cause of this loneliness was rooted in their pursuit of conformity, their need to belong.

The Lonely Crowd is remembered mostly for its title, and partly for a term Riesman introduced to account for this loneliness. The term is "other-directedness," and it describes an individual whose sense of belonging depends on the preferences and expectations of others. Riesman contrasts "other-directedness" with "inner-directedness," a mentality that is driven by a set of goals or principles that are internalized at an early age.

The quintessential inner-directed personalities are men such as Benjamin Franklin and George Washington, who in life and in legend lived by codes that they actually wrote out and carried around with them in order to regulate their actions. These codes did not neglect the importance of appearances, but they did not change with the reactions of others, nor with fads and fashions. If Franklin made a point of being seen hauling a wheelbarrow full of printer's paper through the streets of Philadelphia, it was because he wanted to remind his neighbors that he was still a printer, and that he still adhered to his ethic of industriousness. He was not looking for their approval, merely the admiration that he deserved. It was all part of his inner-directed plan.

In his *Autobiography*, Franklin describes his method of self-perfection, a method which he scrupulously followed from his youth. In a notebook he always carried, he had written out thirteen principles or maxims of ideal conduct. Each week he would choose one maxim to work on, and carefully note how his actions accorded with, or fell short of it. Through this process of relentless reflection, criticism, and self-correction, Franklin proposed to refine his character continually, thereby achieving the satisfaction of having lived a good life.

Franklin did not invent this method of self-improvement. Since Chaucer's day (and very likely even before that), many advice books contained the word "mirror" (or its Latin equivalent *speculum*) in their titles, metaphorically suggesting that one's personality could (and should) be subjected to daily examination so that any blemishes might be detected. In this spirit of self-examination, George Washington, at the age of sixteen, painstakingly copied out "The Rules of Civility and Decent Behavior in Company and Conversation"—110 rules of good character contained in a sixteenth-century Jesuit conduct book. He continued to refer to these rules throughout his life because character—that highly subjective measure of a man's worth—consumed him more than any other attribute.

It is certainly not the case that Franklin and Washington had no concern for their reputations. This is not the point of inner-directedness. They built their public image around their principles instead of allowing public opinion to dictate those principles. They assumed (correctly) that good character of itself would earn them respect.

If Franklin and Washington are the quintessential "inner-directed" personalities, any of today's politicians might be chosen as the essence of other-directedness. "While all people want and need to be liked by some of the people some of the time," writes Riesman, "it is only the modern other-directed types who make this their chief source of direction and chief area of sensitivity." Advertising is usually blamed for this—for the elevation of image over substance. And so it might also be blamed for the declining popularity of statements of principles, ideals, and values—for the disappearance of character. The inner-directed type is becoming more and more rare because American popular culture keeps hammering away at the idea that who you are is defined by what you own, and how fulfilled you are is a matter of how fulfilled you appear to be.

Although the 1990s have witnessed a revival of interest in values and classical virtues, the decade has seen little decline in the worship of image over substance. This does not mean that the inner-directed personality is becoming extinct. People continue to idolize those who demonstrate through their words and deeds a strong commitment to bedrock principles and an indifference to public opinion. In people such as Cal Ripken, Jr., Colin Powell, and Rosa Parks, the character ideal embodied by Franklin and Washington lives on. But virtue and character are increasingly being treated like commodities which get attention because they sell, and cease to get attention when sales decline. It is proving difficult to revive the idea of virtue as anything but a commodity in a culture where popular tastes are always moving on to something else.

HORATIO ALGER

Before other-directedness displaced inner-directedness and showed how being popular counted for as much as being virtuous (if not more), the American ideal of success was linked to a name that symbolized pluck, determination, and the prospect of the American dream. The name still conjures up this image, but it is an image that is mired in nostalgia.

The Horatio Alger myth belongs to another era. It is the original rags-to-riches saga, in which a young boy is cast adrift in the big city and falls prey to all kinds of malingerers and crooks. But buoyed by his fundamental sense of honesty and his dogged belief in the opportunities that America lays at everyone's doorstep, he pulls himself up out of the gutter by his own bootstraps, and climbs the ladder of success to become a rich man, whereupon he extends a benevolent hand to others like himself, and he tells them to have faith that determination and hard work will be rewarded.

This is somewhat exaggerated, but not by much. Few Americans have read any of Alger's novels; in fact it is widely believed that Horatio Alger is the hero's name in these sagas. The name stands for the idea that through hard work, anyone in American can get rich. It is a potent myth, to which many people still cling. But not surprisingly, it does not accurately reflect Alger's work.

Horatio Alger, Jr., did write success novels. He found a formula and stuck to it. Of the 119 titles he is credited with, one critic was moved to say, "Actually, he wrote one book and rewrote it 118 times." Certainly he recycled material. But what he recycled was not quite the rags-to-riches saga with which he is associated. One of his most successful plot lines, the one that comes closest to providing the model of a "Horatio Alger hero" comes from *Ragged Dick; or Street Life in New York with the Boot-Blacks* (1868), which gives an idea of what the Alger myth would be if it were faithful to the man's work.

Ragged Dick is Richard Hunter, Esquire, a self-reliant and trustworthy teenager who indulges in a few vices such as gambling and smoking, but can otherwise be counted on to work hard and play fair. The plot of this first in a series of Ragged Dick novels allow Alger to describe the pitfalls of city life, as Dick becomes a tour guide to a newfound friend, and shows him both the high and low points of New York. With many farm boys setting out for the big city in search of work, Alger's books provided one of the few sources of information on what sort of world awaited them.

Dick gets his big break by luck and by pluck, to paraphrase another Alger title, and shows how the typical Alger hero depends completely on fate, rather than determination, to turn his life around. When a boy falls off a ferryboat, Dick leaps in to save him. The boy's father turns out to be a wealthy merchant who offers Dick his first respectable job. When the book ends, Dick has the prospect of a career, but he is by no means rich.

ALGER'S BOOKS SOLD moderately well, but never quite enough to allow him to rest upon his success. Which is to say that Alger did not enjoy fame and fortune during his own lifetime. He concentrated on juvenile fiction because it paid more than serious fiction, and because he was good at it. But his reputation did not extend beyond his youthful readership.

It is possible to find hints of the Alger myth in many of his titles, which include *Risen from the Ranks, Winning Out by Pluck,* and *From Canal Boy to President, or the Boyhood and Manhood of James A. Garfield. Risen from the Ranks,* which is loosely modeled on Benjamin Franklin's *Autobiography,* does come close to the myth. It relates the tale of a boy who starts out as a printer's devil, then becomes a writer, an editor, and finally, a congressman. But even this cannot compete with the breathtaking rise of an Andrew Carnegie or a Charles Schwab, whose lives are considered to be classic Horatio Alger success stories.

Neither Alger's modest sales record and mediocre writing skills, nor his diminutive stature and retiring personality made him a likely candidate for the American model of success. Debunkers could have a field day exploring the seamier side of his career. But his persistence and his prolific output did pay off after his death in 1899. Edward Stratemeyer, the creator of the Hardy Boys series and an entire industry of juvenile fiction, finished a dozen of Alger's plot outlines and issued them under Alger's name. As the demand for success literature and coming-of-age novels increased, Alger's titles began to sell better than they had during his lifetime. He posthumously carved out a niche, and slowly the myth began to grow.

In a 1931 *New Yorker* cartoon, a man is shown wielding a shovel in a trench on Park Avenue as limousines roll by. He turns to his fellow ditch digger and says, "And me brought up on Alger stories!" The juxtaposition—rags to riches, ditch digger and corporate executive—was firmly established by the time of the Great Depression, but the Alger myth really took off in 1947, when the American Schools and Colleges Association created the Horatio Alger Awards. By singling out men "who by their own efforts have pulled themselves up by their bootstraps in the American tradition," the awards celebrated free enterprise, equal opportunity, and the virtues of hard work and thrift extolled by Benjamin Franklin. They also brought Alger's name to center stage, planting it in the minds of post-war generation Americans as a symbol of hard-earned success.

The reality behind the myth may seem to be a moot point, but it is nonetheless interesting. Most of Alger's novels deal with the fast-growing urban scene of the late 1800s, and reveal many of the hardships and pitfalls that lie in hiding to trip up the honest soul. His heroes were teenagers, not grown men or little boys. And they did not generally rise from rags to riches. Many of them came from solid backgrounds, and almost all of them achieved nothing more than respectability by landing a good job (usually in a store or bank), and by getting their first good set of clothes. Their big break does not come solely through perseverance and pluck, but instead by pure dumb luck—the hero is befriended or taken in by a wealthy benefactor who sets him up in a steady job.

What the novels succeed in doing is establishing the idea that a young man of good character and solid values can reasonably expect to get a break. They perfectly illustrate Benjamin Franklin's inner-directed philosophy of success, as summed up in this passage from a letter to John Alleyn:

> Be studious in your profession, and you will be learned. Be industrious and frugal, and you will be rich. Be sober and temperate, and you will be healthy. Be in general virtuous, and you will be happy. At least, you will, by such conduct, stand the best chance for such consequences.

After the Depression, the Alger hero would become associated with a more innocent era. In fact the Alger myth is now being displaced by the attention given to athletes who go from rags to riches when they sign professional contracts, and by winners of state lotteries who become instant millionaires. The modern rags-to-riches saga still relies on a good deal of luck, but character has little or nothing to do with it. Persistence is still considered a virtue, but the essence of Franklin's advice has been boiled down to a much simpler hit-or-miss formula that has become a success mantra of the modern age: just do it. What it means is anyone's guess.

THE CHARACTER ETHIC

Popular wisdom, especially in the field of success literature and advice books, has steadily changed with the times. The most noteworthy trend, which is related to the shift from inner-directedness to other-directedness, is the transition from a success ethic based on character to one based on personality. These are the terms used by Richard M. Huber in his 1971 book *The American Idea of Success*, which tracks American attitudes toward success through the history of success literature, and relates the fascinating stories of men and women who produced the most influential examples of the genre.

The pivotal figures in this saga are Franklin, who built a career around the character ethic; Dale Carnegie, whose *How to Win Friends and Influence People* redefined success as the ability to project a winning personality; and the Reverend Norman Vincent Peale, whose *Power of Positive Thinking* set out to prove that failure is only a state of mind. Each of these men popularized trends rather than inventing them, and these trends signaled changes in the way people went about the business of giving and taking advice. But Huber is careful to point out that he is only providing helpful labels—that the character ethic, the personality ethic, and what he calls the mind power ethic (the New Thought philosophy that the mind must be conditioned for success) are not distinct and mutually exclusive categories. Like inner- and other-directedness, they are useful terms, but not exact labels. An individual can exhibit aspects of all three. A good example is found in Charles Schwab's "Ten Commandments of Success," which begins with directives to "Work Hard" and "Study Hard," but jumps the track in the seventh commandment: "Cultivate Personality." In the late 1930s Dale Carnegie would move this commandment to the top of the list.

DALE CARNEGIE

In *The American Idea of Success*, Richard Huber sketches the career of Dale Carnegie with a special emphasis on showing how his best-seller, *How to Win Friends and Influence People*, was a watershed event in the history of advice and etiquette books. It was certainly the final breakthrough for the personality ethic, as Huber calls the idea that manners are more important than morals. The character ethic promoted by men such as Benjamin Franklin and George Washington had for some time been yielding to an ethic founded upon popularity. Not that popularity for its own sake was something entirely new. It had been promoted by Shakespeare's Polonius, by Lord Chesterfield, and even by Franklin himself. It has always been deemed wise to make a good impression, but Carnegie-ism represented the complete triumph of style over substance.

The secret of success, according to Carnegie, lies in the ability to praise and flatter other people. In capsule form, this was the Carnegie canon:

1. *Be genuinely interested in other people.*
2. *Smile.*
3. *Remember that a man's name is to him the sweetest and most important sound in the English language.*
4. *Be a good listener. Encourage others to talk about themselves.*
5. *Talk in terms of the other man's interest.*
6. *Make the other person feel important—and do it sincerely.*

In all of the anecdotal evidence that Carnegie musters to illustrate these simple rules, intentions and actions are obscured by a layer of deception. As a code of ethics, Carnegie's advice suffers from an inherent contradiction—to be "genuinely interested in other people," or to be "a good listener," or to be sincere is easier said than done. One cannot be instructed to be sincere or genuine, but only to appear to be so, which is then nothing more than an affectation.

Still, Carnegie had hit upon a successful formula and a brilliant title, and he won over many admirers and disciples. What does not come through in Huber's story of Carnegie's meteoric career is how late in life big-time success came to him, and how it was brought about by a small and somewhat compressed aspect of his life's work.

UNTIL 1912 (when he turned twenty-four years of age), Dale Carnegie had been making a living as a salesman of cars and neckties while pursuing his dream of becoming a great public speaker. In that year he decided to try teaching a course in public speaking, and he took the idea to the director of a New York City YMCA. The man was initially lukewarm, but finally gave Carnegie a chance. From this humble beginning Carnegie built a small public-speaking empire which eventually gave birth to his Institute of Effective Speaking and Human Relations. One of his more inspired decisions was to change the spelling of his name from Carnagey to Carnegie, which made a great deal of sense when he began renting space in the great hall built by the celebrated philanthropist Andrew Carnegie.

Dale Carnegie did very well in the public-speaking trade. He taught, lectured frequently, opened more and more schools of public speaking, and wrote several books. The culmination of these efforts is his 1926 magnum opus *Public Speaking and Influencing Men in Business*—a series of lessons and anecdotes woven into textbook form. It represents twenty years of investigation, lecturing, and practice.

Although this work sold well enough to merit several new editions, Carnegie still lacked a formula that would allow him to break through to a larger audience. But in 1937 he got his break with the help of an editor from Simon & Schuster. The formula they hit upon called for a series of succinct rules, much like commandments, accompanied (in Machiavellian style) by anecdotes illustrating how famous men had prospered by such advice. The six tenets listed above were grouped under the title "Six Ways to Make People Like You." They formed the backbone of his new book.

In its first year, *How to Win Friends* sold over 700,000 copies. It would go on to sell millions, to be widely translated, and to make Dale Carnegie a household word. A newspaper column came his way, and soon he was distilling and dispensing such bracing tonics as "Seven Rules for Making Your Home Life Happier," and "Eight Ways by Which You Can Be Braver." At the age of fifty, Carnegie had discovered the selling potential of lists.

Dale Carnegie's life's work is best represented by his textbook on public speaking. By comparison, *How to Win Friends* gives a skewed outlook on the personality of a man whose great strength was in teaching others to present themselves well by speaking forcefully, knowledgeably, and with flair. His best seller brought him fame, but also a kind of Machiavellian infamy.

Sinclair Lewis, the man who had skillfully captured the hypocrisy of tired businessmen in *Babbitt*, wrote a scathingly sarcastic profile of Carnegie for *Newsweek* just as *How to Win Friends* was topping the best-seller list. Lewis summarizes the book as "130 pages of telling people how to smile and bob and pretend to be interested in people's hobbies precisely so that you may screw things out of them." He sums up by saying, "Conceivably one may sell 600,000 books and still be a failure."

Lewis may be accused of being overly cynical, perhaps even overly jealous, but the difference a decade made on Carnegie's outlook is profound. His public-speaking text is both useful and sincere. His success book is useful as well, but also calculating and manipulative. This is because one book is about how to entertain an audience with an effective speech, the other about how to fire employees or reject the rank-and-file's request for a pay hike while making them feel good about it.

Carnegie, as had Machiavelli before him, explained how successful men climbed to the top and managed to stay there, and he did it using their own words, thereby advertising his own access to them. He traveled freely in the exclusive company of the rich, and this access is what people bought, as much as the advice itself. As the reputations of its subjects faded, so did Carnegie's book. The schools of public speaking lived on, but the book has been displaced by newer success bibles. Its creed is now used primarily in the cynical game of selling.

THE CYNIC'S ETHIC

The Italian novelist and semiotician Umberto Eco once noted that, "In the United States there's a Puritan ethic and a mythology of success. He who is successful is good. In Latin countries, in Catholic countries, a successful person is a sinner." This dichotomy no longer seems so clear cut. America has produced its share of Olympian sinners and hypocrites—evangelizing ministers and values-promoting public officials with hands in cookie jars— who would seem to refute Eco's theory. They have not changed the mythology so much as overthrown it, along with the Puritan ethic that sustained it.

Cynicism is nothing new in American life, but the cult of cynicism is. The decline of the character ethic, to many minds, coincided with the disappearance of character in public life. The personality ethic, even as it was being popularized by Dale Carnegie, drew harsh criticism for its hypocrisy. It claimed its authority from the fledgling field of social science, which initially promised to codify human behavior and unleash society's greatest potential. Instead it produced the manipulativeness of Carnegieism, which in the 1960s led to a form of pessimism rooted in life's vicissitudes, in the failings of human nature, and in the perverse nature of inanimate objects. Cynicism was the catalyst which morphed success literature into a literature of failure and frustration—a genre whose prophets go by the names Murphy, Parkinson, and Peter.

To carry this capsule (and highly speculative) scenario to its logical conclusion, one has merely to take the short leap from the cult of Murphy's Law to one whose sense of helplessness and whose moral agnosticism is embodied by a slogan such as "Shit happens," and whose lack of prospects is best conveyed by the equally popular "Don't worry, be happy." If nothing else, even the suggestion that such a trend is real and ineluctable keeps many a hand-wringing cultural watchdog gainfully employed obsessing over how we are either "slouching towards" or "limping into" the next century.

In what sense people "live by" such slogans is hard to pin down. Bumper stickers can only tell so much about the national psyche. But Murphy's Law and its cousins are more than slogans, and are worth a closer look. They now dot the landscape of working America to the extent that they are cited as often as the Ten Commandments. Of course, they are not commandments. Rather, they are advice masquerading as theory. And like the more traditional forms of advice, they have been adapted by contemporary American culture to suit its particular needs.

MURPHY

In 1977 an enterprising writer by the name of Arthur Bloch hit upon the idea of putting together a short collection of popular sayings which he grouped under the title *Murphy's Law.* Twenty years later, the law requires no explanation. It would be hard to assemble a dozen Americans who have never heard of it. This is partly due to Bloch himself. His little paperback became a best-seller, begat two follow-up best-sellers and three calendars, not to mention an entire line of gift items, all of which made him a rich man and Murphy's Law as ubiquitous as the Golden Rule. Bloch did not discover Murphy's Law; it had been circulating for years in research laboratories and corporate offices. He merely stumbled upon it, and turned it into an everyday expression, if not a gold mine. What he did not know, however, was that he had it all wrong.

"If something can go wrong," says the law as related by Bloch, "it will." Murphy's Law is a confirmation of everyone's gloomiest suspicions, which accounts for much of its appeal. To most people, it is reassuring proof that the fault is not in ourselves, but in our stars; that things fall apart, go from bad to worse, and conspire to break down when they are most needed; that the toast always lands with the jelly side down. It is a simple fact of life.

Captain Edward Aloysius Murphy, Jr. (U.S. Air Force, retired) was philosophical about this when a *People* magazine reporter tracked him down in 1983 to interview the man behind the myth—the man who made no money from his invention. The expanded Murphy's Law—everything that can go wrong, will, and at the worst possible moment—had come back to haunt him in the form of a corollary: "Whoever can be misquoted will be, and at the worst possible moment." Murphy was claiming to be the eponymous lawgiver, and the strength of his claim lay in his insistence that what he originally said was something very different from what people assumed he said.

As a performance engineer working at Edwards Air Force Base in 1949, Murphy one day discovered that somebody had installed some sensing devices backward in a rocket sled designed to test the effects of deceleration on humans. Of the two possible positions in which the switches could have been set, a technician had opted for the wrong way. A harrowing test run that nearly killed the test driver yielded no data whatsoever.

"If there is more than one way to do a job, and one of those ways will end in disaster," Murphy concluded at the time, "then someone will do it that way." This, according to the man himself, was the original Murphy's Law.

What it soon became was something quite different. Murphy was making a useful point about systems design: do not build into a system a multiplicity of options, only one of which is correct, because if it is possible for the system to be hooked up incorrectly, someone will eventually come along and do just that. At a press conference following Murphy's revelation, however, his immediate superior, Major John Paul Stapp, the man who took the ride in the malfunctioning rocket sled, relayed Murphy's Law to a reporter as: "If something can go wrong, it will," which implies that it always will, or at least that it will most of the time. Thus Murphy's Law, as Americans have come to understand it, was born.

Even if Bloch had known this, he would probably have run with Stapp's revision. Edward Murphy's maxim is useful and technically correct, if not obvious (in retrospect). But it fails to lay any blame on the perverse nature of nature, which has been a firm tenet of human faith since prehistoric times. People worship objects in order to get them to act less capriciously. Bloch played this to the hilt, and expanded the theory of life's essential unfairness with many corollaries and lemmas. In effect, he followed the newsman's dictum from the film *The Man Who Shot Liberty Valance*: "When the legend becomes fact, print the legend."

Edward Murphy, an engineer to the core, refused to be consumed by bitterness. After all, he had simply been a victim of his own law. The point of the real Murphy's Law is that people will ultimately get things wrong, not that nature acts to confound their efforts. But the popular version has it backwards. In so doing it provides a good demonstration of how people tend to react to complexity by seizing upon the simplest explanation they can find. This is sometimes referred to as Occam's Razor, a rule which says that the simplest explanation is always the best.

Appropriately enough, William of Occam, a thirteenth-century church scholar, never actually said or wrote this. Nor did he name anything Occam's Razor. What he did say was that "entities should not be multiplied unnecessarily," a rule which seems to justify the kinds of oversimplifications that people are prone to. But it does no such thing. In reality, Occam was arguing that in any investigation of phenomena, the simplest of competing theories is always preferable to the more complex. He did not say that oversimplification to the point of error is desirable. Occam, it seems, occupies a place in history not unlike that of Edward Murphy.

What both men's legacies also illustrate is the fact that people like to be able to attach simple names to complex events, and scientists, knowing that immortality is granted to the discoverer, scramble to provide them. Maxwell's Equations, Heisenberg's Uncertainty Principle, and the Pythagorean Theorem have preserved what would otherwise be names known only to specialists in the field. Newton's Laws of Motion are so reassuring that they are often invoked as proof of such nonscientific propositions as the Golden Rule.

It is no accident that Murphy's Law has its origins in science (as opposed to business), and that prior to Bloch's blockbuster it first gained popularity among academics. Scientists are as eager to seize upon ready-made opinions as the lay person, if not more so. In fact the earliest widely circulated reference to Murphy's Law (but not to Murphy) appears in a 1956 issue of *Scientific American*. In a parenthetical afterthought, a writer refers to what he seems to accept as a bit of commonly known wisdom—specifically: "(1) If something can go wrong, it will, (2) When left to themselves, things go from bad to worse, and (3) Nature always sides with the hidden flaw." Four years later, a recent Cornell graduate and soon-to-be-celebrated novelist named Thomas Pynchon wrote a short story entitled "Entropy," in which a young man at Princeton "learned a mnemonic device for remembering the Laws of Thermodynamics: you can't win, things are going to get worse before they get better, who says they're going to get better."

This is the type of connection that consumes the energies of many scientists in their spare time—the possibility that Murphy's Law is somehow implicit in the three Laws of Thermodynamics. When such ruminations bubble up to the surface of popular culture, they fuel endless speculation, and allow enterprising writers like Arthur Bloch to cap the well and reap huge profits.

THE PROLIFERATION OF LAWS

Although the discussion of popular, humorous, or pseudoscientific laws begins with Murphy in a strictly chronological accounting, the way was paved for the Murphy phenomenon by C. Northcote Parkinson, an English historian and novelist, who in 1955 wrote an article for the staid journal, *The Economist*, in which he introduced a famous law.

"Parkinson's Law" the article, begat *Parkinson's Law* (1958) the book, which begat Parkinson's Second Law (and the book *The Law and the Profits*, 1960), Parkinson's Third Law (from *In-Laws and Outlaws*, 1962), Parkinson's Fourth Law (*The Law of Denial*, 1970), and even *Mrs. Parkinson's Law* (1968). The original law, however, is the one that is embedded in popular culture. And because of Parkinson's academic credentials and the scientific methodology with which he argued his theory, many people think of his law as a proven fact, an essential pillar of social science.

In 1971, when Professor Laurence J. Peter contributed the Peter Principle to public discourse, the same impression surfaced—that this law has a basis in scientific experimentation and statistical proof, and had been waiting to be discovered, much like the Law of Relativity. And like any important theory, it opened a door on all kinds of corollaries, such as Peter's Inversion, Peter's Paradox, and Peter's Theorem.

For all of their academic trappings, however, Parkinson's and Peter's books are shelved in the humor sections of libraries and bookstores. This was the intent of their authors all along. As with Murphy's Law, the ideas simply ran away from their inventors.

PARKINSON'S PREMISE

Parkinson's Law, like Murphy's Law, has been oversimplified by the public, as a glance at either the original *Economist* article or at the book it inspired will show. Replete with charts, graphs, and imposing mathematical formulas, both the article and the book attempt to establish the scientific basis of a bureaucratic theory. The deadpan academic style adopted by Parkinson was well suited to the pages of *The Economist*, and it helps to drive his point home in a mercilessly funny way. But what, exactly, was his point?

A close reading will show that the point of both works—the real Parkinson's Law as Parkinson himself defined it—is now lost even on expert commentators who invoke it. The idea that is now accepted as the law itself—that work expands to fill the time allotted to complete it—occupies Parkinson for little more than a paragraph. He dispenses with it as nothing more than a preliminary commonplace observation. That work is elastic in its demands on time is, in fact, merely his opening premise.

The actual law builds upon this point of departure by tracing the cumulative effect of the elasticity of work on a modern bureaucracy. Specifically, when the number of administrative workers increases, people assume it is because there is more work to be done, that everyone pulls their fair share. But in fact, "the number of the officials and the quantity of the work to be done are not related at all." Because work can expand indefinitely, it can be used by any civil servant to justify the hiring of two subordinates, and this process can (and will) continue until it produces a bloated administration.

This was Parkinson's observation when he was a British Army staff officer during World War II, and he pursued his theory by gathering statistical data on the post –World War I British Navy to show that the command structure had become top-heavy while the work load did not increase proportionally.

As an example of Parkinson's original law, consider a civil servant who is given the task of analyzing census data. Feeling overworked, he asks for two assistants and a promotion (so that he has indisputable authority over his assistants). Because he has produced good work to this point, the request is granted, and his office continues to send out the same number of census reports. A few years later the civil servant is an executive vice-president in charge of census reports with a staff of sixty-two, and with no time to look at any census data because he is too busy managing the people he has hired. His office produces the same level of output it did when he handled it himself.

Thus Parkinson's Law, as originally stated, dealt with the multiplication of subordinates. Specifically, the law as Parkinson himself coined it says that in any public administrative department not actually at war, the staff increase each year can be expected to be "between 5.17 and 6.56 per cent, irrespective of any variation in the amount of work (if any) to be done." The work will simply expand so as to consume the energies of everyone hired to do it.

When Parkinson expanded this idea into a book, the public and the press fixated upon the book's first sentence—"Work expands so as to fill the time available for its completion"—and never quite made it to the actual statement of Parkinson's Law. Recognizing this, Parkinson fell into step, renamed his premise the Law, and produced more laws in the same vein, including, "Expenditure rises to meet income" (Parkinson's Second Law) and "Delay is the deadliest form of denial" (Parkinson's Fourth Law), which served as points of departure for subsequent books. By the time he collected all of his laws into one omnibus volume entitled *Parkinson: The Law* (1979), he saw Parkinson's Law as the public saw it, and the original theorem was shunted aside.*

THE PETER PRINCIPLE

With the Peter Principle, Laurence J. Peter hit the nail on the head with the first swing. In his 1969 book of that title, written with Raymond Hull, he unburdened himself of years of investigative research. Peter's basic premise is that "in a bureaucracy every employee tends to rise to his level of incompetence." This is a direct extension of the original theory put forth by Parkinson. The bulk of Peter's book is taken up with the careful elimination of all exceptions to this rule. "My law was a product of a twenty-five year study I did on teacher incompetence," he said. Because it sprang from reality, he added, it has lasted.

The idea for the Peter Principle was not entirely original. David Riesman had noticed it as early as 1951 in *The Lonely Crowd*. Riesman writes in the style of an academic, a careful social scientist, yet he can't resist italicizing the occasional important conclusion.

> The pressure toward social competence, with its concurrent disregard for technical competence, suggests . . . the emergence of a new pattern in American business and professional life: *if one is successful in one's craft, one is forced to leave it.*

Riesman then shows how the hands-on engineer who is promoted to sales manager, or the college professor who is promoted to dean, leaves behind

---

*To its credit, the Merriam-Webster Collegiate Dictionary is the only reference work to get this right. It is the policy of Merriam-Webster to list definitions in the historical sequence of the meanings the word has assumed. Quite correctly, the Collegiate lists two definitions for Parkinson's Law, and in the proper order: (1) an observation in office organization: the number of subordinates increases at a fixed rate regardless of the amount of work produced and (2) an observation in office organization: work expands so as to fit the time available for its completion.

the skills that first attracted them to their professions and made them successful. Now they must learn to master "people skills," and gradually they will lose touch with the functional aspect of their fields. A similar idea has recently been repackaged by cartoonist Scott Adams, whose protagonist Dilbert must daily endure the fallout from the Dilbert Principle: "The most ineffective workers are systematically moved to the place where they can do the least damage: management." Of course, Adams and Peter see this in a humorous light, while to Riesman it is a dead serious matter.

TOM SAWYER'S LAW

As dangerous as it is to try to analyze humor, it is worth noting that Parkinson's Law and Peter's Principle rode the crest of a wave of enthusiasm for social science that was beginning to break upon the rocks of skepticism in the 1960s, turning "science" into humor.

Since the outset of the century, academic writers had been trying to quantify the unquantifiable—to explain cultural trends in much the same way that Darwin had explained evolution, or to chart mass psychology in the way Freud had charted the inner mind. The American public had come to embrace the identification of trends, from David Riesman's *Lonely Crowd* and William Whyte's *Organization Man* of the 1950s, to Marshall McLuhan's Global Village of the '60s, to the Me Decade, and so on. The practice of trying to coin a name for one's era was not new, but it was generally done in hindsight. The trick became to summarize the spirit of an age as it was unfolding. The Renaissance, the Enlightenment, the Industrial Revolution were all named after the fact (although Thomas Paine got on board just before the doors closed with *The Age of Reason*). Some writers managed to strike the right note and thereby enter the quotation dictionaries by attaching an easy handle to a complex idea. Joseph Heller's "Catch-22" is a good example.

History shows that names are frequently as important, if not more important, than the things named. It is difficult to define a Catch-22 other than through examples, which is how Heller did it, but the idea is universally understood, within certain limits. (With the passage of time the definition of a Catch-22 becomes less distinct. What began as a description of an unbreakable circle of illogic is now used to describe nothing more than a dilemma or a bureaucratic snafu.) No one can quite agree on the proper statement of the Golden Rule, while almost everyone concedes its importance as the fundamental moral principle. Occam's Razor is yet another idea that it is far easier to refer to than to state.

Conversely, the lack of a catchy name has doomed many a clever observation to obscurity. This has led many writers inspired by the success of Murphy's Law to retroactively attach names to isolated observations, usually to little effect. Still, it is a tempting game to play.

When Tom Sawyer joins a new order of the Cadets of Temperance ("being attracted by the showy character of their 'regalia'") in *The Adventures of Tom Sawyer*, he has to promise "to abstain from smoking, chewing, and profanity." He quickly learns what could be called Tom Sawyer's Law: "that to promise not to do a thing is the surest way in the world to make a body want to go and do that very thing." If the author had seen clear to give this observation a name, he would have assured himself yet another entry in the quotation books.

NEVER EAT AT A PLACE CALLED MOM'S

What some writers have understood since Machiavelli's time, and others have missed entirely, is that wisdom must be condensed, even distilled, and given a distinctive label if it is to thrive in the marketplace of ideas. Even then it may not catch on. But if the wisdom is compelling enough, the market may do the distilling and packaging on its own. Machiavelli focused on two words, *virtu* and *fortuna*, and ended by being remembered for something else entirely. Shakespeare composed a wicked parody of paternal advice, and wound up being lauded for producing the finest example of the genre. Edward Aloysius Murphy, Jr., got an idea right, only to discover that the world preferred to get it wrong. Cyril Northcote Parkinson discovered in time that his premise was more compelling than his conclusion, so he chucked the conclusion.

ERNEST HEMINGWAY once offered this cynical piece of advice: "Always remember this: if you have success you have it for the wrong reasons. If you become popular it is always because of the worst aspects of your work. They praise you for the worst aspects. It never fails." In other words, when you let go of your work, you cannot dictate how the public will respond to it. The American public in particular still tends to seize upon the most accessible explanations and labels, those which are ready-made for their consumption. If an idea doesn't have such a handle, they often invent one. And even if the inventor stamps his creation with his name, he still cannot ensure that people will get it right.

Raymond Chandler once wrote a magazine article for the *Saturday Review* in which he described what was wrong with the art of mystery writing and detective fiction at that time. He derisively coined a formula which summarized the hackneyed approach of the hapless amateur: "When in doubt have a man come through a door with a gun in his hand." But the comment backfired. It became the most famous piece of advice Chandler would ever give, and even came to define the Chandler style for many of his readers. His put-down became the signature of his own work.

Nelson Algren was more careful. After achieving fame from his novels, he toured the college lecture circuit for years, closing every lecture with the same piece of advice, which he claimed had been given to him by "a nice little old Negro lady" from the South. He used the line in his novel *A Walk on the Wild Side,* and made sure he repeated it countless times, so as to turn it into his epitaph:

> *Never play cards with a man named Doc.*
>
> *Never eat at a place called Mom's.*
>
> *And never lay down with a woman whose troubles are worse than your own.*

The last word on the art of being clearly heard belongs properly to generations of mothers, who by their collective refusal to be misunderstood have managed to hammer home a core of parental advice that no child or former child could claim to be unfamiliar with, and without which no treatment of advice could be considered complete. This canon has appeared in many forms, but one of the best was compiled by the owner of New York's Empire Diner, who, in an effort to provide solace to lone diners and stranded tourists, placed this message at the bottom of the menu. Some might consider it the only advice anyone could ever need. It reads:

> *Be nice.*
>
> *Don't shout.*
>
> *Sit up straight.*

Smile.

Don't play with your food.

Have a nice day.

Take care.

Don't be a stranger.

Murray, call your mother.

BIAS OF PRIENE IN SONIA: MOST MEN ARE BAD.

CHILO OF SPARTA: CONSIDER THE END.

CLEOBOLUS OF LINDOS IN RHODES: THE GOLDEN MEAN,
OR AVOID EXTREMES.

PERIANDER OF CORINTH: NOTHING IS IMPOSSIBLE
TO INDUSTRY.

SOLON OF ATHENS: KNOW THYSELF.

PITTACUS OF MITYLENE IN LESBOS: KNOW THY
OPPORTUNITY (TAKE TIME BY THE FORELOCK).

THALES OF MILETUS: SURETYSHIP IS THE
PREDECESSOR OF RUIN.

CHAPTER SEVEN

SEMPER FI

MOTTOES, MAXIMS, AND SLOGANS

ALL THE NEWS THAT'S FIT TO PRINT

In 1981 the *Washington Post* returned a Pulitzer Prize when it was revealed that their winning article was based on a reporter's fabrications. This incident was the first in a succession of crises that drew attention to the *Post's* ethics and the ethics of journalism as a whole. One veteran *Post* reporter, commenting on the paper's ordeal, noted:

> If you have a theme, a common thread in these episodes, it is the question of how we define our mission; we don't. For the *New York Times*, it's "All the News That's Fit to Print." Now, they don't always do that. . . . But what they have is a unifying, coherent goal that they are reaching for. It is a solid effort, even if flawed, to put on page one with some kind of balance, things about our life on earth that matter. . . . Whatever achievement the *Post* is trying to bring about is not defined. What is it? We're never told.

Ironically, the *Post* did indeed have a brief code of ethics as well as a detailed editorial policy statement, both of which had been in effect long before this crisis. But few writers knew of their existence. Maybe the code wasn't pithy enough, or the policy was simply too long. But clearly, a well-written motto can ease the burden of uncertainty that weighs down everyday decisions. "All the News That's Fit to Print" may be something of a catchall open to a wide range of interpretations, but it is easy to grasp, easy to see, and, in a morally aware environment, people can generally agree on what it means. The writers and editors of the *Times* may sometimes take their slogan for granted, yet they must be grateful for it, because it sets them apart.

THE *TIMES*'S SLOGAN is a good example of how a few seemingly innocent words commanding a place of prominence can go unnoticed and perhaps unappreciated, at least until something goes wrong. Other examples of the power of mottoes seem to crop up with regularity.

In late 1995, five weeks after the Quebec referendum nearly split Canada in two, a slight change in the motto on the Canadian coat of arms went into effect, causing a stir in the House of Commons, which hadn't been informed. What occasioned the tempest was the addition of three Latin words—*Desiderantes meliorem patriam* (Desiring a better country)—to the existing motto, *A mari usque ad mare* (From sea to sea). The change, which would gradually appear on Canadian currency and passports, threatened to antagonize Quebecers who had voted to split from the country. The situation was defused somewhat when someone pointed out that Queen Elizabeth had approved the motto eighteen months prior to the event, and that it had been submitted for approval years earlier in order to give the coat of arms a more Canadian character. The change just happened to come along at a tense moment, when it did not seem to be a good idea to be tampering with national symbols.

What surprised onlookers was that a seemingly insignificant device—a few Latin words that most people were unable to translate—could cause such a commotion. But it is in the nature of ready-made opinions that, in the midst of a crisis, especially an identity crisis, a few words can become a fulcrum through which a small gesture dislodges a mass of righteous indignation.

AS THESE TWO EXAMPLES SHOW, the practice of adopting brief sentiments or maxims as something to go by is widespread. In the corporate sphere, in academia, in associations and clubs, in the military, and in the public forum, mottoes help people to set their bearings. While only a small percentage of people actively espouse mottoes, the majority are quick to defend them, and are generally pleased to have them.

This is because mottoes and slogans are the most succinct ready-made opinions—perhaps what Tocqueville had in mind when he coined the term. He must have come across them everywhere. Even by the 1830s, when he made his historic trip to America, the landscape was studded with them—political slogans, advertising jingles, and patriotic mottoes.

Where did they come from, and what role do they play in American culture? These questions turn out to be more manageable than they may at first appear. Although the origin of mottoes is somewhat murky, their present role is well defined. They are most usefully thought of as rousing and inspirational rallying cries. In fact it is as battle cries that mottoes and slogans got their start, and they continue to serve very effectively in that capacity.

FIGHTING WORDS

According to the *Oxford English Dictionary*, a motto is a word, sentence, or phrase attached as a legend to an emblematic design. In a wider sense it can be a sentence, word, or fragment appropriate to some occasion or purpose. It might be a short quotation or bon mot that serves as a useful or witty interjection. But it can also be a "pithy maxim adopted by a person as his code of conduct."

This last sense alone gets at the idea of a motto as something to live by—a highly abbreviated code of ethics that serves as a reminder of a larger philosophy, a token of shared commitment, or as a guide to life and duty. It can evoke a founding idea, such as *E pluribus unum* ("One composed of many"), a goal to live up to, such as the Postal Service's unofficial motto "Neither snow nor rain nor heat . . . stays these couriers . . . ," or a commitment to a standard of excellence such as the *New York Times's* "All the News That's Fit To Print."

Like all words to live by, mottoes and slogans once functioned in a much narrower and more specific sense than they do today. Among historians there is a general consensus that they originated as battle cries of Scottish and Gaelic clans sometime in the early Middle Ages. The slogan started out as the *slughorn*, a Gaelic word that connotes the mustering of an army. The *motto*, the slughorn's more refined cousin, comes from the French and Italian words meaning "word" (*mot*), which in turn derive from the Latin *muttum*, or utterance.

There undoubtedly were formulas that functioned as mottoes in antiquity. The Romans, it can be said, used the device S.P.Q.R. ("the Senate and the People of Rome") as their identifying symbol—arguably as their motto. Each of the Seven Sages of ancient Greece is linked with a brief maxim. The inscription over the library of Thebes is reputed to have read "Medicine for the Soul." To call these mottoes in the modern sense, however, is to look too closely for precedents that technically do not exist. Whoever adopts a classical or biblical maxim for their personal use updates it simply by calling it a motto.

This is because the tradition of what are properly called mottoes begins with the rallying cries of chiefs, kings, princes, and knights. Strictly speaking, mottoes and slogans came into being when the words used to describe them were invented.

THE FIRST TRUE MOTTOES (or slughorns) appear in the twelfth century. One of the earliest, *Crom a boo*, rallied men into battle (although historians are at a loss as to what it means). Richard the Lion-Hearted supplied England with the motto of the British royal house when he shouted the battle-cry *Dieu et mon droit* (God and my right), as he set off to attack the French at the Battle of Gisors. By the thirteenth century such devices had become well established, and the idea of a rallying cry merged with military regalia to produce heraldic coats-of-arms and the clan mottoes that were passed on as part of family legacies.

Among the clans of the north, a king's war cry was his alone, and his followers' cry took the form of a response. The chief of the Scottish Grant clan would announce, "Stand sure," to which his followers, the Grants of Corrimony, would answer, "I'll stand sure." By the fourteenth century mottoes enjoyed such great popularity that King Edward III indulged in creating new ones for special occasions. When he founded the Order of the Knights of the Garter in 1348, he adapted a French expression that has since become one of the best-known chivalric mottoes: *Honi soit qui mal y pense* (Shame to him who thinks evil of it).

Such mottoes were typically handed down from above, and then handed on to succeeding generations. That is, they belonged to royalty or nobility, and were passed along as a venerable tradition within the family. But they would soon spread beyond the domain of the hereditary elite. Personal mottoes became clan mottoes, which naturally led to corporate mottoes—slogans of guilds, of secret societies, of monastic orders. This tradition lives on, primarily in the modern military, but also in certain institutions that adopted the trappings of heraldy and medieval culture—universities and Greek letter societies, for example. Along the way, the motto and slogan have become democratized. In American culture especially, they are no longer the sole province of the privileged. "Every man a king," the slogan of Louisiana's Huey Long, reflects an American sense of proprietorship—every man is king of his castle, and any king can have a motto.

IN CEREMONIAL SETTINGS, mottoes function in much the same way as creeds, codes, or oaths. They may serve as tests of loyalty (rather crucial in the case of a call to arms), as tokens of membership (which can be useful as formal greetings or as passwords), and even as rules of life. Where mottoes are most often cited as words to live by, however, is in the inculcation of morals. A motto can be a form of encouragement, or something to reflect upon in times of trouble. It can serve as advice, as a practical rule for deciding the proper thing to do, or as reminder of duty.

For all but the extraordinary few, mottoes are received ideas, and the way they are received determines how effective they will be. Some mottoes come with the territory. Where membership has its privileges, it also entails an expectation of duty, which may be summarized by a motto. The attainment of status or position within an organization may also merit the awarding of a motto. And such simple affiliations as attendance at a school, or residence in a town, county, or state earns one the right to a series of accompanying mottoes.

Thus everyone has many mottoes, at least in theory, although most people would be at a loss if asked to recite them all, or to explain what each one means. College students tend to know their school mascot better than the school motto. A few schools, like Harvard University, whose motto is *Veritas* (Truth), make a point of displaying it prominently, although it is unclear what it means to the student body.* The Greek letter names of fraternities and sororities are abbreviations of secret mottoes that usually remain a secret even to members. They have become the province of spe-

*Harvard actually has three mottoes, of which *Veritas* is the most recent. *Christo et Ecclesiae* and *In Christo Gloriam* have been used by the college since the seventeenth century. Some commentators have suggested that they serve as a reminder that *Veritas* signifies the divine truth, as it did to Dante. See Samuel Eliot Morison, *The Founding of Harvard College* (1935), pp. 250 and 329 ff.

cialists. Only genealogy buffs can recite their ancient family mottoes, and the house motto, once common in Victorian-era parlors, has become a museum piece. The average American is hard pressed to state the motto of his town, city, state, and possibly even the country itself.

Consequently, at first glance, it may seem that mottoes are nothing more than a curiosity, a pretentious vestige of a distant past. But a closer look reveals something surprising and subtle at work: there exist certain mottoes and slogans that do provide a sense of identity, and actually manage to function effectively as concise codes of ethics. Many of them continue to serve as battle cries.

DE OPPRESSO LIBER

When President Clinton committed the United States to the enforcement of the peace accord in Bosnia in late 1995, the U.S. First Armored Division had the honor of going in first. There was some ambivalence among the troops, but no uncertainty about how they would respond. One soldier, explaining the division's attitude about the mission to a television reporter, summed it up by reciting their motto: "We Will Not Fail Those With Whom We Serve." It seemed tailor-made for the occasion.

Clearly many members of the First Armored did not support the president's decision. Some did not respect President Clinton himself. But their motto is indifferent to that. To these troops, "We Will Not Fail Those With Whom We Serve" means that they are in it for each other, and consequently will not fail to carry out any mission. There were no ambiguities, no inner conflicts, and no contradictions, at least not publicly.

A few months later the U.S. Special Forces arrived in Bosnia to begin the task of patrolling the zone of separation. A radio reporter tagged along with an American patrol as they searched for a Russian unit assigned to the same mission. The major in charge explained to the reporter how several weeks earlier his counterpart, a Russian special forces colonel, had presented him with a tee shirt featuring his unit's logo. Wishing to return the favor, the major had written home to his wife, asking her to send a Special Forces green beret. Within a few days, the American patrol caught up with the Russians, and the major got the opportunity to present his gift. In a modest show of ceremony, he explained to the Russian (and to a national radio audience) the meaning of his gesture by pointing out the motto displayed on the cap's insignia. "It says *De oppresso liber*," he said, "which means to liberate the oppressed." The reporter left unspoken the irony that troops who were trained to fight each other now found themselves on the same side of a cause, united behind the same principle.

WAR NATURALLY GIVES RISE to mottoes and slogans. Every division, battalion, company, regiment, and command has one, and the military continues to supply some of the most stirring examples of the genre. Some resurrect the fighting words of famous armies; others are inspired by contemporary events. "Remember the Alamo" and "Remember the Maine" aroused public support for two American wars. "Hit hard, hit fast, hit often" was known as the Halsey battle cry in World War II, after Admiral William F. Halsey, the U.S. commander of the Pacific theater. "Damn the torpedoes, full speed ahead" is the popular version of Farragut's orders at Mobile Bay in 1864.* "Don't give up the ship" is attributed to Captain James Lawrence—his dying words as he was carried to the wardroom after being mortally wounded during a skirmish with a British frigate in 1813. The U.S. Navy has had an even longer association with the motto "I have not yet begun to fight," the famous reply of John Paul Jones to the British commander of the *Serapis*, which appeared to have disabled Jones's *Bonhomme Richard* in a battle of 1779. The American commander and his men fought on until they secured a British surrender.

These words, whether they were actually spoken in the way they have come down to us or not, constitute a useful mythology—one that builds esprit de corps. They surface in the wake of the horror and heartbreak of battle, and are salvaged as tokens of courage, duty, leadership, and persistence.

Other fighting words may not be forged in the heat of battle, but are carried there and tempered under fire. "The difficult we do at once, the impossible takes a little longer," was a popular slogan in World War II. The Army Corps of Engineers, the Army Air Forces, and the Seabees have all laid claim to it, or at least some variation of it. General Douglas MacArthur, in an address to the cadets of West Point in 1962, on the threshold of the American escalation in Vietnam, showed how mottoes function at their best when he said:

*The phrase "Damn the torpedoes" is usually misconstrued because of the modern connotation of the word "torpedo." In its original sense it refers to a partially or fully submerged mine. In his initial approach to Mobile Bay, Farragut looked on as his lead ship was destroyed trying to cross a line of torpedo mines. Knowing that he had to get beyond the line he issued his celebrated order, although not in these precise words. The recorded version is "Damn the torpedoes! Captain Drayton, go ahead! Jouett, full speed!" Miraculously, Farragut made it through intact.

Duty, Honor, Country:

> *These three hallowed words reverently dictate what you ought to be, what you can be, what you will be. They are your rallying post to build courage when courage seems to fail, they regain faith when there seems to be little cause for faith, to create hope when hope becomes forlorn.*

Such mottoes are particularly compelling because even if the cause is not universally perceived to be noble or just, the mission usually is. That is, the motto belongs to young men and women who are sent into situations of desperate danger and struggle. If they are cut off from the chain of command, their motto may be the only directive they have. The U.S. Marines live by the words *Semper Fidelis,* or *Semper Fi,* which needs no translation, and in fact is completely undone by it. "Always Faithful" doesn't stir the blood. But *Semper Fi* is a rallying post, a point of identification, a solemn bond, a creed, and a form of greeting all in one.

Most hierarchical organizations have mottoes. The more hierarchical, the more weight the motto usually has. This is why mottoes are so appropriate to the military and to law enforcement, and so ineffective in ceremonial settings, as for example when they are adopted by states, towns, and colleges.

Hierarchies use mottoes like they use creeds, oaths, and codes of conduct—to instill allegiance, test loyalty, and to establish solidarity. When corporations have tried to accomplish this with their logos and slogans, only the more highly structured ones have had any success. For many years the IBM corporation was identified with the one-word motto "Think," which acted as a kind of corporate mantra. It created a bond of company loyalty that would now be considered unusual. But the modern corporate world has given up on loyalty of this kind, and can no longer expect it from its employees in return. Hence corporate slogans tend to ring somewhat hollow—a problem that *Semper Fi* doesn't face.

LIBERTY OR DEATH

Not all fighting words originated on the fields of battle or within the ranks. In some instances, politicians rather than generals provided the troops with their rallying cries. In May of 1775, when the Virginia volunteers of the Continental Army first mustered in response to Patrick Henry's call to service, the 350 minutemen marched under a banner inscribed with a motto inspired by Henry's most famous words, spoken just two months earlier. "I know not what course others may take," said Henry, "but as for me, give me liberty or give me death." So electrifying was the speech that the soldiers immediately took it up as a battle cry. The motto "Liberty or Death" was also adopted by the Second Regiment of Infantry of South Carolina, who made it part of their insignia.

"Liberty or Death" is a straightforward slogan that needs little explanation. It is an unequivocal call to arms, which can still serve as an American motto with no loss of its original meaning. It inspired the battle cry "Victory or Death," used by American soldiers under Andrew Jackson in 1815 at the Battle of New Orleans. A similar motto, this one of the French Revolution, may also have been inspired by Patrick Henry, but its story is far more convoluted. It is a good example of how ready-made opinions can change their meaning to suit the tenor of the times. It also shows how national mottoes are never as simple as they seem.

FRATERNITY OR DEATH

The French national motto—Liberty, Equality, Fraternity—is so indelibly associated with the country, with its revolution, with its tricolor flag, and with the Delacroix painting *Liberty Guiding the People*, that it is natural to assume that the three ideals have always been dear to the French people. And yet while liberty and equality had been at the heart of the revolutionary spirit from the start, fraternity was something new—a last minute addition that initially had a very specific meaning quite different from the generic sense of brotherhood it carries today. At the outset, the French did not quite know what to make of it.

There is a consensus of scholarly opinion that fraternity, while not invented by the Masons, was popularized by them throughout Europe during the Enlightenment. When the French National Guard decided to adopt it as a motto in 1790, they did so not as an homage to Freemasonry, but instead as a recognition of the birth of the citizen's army. That is, "fraternity" referred specifically to a new policy of assembling a standing army from the ranks of citizens, as opposed to professionals and foreign mercenaries.

As historian David Thompson has observed, "within the citizen-body [the National Guard] represented the principle that the best way to make a soldier a brother was to make your brother a soldier—and that was what fraternity meant in 1790." When the full slogan—*Liberté, Egalité, Fraternité*—first appeared in 1791, according to Thompson, fraternity acknowledged that the French army could not be used against the French people, a possibility which had been of real concern under the monarchy.

By 1792 revolutionary enthusiasm expanded the ideal of fraternity through the well-meaning but politically shortsighted "Edict of Fraternity," by which the French promised to come to the aid of any of the peoples of Europe who wished to gain their freedom. As the recent efforts of the United Nations have shown, such an ideal, while laudable, is difficult to carry out, and impossible for a lone emerging government. The French quickly backed down from their promise, but not before the notion of fraternity had been expanded.

In 1793 the government of Paris, in a display of growing revolutionary fervor, declared that every householder would be required to paint the front of his house with the slogan, "Unity, Indivisibility of the Republic, Liberty, Equality, Fraternity, or Death." This rather unwieldy sentiment was soon shortened to "Fraternity or Death," and initially it implied a resolve to die rather than to cede the ideals of the revolution. But the motto would soon acquire a sinister twist. As the reign of terror swept through France, and the Jacobins began to send countless Frenchmen to the guillotine, fraternity began to take on the very opposite of its literal sense. The motto, which had once been a spirited rallying cry, was now regarded as a threat. Fraternity had become a macabre joke. Thompson quotes the famous remark of Prince Metternich, the Austrian statesman, who, upon observing what had been done by the French in the name of fraternity, said, "If I had a brother I would rather call him cousin."

It took several decades for this ghastly connotation to fade away. It was only with the onset of French Romanticism in the 1830s that writers began to reflect positively on the ideal of fraternity by glossing over its former shades of meaning, and they again championed it as the ideal of universal brotherhood it remains today. The process was made complete when the tripartite motto was officially incorporated into the French Constitution of 1848, by which time the meaning of fraternity had run the gamut, and was no longer considered offensive.

As this example shows, a slogan's meaning can run away from the words. Fraternity, in revolutionary France, became a code word for fratricide. In the twentieth century "Think," as it was understood by the employees of IBM, really meant "conform." This kind of accommodation is not unusual with mottoes. Times change, sentiments change, but because the words cannot change, they are often forced to fit the demands of the situation. The fit is not always perfect.

Something to Go By

In a 1911 essay in *Lippincott's* magazine, a writer named Churchill Williams reflects upon the disrepute mottoes had fallen into at the turn of the century, noting that while they were once commonly found framed and mounted in people's homes, they seemed to have passed out of style. "I wonder sometimes if we have progressed so far that we no longer need these writings on the wall," he asks. In answer to his own question, he relates the story of an eight-year-old boy who asked his father for "something to go by." His friends have mottoes, he said, and he'd like one too. After giving it due consideration, the boy's father gave him the motto: "Know the truth and speak the truth." The rest of the essay is a rumination on the appropriateness of this sentiment.

The power of such a motto derives from the circumstances which give rise to it—the context is an exchange between father and son. The boy cannot choose his own motto; it must be chosen for him. But he can choose to keep it, and use it hopefully as a moral yardstick.

While the entire genre of advice to sons seems to promote the idea (easily disproved by the example of Lord Chesterfield) that if you throw enough aphoristic wisdom at the wall, some of it will stick, this story underlines a different idea: choose advice carefully, give it sparingly. The father wisely selects a single motto rather than giving the boy a book of mottoes to choose from, knowing that the boy's future will be shaped in part by this gesture.

This story recurs in many settings—a youth receives a piece of wisdom from an elder, and it serves him well, or perhaps serves him only once, but in a crucial situation. It provides courage, faith, hope, or direction when these are in short supply. Its strength lies in the bond between bestower and recipient, whether it is from parent to child, teacher to student, commander to troops, corporation to employee, or great leader to a nation. Such a motto has an emotional resonance that a simple slogan or sound bite lacks.

In every era, those who earn praise for wisdom, courage, and honor are invariably those who follow specific principles of conduct which often take the form of mottoes or maxims that they learned in youth. By constantly testing their actions against a fixed standard, such individuals conscientiously seek to attain virtue through practice. The motto serves as the metronome which regulates that practice.

George Washington, as mentioned in Chapter Six, followed "The Rules of Civility," which helped him establish notions of social propriety and everyday virtue that he would use for the rest of his life. Thomas Jefferson compiled his Decalogue—his ten rules of decent behavior. Benjamin Franklin carried his book of thirteen virtues which he used daily to practice relinquishing his faults. "I always carry my book with me," he wrote in the *Autobiography*, "and it may well be my posterity should be informed that to this little artifice . . . their ancestor owes the constant felicity of his life." Colin Powell, in his autobiography, claims to have done the same, also with thirteen precepts.

Franklin had no idea just how much his posterity would be informed by his little artifice. His proverbs have turned out to be his greatest legacy— more influential in popular culture than his inventions or his political writings. One idea in particular captures Franklin's ethic in three words. There are several maxims that hint at it—"Lose no time; be always employed in something useful," "Lost time is never found again," and "Never leave that for tomorrow which you can do today." But the most complete expression of the idea can be found in *Advice to a Young Tradesman*, where Franklin says, "Remember that *time is money*." This motto evolved into nothing short of a cultural standard, the foundation of what the German sociologist Max Weber would define as the American work ethic. In his 1905 book, *The Protestant Ethic and the Spirit of Capitalism*, Weber credits Franklin's maxims, and "time is money" in particular, as the seeds from which the American approach to work and to the enjoyment of life grew.

Success philosophies are driven by maxims and mottoes, but not just any maxims or mottoes. Other men might have said "time is money," but the success of this ethic owes to the example of Franklin's life, the quirks (and strengths) of his personality, and his place in American history. Franklin invented himself through his *Autobiography*, and through such works as *Poor Richard's Almanac*. His legacy gained considerable momentum in the nineteenth century through such vehicles as the McGuffy readers, and in this century by that great repository of aphoristic wisdom, the dictionary of quotations.

Second only to Franklin, Ralph Waldo Emerson represents an American ethic through his maxims of transcendental idealism. He once wrote, "I hate quotation. Tell me what you know." But what remains of Emersonianism in popular culture can be expressed in a relatively few lines that are at once hopeful—"Hitch your wagon to a star"—inspirational—"The only way to have a friend is to be one"—uplifting—"Character is higher than intellect"—and pragmatic—"A foolish consistency is the hobgoblin of little minds." In his best-known maxim (an attribution), he states that, "If a man can write a better book, preach a better sermon, or make a better mousetrap than his neighbor, though he build his house in the woods, the world will make a beaten path to his door." This is the essence of the work ethic pioneered by Franklin.

As secure as Franklin's place may seem in the American pantheon, he was not above criticism or parody. Mark Twain skewered the American success ethic, squaring off against Franklin in *Pudd'nhead Wilson* (1905), which provides a twist on *Poor Richard* by prefacing each chapter with aphorisms from "Pudd'nhead Wilson's Calendar." The maxims of Pudd'nhead Wilson appear as a welcome antidote to the sometimes over-bearing exhortations of Franklin's success philosophy. (This is only because Franklin's wittier, bawdier, and more caustic observations were kept out of children's primers. Franklin, it should be remembered, was the one who said, "In this world nothing can be said to be certain except death and taxes"—an observation that in style and content could easily be attributed to Twain.) What Twain targeted was not Franklin himself, but his reputation as a grandfatherly scold. Some of Twain's better maxims include:

Put all of your eggs in one basket and—WATCH THAT BASKET.
When angry, count four; when very angry, swear.
Let us endeavor so to live that when we come to die even the undertaker will be sorry.

Every generation has its slogans. Some of them defy time and tastes and manage to stay around for a while. "Time is money" and "Hitch your wagon to a star" have held up well. There have been other, lesser mottoes that dazzled the public imagination for a time, but soon burned out. One such motto swept through the United States in the 1920s, and although it may still sound familiar to some ears, the story behind it is mostly forgotten. Yet it was the first self-help mantra and the forerunner of flash-in-the-pan mottoes that have come to the fore in subsequent generations, which makes its story worth retelling.

EVERY DAY IN EVERY WAY I AM GETTING BETTER AND BETTER

In the summer of 1923 an unpretentious Frenchman named Emile Coué visited the United States to promote a technique which had caused a sensation in France and in London. The former apothecary's trip to America occasioned an outpouring of emotion that finds its modern counterpart in the receptions given to rock stars and popes, and the press turned out in force.

Coué gave his name to Couéism—a term that had entered the American language long before the man himself set foot off the boat. Millions of Americans were reciting his soothing self-help motto as part of a method he called "autosuggestion," a form of healing in which the conscious mind sells an idea to the unconscious mind, which converts it to reality. A cultural phenomenon of the mid 1920s, Coué's motto—Every day in every way I am getting better and better—inspired a surprising outpouring of serious criticism in the press; surprising because of how silly it sounds today. Yet Couéism was all the rage, and even if the diminutive Frenchman is not remembered, his motto still rings a bell.

To be fair, Coué's motto needs to be considered in the context of his method, for which he made only modest claims. The authorized translation of his book, prepared for his U.S. visit, gives the core of his method as a simple prescription:

> Every morning before getting up and every evening as soon as you are in bed, shut your eyes and repeat twenty times in succession, moving your lips (this is indispensable) and counting mechanically on a long string with twenty knots the following phrase: *"Day by day, in every way, I am getting better and better."* Do not think of anything in particular, as the words, "in every way," apply to everything.

To give a simple idea of what he meant and of what powers of the inner mind supported his thesis, he asked a simple question: Why is it so easy to walk confidently along a one-foot wide plank laid upon the ground, but not on the same plank when it spans the towers of a cathedral? His answer: in the first instance we imagine we can do it, and in the second that we cannot, thus proving that willpower cannot overcome imagination.

The importance of the Coué phenomenon to the discussion of mottoes is simply this: twenty years earlier his motto and method would not have succeeded because the culture was unprepared for it. At the turn of the century, most people still believed in the principles of hard work, stick-to-it-iveness, and prayer. Mysticism flourished, to be sure, but Coué's form of healing relied heavily on the public's newfound belief in the subconscious, made possible by the breakthroughs of Sigmund Freud. In the 1920s the American public had become susceptible to the notion that there was another self—the unconscious self—that they could work to improve. With the discovery of the unconscious id, mottoes such as Coué's could now work as magic passwords to success, health, and happiness.

Coué claimed that the will is no match for the imagination. In fact the great enemy of the method of auto-suggestion is effort. The technique should be simple and unforced, and this constituted a large part of its appeal. But Coué also benefited from a succession of minor miracles. The ecstatic throngs that greeted him spewed forth disabled believers who threw away their crutches, as well as victims of paralysis who rose from their wheelchairs. The method drew ringing endorsements from such work ethic stalwarts as Thomas Edison and Henry Ford. In a very specific way, this is not surprising. Corporate leaders had a great interest in motivating an ever-expanding work force charged with performing numbingly repetitive tasks. The ethics of individualism or Horatio Algerism, which held out the hope of rising above others, was not suited to an industrial society. But Coué promised a better world with no effort and no expenditure of energy. Many people soon latched on to the idea that they could even learn in their sleep, and they bought machines that would soothingly whisper reassuring mottoes in their ears during the night.

The brilliance of Coué's method lay in its simplicity. Some of the credit, however, should go to his translator. In the first American edition of his book, *Self-Mastery through Conscious Autosuggestion,* the motto is rendered as: "Every day, *in every respect,* I am getting better and better." It is not clear who saw a catchier line buried in this one—whether it was an American editor or simply the public itself that gave an awkward phrase some rhyme and rhythm. In any event, as one magazine columnist noted at the time, the change to "in every way" made the slogan "go," and so "put Coué over" with the American public.

Mottoes as tools of indoctrination did not begin or end with Emile Coué. His popular slogan, however, implanted itself into the nation's consciousness, although perhaps not, as he had hoped, into its subconscious. Coué died in 1926, and his method more or less died with him, although the basic idea has been revived by many other charismatic personalities in a wide variety of forms.

HONEST LABOR NEEDS NO MASTER

In the mid 1800s the average American home featured at least one house motto, usually embroidered on a sampler and hung in the entryway, the parlor, or over the hearth, proclaiming some banality such as "Home Sweet Home" or "Forget Me Not." By the turn of the century publishing companies churned out thousands of printed mottoes suitable for framing, many of them drawn from the Bible, of course, although homegrown wisdom also claimed its share of wall space.

Enthusiasm for house mottoes even spread to artists and intellectuals, particularly those who were caught up in the Arts and Crafts movement. Most notably, the architects Louis Sullivan and Frank Lloyd Wright sought out expressions of hope and encouragement to place on the walls of the homes they designed. Inspired by Ralph Waldo Emerson, their efforts reflected a serious and purposeful form of idealism. But in retrospect, even transcendentalists could not transcend greeting card sentimentality.

Wright provided one of the most striking uses of slogans when he designed his first office building in 1904. The Larkin Building, built at the height of American neoclassicism, was stylistically about three decades ahead of its time. One of its greatest (and most overlooked) innovations was the introduction of motivational mottoes into the workplace. Although too much of a one-of-a-kind oddity to have started a trend, the Larkin Building *anticipated* a trend that soon became a staple of the workplace (and still is).

Wright's clients, the Larkin brothers, made soap and sold it through a clever mail-order marketing campaign which also sold the idea of cleanliness to the American public. When they decided to build a new corporate headquarters in Buffalo, New York, they hoped that the building would reinforce the connection between cleanliness and godliness. To this end, Frank Lloyd Wright concocted an inspirational work environment whose most spectacular feature was an atrium that ran up through the entire six-storey height of the building, affording every floor a view of the central clerical work area on the main level. The Light Court, as it was called, displayed Wright's signature use of geometric ornamentation, and also his predilection for Arts and Crafts motifs—in particular the use of stylized lettering.

To complement the design, Wright included inscriptions overlooking the central work space. These took the form of one-word mottoes, grouped three to a panel and intended to be sequential in meaning. They extolled selected virtues in a way that permitted "independence of thought and individuality of interpretation," according to the office manager,

William Heath, who chose the words. There were fourteen such panels lining the central Light Court at the fifth-floor level, and they conveyed such sentiments as:

INTELLIGENCE	COOPERATION	INTEGRITY
ENTHUSIASM	ECONOMY	LOYALTY
CONTROL	INDUSTRY	FIDELITY

There were two other panels at the front and back of the atrium, each of which contained an adage from the Sermon on the Mount. (One of them, naturally, was the Golden Rule.) At each entrance to the building, sculpted friezes greeted employees with the inscribed mottoes:

HONEST LABOR	FREEDOM TO EVERY
NEEDS NO MASTER	MAN AND COMMERCE
SIMPLE JUSTICE	WITH ALL THE WORLD
NEEDS NO SLAVES	

The entire scheme reflects the Larkins' and Wright's identification with American idealism, and particularly with Emersonianism. Their goal was to create a transcendental atmosphere, one that would have a spiritual effect on its occupants. The result, notes one writer, "can be seen to exemplify Emerson's belief in the unity of all things in nature and in the aspiration of all matter to a spiritual ideal."

Unfortunately, the Larkin Building can now only be judged through photographs (the building was demolished in 1950), and these only hint at the mottoes' effect. The interior inscriptions, because their point of reference is a decorative style that has little meaning today, appear almost patronizing, if not controlling. To a modern observer, the inscribed panels seem to hover over the workplace in a Big Brotherly way, incessantly urging the staff to live up to impossible expectations.

Whether the workers felt inspired or unnerved by this is not known. What the Larkin Building does show is that Wright's motif of incorporating inscribed mottoes into mantelpieces and other woodwork in the private homes he designed (including his own) can appear condescending and threatening in an impersonalized setting. Yet the Larkin Building is not considered a failure, or even a cautionary tale. It merely reflected the popular tastes of its time, and it served as a precursor of the corporate use of mottoes that would reach its apogee in the hands of Thomas J. Watson—

the man who brought IBM to the height of its success, and made it synonymous with a single word.

THINK

For most of this century the company most closely associated with a motivational motto (as opposed to an advertising slogan) and a single dominating personality who shaped a corporate ethic, was IBM. Thomas J. Watson did not found International Business Machines, nor did he originate the idea of posting signs throughout its offices urging its employees to THINK. Yet he is famous for both of these things. Watson is synonymous with IBM in the way Henry Ford personified his car company. The motto he made famous is now part of IBM legend, and by extension has become a part of American business mythology.

Although not much in evidence these days, at one time the IBM motto was so closely identified with the company that a promotional film shown at the IBM Pavilion at the 1964 World's Fair was simply entitled "Think." Later, during the company's heyday as the preeminent maker of mainframe computers, its philosophy became more sophisticated—the slogan reemerged as "Machines Should Work, People Should Think." The implication of this revised motto, however, is far from that of the original. Today the company is merely identified with the rather uninspiring nickname of Big Blue.

But during its early period of market dominance IBM's one-word corporate philosophy represented a code of behavior that permeated the workplace. To present-day sensibilities (or sensitivities) it carries the onus of overbearing authority. Yet during Watson's tenure as CEO, and to a lesser extent during his son's reign, IBM held the highest esteem among its employees and its competitors. It was considered one of the best companies to work for, a solid employer renowned for never laying off workers during slow times, and for treating its employees like a large extended family. The price to be paid for this paternalism was loyalty. An IBM man followed the rules, always wore a white shirt with a club tie, and was happy to do so. The single most important sign of that loyalty was the THINK sign on his desk, and he was proud to display it.

THOMAS WATSON WAS HIRED as a branch manager at National Cash Register in 1899. Legend has it that he failed to sell a single machine in his first two weeks on the job, and here the legend rings true. It wasn't the word "think" that brought him out of his funk, however. Watson's employer, John Henry Patterson, a somewhat tyrannical entrepreneur who had founded NCR, had enough patience with the young salesman to keep him on, and eventually promoted him to sales executive. Watson absorbed the Patterson sales philosophy and perfected it. He managed to dodge Patterson's mercurial wrath through a Machiavellian combination of quiet subservience around the boss and an aptitude for implementing Patterson's best sales strategies.

During his weekly chalk talks to the sales force, Watson took to using mottoes such as DO RIGHT and THINK, which he would write in large block letters on his demonstration pad. One day, Patterson walked in on one of these talks and was taken with the THINK motto. He decided to have it printed on cards and placed in every department in the company. When Watson moved on to IBM many years later, he took the idea with him, and made a THINK sign mandatory on every desk, going so far as to insist that it be placed in plain view of the desk's occupant at all times.

The message was not meant to be taken literally. To "think" means to be original, to improvise, to come up with innovative solutions. To Watson, the THINK sign was a badge of loyalty to the company and to the Watson philosophy, which was noted for its strict codes of business ethics and personal behavior.

One story has it that Watson once entered the company's headquarters with a group of junior executives in tow, only to find that a vandal had pulled down the THINK sign in the lobby. The CEO noticed it immediately and was visibly upset. A member of the group took it upon himself to remove the THINK placard at his own desk to replace the missing sign, which, after all, occupied a place of greater prominence. Later that day the young man's supervisor happened by and, noticing the absence of the obligatory sign, berated his subordinate, accusing him of disloyalty.

Somewhat chagrined that his self-sacrifice had earned him such rough treatment, the young man bought some paint and returned to the building that night, and in an act of defiance he painted THINK on the sales meeting room wall in six-foot-high letters. When Watson saw this the next day, he took it as an act of anonymous enthusiasm and corporate spirit. He ordered that it should remain in place as an inspiration.

The story might well be company folklore, but it gives a good idea of what THINK meant to Watson, and what inspiring mottoes meant to other executives. Thomas Edison, according to Dale Carnegie, had a quotation from Sir Joshua Reynolds posted in each of his factories. It read, "There is no expedient to which a man will not resort to avoid the real labor of thinking." It is a rare motto that makes one pause and think in the way this one does. It is, of course, an interesting commentary on the IBM motto. Ironically, it explains precisely why Watson is famous for his motto while Edison is not. The Reynolds quote requires more thought than most people are willing to expend.

IGNORANCE IS STRENGTH

Today executive offices are regularly festooned with framed posters featuring odd juxtapositions of images and one-word mottoes: a magnified water droplet accompanying the word "Attitude"; a canoe aground on a lake shore illustrating "Success"; a sloop under sail at sunrise with the word "Opportunity." Many of today's CEOs buy right into this idea. They support a thriving mail-order industry that deals in breathtakingly unspectacular motivational paraphernalia—everything from posters and mugs to molded rocks inscribed with such platitudes as "Attitude Is Everything" and "We Can't Spell Success Without U."

And yet "unspectacular" may be too harsh a judgment when the trajectory of workplace mottoes is taken into full account. In a century that began with the Larkin Building's INTELLIGENCE, ENTHUSIASM, CONTROL, and Thomas Watson's THINK, and that gave birth to Couéism and unconscious auto-suggestion, and finally bottomed out in the era of Nazi and fascist propaganda, the new workplace mottoes have the singular advantage of being inoffensive and nonthreatening—an advantage in light of historical events that have eclipsed the innocence that once informed motivational methods. After two world wars, attitudes have changed so profoundly that few people can look at photographs of the Larkin Building without being reminded of George Orwell's chilling vision of the year 1984. In this nightmare world ruled by the ubiquitous face of Big Brother, a doomed hero works in the department of propaganda, which is ironically called the Ministry of Truth, and which lays down the Party line using the slogans

WAR IS PEACE
FREEDOM IS SLAVERY
IGNORANCE IS STRENGTH

With Orwell, the history of inspirational mottoes runs its course from HOME SWEET HOME to THINK to BIG BROTHER IS WATCHING YOU. Thus it made perfect sense to Apple Computer, when it unveiled its Macintosh model in 1984, to launch an advertising campaign with a nod to Orwell and a swipe at their biggest competitor. In an infamous commercial that ran during the first half of the Super Bowl, Apple portrayed IBM's clients as Orwellian automatons worshipping a bluish Big Brother figure. A lone defiant figure, a female athlete, sprints through this demoralized landscape and hurls a missile which smashes the huge televised image that has transfixed the audience. It was a big concept, but also a big failure. Not many viewers in the television audience had any idea what it meant.

More effective by far in deflating IBM's image had been a one-word slogan that someone cooked up years earlier. It was subtle, yet effective and to the point.

It simply read: THIMK!

LET'S HAVE BETTER MOTTOES

The executive who goes in for motivational mottoes may not appreciate the full history of the idea, or how little it has changed. The corporate version of the house motto began to appear in workplaces shortly after the turn of the century. By the 1940s IBM's THINK had led the way to a widespread corporate use of motivational slogans, to the extent that the business world employed a good number of "motto-men" as CEOs and managers. Their enthusiasm produced a workplace littered with such admonitions as "Keep Smiling!", "Nothing Takes the Place of Experience," and "Knowledge Is Power!" It was only a matter of time before someone thought to lampoon this practice and make money from it.

The someone turned out to be Frederick E. Gymer of Cleveland, a former canal boat worker and tuba player turned advertising man, who had nothing against self-improvement, but had trouble swallowing it when it was forced down his throat. So Gymer decided to create some mottoes of his own, only in reverse. "Think! It may be a new experience," was one of his early efforts. "Smile! Later today you won't feel like it."

Pleasantly surprised at the enthusiastic response that greeted these spoofs, Gymer quit the ad game in the late 1940s in order to found a direct mail business which supplied his clients with a motto every month. These

were embellished with a cartoon horse named Joe, and mailed out in pack-
aged sets to business executives who then had the privilege of being "sec-
retaries" of the organization. They in turn would hand out the mottoes to
their clients and friends. Thus was born the Let's Have Better Mottoes
Association.

Gymer's business flourished during the booming post-war years, as
companies proliferated and white-collar workers found life to be increasingly regimented. In many workplaces the monthly arrival of Gymer's
mailing was a welcome relief from the standard motivational doctrines.
Gymer bucked conformity, but in a safe way. Hardly iconoclastic, and
somewhat corny by design, his brand of humor can still be found on greeting cards, bumper stickers, and in the pages of *Reader's Digest*. Here are a few
of his gems:

> *Someone said it couldn't be done—So the hell with it.*
> *Accuracy is our watchword—We never make misteaks.*
> *Work fascinates me—I can sit and look at it for hours.*

Although they began as a white-collar diversion, Gymer's mottoes filtered
down from the boardroom to the secretarial pool, and are now most popular with those who have to suffer the latest motivational fad or spiritual
success doctrine dragged in by the boss.

It should come as no surprise that when self-improvement philosophies
and meaningless motivational platitudes become part of corporate indoctrination, humor is the only effective response. Dale Carnegie's rules for
success and "the power of positive thinking" espoused by Norman Vincent
Peale, both of which were in earnest, soon gave way to Murphy's and
Parkinson's laws, which were not. After Fred Gymer, a long-suppressed capacity for fun and outright silliness flourished in corporate America. ("Next
week, we've got to get organized!") Gymer himself enjoyed his fifteen minutes of fame. He made a business out of doing what a million other white-
collar workers wished they had thought of first.

OTHER-DIRECTEDNESS

If the Let's Have Better Mottoes Association didn't usher in the era of joke
mottoes (and it's not entirely clear that Fred Gymer deserves all of the
credit), it at least marked a trend that alarmed some cultural watchdogs. In

the late 1950s an English professor named L. W. Michaelson ruminated on the motto phenomenon in a piece for *Catholic World* magazine. "It would be a waste of time," he wrote, "to try to judge the tone, temper, and sentiment of a nation simply by observing the mottoes hung upon the walls of its citizens." Apparently unconvinced by this opening premise, Michaelson goes right ahead and attempts it anyway.

Cynical mottoes in reverse such as those produced by Fred Gymer and others of his ilk, Michaelson asserts, can be seen as youthful protests, as an antidote to 1950s anxiety, or simply as a rebirth of the "Yankee frontier-style humor of Mark Twain, Bret Harte, George Ade, and Will Rogers." Yet to Michaelson they seem instead to be "a rather painful reminder that David Riesman's *The Lonely Crowd* is a bit more prophetic and accurate than most of us would care to believe. That is to say, in these reverse-English maxims we can see additional proofs of the rise of 'other-directedness.'"

Michaelson's point is that the reverse-motto, the cynic's retort, is a rejection of rugged individualism and the success-driven maxims of the past. It concedes that the modern corporate world rewards conformity and obedience, and has no place for a Horatio Alger or even a Ben Franklin. The work ethic remains, but it discourages inventiveness and initiative. William Whyte, in *The Organization Man* (1958), quotes an IBM executive as saying, "the training makes our men interchangeable." In Riesman's other-directed world, to be different, to maintain a personal set of goals and standards that sets you apart from the rest, leads ultimately to loneliness. Quoting Tocqueville, Michaelson concludes, "The same equality that allows every citizen to conceive lofty ambitions renders all citizens less able to realize them." Ironically, it is Fred Gymer, a modern-day Poor Richard, who is the glaring execption to this rule.

AS FADS AND FASHIONS in mottoes and slogans come and go, one set of mottoes remains a fairly constant part of American life. This took some doing, and did not happen overnight, but there are now four brief formulas that function as the nation's mottoes, and it looks like they are here to stay. They are not rallying cries so much as points of identification. Most Americans have little idea what they mean. How these few seemingly innocuous ready-made opinions became national institutions is the subject of the next chapter.

AND THIS BE OUR MOTTO,
"IN GOD IS OUR TRUST."

FRANCIS SCOTT KEY,
"THE STAR-SPANGLED BANNER"

CHAPTER EIGHT

IN GOD WE TRUST

THE NATIONAL MOTTOES

It would seem only natural for an American businessman, finding himself stranded overseas, to seek some confirmation of his own identity. Flipping through his wallet, he might come across some pictures of his wife and children, perhaps a subway pass, a health club membership, or a library card. Although these items might evoke a pang of remembrance, this will soon give way to a detached inventory of personal effects: he will naturally be led to examine the photographs closely for the first time, to read the back of his driver's license, or to see when his library card expires.

Digging deeper, he will undoubtedly take comfort in the sight of the American money he kept in reserve—greenbacks, legal tender, cold hard cash. It will look much more solid and dependable than the funny money he has been spending on his trip. But it will also be thrown into relief by strange surroundings. Because of this, he might examine it more objectively than ever before, and he will find a surprising wealth of information there.

The dollar bill in particular, that most enigmatic of all denominations, seems to have a story to tell. But what is it? How would he explain to an inquiring foreigner the presence of the pyramid capped by an eye within a triangle? What does the eagle hold in its claws and in its beak? What are those Latin words, and what do they say about the country?

A sad aspect of the American sense of civics is that most Americans cannot answer these questions. But they have an excuse: the story is not taught in schools, nor is it particularly well understood by the writers of history texts. It is a story that has been left untold because it exposes the machinery behind part of the American myth. This is too bad, because with a little bit of investigation, what unfolds is a plot that is operatic in scope, and, despite a few gaps in the narrative, one that plays well in Peoria.

THE GREAT SEAL

On the afternoon of July 4, 1776, the Continental Congress, having dispensed with the matter of signing the Declaration of Independence, assembled a committee to attend to the pressing task of designing an official seal for the new nation. Although the Founders were breaking away from England, they were not about to abandon all of its traditions, and the idea of a heraldic seal, while not absolutely necessary to validate documents and treaties, would go some way toward legitimizing their endeavor.

The first committee consisted of no less distinguished a trio than Benjamin Franklin, Thomas Jefferson, and John Adams. Jefferson had been working on the idea of a seal and a national motto since 1774, which may seem surprising. Yet it goes to show that well before the nation existed, its founders were consumed with creating symbols to represent it.

The committee produced several designs. Adams proposed a tableau featuring Hercules contemplating a choice between two allegorical figures representing Virtue and Sloth. Jefferson proposed a depiction of "The Children of Israel in the Wilderness." Franklin suggested a device showing Moses parting the Red Sea. For the motto, he chose the words of Oliver Cromwell: "Rebellion to Tyrants Is Obedience to God." Jefferson liked it so much that he adopted it as his personal motto. (The motto is also credited to John Bradshaw, the chief of the Regicides who executed Charles I.)

Getting no closer to an acceptable design, the committee called upon Pierre Eugene du Simitière, a Swiss-born silhouette cutter and portraitist who had some knowledge of heraldic devices. Du Simitière attempted to combine the committee's suggestions into a design that drew upon some common symbols and popular mottoes, which meant throwing out most of the committee's suggestions. In his first proposal he tried to convey the idea of six European nationalities joined in one divinely ordained venture. Two features survived this initial process. One is the motto *E pluribus unum*, which means "One, from many." The other is the all-seeing eye of Providence, which was a common motif in medallic art as well as a Masonic symbol. (Franklin was a Freemason, and Jefferson probably one as well, so it would have seemed natural to them to use this familiar allegorical image.)

Several other mottoes and symbols vied for space on designs submitted to the committee, but none seemed to take hold. When Jefferson combined Du Simitière's and some of Franklin's ideas into a final proposal and submitted it to Congress, they tabled it. The issue came up again in 1779, when the Congress appointed a second committee, but it too failed to come up with an acceptable design. Finally, with the War of Independence coming to a close and with pressure mounting to get the job done, Congress formed a third committee which, like the first, immediately sought the help of an outside consultant. In this instance they brought in a young Philadelphia lawyer named William Barton, who is known to have had an aptitude for drawing as well as a passing knowledge of heraldry.

In his first attempt, in 1782, Barton came up with an overly elaborate design for the observe, or front, of the seal. His much simpler design for the reverse, however, was kept (after some refinement and a change in mottoes). It included the now familiar unfinished pyramid (suggesting a solid foundation with work yet to be done) surmounted by the all-seeing eye of Providence (retained from Du Simitière's design). While both of these are thought to be Masonic emblems, there is convincing evidence that Barton had no intention of promoting any form of fraternalism. At that time both symbols circulated in other contexts, and it seems likely that the Masonic connection is a coincidence. Much of the Masonic lore attached to the Founding Fathers, in fact, was augmented considerably through the energetic hindsight of Masonic hagiographers, who succeeded to the extent that Barton and Du Simitière's symbolism on the Great Seal is now widely considered to be Masonic in origin, whatever their original intentions may have been.

While the simple scheme of the reverse went over well, Barton's design for the obverse of the seal was far too ambitious. It did contain an eagle and a crest, but with far too much additional symbolism. When Barton submitted it to Charles Thomson, the Secretary of the Congress, Thomson decided to expedite matters by extracting from Barton's scheme what he thought would work, and finishing it himself. Although a man of many talents, Thomson knew nothing of heraldry and was no artist, but he approached the task of refining Barton's proposals in the same businesslike way that he ran the Congress from behind the scenes. He was particularly attuned to the importance of symbols. With the war over, and the government beginning to set up shop, the seal had become a high priority, and Thomson was determined to get it done.

From Barton's design for the obverse, Thomson kept only the eagle, on whose chest he mounted a shield. In one claw he placed an olive branch (signifying peace), in the other a bundle of arrows (representing war). In its mouth he inserted a banner inscribed with the words *E pluribus unum*. To round out the design, he replaced the mottoes Barton had chosen for the reverse, substituting two phrases from Virgil—*Annuit coeptis* and *Novus ordo seclorum*—to be placed at the top and bottom respectively.

OF THE THREE MOTTOES of the Great Seal, *E pluribus unum* is the most familiar. Not only does it appear on the front of the seal, but it has been used on United States currency throughout the nation's history, as well as on commemorative coins, the presidential seal, and other ceremonial emblems. It is sometimes called the "federation motto" because it connotes the joining of thirteen separate colonies into a single nation. The literal translation—"From many, one" or "One, from many"—conveys not only the idea of many commonwealths joined as one nation, but also the more modern concept of many different peoples joined as one nation. This last sense of the motto, which the vagueness of the Latin easily accommodates, is a twentieth-century interpretation. The Founding Fathers who approved the motto merely had in mind "the several states all joined in one solid compact entire, supporting a Chief, which unites the whole and represents Congress." They had no idea just how diverse the "pluribus" would eventually be.

The two additional mottoes of the reverse side are vaguely familiar to most Americans, and not very well understood. Both were adapted by Thomson from the Roman poet Virgil. *Annuit coeptis* sweeps over the all-seeing eye of Providence and translates as "He favors our undertaking." Below the unfinished pyramid appear the words *Novus ordo seclorum*, which means "A new order of the ages," although it has recently been construed to mean "A new world order."

These mottoes would be virtually forgotten but for one of those quirks of fate that caused them to be distributed more widely in this country than the Bible. Since 1935, the reverse side of the Great Seal has been printed on the backs of dollar bills. This marked the first time both sides of the seal had been publicly displayed, and because of this decision the mottoes found their way into every wallet, purse, and pocket in America. Exactly how this happened and why is not entirely clear, which opens the door to all manner of conspiracy theorists who see apocalyptic doom in the words "new world order," if not in the New Deal itself. For it was Franklin Roosevelt who brought this about, and of course Franklin Roosevelt was a thirty-second-degree Mason.

THE SILVER CERTIFICATE

To fully appreciate Roosevelt's decision to use both sides of the Great Seal, it should be pointed out that Barton and Thomson's design for the reverse side, although approved by Congress in 1783, was never cut into a usable seal, and thus was never affixed to state documents, or attached to any state symbols. In fact it had never been seen by the public.

In 1841 the seal was redrawn and recut, but the reverse was omitted. Before the World's Columbian Exposition in Chicago in 1893 an enlarged and touched-up version of the seal was prepared for public display, but again the reverse was considered too problematic and was not exhibited. A committee of scholars appointed by Congress in 1884 had concluded that it could not and should not be salvaged. In their report, art historian Charles Eliot Norton wrote: "As to the reverse, the device adopted by Congress is practically incapable of effective treatment; it can hardly (however artistically treated by the designer) look otherwise than as a dull emblem of a Masonic fraternity." The committee recommended that the reverse should be displayed as little as possible, and should never be cut. "It has been so long kept in the dark," they concluded, "a few more months of shade will do it no harm."

The American public would have been none the wiser had not the issue surfaced again in the 1930s, when someone proposed that the Great Seal appear in its entirety on the back of the silver certificate. The proposal, of course, had to be approved by the president.

Franklin Delano Roosevelt was a Shriner, an honor open only to thirty-second-degree Masons. During his political ascendancy, the Masons were at the height of their power and influence, and membership for someone of Roosevelt's station was a formality, just as it is today for someone like Bob Dole. As Masonic ritualism declined in the 1920s and '30s, the lodges turned to more entertaining diversions such as parades and conventions, activities that were noted for a conspicuous consumption of alcohol. Roosevelt understood his brothers well enough to make a point of being out of town when they held their annual convention and parade in Washington. He knew better than to become associated with drunken revels, accosting of women, and flouting of the laws of society and common sense.

But when the Great Seal came to his desk as part of a proposal to change the dollar bill, the president had a chance to make a good impression on his fellow lodge members, who constituted a significant proportion of the political and corporate elite in America. The president considered the proposal, and signed off on it. Then he scratched out his signature.

Whether he was agonizing over the decision is hard to say. His hesitation seems to have been due to his artistic sense, however, because he proceeded to amend the design by suggesting that the positions of the reverse and obverse be switched—the reverse should appear on the left, he decided, over the words "The Great Seal," and the obverse on the right, over the words "of the United States." He then initialed the changes, and with that the reverse of the Great Seal, along with the pyramid, *Annuit coeptis*, and *Novus ordo seclorum* appeared for the first time in the full light of day.

THE QUESTION OF WHO SUGGESTED using the seal on the dollar bill may never be completely resolved. Certainly Roosevelt played a key part. The instigator may have been former Vice President Henry A. Wallace, who made the claim on his own behalf in a letter dated February 6, 1951, and in a follow-up letter of 1955. The text of the first letter is worth reprinting in its entirety not only because it tells an interesting story, but because it shows that whatever William Barton and Charles Thomson may have intended, the man who put the Great Seal on the dollar bill (and gave it the name "great") definitely interpreted it as a Masonic symbol. This is how Wallace remembered it:

> In 1934 when I was Sec. of Agriculture I was waiting in the outer office of Secretary [of State Cordell] Hull and as I waited I amused myself by picking up a State Department publication which was on a stand there entitled, "The History of the Seal of the United States." Turning to page 53 I noted the colored reproduction of the reverse side of the Seal. The Latin phrase *Novus Ordo Seclorum* impressed me as meaning the New Deal of the Ages. Therefore I took the publication to President Roosevelt and suggested a coin be put out with the obverse and reverse sides of the Seal. Roosevelt as he looked at [the] colored reproduction of the Seal was first struck with the representation of the "All-Seeing Eye," a Masonic representation of The Great Architect of the Universe.

Next he was impressed with the idea that the foundation of the new order of the ages had been laid in 1776 but that it would be completed only under the eye of the Great Architect. Roosevelt like myself was a 32nd degree Mason. He suggested that the Seal be put out on the dollar bill rather than a coin and took the matter up with the Secretary of the Treasury. When the first draft came back from the Treasury the obverse side was on the left of the bill as is the heraldic practice. Roosevelt insisted that the order be reversed so that the phrase "of the United States" would be under the obverse side of the Seal. I believe he was also responsible for introducing the word "Great" in the phrase "The Great Seal" as it is found under the reverse side of the Seal on the left of our dollar bills. Roosevelt was a great stickler for details and loved playing with them, no matter whether it involved the architecture of a house, a post office or a dollar bill.

E PLURIBUS UNUM

The Great Seal of the United States, because it is essentially a heraldic device, is generally forgiven its eccentricities. Barton's Masonic symbolism has not raised too many objections, nor have the mottoes. Thomson adapted the phrases from Virgil to fit Barton's imagery, and explained them in this way: "The pyramid signifies strength and duration. . . . The eye over it and the motto allude to the many interpositions of providence in favour of the American cause. The date underneath [MDCCLXXVI] is that of the Declaration of Independence and the words under it signify the beginning of a new American era."

The "new American era" has lately given rise to the "new world order," which serves as a code word for those who believe that the United States is helping to bring about a cabalistic world government through the United Nations. The talisman on the back of the dollar bill is cited as evidence of this. Both Franklin Roosevelt and Charles Thomson might have been surprised at this development, but it seems that if conspiracy theorists did not have this to focus on, they would simply latch onto something else.

E pluribus unum is a more difficult phrase to trace to its true source than its companion mottoes. It is also the more important by far. George Shankle, in *American Mottoes and Slogans* (1941), cites an early use of the phrase by the *Gentleman's Magazine*, a popular English journal that circulated widely after the 1730s. The magazine's masthead featured an emblem of a hand grasping a bouquet of flowers, accompanied by the inscription *E Pluribus Unum*. This undoubtedly is where Du Simitière found it. As to what inspired the magazine's use of the motto, the best guess is the line *color est e pluribus unus*, which appears in Virgil's *Moretum*. It refers to the making of a salad, which some modern observers have found to be a more appropriate national metaphor than "the melting pot." Similar phrases can also be found in Horace, so it cannot be said for certain who coined the term. It was literally coined very early in this country's history: it first appeared on a U.S. coin in the 1790s, and by 1798 it was on the silver dollar.

Because of its longevity, and because it falls so easily off the tongue of Americans who have no idea what it really means, *E pluribus unum* is often thought of as the national motto. But it is not. The national motto lies elsewhere on the dollar bill—not the one that Franklin Roosevelt redesigned in 1935, but a much newer one. The phrase first appeared on paper money as recently as 1957, two years after it was declared the official national motto by Congress. It can now be found on the reverse side of the dollar bill in prominent letters engraved above the word ONE.

God, Our Trust

There are three inscriptions that are now required on all United States coinage. They are LIBERTY, E PLURIBUS UNUM, and the words, IN GOD WE TRUST. The first two seem clear enough. The last, however, is the most recent and by far the most controversial. Some coin experts grumble that it owes its place in this exclusive club to the efforts of a country bumpkin—a religious fanatic who pressured the secretary of the treasury during a time of civil war. There is some truth to that. Many civil libertarians claim that a reference to God has no place on U.S. currency, that it violates the separation of church and state, and that its origin is nothing more than a historical aberration. There is also something to that. There have been a few people in high places who worried about its propriety, and thought the country would hardly miss it if they quietly eliminated it. They were quite wrong about that. The motto is here to stay; even the Supreme Court has signed off on it.

All of which raises a good question: how did four words that few people seem to notice wind up as the official and permanent motto of the United States of America? The answer, of course, is that like many other cultural icons, it resulted from the well-timed efforts of a few well-connected men. And it did not happen all at once.

IN 1861 SECRETARY OF THE TREASURY Salmon P. Chase received a letter from the Reverend M. R. Watkinson of Pennsylvania. In the letter Watkinson suggested that in this time of civil strife the Union risked being misinterpreted by posterity. "What if our Republic were now shattered beyond reconstruction? Would not the antiquaries of succeeding centuries rightly reason from our past that we were a heathen nation?" To head off this possibility, he made a suggestion that God be invoked on the country's coinage. "What I propose is . . . a ring inscribed with the words . . . 'God, liberty, law.'"

Chase took the suggestion seriously enough to send a directive to James Pollack, the director of the U.S. mint. "The trust of our people in God shall be declared on our national coins," he wrote. "You will cause a device to be prepared without unnecessary delay with a motto expressing in the fewest and tersest words possible this national recognition."

It may be argued that the result is solely due to the Reverend Watkinson. He is credited with the very first letter received by Chase suggesting the idea. But apparently Chase had felt some pressure from others, although the exact nature of this pressure is not known. Some historians claim that it came from Pollack, who later became governor of Pennsylvania. In any case, Pollack came back to Chase with a few suggestions for a new issue. One read "Our country, our God," the other "God, Our Trust."

Chase replied, "I approve your mottoes, only suggesting that on [one coin] the motto should begin with the words 'Our God,' so as to read: 'Our God and our country.' And on that with the shield, it should be changed so as to read: 'In God We Trust.'" The first coin mentioned by Chase was never minted. The one "with the shield" was the 1864 two-cent piece, which carried the new motto.

O'ER THE LAND OF THE FREE

As satisfying as this account may sound, it stops short of revealing Chase's inspiration for the exact wording. He did not invent the motto out of thin air. It had, in fact, been in the air for some time. It first appears, appropriately enough, in the words to the "Star-Spangled Banner"—only not in the one and only verse that Americans ever hear. Francis Scott Key, when he composed the song in 1814, wrote out four verses, and in the final stanza of the fourth verse he included the words, "and this be our motto, in God is our trust." Key may have taken this from the fifty-sixth Psalm, which contains the phrase, "In God I have put my trust." If he didn't invent the sentiment, he at least was the first to suggest it as a national motto.

Key's suggestion took a half-century to catch on, but exactly how it filtered down through the next few generations is unclear. Certainly his fourth verse was more well-known in nineteenth-century America than it is today. The national anthem circulated widely in sheet music form, and carried all four verses. Before there was a national pastime, the song had a greater chance of being sung in its entirety, but this does not seem to have inspired support for a new national motto. "In God We Trust" would not get much attention until the 1860s, when it became the battle-cry of a group known as the Huntington Bible Company.

The name is a bit deceptive. The Huntington Bible Company was not a publisher of holy books, but was instead the nickname of the Fifth Pennsylvania Volunteers, who distinguished themselves at the Battle of Antietam. They had adopted "In God We Trust" as their battle cry in 1862. Because of their heroics, it had become quite popular by the time that Salmon P. Chase suggested it for the new two-cent piece, and it remains the best guess for the source of the coin motto.

This coin, with the new motto prominently displayed within a banner above a seal on the obverse, was introduced in 1864, and remained in circulation until 1873. It turned out to be very popular (although Chase initially drew some criticism for including a reference to God). The motto was subsequently incorporated into designs for other denominations, so that by the turn of the century, it was a standard feature on many coins. Still, it was not mandated by law, did not appear on paper money, and it was not the national motto, Francis Scott Key notwithstanding.

The legality, not to mention the propriety, of a reference to God on coins has been a delicate point from the start. Chase successfully avoided the controversy, but in 1907, the president himself began to have misgivings about commingling God and Mammon. When faced with the task of designing new ten- and twenty-dollar gold pieces, Theodore Roosevelt and the sculptor Augustus Saint-Gaudens conspired to leave the motto off the coin. Sculptors like Saint-Gaudens did not relish the idea of accommodating mottoes within their coin designs. He viewed them as inartistic intrusions that are difficult to incorporate into a compact scheme that is already overburdened with symbolic content. The gold coins he did produce, typical of all of his work, are very elegant, and Roosevelt was extremely happy with them. But the public was not.

A heated debate over the exclusion of the motto ensued, and it played itself out not only in newspapers, but in Congress. There, in a lengthy floor debate, a Virginia representative delivered an exhaustive summary of the historical uses of religious mottoes and insignia on coins dating back to the time of the emperor Constantine. In response, dissenters tried to stress the importance of not trivializing the name of God. Enthusiastic applause greeted both sides of the argument, but the pro-motto faction clearly had the stronger hand, and parlayed their religious mandate to an overwhelming victory—one which restored the motto to all coins on which it had previously appeared (although not to paper money, on which it had not yet appeared).

In an interesting postscript, a letter written to the *New York Times* pointed out, incorrectly, that Oliver Cromwell had commissioned a coin which read THE COMMONWEALTH OF ENGLAND on one side, and IN GOD WE TRUST on the other, prompting the witticism that God and the Commonwealth appeared to be on opposite sides. The coin, minted in 1650, was the only English coin to abandon Latin in favor of English. It actually read "God with Us," but the joke still connects, as it does with American coins.

Evidently the fervor that follows such symbols waxes and wanes. The Buffalo Nickel, designed in 1913 by James Earle Fraser, never included the motto in its twenty-five years of minting. In fact the motto question did not resurface until the 1950s, and once again the issue was broached by a letter writer.

THE NATIONAL MOTTO

The use of "In God We Trust" on coins but not on paper money had long been largely a matter of cost. It was not a simple matter to redesign the plates for all denominations and to introduce them into use. But when a new form of religious enthusiasm swept the country in the 1950s, driven in large part by the threat of Communism, the time was ripe for another crusade on behalf of the unofficial currency motto.

In 1953, while attending services at a Christian Science church in Chicago, an Arkansas businessman noticed that the motto "In God We Trust" appeared on the coins in the collection plate, but not on the paper money. It occurred to him that the nation's currency, which circulates to all countries of the world, did not carry this important message.

The same thought may have occurred to other pious souls, but Matthew Rothert, Sr., knew some well-placed individuals who managed to get the suggestion worded into a bill that was passed by the 84th Congress. President Eisenhower signed it into law in July of 1955. From that day forward the treasury department was to gradually work the motto into all new currency plates.

The quest to place God squarely into the daily routine of all Americans started out as a small crusade, but because it was politically unwise to stand up to mainstream religious enthusiasm in the mid 1950s, a few crusaders managed to storm the gates with little opposition. In 1954 Dwight D. Eisenhower had been pressured into amending the Pledge of Allegiance. On Flag Day of that year, he had signed into law a bill that inserted the words "under God" after "one nation." And if Americans thought they had a national motto in *E pluribus unum*, they were wrong. Thanks to Rothert's initiative, "In God We Trust" took its place as the national motto through an act of Congress in 1955. Finally, in 1957, it earned a place on every form of American currency with a stroke of the president's pen.

The changeover could not be made at once. The Bureau of Engraving and Printing initiated a plan to work in a new series of bills over the next decade, as they went about replacing their old printing process with a new experimental one. The first bill on which they used the motto was the silver certificate of 1957. Thus in 1957 there were two silver certificates, and oddly enough, those with the motto—the ones printed on the new plates—were in the minority, and therefore are of greater value to collectors.

From there the story takes on a strange twist. The plan to change over all denominations of bills called for a gradual replacement of plates over a dozen years or so. But the phasing-in process was hastened by the very people who opposed government-sponsored forms of worship, and the national motto in particular. Because of yet another national scare, this time from within the country's own borders, the motto was rushed into production.

THE SEPARATION OF CHURCH AND STATE

At the end of a decade that saw God legislated into public life, Madalyn Murray O'Hare, the famed atheist, began a crusade to get Him back out again. In 1962, in a decision that took the nation by surprise, the Supreme Court upheld her challenge to school prayer, and this sent many people into a panic. Fearing that "In God We Trust" might be the next to fall (even before it was fully implemented), the director of the Bureau of Engraving and Printing took to the offensive. To avoid the expense of redesigning plates and reintroducing bills all over again, he ordered that the new printing process be rushed into use, and that the plates for every denomination be immediately redesigned to incorporate the new motto. Thus the loss of school prayer was quietly compensated for with the inclusion of God in another area of public life.

O'Hare did go after the motto in the 1970s, but by then it was too late—it had become firmly entrenched, and the lawsuits never went beyond the appeals court level. In each challenge, the courts defended the motto at the expense of its meaning. In the same type of legal reasoning that supported the Pledge of Allegiance in court decisions of the 1970s, "In God We Trust" was ruled to have no specific religious content, to promote no single religion, and therefore to be a neutral statement that had lost much of its meaning through wide exposure. In 1983, Supreme Court Justice William Brennan observed that slogans such as "In God We Trust" have "lost any true religious significance." But obviously they have some significance, or there would be no particularly compelling reason to retain them.

THE GALLING FACT for atheists and believers in a strictly enforced freedom to worship (or not worship) is that "In God We Trust" has become a national symbol much like the Declaration of Independence, the American flag, and the Statue of Liberty. To attack it is to risk being called un-American. It matters little that the U.S. Constitution laid down a clear separation of church and state, or that one of the country's most revered founding principles is religious toleration.

The courts may claim that the motto has lost any significance that is specifically religious, or deny that it promotes any particular religious belief, but by protecting it, they ultimately acknowledge that it is central to the patriotic fervor that zealously guards national symbols. The courts undoubtedly found in favor of the motto and the Pledge for this reason. Their exoneration of the words, purchased at the expense of declaring them to be meaningless, was considered by most Americans to be a bargain.

In the end, "In God We Trust" achieved the widest possible circulation and immediately legitimized a collective belief in the divine sanctioning of the country's founding. The God "we trust" is the one whose all-seeing eye looms over the unfinished pyramid on the back of the dollar bill. Tempting as it might be to write off the motto as so much bunk, it is here to stay, as Theodore Roosevelt and Madalyn Murray O'Hare discovered.

Yet the courts engaged in a curious trade-off because such mottoes do, in fact, lose their significance through universal exposure. Still, the idea that Reverend Watkinson passed on to Salmon P. Chase remains viable. The currency of the United States does signify to the rest of the world that this is not a heathen nation. At the same time it seems to be saying that it is a nation of Freemasons, which is another matter altogether.

LIBERTY HAS BEEN THE KEY TO
OUR PROGRESS IN THE PAST
AND IS THE KEY TO
OUR PROGRESS IN THE FUTURE
IF WE CAN PRESERVE LIBERTY
IN ALL ITS ESSENTIALS
THERE IS NO LIMIT TO THE FUTURE
OF THE AMERICAN PEOPLE

INSCRIPTION — ROBERT A. TAFT
MEMORIAL, WASHINGTON, D.C.

CHAPTER NINE

NEITHER SNOW NOR RAIN NOR
HEAT NOR GLOOM OF NIGHT

ARCHITECTURAL INSCRIPTIONS OF THE
AMERICAN RENAISSANCE

The most famous post office in America is also its most legendary—in a surprisingly literal way. Few Americans have any idea where it is or what it looks like; who built it, or why. Some might be surprised to learn that it actually exists. The average person, standing in front of it, would probably not even recognize it—unless they happen to look up at the building's entablature, which holds the key to the building's fame. It's the inscription. Sweeping across the building's entire width in magisterial Roman capitals, it reads:

NEITHER SNOW NOR RAIN NOR HEAT NOR GLOOM
OF NIGHT STAYS THESE COURIERS FROM THE SWIFT
COMPLETION OF THEIR APPOINTED ROUNDS

The U.S. Post Office Building in New York was dedicated in 1912 at the height of "academic classicism," the dominant style of American civic architecture during the early part of this century. It is one of the best examples of a building that dignifies its purpose by quoting not just the architecture of antiquity, but its literature as well—in this case the Greek historian Herodotus. No other building in the world has so successfully uses words to instill a sense of pride and purpose. It supplied the Postal Service with what they are quick to point out is their *unofficial* motto. Unofficial or not, postal workers take great pains to live up to it. So fitting is this inscription that it has probably saved the building from the wrecking ball.

There are many other examples of architectural inscriptions on public buildings in the United States. The practice is now in decline, but between 1890 and 1940 classicism dominated American civic architecture, and Roman-style inscriptions seemed to turn up everywhere. They appeared on banks, libraries, schools, museums, monuments, post offices, courthouses, and state capitols. Most of them simply state the name of the building and its date of dedication. Yet in many instances, the words convey uplifting and presumably timeless messages.

Because the average American does not often stop to "read" buildings, such inscriptions may seem at first to be an unusual source of words to live by. Yet most of these buildings still stand, and a significant few still manage to stand *for* something.

The New York Post Office is probably the best illustration of the power of words to elevate a visual symbol to mythical proportions. It conjures up images of ancient Greece and Rome, but in doing so it gives rise to some common misconceptions about the practice of inscribing words onto buildings. The Greeks and the Romans may have originated the practice, but nothing like the New York Post Office was ever seen in the ancient world. Nor is there anything like it among the neoclassical buildings of Europe. Although the classical revival in the United States seems to be entirely derivative—a movement inspired by European architecture—there is no precedent for such inscriptions as the Supreme Court's EQUAL JUSTICE UNDER LAW or the National Archive's ETERNAL VIGILANCE IS THE PRICE OF LIBERTY. To the casual observer these may look like faithful imitations of European classicism, but they differ in one important respect: they use inscribed text to inspire civic virtue, to promote republican ideals, and to teach good citizenship. In this way, they play an important role in creating a national identity through public art.

This might seem to be an overambitious claim, until one realizes just how unique the practice is, how deliberate it was, and just how important inscribed words were in defining what are still some of the country's most important symbols. Buildings and monuments from America's classical revival represent an attempt by a relatively small group of innovators to shape a national consciousness. In an ironic turn of events, the extent to which they succeeded is measured by the extent to which they are taken for granted today.

ARCHITECTURE AS ICON

The most conspicuous vestige of a culture is its architecture, especially its civic architecture. This is a lesson that most dictators and autocrats have understood, and it has been heeded by democratic governments as well: the state needs to be able to rally its citizens behind clear symbols which employ simple visual cues that trigger an emotional response. They can be vague, even ambiguous, but if they are easily identifiable, they can unite a group or inspire an entire nation. This description fits not only the greatest and most visible symbols of ancient cultures—the pyramids, the Coliseum, and the Parthenon—but such modern icons as the Eiffel Tower, the Sydney opera house, and Big Ben. It motivates the design of every state capitol building, city hall, and county courthouse.

The Statue of Liberty is one of the best examples of a structure that has merged with simple words to become a symbol for the entire nation. There are a handful of basic American ideas, and this is one of them: GIVE ME YOUR TIRED, YOUR POOR, YOUR HUDDLED MASSES YEARNING TO BREATHE FREE. Few Americans know the entire sonnet, or even the precise statement of its most famous line, but everyone knows what it stands for. It is hard to imagine an America without it.

Yet the symbol of Liberty is easy to take for granted. Like the New York Post Office, it is famous for being famous. Any visual treasury of the familiar would have to include it. But a truly comprehensive dictionary of received ideas would also have to note how its meaning has changed over time. It doesn't "read" the same as it once did. The French sculptor Frédéric-Auguste Bartholdi conceived of it as a celebration of American independence and democracy. The name he gave his work—"Liberty Enlightening the World"—conveys his original meaning, as does a little-known detail: the figure of Liberty has just cast off the chains of oppression, which lay broken beneath her sandaled feet. But this was quickly forgotten. Emma Lazarus's sonnet, "The New Colossus," written to help raise funds for the construction of the pedestal, soon overshadowed the sculptor's intentions. Although the words were not affixed to the base until two decades after the statue's unveiling, by then they were already stamped into the public imagination.

Once in place, the gift celebrating American independence quickly turned into a symbol of hope for all oppressed people, and a welcome sign hung out to greet new immigrants. How this symbol took hold so quickly has much to do with the age that produced it. When it was new, it had surprisingly little competition.

CIVIC VIRTUE AND NATIONAL IDENTITY

The only way to fully appreciate classical civic architecture in the United States is to try to imagine what the country was like without it, which only requires stepping back about a hundred years. Most Americans would have trouble recognizing the urban landscape as it would have appeared to their great-grandparents.

In 1880 the United States of America did not look particularly American. At that time the Statue of Liberty was still in the planning stages, as was the Brooklyn Bridge. Just over a century ago city skylines barely met the sky, especially in Chicago, which had been decimated by fire. The White House and the Capitol were completed (in their original conceptions), as was the Smithsonian castle, but the Washington Monument was still under construction. There were no great national memorials or art galleries, no metropolitan museums, grand public libraries, or elegant symphony halls. The most opulent structures the country could boast of were the mansions of Newport and Long Island, which hardly counted as national symbols. It was, simply put, an age in search of a style.

This shortage of national symbols was related to a shortage of national symbol makers. In 1880 there was no national academy of architecture, and no home-grown school of art that could compare with the academies of Europe. American artists and architects of distinction, of whom there were few, had learned their trade in the ateliers of Paris and Rome. Many of them stayed there to earn their living, but a few had come back to design homes for a new moneyed class.

When the country was swept up in a frenzy of erecting Civil War monuments, most small towns could not afford a trained artist, and instead went shopping for boilerplate memorials that were sold through catalogues. In 1880 mass-produced statues and surplus ordnance accounted for most of the country's public art, and these primitive monuments drew about as much attention as a howitzer in an American Legion parking lot does today.

Abraham Lincoln had doggedly pressed on with the completion of the

United States Capitol during the war years, knowing that such a symbol was crucial to national unity, and well worth the diversion of funds. But Reconstruction had left the nation bitterly divided, not just over the issue of slavery and the economic deprivation of the South, but about what it meant to be an American. As the centennial year approached, members of the social elite began to express alarm over the swiftness of social change that was overtaking the country. Immigration and industrialization were transforming the character of American communities, making cities into haphazardly built centers of population, and the rapidly growing economy produced a middle class with no true identity. Without a sense of community pride, leaders feared, there could be no civic responsibility. Without national unity, the Union appeared to be at risk.

This was the situation the country faced on its hundredth birthday, and although much has changed in a century, the plight of post-Civil War America reads surprisingly like a litany of today's problems. In late-twentieth-century America yet another highly divisive war has tested traditional values and overturned many cultural assumptions; memorials to that war have opened as many wounds as they have healed; immigration and technological progress are feared as threats to the status quo; and mass production is providing most of the icons to which Americans relate. The same fears have arisen: that the country has no clear vision, no common standards, and thus an uncertain future.

But there are significant differences as well. In 1880 the United States had not yet come of age as a nation. It had no clear image of itself because it had not defined a national culture. It was an agricultural nation on the verge of becoming an urban manufacturing nation, and it was looking to Europe to see how it should be done.

THE AMERICAN RENAISSANCE

The problem of national identity and civic ideals a century ago came down to a search for effective cultural reference points. It began not in the public sector, but in the private sector, when a new wealthy class of industrialists discovered philanthropy. After building and furnishing palatial estates and townhouses in a suitably cultivated style, they founded cultural institutions—libraries, symphony orchestras, and museums—and housed them in ornately decorated buildings, many of which are still in use. The artistic tastes that informed these ventures were supplied by European-trained artists and architects whose chosen point of reference was the Italian Renaissance. For educated Americans, the age of Leonardo, Michelangelo, and Raphael represented the high point of Western achievement. It was only natural for the Rockefellers, Carnegies, Morgans, and Vanderbilts, having made their fortunes, to cast themselves as modern-day Medicis, sponsoring public art in order to express notions of order, national identity, civic-mindedness, and cultural unity.

This reverence for Rome and Renaissance Florence was not simply aesthetic. Along with a new generation of architects and decorative artists, these philanthropists believed they possessed a vision of the country's future, and they wanted to shape that future. Classicism, in the eyes of this select group of highly influential men, represented not only the apogee of civilization, but it embodied certain timeless ideals, not the least of which was the ideal of republicanism. This enthusiasm for defining a national identity modeled on classical motifs set the stage for a fifty-year period of nation building, during which most of the recognizable symbols of the American republic, and in fact its predominant urban civic style, took shape. The response was not simply an imitation of ancient Greek, Roman, or Renaissance motifs, but a careful adaptation of the classical style that inspired the nickname of the American Renaissance.

Although this Renaissance embraced all of the arts—literature in the works of Nathaniel Hawthorne, Ralph Waldo Emerson, and Walt Whitman; art, in the paintings of Thomas Eakins, John Singer Sargent, and Winslow Homer—its claim was strongest in the field of architecture, architectural sculpture, and landscape design. And unlike their counterparts in painting and poetry, the men who built and decorated buildings understood very well the historical implications of their work. Speaking to the Chicago Art Institute in 1912, the American classical muralist Edwin Howland Blashfield summed up the sentiment of the age when he stated:

The decoration of public buildings is the most important question in the consideration of that art of the future, just as it has been in the past of any and every national art form from the time of the pyramid-builders down. Indeed, it passes beyond the question of art to the question of morals and patriotism and general culture . . . wherever the footprints of the spirit of civilization have rested most firmly some milestone of human progress has risen . . . to celebrate patriotism, inculcate morals, and to stand as the visible concrete symbol of higher endeavor.

In the late 1800s American architects seized upon the classical Renaissance style because they saw it as a vehicle for civic education and moral improvement. In particular, they used inscriptions to eliminate any doubt about the purpose of a building or monument, and thereby initiated a national style. As new libraries, museums, railway stations, courthouses, state capitols, schools, colleges, and post offices went up, so did messages of inspiration, exhortation, and civic pride. Like many popular movements that reached a golden age in the late 1800s—such as fraternalism, the temperance movement, and the establishment of professional societies with codified standards of practice—academic classicism in architecture gravitated toward visible and sometimes ornamental statements of principle and purpose. In this way, a select few American architects and city planners created a new type of monumental inscription which is not given much credit as innovative design even though it does constitute a distinctively American style.

FROZEN MUSIC

If architecture is "frozen music," as the German poet Goethe proposed, then it is natural to think of lettering on architecture as words set to music. The comparison is apt. Whoever thinks of such Roman antiquities as the Pantheon or Trajan's Column thinks also of inscribed text—words which impress the viewer with their monumentality and mystery. To the foreign visitor making the grand tour, the ruins of Rome and the architecture of Renaissance Florence speak volumes about the spectacle of empire and the height of cultural achievement. The effect is enhanced by the impenetrability of the texts. What do the inscriptions say? Like the words to an opera, they are difficult to make out, which only heightens their exoticism. And like most opera librettos, once translated and examined apart from their setting, they often turn out to be remarkably uninspiring.

This flies in the face of a modern stereotype of classical inscriptions, which consists of a Greek temple or Roman arch decorated with a dignified word or phrase such as LOYALTY, TRUTH, or COURAGE. But this stereotype is a purely romantic invention. There were no such inscriptions on Greek architecture, and the monuments of Rome, instead of conveying Platonic ideals or stoic maxims, were instead inscribed with highly abbreviated dedications or cryptic and often false boasts.

The Pantheon, for example, considered by many to be the finest example of the incorporation of lettering in ancient Roman architecture, has a prominent inscription that reads: M . AGRIPPA . L . F . COS . TERTIVM . FECIT. Deciphered, it says "Marcus Agrippa, three times consul, built this," which is neither obvious nor true. The Pantheon was not built by Agrippa, but by the emperor Hadrian, who disdained having his name inscribed on public buildings. Because a sanctuary built by Agrippa, Augustus Caesar's minister, previously occupied the site, Hadrian had Agrippa's original inscription copied onto his new building. Neither the words nor the building profit by the translation.

The column of Trajan, whose spiral frieze depicts the victorious Roman campaign against the Dacians in A.D. 117, also has a celebrated inscription. The six lines inscribed on its base are considered the model of perfection in the execution of monumental lettering, and the inspiration for the Roman letter form still used to inscribe text in stone. The words themselves, however, are less than inspiring. The first four lines provide the kind of information typical of Roman monuments: first acknowledging the commissioning of the column by the senate and the people of Rome, then listing Trajan's imperial titles. Scholars cannot quite agree on the meaning of the last two lines, which seem to declare how the site for the monument was prepared. At the very least, the Trajan inscription makes one thing abundantly clear: the text of Roman inscriptions is incidental to their symbolic impact. Their meaning and evocative power reside mostly in the shape and composition of the letters and not in the words themselves.

The Romans had been the first to use architectural lettering on a monumental scale, and they designed an alphabet for this very purpose. It is a surprising irony that the most commonly used modern uppercase text font, in fact the very font used in this book, was inspired by Roman stonecutters. It is an alphabet that was shaped by the requirements of the medium, just as the stonecutter's choice of text and the wildly haphazard system of abbreviations was dictated by the predetermined dimensions of the spaces to be inscribed. The effect of such letters is somewhat lessened on the printed page, but when cut into stone, they take on the durability and sometimes the impenetrability of the medium. As Nicolete Gray writes in *Lettering on Buildings*:

One forgets that the Roman alphabet was not to the Romans, as to us, a taken-for-granted inheritance. It was their creation, even if they owed much to the Greeks. That is why, surely, a simple procession of letters on a great monument such as the Pantheon . . . has such power. It derives, one feels, . . . from the letterer's immediate sense of common basis of some geometrical forms in architecture and letter, of the stability, firmness and objectivity of that basis, and of both as a symbol of Rome.

The omnipresent symbol of the Roman Republic consisted of the inscribed letters S.P.Q.R., which stand for SENATUS POPULUSQUE ROMANUS (The Senate and the People of Rome). This symbol was by far the most frequently inscribed legend during the republican era, and even survived the transition to the Empire, where it served as a kind of corporate logo for the Roman people. According to art historian Alan Bartram, such lettering may have been self-glorifying propaganda, "but it was done magnificently, and became of the utmost importance in the history of Western civilization."

The Greeks did not use inscriptions as an architectural motif, but they did try to make buildings speak their purpose. In *Pericles of Athens and the Birth of Democracy*, Donald Kagan explains how the great Greek ruler of the fifth century B.C. used architecture to convey his vision of civic virtue to the people. When he commissioned the Parthenon, Pericles instructed his master builder Phideas to celebrate democracy through visual means.

> The entire artistic endeavor . . . must be seen as part of a broad educational program meant to instill in the Athenians the love for their city that Pericles required and to instruct them in the virtues they needed. For Pericles knew that any successful society must be an educational institution. However great its commitment to individual freedom and diversity, it needs a code of civic virtue and a general devotion to the common enterprises without which it cannot flourish or survive. It must transmit its understanding of good and bad and a sense of pride, admiration, and love for its institutions.

In this passage, if the word "Athenians" is replaced with "Americans," and "city" with "nation," then Kagan's description of Pericles' building program sounds very much like the fusion of art and morals initiated by American civic leaders in the late 1800s. It may not have occurred to the Greek builders to communicate inspiring or sublime ideas through words. It is easy to forget that written text has a different symbolic weight today than it had prior to the time of the Romans. But American academic classicism should be seen as a revival of the aesthetic of Periclean Athens grafted onto the visual splendor of imperial Rome. Fittingly enough, this fusion would first appear in the city known as the Athens of America.

CHARLES MCKIM AND THE BOSTON PUBLIC LIBRARY

In 1887 the prestigious New York architectural firm of McKim, Mead & White received a commission from the city of Boston to design a public library. At that time the Library of Congress did not have its own building, so Boston's would be the largest library in the country.

Charles McKim, then forty years old, assumed the role of principal designer. A decade earlier he had worked for Henry Hobson Richardson, the country's most innovative architect, on Boston's Trinity Church, which faced the site of the proposed building. This presented the obvious possibility of using Richardson's signature Romanesque style, which was dark, heavy, and solid. But McKim had another idea. Instead of ponderousness, he opted for the uplifting style of the Italian Renaissance.

McKim studied engineering for a year at Harvard in the 1860s, but dropped out to pursue a career in architecture. As any hopeful architect did in those days, he promptly left for Europe. From his atelier in Paris, he learned the design principles of the Académie des Beaux-Arts, the French national academy of art, which provided him with technical skills, a reverence for historical precedents, and more importantly, with a design philosophy that stressed function as an elemental part of design. The "Beaux-Arts style" he studied is not so much a specific decorative style as a philosophy of laying out a building in a way that leads a spectator through a series of interior vistas. The idea is to create artistically satisfying interior spaces and exterior views. The decorative style of a Beaux-Arts building might be Greek, Egyptian, Roman, Romanesque, Renaissance, Gothic, Baroque, or even Richardsonian. That was up to the architect or the client.

Having made his pilgrimage to Italy, McKim found himself drawn to Renaissance classicism. He was especially impressed with Donato Bramante, who in the fifteenth century redesigned St. Peter's in Rome. An audacious architect, Bramante displayed an affinity for inscriptions. According to one story, he tried to persuade Pope Gregory II to allow him to include hieroglyphic inscriptions in the Vatican. The pope wisely and patiently talked him out of it. (Bramante, it should be noted, was McKim's nickname around the offices of McKim, Mead & White.)

In his design for the Boston library, McKim quoted two of his favorite

Renaissance buildings. One was the Cancellaria in Rome, which in McKim's day was attributed to Bramante. The other was the Bibliotheque Ste-Geneviève in Paris. Both of these buildings make generous use of inscriptions. The Paris library, designed by Henri Labrouste in 1843, takes the form of a rectangular box with its front facade broken up by a series of arched windows, below each of which sits a panel featuring the inscribed names of great authors, over eight hundred in all. The building effectively serves as an outdoor card catalogue. McKim chose the same motif for the Boston library.

From the Cancellaria he took the inner courtyard scheme and one exterior detail that had not been used on Labrouste's library. This was a long inscription that filled the entire width of the front architrave, which runs just under the roof line.

Free to All

A quick comparison of the Boston Public Library with its European predecessors reveals immediate points of comparison. It also reveals McKim's innovations. Little remarked upon by architectural historians is the architrave inscription.

McKim's preliminary rendering of the building in 1888 shows the vague outlines of a Latin inscription. But the final inscription is not in Latin. The text that fills the front architrave reads:

THE PUBLIC LIBRARY OF THE CITY OF BOSTON BUILT BY THE PEOPLE AND DEDICATED TO THE ADVANCEMENT OF LEARN-ING A.D. MDCCCLXXXVIII

This is a typical dedicatory inscription except for two things: it is dedicated to the American ideal of public education and, more importantly, it is in English. The inscription on the side architrave is more noteworthy. It reads:

THE COMMONWEALTH REQUIRES THE EDUCATION OF THE PEOPLE AS THE SAFEGUARD OF ORDER AND LIBERTY

This inscription has probably not had a close reading since it went onto the building, but it says a great deal about some fundamental assumptions that still apply. "Order and Liberty," two potentially conflicting concepts, are at the core of the American creed. They juxtapose the fundamental tenet of individualism with the necessity of the rule of law. In modern parlance, they echo the mantra of "rights and responsibilities." The only way to reconcile these, the very purpose of the library, is through an enlightened citizenry. That is, universal education is essential to a well-ordered society, and a society must be well-ordered if it is going to sustain and protect individual liberty. Furthermore, access to education should be FREE TO ALL, as the inscription over the library's front entrance proclaims.

Observers of American civic architecture see nothing noteworthy in these inscriptions. Many think them trite. Perhaps the extent to which inscriptions with a message are taken for granted attests to their overuse. What is often overlooked, however, is that neither the Greeks, the Romans, the Italian Renaissance architects, the British neoclassicists, German Romantics, or the French Beaux-Arts designers consistently used inscriptions to clearly state a principle or higher purpose in a language and format that could be understood by the people. And none of these cultures advertised democratic principles or classical virtues through inscribed text. This was an American innovation.*

Prior to the classical revival, inscriptions had been used to label, describe, dedicate, identify, and impress, to praise God, and even to boast. Yet they were not used to convey principles other than allegorically. Charles McKim may not have been the first to do this, but his Boston Public Library is considered a landmark for its innovative melding of cultural references. It was the first public building in America to display the ornate Italian Renaissance style that had previously been reserved for Newport mansions and private clubs. In bringing this aesthetic to the people, McKim decided to include an unambiguous statement of the building's democratic purpose as part of its symbolic artistic program. He decided to have the message inscribed where no one could miss it.

The Boston Public Library was also the first public building in America to follow a thematic program directed by the architects, who employed the talents of some of the country's finest artists. It features murals by John

*There is one possible exception worth noting. In his *Description of Greece*, Pausanias writes, "In the foretemple at Delphi there are inscribed useful maxims for the conduct of life. They were inscribed by those whom the Greeks call the Sages. . . . These men came to Delphi and dedicated to Apollo the famous maxims 'Know thyself' and 'Nothing in excess.'" Pausanias probably took the story from Plato's *Protagoras*. Other authors, including Diodorus, Pliny, and Plutarch, corroborate its substance, but differ on many of the details, including the location of the inscriptions. This seems to be an isolated instance which did more to establish the reputation of the Sages (whose maxims are given on p. 156 in Chapter Seven) than to inspire the use of architectural inscriptions elsewhere.

Singer Sargent, Edward A. Abbey, and Pierre Puvis de Chavannes; and sculpture by Augustus Saint-Gaudens, Louis Saint-Gaudens, Frederick MacMonnies, Bela Pratt, and Daniel Chester French. It was built not only to house books and provide a place to learn, but to expose the citizens of Boston to art and culture. Like the Parthenon, it was intended to inspire and instruct. Its entire philosophy and execution recalled the greatness of the age of Pericles, and helped to secure Boston's reputation as the Athens of America.

While McKim deserves much of the credit for having initiated a trend, the Boston Public Library was not a sufficiently important building to launch a national style. It did set a standard for public libraries that would be built within the next decade, but for McKim it was a stepping stone. While the decoration of the library was being carried out, he was called to Chicago to participate in the event that would give him a much more commanding platform from which to preach his vision of civic America.

THE WHITE CITY

In 1892 Chicago made ready to host an exposition celebrating the four-hundredth anniversary of Columbus's discovery of the New World. Recently, what would have been the hundredth anniversary of this exposition naturally coincided with the five-hundredth anniversary of Columbus's landing, an event which in 1992 was no longer regarded as a cause for celebration. Consequently, the centennial of the great World's Columbian Exposition went largely ignored. This was too bad, because the 1893 exposition was not about Columbus as much as the emergence of a powerful nation. It was a watershed event in the nation's cultural history, and its effects are still felt. Among other things, it introduced Cracker Jack, the Pledge of Allegiance, the Ferris Wheel, and Dvořák's *From the New World* symphony to Americans. It also introduced America to the rest of the world. Like the London Exposition of 1851 and the Paris Exposition of 1889, the Chicago fair displayed the world in microcosm. Not merely a victorian Epcot Center, it showcased America's greatest technological, intellectual, and cultural achievements. In particular, it featured the largest collection of American art ever assembled.

The great expositions left behind many impressions and a few monuments: London briefly enjoyed its Crystal Palace; Paris decided to keep Gustave Eiffel's tower. The most lasting image of the Chicago Exposition is its great, white, Beaux-Arts Court of Honor—a grand courtyard and lagoon surrounded by a series of highly ornamented pavilions designed by some of the country's leading architects.

The master planner for the exposition was the Chicago architect Daniel Burnham, a pioneer in the Chicago school of skyscraper design. The consortium of architects he assembled drew heavily on the established New York firms, a group that naturally included Charles McKim. Although American designers were at that time establishing a new style of steel highrise construction, the consortium agreed, with McKim's urging, to adopt a Renaissance style for the central core of exposition buildings. This choice was crucial, because it would provide a forum (literally) for an innovative use of architectural inscriptions that would carry over into the decades to follow.

Burnham, who is associated with the famous advice "Make no little plans," lived up to his motto. The Renaissance-inspired architecture of the exposition housed a display of industrial and cultural achievement on a scale never seen before. The millions who attended came away with vivid memories of splendor and spectacle. The fair was a sensation.

Built with a stiff plaster called staff, the Court buildings went up very quickly over their steel superstructures. A battalion of sculptors, painters, and assistants, fresh from their academic training in Europe, collaborated on an ambitious program of freestanding sculpture, decoration, and murals. For these emerging artists, the Chicago fair provided an opportunity to design and execute a large amount of work in a very short period of time. Architects and artists who might otherwise have spent years trying to get commissions that would allow them to advance their craft worked side by side to realize projects that drew on the full range of their Beaux-Arts training. What they produced in one year in plaster would have required a decade or two to build in stone, bronze, and marble. When they were done, the ensemble looked like a fantastical wedding cake, and inspired the nickname of the White City.

PRESIDENT ELIOT OF HARVARD

Scarcely mentioned in accounts of the building of the great White City is the contribution of Dr. Charles W. Eliot, the president of Harvard University. Like very few men of his generation, Eliot's accomplishments still resonate in American life while drawing little attention to his name, which is how he would have wanted it. A public man in the most noble sense of the term, he had a vision not just for Harvard, but for American society as a whole, and he communicated this vision partly by example, and partly through his writings. Ironically, what would prove to be his most enduring legacy started out as nothing more than an interesting diversion, albeit one he took very seriously.

Eliot began his career at Harvard as a professor of mathematics and chemistry in 1858. Offered the presidency in 1869 at the age of thirty-five, he became the youngest president Harvard has ever had, and in his forty years at the helm he turned the university into the renowned institution it is today. It was Eliot who built Harvard's graduate schools into world-class institutions. He also scrapped the undergraduate curriculum and replaced it with the elective system, which became a standard throughout the country. In all of his activities, both in academia and on the national stage, he commanded the kind of respect that encouraged others to seek his advice and ask his opinion.

Part of Eliot's duties as a college president involved writing introductory remarks for invited speakers and brief words of praise for honorary degree recipients. These compositions, much like ancient Greek epigrams, constitute a demanding and precise literary genre, and Eliot excelled at it. He possessed a talent for writing simple yet effective words, and because of this reputation he was asked in 1877 to provide an appropriate inscription for a Civil War memorial being built on the Boston Common. So successful was this venture that other requests began to pour in, and Eliot found yet another educational outlet available to him.

From the start, he accepted no fee for his efforts, but he did insist that if his advice was sought, then his recommendations should be carried out to the letter. Priding himself on his ability to meet the exacting requirements of inscription writing, he carefully measured his texts, both figuratively and literally. Never exaggerating for effect, he weighed each word against the facts and the demands of the occasion. Constrained by the physical limitations of the spaces provided by architects and sculptors, he insisted that the words should be meaningful to the average viewer. "The lettering ought to be plain," he wrote, "and the size of the letters should be whatever will make them easily legible from the ordinary or most probable standpoint of the reader." And obviously, the words should be in English.

Prior to Chicago, Eliot had called upon McKim for advice relating to architectural matters at Harvard. (McKim designed many of the gates of

Harvard Yard, as well as several academic buildings.) And McKim had sought out Eliot for advice on inscriptions and classical motifs. (It was Eliot, for example, who anonymously composed the architrave inscriptions for the Boston Public Library.)

For the Chicago Exposition, Daniel Burnham asked Eliot to provide a series of inscriptions for the Watergate, a triumphal arch which anchored one axis of the central Court of Honor. The result was a monument to a wilderness transformed into a democratic and free society. Rather than celebrating Columbus, Eliot's Watergate cited the pioneers who explored the "lakes, rivers, mountains, valleys and plains of this new world," as well as those who pioneered "civil and religious liberty." It was remarkably inclusive. It saluted explorers "of many races, tongues, creeds, and aims, but all heroes of discovery." It acknowledged the "brave women who in solitudes, amid strange dangers and heavy toil, reared families and made homes." It included a passage from the Gettysburg Address, and also praised freedom, culture, and toleration in religion. One panel lauded civil liberty as "the means of building up personal and national character."

The Watergate, like all of the fair's buildings, was a temporary structure—one of the few examples of Eliot's handiwork that no longer stands. But it was only a beginning. For Eliot, it led to more collaborations with architects (notably with Burnham and McKim), which would secure his reputation as the preeminent inscription writer of the American Renaissance.

Anyone who stops to admire a classical civic building in an American city, especially a building that contains inspirational inscriptions, is contemplating the legacy of Charles McKim, Daniel Burnham, and Charles Eliot, three men who nurtured an inspired vision of the nation's greatness. Because they were motivated by civic ideals instead of self-promotion, their contribution is easily overlooked (as are the inscriptions themselves). But their influence on succeeding generations cannot be denied, as a glance at the works produced by their disciples will attest.

LESIONS SIGNIFICANT OF DEMENTIA

Architectural historians generally decry the lasting significance of the Chicago Exposition, often by invoking Louis Sullivan's famous dismissal of the event. "The damage wrought by the World's Fair," Sullivan wrote, "will last for half a century from its date, if not longer. It has penetrated deep into the constitution of the American mind, effecting there lesions significant of dementia." Sullivan, who was Frank Lloyd Wright's mentor, was also one of the most talented architects working in Chicago. His Transportation Building was a critical success, and stood apart from the wedding cake compositions of his colleagues. (It did feature an inscription chosen by Charles Eliot.) Yet Sullivan's opinion should be taken with a grain of salt; it was not offered until thirty years after the fair, at which point the overuse of the classical style had become a firmly established fact of American civic architecture.

While the Chicago school of skyscraper design became the dominant commercial style in the twentieth century, the Chicago Exposition's classicism set the example for most of the civic architecture that followed. After the success of the fair, Beaux-Arts principles dictated the design of state capitols, office buildings, and courthouses, extending well into the 1930s through such monumental projects as the Federal Triangle complex in Washington, D.C., and Rockefeller Center in New York City. This was partly due to the forceful attitude of certain leading architects, but mostly due to the conservative impulses of their influential clients. The team of architects that produced the White City fanned out across the country, leaving behind innumerable classical edifices because that was what government officials and private benefactors wanted. To what extent these architects created this taste is debatable. At the very least, they recognized what Sullivan referred to as its "commercial possibilities."

THE CITY BEAUTIFUL

The Chicago World's Fair not only developed the talents of a new generation of American architects and sculptors, but served as a launching pad for their careers. McKim, Mead & White became the largest and most prominent architectural firm in the country, at one time employing over a hundred draftsmen. Many of them left to establish firms of their own, and to perpetuate Charles McKim's vision of classicism and his use of inscriptions. Some of the more noteworthy alumni are Henry Bacon (the Lincoln Memorial), Cass Gilbert (the Supreme Court Building), John Carrère and Thomas Hastings (the New York Public Library and the Arlington Memorial Amphitheater), Harold van Buren Magonigle (Kansas City's Liberty Memorial), and Wallace K. Harrison (Rockefeller Center and the United Nations Headquarters). In their heyday, McKim, Mead & White themselves designed such landmarks as New York's late and lamented Pennsylvania Station (designed 1902–5, demolished 1962), the original Madison Square Garden (1887), Boston's Symphony Hall (1900), the Army War College (1904), and the Rhode Island State Capitol (1903).

After the Chicago Exposition, Daniel Burnham continued his career as a civic planner and architect, promoting a vision of urban design that came to be known as the City Beautiful movement. In 1901 he brought McKim and the landscape designer Frederick Law Olmstead, Jr., onto his team to revise Pierre Charles L'Enfant's original master plan for Washington, D.C. They proposed that all buildings on the Mall should be strictly neoclassical, to the extent of relocating James Renwick's gothic Smithsonian castle. Their plan included a railway terminal and a new post office, which Burnham eventually designed, and for which Eliot would select the inscriptions.

Later, Burnham would produce similar grand schemes for Chicago, Cleveland, and San Francisco. These are characterized by wide tree-lined boulevards anchored by classical structures housing museums and libraries, and accented with fountains, monumental sculpture, landscaped gardens, and of course, inscriptions. This model was widely imitated, and although most of these grand schemes were never fully realized, they still define what for most visitors is the distinctive splendor of many older American cities.

CLASSICAL WASHINGTON

After 1893 Charles Eliot kept busy with his reforms at Harvard and with his sideline of inscription writing. At the special request of McKim, he composed words for the Robert Gould Shaw Memorial in Boston, and he was also asked to select texts to accompany allegorial statues in the rotunda of the new Library of Congress in Washington. Of all of the highly artistic collaborations that grew out of the Chicago Exposition, this building was the most spectacular. To execute its decorative program the builders employed over forty of the greatest sculptors and muralists of the day. Its aesthetic is quite clear—the thematic decor of the reading room of the nation's library pays homage to man's highest intellectual achievements as personified by the great thinkers of the Western tradition. It is an inspirational Pantheon.

In the one known instance of an Eliot text undergoing editorial changes, the verses he submitted for Burnham's Washington, D.C., Post

Office had to pass the scrutiny of the president of the United States. Eliot claimed that the words came to him in a sudden revelation while sailing in Maine, and he quickly wrote them down.

> *Carrier of news and knowledge*
> *Instrument of trade and industry*
> *Promoter of mutual acquaintance*
> *Of peace and of goodwill*
> *Among men and nations*
>
> *Messenger of sympathy and love*
> *Servant of parted friends*
> *Consoler of the lonely*
> *Bond of the scattered family*
> *Enlarger of the common life*

When the proposed inscription came across the desk of Woodrow Wilson, the President changed a few lines without knowing whose text he was editing. (The revised text appears in Part II.) In this instance Eliot, who sometimes labored over a single inscription for years and fought tenaciously for his texts, graciously yielded.

THE FIVE-FOOT SHELF

Upon his retirement from Harvard in 1909, Charles Eliot embarked on a project that would bring him his greatest fame. It did not involve inscriptions, but did draw upon the same philosophy of public education and civic idealism that had motivated his selection of quotations for the Library of Congress and other bulidings.

Near the end of his tenure as a college president, Eliot made an offhand remark that a man could obtain a liberal education by reading just fifteen minutes each day from a collection of books that would fit on a standard bookshelf. An enterprising publisher took him at his word and asked him to make such a selection. Thus was born the Harvard Classics—Dr. Eliot's celebrated "five-foot shelf."

Eliot's canon of philosophy and literature proposes that there is a core of knowledge, rooted in the Western tradition, that expresses universal truths, and forms the proper basis of an enlightened education. This is, not coincidentally, the same idea that informs the thematic program of the Boston Public Library, the Library of Congress, and other buildings featuring quotations, either biblical or classical. It is an idea that has come under attack in the last two decades, although Eliot, his canon, and his inscriptions have passed through the multicultural wars relatively unscathed, possibly because they have gone largely unnoticed, but probably because these projects were so well executed.

On close examination, Charles Eliot, contrary to appearances, was not simply a Protestant propagandist. His five-foot shelf included Chinese philosophers and sacred books of the Near East. His gaze came to rest on whatever was useful, whatever the source. As historian Bernard Knox has taken great pains to show, classicism is a remarkably diverse and (one hesitates to say) multicultural phenomenon, that is nothing if not liberal in its celebration of reason, rights, and the pursuit of happiness. It is true that some twentieth-century dictators—notably Hitler and Mussolini—favored classicism for state architecture, and each made use of inscriptions. But to Eliot, McKim, Burnham, and others, classicism stood for enlightenment, freedom, republicanism, and the cultural achievements of the Italian Renaissance masters they so admired.

DR. HARTLEY BURR ALEXANDER OF NEBRASKA

Charles W. Eliot was not the only composer of inscriptions, but he was the father of the genre. Like any good father, he was strong-willed yet broadminded. If he privately harbored prejudices, he hid them publicly. His aim was to educate and to inspire, and if for him inscription writing was not a vocation, it was certainly a calling—one that required dedication and adherence to a set of guidelines.

His most noteworthy successor in this specialty was also an academic—a professor of philosophy from the University of Nebraska who developed the art of inscription writing to an even greater involvement with the themes and aims of monumental civic architecture.

Hartley Burr Alexander began his academic career teaching philosophy at the University of Nebraska in 1908. In his nineteen years there he developed a reputation as a classicist, a poet, and an expert on native American cultures. In 1920, he would get a chance to bring all of these talents to bear on a unique project.

Not far from the Nebraska campus, a new state capitol building—a grand Beaux-Arts palace—began to take shape under the direction of ar-

chitect Bertram Grosvenor Goodhue. It featured a four-hundred-foot
tower sitting upon a four-hundred-foot wide base. Although classical, it
hardly resembled any of its heavily ornamented Beaux-Arts predecessors.
It relied on some highly stylized architectural sculpture that suggested a
cross between pure classicism and art deco. The sculptor on the project,
and the originator of this hybrid style, was Lee Lawrie, who had inherited
the mantle of dean of American sculptors from Daniel Chester French (for
whom he had worked as an assistant at the World's Columbian Exposition).

In his grand scheme Goodhue left space for many inscriptions in order
to complement a full program of sculpture and murals, but he was having
trouble finding the right words or even suitable themes for the artwork.
Sympathizing with his plight, the Capitol Commission decided to look for
an expert of the caliber of Charles Eliot—someone who understood the
classical heritage, but who also understood American history, including
the history of the native peoples of Nebraska. The logical choice was Dr.
Alexander.

Where Eliot had been called in to put the icing on the cake, Alexander
presided over the mixing of the ingredients. For the Nebraska Capitol, he
chose the subjects of murals, freestanding sculptures, and decorative
friezes, suggested motifs and provided accompanying text. The result is
another of the country's great artistic collaborations—a grand vision of
American history and culture. Like Eliot before him, Alexander pored over
scriptural and classical texts searching for brief passages that would complement the themes of the artwork. His texts emphasize justice, law and
order, and reverence for the Constitution. The most prominent inscription, placed above the arch over the front portal, states:

WISDOM JUSTICE POWER MERCY
CONSTANT GUARDIANS OF THE LAW

Its complement, on the opposite side of the building, reads:

POLITICAL SOCIETY EXISTS FOR THE SAKE OF NOBLE LIVING

Alexander would team up with Goodhue and Lawrie again, notably on the
Los Angeles Public Library, for which he wrote a number of fine inscriptions, including

IN THE WORLD OF
AFFAIRS WE LIVE IN OUR
OWN AGE : IN BOOKS
WE LIVE IN ALL AGES

Lawrie and Alexander also worked together on New York's Rockefeller Center. Alexander submitted a thematic design for the Center's artwork, then withdrew early in the project, yet many of his ideas were executed. In particular, the striking entrance to the RCA Building, which houses NBC studios, has become a familiar icon to viewers of late night television. Lawrie's polychrome frieze, forbiddingly titled "Genius, Which Interprets to the Human Race the Laws and Cycles of the Cosmic Forces of the Universe, Making the Cycles of Light and Sound," consciously quotes a drawing by William Blake, one that Alexander had suggested as an appropriate image. John D. Rockefeller, Jr., involved himself in the choice of inscription. After rejecting over fifty suggestions, he gave the nod to a verse adapted from Isaiah:

WISDOM AND KNOWLEDGE
SHALL BE THE STABILITY OF THY TIMES

These inscriptions may not come off quite as well as the words on the New York Post Office or the Supreme Court Building, but few inscriptions do. None of Eliot's and Alexander's inscriptions are particularly well-known. They serve well enough the exacting demands of time and place required by local monuments and civic structures, but they are far less noteworthy as texts than as reminders of very general ideals. Both men contributed words that people expect to see when they visit Washington or any of the state capitals—words of lofty purpose and appropriate gravity, although some can veer towards the bizarre. For McKim's Rhode Island State Capitol (1903), Eliot came up with this:

TO HOLD FORTH A LIVELY EXPERIMENT
THAT A MOST FLOURISHING CIVIL STATE MAY STAND
AND BEST BE MAINTAINED WITH FULL LIBERTY
IN RELIGIOUS CONCERNMENTS

THE FEDERAL TRIANGLE

An inscription does not have to produce a celebrated icon to be considered successful. Hartley Burr Alexander and Charles W. Eliot viewed their task as collaborative—a creative process shared with sculptors and muralists—and also as somewhat anonymous. They attempted to convey ideals through words that complemented the activities that would take place within a building, mindful of the purpose of the building itself within the urban scheme. Some structures afforded bigger stages than others. Two of the biggest—Rockefeller Center and Washington's Federal Triangle—were Alexander's last major projects.

The Federal Triangle was conceived as an extension of Daniel Burnham's 1901 master plan for Washington, and took its inspiration from the Chicago Exposition. Like the Court of Honor, it features a grouping of white buildings of nearly uniform cornice height, showcasing a wide variety of artistic talent within a rather narrowly conceived classical plan. It was begun in 1922 as a solution to the vexing problem of permanently housing some of the larger federal agencies—notably the Departments of Justice and Commerce, the Internal Revenue Service, and the Federal Trade Commission.

Alexander served as thematic consultant for the Justice Department Building, and submitted inscriptions and suggestions for sculptural subjects. In one of his letters to the project's sculptor, Carl Jennewein, he explains his motivation for departing from the traditional use of Latin, and in so doing explains how American classicism democratized the Roman style. "Latin is the best inscription language because of terseness and the absence of articles and minor connectives," he wrote, "but after all this is America and our own language ought to carry the main meanings. . . . Where the passage is more than a mere motto, I believe that English should be employed."

It rarely occurred to Europeans to use the people's language on buildings. Latin, after all, was once the universal language of the educated class. American architects, however, did not assume the existence of a cultivated audience, and correctly made the assumption that if the people can't understand it, it shouldn't be up there.

Alexander's contributions to the Justice Department Building, as well as the inscriptions on the nearby National Archives Building, come off very well. The architects and sculptors working on the Archives labored over motifs and texts, and produced such inscriptions as STUDY THE PAST and ETERNAL VIGILANCE IS THE PRICE OF LIBERTY to accompany allegorial sculptures. The Archives Building still serves as an inspirational reminder of the importance of documenting the nation's past. But elsewhere in the Federal Triangle, inscriptions are grossly overused, carelessly written, and poorly placed. Many of the blocks of inscribed text, especially those on the Commerce Department, are much too long and difficult to read. They betray an infatuation with a motif that can be overdone even when presented in small doses.

Perhaps in reaction to this particular building, the editors of the *Federal Architect* of October 1933 complained that inscriptions had sunk to the level of superfluous decoration, wherein the choice of text is too often "a painful insult to the intelligence of the public reading it." While acknowledging the New York Post Office as "the very zenith of achievement in inscriptions," they lament the fact that most inscriptions make no appeal to the mind or the emotions. "When an inscription becomes an absolute necessity," they conclude, "we believe there should be some fund set aside for payment to a competent authority to select or compose it. But, generally, under the head of 'Advice to architects about to call for an inscription,' we believe the proper reply is 'Don't.'"

BY THE MID-1930S even conservative federal architects recognized the limitations of the classical style. In a span of forty years Washington had become a bastion of tastes that many critics had deemed stale as early as the Chicago Exposition. Louis Sullivan's backward-looking comment was now proclaimed to be prophetic. The fashion inspired by the great Chicago World's Fair had in fact lasted almost half a century. It had inaugurated an era of American identification with the Roman Republic and the Italian Renaissance, and in particular with the use of architectural inscriptions executed in Roman capitals. And people were sick of it.

But such harsh views are being reconsidered. Some critics now contend that the finest examples of academic classicism are those found in the United States. McKim especially is credited with originating an American classical style that rivaled the Europeans, and with designing buildings that rank with any in Europe. His Pennsylvania Station, which was demolished in 1962, is now regarded as a tragic loss to New York City. In fact its destruction was a catalyst in the formation of the historic preservation movement. There are now plans (recently stalled in Congress) to renovate

McKim, Mead & White's Post Office Building, which stands adjacent to the site, into a new Pennsylvania Station. It is not likely to happen, but if it did the inscription would stand to retain some of its relevance, if not gain new meaning.

EQUAL JUSTICE UNDER LAW

Charles Eliot and Hartley Burr Alexander were among the few competent authorities of their day, but there are a few others worth mentioning. Each of them can claim credit for making a single lasting contribution to the landscape of national icons, and their words have outlived their names. This comes with the territory. Unlike the architect or sculptor, the inscription writer receives little credit for his work.

ROYAL CORTISSOZ STARTED his career as an office boy for McKim, Mead & White in 1885. From that humble beginning he rose to become the art critic for the *New York Herald Tribune*, a position he held for more than fifty years. In that time he earned a reputation for elegant and unpretentious writing, and like Eliot was asked to compose words for a number of memorials. When his friend Henry Bacon, the architect of the Lincoln Memorial, began to work up his decorative scheme for the monument, he turned to Cortissoz for an inscription that would complement Lincoln's own words.

The task seemed daunting. The placement of the text, right over Daniel Chester French's great seated statue, magnified the challenge. Cortissoz understood Bacon's theme, which deified Lincoln by placing him in a Greek temple, and he responded by providing these words, which make the symbolism even clearer:

> IN THIS TEMPLE
> AS IN THE HEARTS OF THE PEOPLE
> FOR WHOM HE SAVED THE UNION
> THE MEMORY OF ABRAHAM LINCOLN
> IS ENSHRINED FOREVER

Like Eliot before him, Cortissoz suffered the editorial meddling of a president who thought he could do better. Warren G. Harding thought he could improve the inscription by changing the third line to read "Of the

Union which he saved." The flurry of correspondence this unleashed provides a disquisition on the art of inscription writing and a defense of the original text, to which Harding eventually relented. Bacon argued for the flow of the original—its progression of last words: *temple, people, Union, Lincoln, forever.* Cortissoz pointed out that Lincoln "saved the Union for the people. . . . It is his phrase that refers to government of the people, by the people, for the people." The inscription was carved as written, and Cortissoz correctly predicted that it would "become utterly anonymous. But long after I am dust it will still be there."

THE MOST SUCCESSFUL INSCRIPTIONS often come about through a painstaking process of research, inspiration, and consultation. At the opposite end of the Mall from the Lincoln Memorial, the U.S. Supreme Court Building portico (1935) bears an inscription which also entailed a struggle, one which was arbitrated by Chief Justice Charles Evans Hughes.

The original proposal, following Jefferson, read EQUAL AND EXACT JUSTICE. Cass Gilbert, the building's architect and another McKim, Mead & White alumnus, suggested EQUAL JUSTICE UNDER LAW. The design commission demurred until Hughes stepped in and announced that Gilbert's phrase had occurred in an early Supreme Court decision, and it was duly inscribed. The inscription on the opposite portico, which gets little attention, reads JUSTICE THE GUARDIAN OF LIBERTY.

AS FOR NEW YORK'S FAMOUS Post Office, due credit for the frieze inscription should go to its author, William Kendall, who was Charles McKim's protégé and the principal designer of the project. The idea occurred to him while he was reading Herodotus. Coming upon a passage that refers to Persian couriers, Kendall thought it could be made to fit the Postal Service, but he was dissatisfied with all of the translations he could find. He went so far as to consult his former classics professor at Harvard, who suggested: "Nor snow, nor rain, day's heat, nor gloom hinders their speedily going on their appointed rounds."

In the end, Kendall wrote out his own translation. By some accounts, he was more thrilled with the inscription than with the design of the building itself. To his credit, he did not try to top it, or even imitate it. He realized that he had created something unique.

LOOK ON MY WORKS, YE MIGHTY

The extensive use of inscriptions on early twentieth-century American civic architecture was, in retrospect, a natural choice. It struck a chord with a public that read something more into it than a simple homage to ancient Rome. Architectural lettering such as that found on the Supreme Court Building or the Lincoln Memorial plays upon certain Romantic conceits about antiquity that first appear in the works of European poets and painters of the early 1800s. In fact a romanticized classicism has played a role in shaping national symbols since the time of the Founding Fathers. Inscriptions took time to emerge, but the stage was set for them by some very specific associations in art and literature.

In 1817 Percy Bysshe Shelley wrote a poem entitled "Ozymandias." Although not considered his masterpiece, it is undoubtedly his most well-known poem: it quickly claimed a spot in the canon of anthologized literature that American high school students at one time had to memorize. The poem tells the brief tale of a visitor to an "antique land," who comes upon the ruins of a once-great civilization. There he finds a statue consisting of two "trunkless legs," and nearby a "shattered visage." On the pedestal he discovers an inscription that reads: "My name is Ozymandias, king of kings. Look on my works, ye mighty, and despair."

Ozymandias is the Greek name for the Egyptian pharaoh Rameses II, whose funerary tomb does contain the ruins of a colossal statue, but does not have any such inscription. It never existed, although it might as well have. (The legend was invented by Greek epigrammists and perpetuated by overenthusiastic historians.) There is no question that the discovery of the ruins of the great civilizations of Assyria, Egypt, Greece, and Rome inspired a wave of romanticized and imitative design in Europe, and eventually in the United States. The Greek revival began in the late 1700s, and was followed by Gothic and Egyptian revivals. In Germany, architect Karl Friedrich Schinkel's neoclassicism complemented the efforts of the German Romantic composers. In France, Claude Ledoux, who designed a series of classical gates for Paris, and Henri Labrouste, who designed the national library, influenced the tastes of the first Americans to study architecture in Europe.

In the United States, the spirit of Romanticism and the attraction of the classical style took longer to develop. It first appears in painting, notably in the works of Thomas Cole, whose imaginary landscapes had a cultural impact in his day comparable to the films of George Lucas and Steven Spielberg today. In a series of five sequential paintings entitled *The Course of Civilization* (1834), Cole attempted to illustrate the cyclical and unavoidable fate of all great empires. In the first canvas, which sketches the very beginnings of society, he depicts a sheltered harbor verging on a savage wilderness. In the next canvas, the same harbor has become an arcadian setting for the first nonnative settlers. At the height of civilization, Cole depicts a vibrant, congested city draped in opulence—a classical Camelot bursting with Greco–Roman architecture. But the culture is doomed. In the fourth canvas, war has broken out, and the city burns while soldiers commit atrocities. In the last canvas, the desolation of centuries-old ruins stand silent watch over the harbor. Nature has reclaimed the land, and there is not a soul in sight—only the barely recognizable remnants of the glory that once was.

This idealized vision of imperial splendor and achievement was a common theme of the Romantic era, and recurs in modern apocalyptic literature. It was also a prophetic vision. Before the century's end, a similar vision took shape at the Chicago World's Fair in the form of the elaborate Court of Honor. Ironically, not long after the fair closed, the abandoned fairgrounds were consumed by fire, as though acting out Cole's imagined drama. In what must have been a scene of breathtaking spectacle, the buildings of the White City were allowed to burn to the ground.

The one thing missing from Cole's tableau, and perhaps the one element whose absence led to his fictional civilization's demise, was the implicit lack of ideals and principles—the lack of a vision. Daniel Burnham supplied part of that vision in Chicago by asking Charles Eliot to compose and select words that would give meaning to what his cohorts had built. In this way Chicago was, in miniature, a model for the future civic landscape of America—a vision of civilization that was perhaps also doomed, if the debris of Charles McKim's Pennsylvania Station were to serve as the final frame. But subsequent events are more encouraging.

The General Services Administration has recently embarked upon an eight billion dollar building and renovation project covering 150 courthouses across the nation. Many of the architects have chosen to work in the classical style. Elsewhere, architectural landmarks are being saved or salvaged. There is no indication that inspirational inscriptions will make a comeback. The principles they promoted, however, seem to be sorely missed.

As Senator Daniel Patrick Moynihan has noted, "Twentieth-century

America has seen a steady, persistent decline in the visual and emotional power of its public buildings, and this has been accompanied by a not less persistent decline in the authority of its public order." Although he hints at cause and effect, Moynihan is instead paying tribute to the standards of design and craftsmanship that went into America's great civic buildings and monuments.* Indirectly, he is praising a group of men who assumed that architecture can inspire civility and patriotism, and who did their best to show how it could be done.

THE PROGRESSION OF THE GREAT MEMORIALS

The story of inscriptions on American architecture is not complete without a few words about monuments and memorials. Three have already been mentioned. The Statue of Liberty, the Shaw Memorial, and the Lincoln Memorial are each complemented by celebrated inscriptions that enhance their symbolic impact. They also serve as a prologue to the most successful modern memorial, and help to explain why it initially met with so much resistance, and also why it ultimately triumphed.

IN 1981 PLANS for a national memorial to U.S. servicemen who died in Vietnam encountered serious opposition from veterans' groups and some conservative politicians. Criticism of the design, by Yale University art student Maya Lin, ranged from accusations of elitism to the charge that it was no more than a "hideous sunken gravestone."

This furor, which escalated to a national debate, was not about artistic taste as much as symbolic content. What did the design say? Unfortunately, it said very different things to different people. Unlike the Iwo Jima monument, to take a famous example of an uncontroversial design, it did not contain the expected visual cues, the lingua franca of monuments and memorials—a representative sculpture, an American flag, and a morally inspiring lesson. Yet Lin's vision has succeeded dramatically by becoming the most visited memorial in Washington, which would seem to imply that the language of monuments is not in fact very well understood by committees and the press.

---

*In 1994, it should be noted, Moynihan sponsored the bill proposing to renovate McKim, Mead & White's New York Post Office Building into the new Pennsylvania Station. It was not fully funded, and remains in limbo.

What most commentators managed to overlook was that Lin's Vietnam Veterans Memorial falls squarely within the trajectory of monument design that leads from the Statue of Liberty to Boston's Shaw Memorial to the Lincoln Memorial. Its use of inscriptions, for example, is far more complex than a simple listing of names. But to fully understand it requires some knowledge of the tradition of American monuments. This tradition begins with a resounding failure—Horatio Greenough's statue of George Washington—a monument designed by committee. It culminates with the success of the Vietnam memorial—a monument almost destroyed by a committee. Between these two extremes are several landmark monuments that illustrate the difficulties architects and sculptors have faced in trying to satisfy a demanding audience.

RHETORIC INTO STONE

The central problem in American monument design lies in the difficulty of reconciling the idea that all men are created equal with the desire to elevate some men above others. The Washington Monument sidesteps this issue in its complete abstraction—the undecorated obelisk invokes the first president in name only. But another monument to Washington—the first important public monument to be made in the United States—stumbled head-on into this problem, and all subsequent figurative memorials have responded to its failure with varying degrees of success.

Horatio Greenough, an American-born sculptor who trained in Europe and eventually established his practice in Italy, was commissioned in 1838 to sculpt a monument to George Washington for the new U.S. Capitol. Greenough did not lack artistic sophistication, but his Washington is a curious, if not comical, juxtaposition of past and present. In what now appears to have been a monumental misjudgment, Greenough, with the encouragement of an informal committee of his literary and political friends, chose to portray Washington as a Greek god. The result is a scandalously bare-chested president who gestures to the heavens with one hand while clasping a sword with the other.

This kind of heavy-handed symbolism drew ridicule from the day of its unveiling. For Greenough it was a colossal embarrassment, a blot on his professional reputation which was not mitigated by the statue's removal to the Capitol grounds. The awkward piece became a favorite target for vandals, and was soon moved to the Smithsonian for safekeeping, where it now keeps company with Archie Bunker's armchair and the ruby slippers from *The Wizard of Oz*.

The reason for the monument's failure seems obvious in retrospect, and even the newspapers of the day hit upon it immediately. This was not the people's Washington, but some remote figure idealized beyond recognition. In elevating Washington to the Greek pantheon, Greenough removed any traces of his humanity, and thus violated the central American tenet that no man is inherently any better than any other. He chose Greek attire partly because the Greek revival was then fashionable, but also because in the opinion of his advisors, the ordinariness of authentic dress—belt buckles, shoelaces, buttons, etc.—would lose credibility if enlarged and rendered in stone.

The inscription selected for the pedestal—Washington's epitaph—was executed in raised block capitals. It reads: FIRST IN WAR, FIRST IN PEACE, FIRST IN THE HEARTS OF HIS COUNTRYMEN. But the stern countenance that gazes out from the cold stone failed to touch the heart of any American viewer. The sculpted figure and the inscribed words contradict each other, and consequently the attempt to create a symbolic point of reference fails. Greenough's rueful remark in *The Travels, Observations, and Experience of a Yankee Stonecutter* (1852) sums up the frustration of the artist charged with creating national symbols: "It is the translation of rhetoric into stone—a feat often fatal to the rhetoric, always fatal to the stone."

DANIEL CHESTER FRENCH AND AUGUSTUS SAINT-GAUDENS

Greenough's debacle proved to be instructive for the next generation of monument builders. Although the Founding Fathers were still occasionally portrayed as Greeks by overenthusiastic mural painters, the medium of sculpture and its very public setting allowed little room for such coinceits.

When Daniel Chester French accepted his first public commission for a sculpture to commemorate the hundredth anniversary of the battle of Concord, he scoured the art museums looking for a classical precedent. His Concord Minuteman (1875) addressed the problem Greenough faced by recasting the famous Greek statue, the Apollo Belvedere, in period New England farmer's dress, while keeping it life-sized. It is an homage to Greek sculpture rather than a copy. French's work was made all the more effective by the addition of Ralph Waldo Emerson's "Concord Hymn" to the otherwise plain pedestal. It is an interesting irony that Emerson, who had championed Emma Lazarus's early poetry, should also have had one of his poems matched with a sculpture to create a national icon.

Despite such successes, sculptors were still torn between the desire to create accurate representations of real persons (as opposed to representative minutemen) and the need to idealize and mythologize the subject in order to impart a moral lesson. Allegorical sculpture representing ideals rather than real people, they recognized, had the disadvantage of not being truly American in concept, while idealized portrayals of contemporary Americans in ancient dress were not sufficiently inspirational. And oversized realistic figures risked seeming ludicrous. (The Statue of Liberty, being purely allegorical, did not have this problem.) As a way out of this paradox, Augustus Saint-Gaudens, French's mentor and the great innovator of this period, tried a different tack.

Saint-Gaudens' solution was to create heroic but accurate life-size portraits of great men in the company of allegorical figures. In his mature works the burden of conveying sentiment or ideals shifts from the principal figure (or figures) to the pedestal or surrounding figures, which typically take the form of ethereal females representing Loyalty, Courage, or Victory. In shifting the burden of philosophizing from the figure to the setting, Saint-Gaudens also made very effective use of inscriptions. Drawing upon his experience in making medallions and bronze portrait friezes, he continued to incorporate sculpted words into his bronzes where possible, and in his collaborations with architects inscriptions play an important role in establishing the proper tone.

His Shaw Memorial, for example, represents a transition in civic art from the sculptural monument toward the architectural monument. Rather than looming over the pedestal like Greenough's *Washington* or French's *Minuteman*, the sculpture is part of it; one exists in balance with the other. This is not to say that the pedestal was an incidental element of his earlier monuments. But in the Shaw Memorial, Saint-Gaudens broke away completely from the conventional standing-figure-on-a-pedestal type of memorial he so detested. He placed Colonel Shaw on horseback, life-sized, and in the company of his men—a phalanx of determined figures that occupied the sculptor for twelve years. A winged angel floats over the head of the doomed colonel, and assumes some of the burden of mythologizing the scene. In this stirring monument the glory is distributed to the regiment, and not just their leader. It is as though the memory of Shaw is sustained and protected by his men.

One consequence of the decision to make the pedestal a more integral part of the monument was to expand the role of the inscription. Saint-Gaudens incorporated a Latin motto—OMNIA RELINQUIT SERVARE REMPUBLICAM (He forsook all to preserve the public weal)—into the Shaw frieze, in keeping with his style of sculpted lettering. He insisted that the inscription be kept brief, and the final choice—the motto of the Society of the Cincinnati, of which the Shaws were hereditary members—was made by Shaw's father. Charles McKim's pedestal is crowded with other inscriptions, most notably on the back wall, where a text by Charles Eliot invokes the words Honor, Pride, Courage, and Devotion. Unlike the words on Greenough's Washington or the Statue of Liberty, the Shaw inscriptions were not tacked on as an afterthought. They are an integral part of the design. At the dedication ceremony, Saint-Gaudens remarked, "It is the finest example of inscription writing I have ever read."

The Shaw Memorial was the first truly classical architectural (as opposed to purely sculptural) monument in America, and one of the last to be attributed primarily to a sculptor alone. It is considered Saint-Gaudens's memorial, not McKim's. More than just a sculpture atop a base, it is an environment, a contemplative setting that incorporates sculpture, architecture, and text. Thus it signals the ascendancy of the architect's influence in monument design, a trend which culminated in the great Washington memorials and the World War I memorials in the United States and Europe.

In This Temple

There are few modern inscriptions that succeed fully as integral components of a monument. The Statue of Liberty and the Concord Minuteman are *associated* with famous inscriptions, but the verses have no visual impact—they were not expressly written with the idea of being incorporated into the design.* Thus they are not part of the visual iconography of the whole in the way that the words on the New York Post Office, the Supreme Court, or the Lincoln Memorial are. The reverse is true of Saint-

---

*In fact, Lazarus's famous sonnet is not inscribed upon the Statue of Liberty or its pedestal. In 1903 the words were set into a commemorative bronze plaque that was placed in the entryway of the fort upon which the statue's pedestal was built. In 1986, as part of the statue's restoration, the plaque was moved into the museum housed within the fort. Most people still assume that the words have always been affixed to the monument itself.

Gaudens's memorials—the inscriptions have visual impact but no textual resonance. This is not to say that many inscriptions fail completely as a visual motif. But the most successful inscriptions are those whose visual effect and literal meaning add to the poetic or philosophical weight of a structure.

The Lincoln Memorial is one the few monuments to have pulled this off. It contains a colossal statue—about nineteen feet high—which is dwarfed by its architectural setting. Here the magnification of the figure is perfectly countered by the scale of Bacon's temple. The approach to the memorial initially focuses attention on the lone monumental sculpture within, but the interior provides a balanced panorama of decorative and symbolic gestures, as well as a dramatic vista encompassing the reflecting pool, the Washington Monument, and the Capitol.

The Lincoln Memorial is an architectural monument which shows how the sculptural problem of idealizing a great figure through magnifying his image could be tempered by a properly monumental setting—one which would have the effect of reducing the figure to human scale, at least when seen from a distance. Up close, of course, the figure looms large, but the inscriptions and decorative murals distribute the focus by providing a frame of reference. Royal Cortissoz's inscription, directly above Lincoln's inclined head, is particularly effective. It is both brief and evocative, and connotes permanence.

THE VIETNAM VETERANS MEMORIAL

In the 1930s enthusiasm for the classical style began to wane. A new generation of glass and steel structures did away with classical motifs, including inscriptions, so that by the end of the decade critics had pronounced classicism dead. As for memorials, the urban analyst Lewis Mumford, in his 1938 book *The Culture of Cities*, sought to eulogize the practice of monument building when he wrote, "The very stones of the ancient tombs are no longer for us true symbols of eternity: we know their secret processes and detect their faltering character. We see their civilizations too, through the perspective of time, perspectives that reveal the feebleness of their boasted power and the frailty of their monuments."

In Mumford's view, the myth of classical greatness promoted by the neoclassicists of the eighteenth and nineteenth centuries had yielded to a myth of dynastic corruption suggestive of Shelley's "Ozymandias." Mumford was reacting in part to the unrestrained proliferation of World War I

memorials that drew upon every cliché available. Even conservative planning boards began to come around to Mumford's views. After the Second
World War, memorials by and large took the form of usable and functional
spaces such as auditoriums, swimming pools, bridges, highways, and ball
parks. But Mumford and others were too quick to bury the classical monument, and perhaps too eager to speak for a public that clearly wanted
places of remembrance. Mumford claimed that a monument could not be
modern by definition. But modern, which he seemed to think meant "not
classical," never implies a complete break with the past.

The Vietnam Memorial, for example, is considered modern, yet is more
closely tied to the tradition of neoclassical memorials than it first appears.
It also falls squarely in the trajectory that leads from the Shaw Memorial—
a sculptor's work fitted into an architectural setting—to the Lincoln
Memorial—an architectural concept augmented by sculpture. Lin's design
takes this progression to its natural conclusion: it is a purely architectural
environment with no figurative sculpture.

As with its predecessors, its principal classical motif is the inscription;
the memorial is essentially a tablet on which the names of almost 58,000
dead are inscribed. But the inscribed text is used in a highly evocative and
effective way that makes visitors participate in the viewing experience.
Lin's choice of incised Roman letters ties the monument into a long-standing tradition, and the polished black granite wall creates the compelling
effect of superimposing the viewer's reflection onto the text. Lin also
wisely saw that it would be best to use a chronological ordering of names,
so that the viewer would have to conduct a search. An alphabetical listing
would have reduced the memorial to a large directory, thereby minimizing
the sobering scale of the loss. By maintaining chronology, she has conveyed the escalating involvement of the United States in the war, as well
as the corresponding toll. She also kept the lettering small, so that visitors
would have to stand close to the wall, making their experience more intimate.

Little noticed, but highly significant, are two inscriptions that serve as
the prologue and epilogue to the memorial. Lin added these so that the
memorial would not be simply a cenotaph acknowledging the dead, but a
point of reference for all who served in Vietnam. The epilogue in particular is noteworthy for its highly traditional exaltation of virtues and ideals
which still have resonance for Americans. It says, in part: OUR NATION
HONORS THE COURAGE, SACRIFICE, AND DEVOTION TO
DUTY AND COUNTRY OF ITS VIETNAM VETERANS.

Reflecting on the monument she designed, Lin has said, "I truly believed that it would help people, and once it was up they would understand." Unfortunately, in a compromise aimed at appeasing the ultratraditionalists, the memorial commission decided to add an accompanying figurative statue of three soldiers. This inclusion fails to heed the lessons learned by Saint-Gaudens and French. The realism of the bronze figures is too literal and too narrowly conceived—it drew an immediate complaint that although it includes a white, a black, and a Hispanic soldier, it does not include women, Asian–Americans, and so on. Partly in response, a sculpture commemorating Vietnam War nurses was added in 1993. Fortunately, both sculptural groups were placed sufficiently far from the wall so as not to intrude on the essential elegance of its design.

CONCLUSION

The viewer of inscriptions in the United States has access to a legacy that connects with the Greek epigrammists, and extends back to the Egyptian tomb builders, and even the Babylonian empire. It does not stretch the point too far to compare the massive black stone on which the code of the Babylonian king Hammurabi is inscribed to the polished granite plaque in the central plaza of New York's Rockefeller Center that contains the Rockefeller family creed. Both feature a text of rules to live by. In one, the Babylonian king is seen receiving the laws from a deity; in the other, John D. Rockefeller, Jr., is proffering wisdom that was handed down to him from his father, the founder of the Rockefeller dynasty. In both instances, the durability of the medium connotes the permanence of the words themselves, while at the same time ensuring their eventual irrelevance.

THE ANCIENT GREEKS invented the epigram as a literary form consisting of words of praise or remembrance that would be suitable for inscribing in stone. In a few instances they actually were inscribed. The Babylonians and the Egyptians had done this as well, but not with didactic verses, and not in a monumental way. The Romans, who did not possess the Greeks' literary talent, converted the metaphor to a visual style and combined it with architecture, but left out the poetry.

But in late nineteenth-century America, a few visionary designers borrowed freely from classical and Renaissance motifs, and combined the poetic and visual potential of inscriptions. Their purpose was to impose on a nation of widely diverse communities a unified vision of commonly shared ideals. Their moral perspective embraced an eclectic mix of classical, biblical, medieval, and modern European influences, which they grafted onto a democratic society. Their hope was to inspire order, civic-mindedness, and cultural unity. Like the Romans, they managed to create some enduring monuments, but within a century their work has drifted into a state of benign neglect. Many Beaux-Arts buildings still serve the purposes for which they were built, a few have been converted to food courts and shopping malls, many have been demolished, and some, like the New York Post Office, silently await their fates.

In modern parlance, words that are "written in stone" have no flexibility, spontaneity, or relevance. They represent the voice of a corrupt and deposed authority, the mystical lure of ancient cultures, or possibly a shard of fragmented memory. They have much appeal, but little clout. The inscriptions produced in the fifty years of the American classical revival still serve to connect present-day America to a not-so-distant past. But to view them simply as cheap imitations of antiquity or random curiosities is to miss an important point. They were created to address a cultural void not unlike the one Americans face today. At the turn of the century they succeeded in contributing to the symbolic landscape of the nation, and in defining the purpose of many of its cultural institutions. In the case of the New York Post Office, a seemingly isolated inspiration grew into a revered code of practice. Few other inscribed words can claim that kind of success.

"ALL OF THE OLD ASSERTIONS get disproved sooner or later," wrote George Bernard Shaw, "and so we find the world full of a magnificent debris of artistic fossils, with the matter of fact credibility gone clean out of them, but the form still splendid." This is one way of looking at the remnants of antiquity—a somewhat more charitable judgment than is found in Shelley's "Ozymandias," and one that celebrates the spirit of creativity, as well as the splendor of America's classical buildings and monuments. Whether inscribed texts found on the future ruins of American civilization will be attributed to arrogance or innocent idealism has yet to be seen. How we view them today depends on whether we choose to see them at all.

PART TWO

THE
TEXTS

GOLDEN RULES

SCRIPTURAL STATEMENTS OF THE GOLDEN RULE
Buddhism
Confucianism
Taoism
Hinduism
Jainism
Islam
Judaism
Christianity
Zoroastrianism

OTHER SOURCES AND STATEMENTS OF THE GOLDEN RULE
Isocrates
Aristotle
Samuel Clarke
John Wise
Immanuel Kant
Thomas Paine
Henry David Thoreau
Henry Sidgwick
Petr Alekseevich Kropotkin
Malcolm X
Alan Gewirth
Louis Armstrong

SCRIPTURAL STATEMENTS OF THE GOLDEN RULE

BUDDHISM

Hurt not others in ways that you yourself would find harmful.

Udanavarga 5:18

CONFUCIANISM

Fidelity to one's self and the corresponding reciprocity are not far from the path. What you do not like when done to yourself, do not do to others.

Li Ki or Book of Rites 28, 1, 32

Tsze-Kung asked, saying, "Is there one word which may serve as a rule of practice for all one's life?" The Master said, "Is not 'reciprocity' such a word? What you do not want done to yourself, do not do to others."

Analects of Confucius 15, 23

TAOISM

Regard your neighbor's gain as your own gain, and your neighbor's loss as your own loss.

T'ai Shang Kan Ying P'ien 3

HINDUISM

Do not do to another what is disagreeable to yourself: this is the summary Law; the other proceeds from desire.

Mahabharata 5(51)39:57

JAINISM

Indifferent to worldly objects, a man should wander about treating all creatures in the world so as he himself would be treated.

Sutrakrtanga (or Book of Sermons) 1, 11

ISLAM

No one of you is a believer until he desires for his brother that which he desires for himself.

Sunna, or the sayings of Muhammed according to oral tradition

JUDAISM

What is hateful to you, do not to your fellow man. That is the entire Law: all the rest is commentary.

Talmud, Shabbath 31a

CHRISTIANITY

All things whatsoever ye would that men should do unto you, do ye even so unto them; for this is the law and the prophets.

Matthew 7:12

As ye would that men should do to you, do ye also unto them likewise.

Luke 6:31

ZOROASTRIANISM

That nature only is good when it shall not do unto another whatever is not good for its own self.

Dadistan-I Dinik 94, 5

OTHER SOURCES AND STATEMENTS OF THE GOLDEN RULE

Do not to others that which angers you when they do it to you.

Isocrates (436–338 B.C.)
Nicocles 61

The question was once put to him, how we ought to behave to our friends; and the answer he gave was, "As we should wish our friends to behave to us."

Aristotle (384–322 B.C.) Quoted in Diogenes Laertes,
Lives and Opinions of Eminent Philosophers,
Book V, xi

In respect of our Fellow-Creatures, the Rule of Righteousness is: that in particular we so deal with every Man, as in like Circumstances we could reasonably expect he should deal with us; and that in general we endeavor, by an universal Benevolence to promote the welfare and happiness of all Men. The former branch of this rule, is Equity; the latter, is Love.

> Samuel Clarke (1675–1729)
> Boyle Lectures of 1705
> Printed in A Discourse Concerning the Unalterable
> Obligations of Natural Religion (London, 1719),
> p. 67

The way to discover the law of nature in our own state, is by a narrow watch, and accurate contemplation of our natural condition and propensions. Others say this is the way to find out the law of nature. *Scil* [that is] If a man any ways doubts, whether what he is going to do to another man be agreeable to the law of nature, then let him suppose himself to be in that other man's room; and by this rule effectually executed.

> John Wise (1652–1725)
> A Vindication of the Government of New
> England Churches (1717), II, 24

The Categorical Imperative: Act only on that maxim through which you can at the same time will that it should become a universal law.
The Practical Imperative: Act in such a way that you always treat humanity, whether in your own person or in the person of any other, never simply as a means, but always at the same time as an end.

> Immanuel Kant (1724–1804)
> Groundwork of the Metaphysics of Morals
> (1785), pp. 421 and 429 in the Academy edition
> (the standard reference for Kant's works)

The duty of man is not a wilderness of turnpike gates, through which he is to pass by tickets from one to the other. It is plain and simple, and consists of but two points. His duty to God, which every man must feel; and with respect to his neighbor, to do as he would be done by.

> Thomas Paine (1737–1809)
> The Rights of Man (1792), Part I

We cannot judge an action to be right for A and wrong for B, unless we can find in the natures or the circumstances of the two some difference which we can regard as a reasonable ground for differences in their duties. If therefore I judge any action to be right for myself, I implicitly judge it to be right for any other person whose nature and circumstances do not differ from my own in some important respects.

> Henry Sidgwick (1838–1900)
> An elaboration on Kant's Categorical Imperative, from
> The Methods of Ethics (1874), Book III,
> Chapter I, section 3, p. 209

By an unprejudiced observation of the animal kingdom, we reach the conclusion that wherever society exists at all, this principle may be found, Treat others as you would like them to treat you under similar circumstances.

> Petr Alekseevich Kropotkin (1842–1921)
> "Anarchist Morality," sect. VI (from Kropotkin's
> Revolutionary Pamphlets, New York:
> B. Bloom, 1927)

I believe in the brotherhood of men, all men, but I don't believe in brotherhood with anybody who doesn't want brotherhood with me. I believe in treating people right, but I'm not going to waste my time trying to treat somebody right who doesn't know how to return that treatment.

> Malcolm X (1925–1965)
> Speech in New York City, December 12, 1964

Act in accord with the generic rights of your recipients as well as of yourself. I shall call this the Principle of Generic Consistency (PGC), since it combines the formal consideration of consistency with the material consideration of rights to the generic features of goods of action.

> Alan Gewirth (1912–)
> Reason and Morality (Chicago: University of Chicago
> Press, 1978), p. 135

I got a simple rule about everybody. If you don't treat me right, shame on you!

> Louis Armstrong (1900–1971)
> *Attributed*

CREEDS

OLD ROMAN CREED (c. A.D. 190)

I believe in God the Father almighty;
and in Jesus Christ, His only Son, our Lord,
Who was born from the Holy Spirit and the Virgin Mary,
Who under Pontius Pilate was crucified, and buried,
on the third day rose again from the dead,
ascended to heaven,
sits on the right hand of the Father,
whence he will come to judge the living and the dead;
and in the Holy Spirit, the holy Church, the remission of sins, the
resurrection of the flesh.

The Latin text of this baptismal formula was recorded by Tyrannius Rufinus in a treatise entitled *Commentarius in symbolum apostolorum*, written in about A.D. 400. In this book Rufinus originated the legend that the twelve Apostles had composed the creed.

THE APOSTLES' CREED

I[We] believe in God the Father almighty, creator of heaven and earth. I[We] believe in Jesus Christ, his only Son, our Lord, who was conceived by the power of the Holy Spirit, and born out of the virgin Mary. He suffered under Pontius Pilate, was crucified, died, and was buried. He descended to the dead. On the third day he rose again. He ascended into heaven, and is seated at the right hand of the Father. He will come again to judge the living and the dead. I[We] believe in the Holy Spirit, the holy catholic Church, the communion of saints, the forgiveness of sins, the resurrection of the flesh, and life everlasting. Amen.

The accepted Latin text of the Apostles' Creed originated at the end of the seventh century in the south of France. It appeared in the city of Rome in the mid-ninth century and finally gained recognition in the West as the Apostles' Creed after the year 1000. The above translation is one of many variants of what is the most widely accepted statement of the Christian faith. Within Protestant and Free Church denominations, the words "holy catholic Church" are replaced by "holy Christian Church" or "holy universal church." The term "Holy Spirit" is now commonly used in place of "Holy Ghost," which has a longer history of use.

CREED OF THE COUNCIL OF NICEA (A.D. 325)

We believe in one God, the Father, All Governing, maker of all things visible and invisible; And in one Lord Jesus Christ, the Son of God, essence of the Father, only-begotten, that is, from the substance of the Father, God from God, light from light, true God from true God, begotten not created, of one substance with the Father, through Who all things came into being, things in heaven and things on earth, Who because of us men and because of our salvation came down and became incarnate, becoming man, suffered, and rose again on the third day, ascended to the heavens, will come to judge the living and the dead.

And in the Holy Spirit.

But as for those who say, There was when He was not, and, Before being born He was not, and that He came into existence out of nothing, or who assert that the Son of God is of a different hypostasis or substance or is subject to alteration or change—these the Catholic and apostolic Church anathematizes.

This creed, written originally in Greek, was preserved by many commentators and observers of the historic council. It introduced the notion of the Son's "consubstantiality," which corresponds to the Greek word *homoousios*, a nonscriptural and therefore highly controversial assertion.

THE NICENO–CONSTANTINOPOLITAN CREED (THE NICENE CREED)

We believe in one God, the Father Almighty, maker of heaven and earth, and of all that is seen and unseen. We believe in one Lord Jesus Christ, the only Son of God, begotten of the Father before all ages. [God from God], Light from Light, true God from true God. Begotten not made, one in being with the Father, through whom all things were made. Who for us men and for our salvation came down from heaven. And by the power of the Holy Spirit he was born of the Virgin Mary, and became man. For our sake he was crucified under Pontius Pilate, suffered, died, and was buried. On the third day he rose again in fulfillment of the Scriptures; he ascended into heaven, and is seated on the right hand of the Father. He shall come again in glory to judge the living and the dead, and his kingdom shall have no end.

We believe in the Holy Spirit, the Lord and giver of life, who proceeds from the Father [and the Son]. Who together with the Father and the Son is to be worshipped and glorified. He has spoken through the prophets.

We believe in one holy catholic and apostolic Church. We confess one baptism for the remission of sins. We look for the resurrection of the dead, and the life of the world to come. Amen.

The creed adopted by the Nicene Council underwent modification by many hands (notably at the Council of Constantinople in 381, and the Third Council of Toledo in 589). The bracketed words are later additions. With many different translations in circulation, the present-day Nicene Creed is recognized by the Roman Catholic Church as well as Lutherans, Anglicans, Methodists, Episcopalians, and many other Christian bodies. In 1969, the World Council of Churches sought to update the translation of the Creed. The result, which is close to the version given above, is now the most commonly used version.

SYMBOLUM QUICUNQUE VULT (THE ATHANASIAN CREED)

Whoever wishes to be saved must before everything hold fast to the Catholic faith. Unless a person preserves it whole and inviolate he will without doubt perish forever. Now this is the Catholic faith, that we venerate one God in the Trinity and the Trinity in unity. Neither mixing the hypostases together nor breaking up the [divine] substance. The hypostasis of the Father is one hypostasis, that of the Son another one, and that of the Holy Spirit still a different one. But there is a single Godhead of the Father and of the Son and of the Holy Spirit, an equal glory, a coeternal majesty. Whatever the Father is, the Son is, and the Holy Spirit is too. The Father is uncreated, the Son is uncreated, the Holy Spirit is uncreated. The Father is infinite, the Son is infinite, the Holy Spirit is infinite. The Father is eternal, the Son is eternal, the Holy Spirit is eternal. Nevertheless there are not three eternal ones, but a single eternal one. Just as there are not three uncreated ones or three infinite ones, but a single uncreated one and a single infinite one. Similarly, the Father is almighty, the Son is almighty, and the Holy Spirit is almighty. Nevertheless there are not three almighty ones, but a single almighty one. In the same way the Father is God, the Son is God, the Holy Spirit is God. Nevertheless there are not three gods, but a single god. In the same way the Father is the Lord, the Son is the Lord, the Holy Spirit is the Lord. Nevertheless there are not three Lords, but a single Lord. Because just as the Christian truth compels us to confess each individual hypostasis singly to be both God and the

Lord, just so the Catholic religion forbids us to talk about three gods or lords. The Father has been made out of no one else, nor has he been created or sired. The Holy Spirit is out of the Father and the Son; he has not been made or created or sired. So there is a single Father, not three fathers; a single Son, not three sons; a single Holy Spirit, not three Holy Spirits. And in this Trinity, nothing is earlier or later, nothing is greater or less, but all three hypostases are coeternal and coequal with one another in such a way that throughout, as it has already been said, both the Trinity in the Unity and the Unity in the Trinity is to be venerated. As a result, let whoever desires to be saved think in this way of the Trinity. But it is necessary for everlasting salvation that he also faithfully believe the Incarnation of our Lord Jesus Christ. This is the correct faith, that we believe and confess that our Lord Jesus Christ, God's Son, is equally God and a human being. He is God sired out of His Father's substance before the ages, and he is a human being born in time out of his mother's substance. He is completely God and completely a human being that consists of a rational soul and of human flesh. He is equal to the Father with respect to his Godhead, less than the Father with respect to his humanity. Even though Christ is God and a human being, he is not two but one. Yet he is not one through the transformation of his Godhead into flesh, but by the taking up of his humanity into God. He is one, admittedly not by a mixing together of substances but through a oneness of his hypostasis. For just as the rational soul and flesh are a single human being, so [here] God and a human being are a single Christ. He suffered for our salvation, went down to the netherworld, rose from the dead, ascended into the heavens, sat down at the Father's right hand, will come from there to pronounce judgment on the living and the dead. At his coming all human beings will have to rise with their bodies, and are going to give an account of their own deeds. Those who acted well will go into everlasting life, those who acted badly into everlasting fire. This is the Catholic Faith. Unless a person believes it faithfully and firmly he will not be able to be saved.

A BRIEF STATEMENT OF FAITH—PRESBYTERIAN CHURCH (U.S.A.), 1990

In life and in death we belong to God.
    Through the grace of our Lord Jesus Christ,
        the love of God, and the communion of the Holy Spirit,
    we trust in the one triune God, the Holy One of Israel,
        whom alone we worship and serve.

We trust in Jesus Christ, fully human, fully God.
Jesus proclaimed the reign of God:
preaching good news to the poor and release to the captives,
teaching by word and deed and blessing the children,
healing the sick and binding up the brokenhearted,
eating with outcasts, forgiving sinners,
and calling all to repent and believe the gospel.
Unjustly condemned for blasphemy and sedition,
Jesus was crucified,
suffering the depths of human pain
and giving his life for the sins of the world.
God raised this Jesus from the dead,
vindicating his sinless life,
breaking the power of sin and evil,
delivering us from death to life eternal.
We trust in God, whom Jesus called Abba, Father.
In sovereign love God created the world good
and makes everyone equally in God's image, male and female,
of every race and people, to live as one community.
But we rebel against God; we hide from our Creator.
Ignoring God's commandments,
we violate the image of God in others and ourselves,
accept lies as truth, exploit neighbor and nature,
and threaten death to the planet entrusted to our care.
We deserve God's condemnation.
Yet God acts with justice and mercy to redeem creation.
In everlasting love, the God of Abraham and Sarah chose
a covenant people to bless all families of the earth.
Hearing their cry,
God delivered the children of Israel from the house of bondage.
Loving us still, God makes us heirs with Christ of the covenant.
Like a mother who will not forsake her nursing child,
like a father who runs to welcome the prodigal home,
God is faithful still.
We trust in the Holy Spirit, everywhere the giver and renewer of life.
The Spirit justifies us by grace through faith,
sets us free to accept ourselves and to love God and neighbor,
and binds us together with all believers
in the one body of Christ, the Church.

The same Spirit
    who inspired the prophets and apostles
    rules our faith and life in Christ through Scripture,
    engages us through the Word proclaimed,
    claims us in the waters of baptism,
    feeds us with the bread of life and the cup of salvation,
    and calls women and men to all ministries of the Church.
In a broken and fearful world the Spirit gives us courage
    to pray without ceasing,
    to witness among all peoples to Christ as Lord and Savior,
    to unmask idolatries in Church and culture,
    to hear the voices of peoples long silenced,
    and to work with others for justice, freedom, and peace.
In gratitude to God, empowered by the Spirit,
    we strive to serve Christ in our daily tasks
      and to live holy and joyful lives,
    even as we watch for God's new heaven and new earth,
      praying, "Come, Lord Jesus!"
With believers in every time and place,
    we rejoice that nothing in life or in death
    can separate us from the love of God in Christ Jesus our Lord.
Glory be to the Father, and to the Son, and to the Holy Spirit. Amen.

CONFESSION OF FAITH—MOSS SIDE BAPTIST CHURCH, MANCHESTER, ENGLAND

God is a Spirit, something that no one can see; he is too mighty for our minds and eyes.

One becomes aware of the reality of God when one sees or becomes involved in some action of genuine unselfishness, where people are lovingly concerned with each other's welfare. God cares for people throughout history, and has ordained that they should be redeemed.

He is loving, caring, just. He understands all about us and can help us. He is great and powerful and controls the earth. He also cares about each individual.

Uniquely and totally we see God in Christ as he became, suffered, died and yet, to the experience of some contemporaries, was alive.

God is a supreme being with whom we can communicate through prayer, brought near to our life of understanding through the life of Jesus.

He teaches us his ways of life.

He longs that all men should worship him on a faith basis of their own free will.

He has allowed each one of us a chance to choose the way we live our lives, but he is also our judge and one day we shall have to face up to him.

ANI MA'AMIN (A JEWISH CONFESSION OF FAITH)

1. I believe with perfect faith that the Creator, blessed be his name, is the Author and Guide of everything that has been created, and that he alone has made, does make, and will make all things.
2. I believe with perfect faith that the Creator, blessed be his name, is a Unity, and that there is no unity in any manner like unto this, and that he alone is our God, who was, is, and will be.
3. I believe with perfect faith that the Creator, blessed be his name, is not a body, and that he is free from all accidents of matter, and that he has not any form whatsoever.
4. I believe with perfect faith that the Creator, blessed be his name, is the first and the last.
5. I believe with perfect faith that to the Creator, blessed be his name, and to him alone it is right to pray, and that it is not right to pray to any one besides him.
6. I believe with perfect faith that all the words of the prophets are true.
7. I believe with perfect faith that the prophecy of Moses our teacher, peace be unto him, was true, and that he was the chief of the prophets, both of those that preceded him and of those that followed him.
8. I believe with perfect faith that the whole Law, now in our possession, is the same that was given to Moses our teacher, peace be unto him.
9. I believe with perfect faith that this Law will not be changed, and that there will never be any other law from the Creator, blessed be his name.
10. I believe with perfect faith that the Creator, blessed be his name, knows of every deed of the children of men, and all their thoughts, as it is said. It is he that fashioneth the hearts of them all, that giveth heed to all their deeds.

11. I believe with perfect faith that the Creator, blessed be his name, rewards those that keep his commandments, and punishes those that transgress them.

12. I believe with perfect faith in the coming of the Messiah, and, though he tarry, I will wait daily for his coming.

13. I believe with perfect faith that there will be a resurrection of the dead at the time when it shall please the Creator, blessed be his name, and exalted be the remembrance of him for ever and ever.

PREAMBLE OF THE DECLARATION OF INDEPENDENCE (JULY 4, 1776)

We hold these truths to be self-evident, that all men are created equal, that they are endowed by their Creator with certain unalienable Rights, that among these are Life, Liberty and the pursuit of Happiness. That to secure these rights, governments are instituted among men, deriving their just powers from the consent of the governed. That whenever any Form of Government becomes destructive of these ends, it is the Right of the People to alter or to abolish it, and to institute new Government, laying its foundation on such principles and organizing its powers in such form, as to them shall seem most likely to effect their Safety and Happiness. Prudence, indeed, will dictate that governments long established should not be changed for light and transient causes; and accordingly all experience hath shown, that mankind are more disposed to suffer, while evils are sufferable, than to right themselves by abolishing the forms to which they are accustomed.

PREAMBLE OF THE CONSTITUTION OF THE UNITED STATES (SEPTEMBER 17, 1787)

We the People of the United States, in Order to form a more perfect Union, establish Justice, insure domestic Tranquility, provide for the common Defence, promote the general Welfare, and secure the Blessings of Liberty to ourselves and our Posterity, do ordain and establish this CONSTITUTION for the United States of America.

THE AMERICAN'S CREED

I believe in the United States of America as a government of the people, by the people, for the people; whose just powers are derived from the consent of the governed; a democracy in a republic; a sovereign nation of many sovereign states; a perfect union, one and inseparable; established on those principles of freedom, equality, justice, and humanity for which American patriots sacrificed their lives and fortunes. I therefore believe that it is my duty to my country to love it; to support its constitution; to obey its laws; to respect its flag, and to defend it against all enemies.

William Tyler Page (1868–1942) composed this Creed in 1917. It was accepted by the House of Representatives on behalf of the American people on April 3, 1918.

AMERICAN CREDO

I believe in America because in it we are free—free to choose our government, to speak our minds, to observe our different religions.

Because we are generous with our freedom—we share our rights with those who disagree with us.

Because we hate no people and covet no people's land.

Because we are blessed with a natural and varied abundance.

Because we set no limit to a man's achievement—in mine, factory, field, or service in business or the arts, an able man, regardless of class or creed, can realize his ambition.

Because we have great dreams—and because we have the opportunity to make those dreams come true.

> *Wendell L. Willkie (1892–1944), "Why I Believe in America,"* North American Review, *vol. 248, no. 2 (Winter 1939–40)*

THE INGERSOLL CREED

My creed is this:

1. Happiness is the only good.
2. The way to be happy is to make others so. Other things being equal, that man is happiest who is nearest just—who is truthful,

merciful and intelligent—in other words, the one who lives in ac-
cordance with life.

3. The time to be happy is now, and the place to be happy is here.
4. Reason is the lamp of the mind—the only torch of progress; and
   instead of blowing that out and depending on darkness and
   dogma, it is far better to increase that sacred light.
5. Every man should be the intellectual proprietor of himself, honest
   with himself, and intellectually hospitable; and upon every brain
   reason should be enthroned as king.
6. Every man must bear the consequences, at least of his own actions. If he puts his hands in the fire, his hands must smart, and not
   the hands of another. In other words: each man must eat the fruit
   of the tree he plants.

Robert G. Ingersoll (1833–1899)
"Creed," Works (New York: The Ingersoll League, 1933),
Volume V, pp. 20–21

THE ROCKEFELLER CREED

I believe in the supreme worth of the individual and his right to life, liberty, and the pursuit of happiness.

I believe that every right implies a responsibility; every opportunity, an
obligation; every possession, a duty.

I believe that the law was made for man and not man for the law; that
government is the servant of the people and not their master.

I believe in the dignity of labor, whether with head or hand; that the
world owes no man a living but that it owes every man an opportunity to
make a living.

I believe that thrift is essential to well-ordered living and that economy
is a prime requisite of a sound financial structure, whether in government,
business or personal affairs.

I believe that truth and justice are fundamental to an enduring social
order.

I believe in the sacredness of a promise, that a man's word should be as
good as his bond; that character—not wealth or power or position—is of
supreme worth.

I believe that the rendering of useful service is the common duty of
mankind and that only in the purifying fire of sacrifice is the dross of self-
ishness consumed and the greatness of the human soul set free.

I believe in an all-wise and all-loving God, named by whatever name, and that the individual's highest fulfillment, greatest happiness, and widest usefulness are to be found in living in harmony with His will.

I believe that love is the greatest thing in the world; that it alone can overcome hate; that right can and will triumph over might.

This is a family creed that John D. Rockefeller, Jr., distilled from the observations of his father. It is also used as the text for an inscription at Rockefeller Center.

ELBERT HUBBARD'S CREDO

I believe in the Motherhood of God.

I believe in the blessed Trinity of Father, Mother and Child.

I believe that God is here, and that we are as near Him now as we ever shall be. I do not believe He started this world a-going and went away and left it.

I believe in the sacredness of the human body, this transient dwelling place of a living soul, and so I deem it the duty of every man and every woman to keep his or her body beautiful through right thinking and right living.

I believe that the love of man for woman and the love of woman for man, is holy; and that this love in all its promptings is as much an emanation of the Divine Spirit, as man's love for God, or the most daring hazards of the human mind.

I believe in salvation through economic, social and spiritual freedom.

I believe John Ruskin, William Morris, Henry Thoreau, Walt Whitman and Leo Tolstoy to be Prophets of God, and they should rank in mental reach and spiritual insight with Elijah, Hosea, Ezekial and Isaiah.

I believe we are now living in Eternity as much as we ever shall.

I believe that the best way to prepare for a Future Life is to be kind, live one day at a time, and do the work you can do the best, doing it as well as you can.

I believe there is no devil but fear.

I believe that no one can harm you but yourself.

I believe that we are all sons of God and it doth not yet appear what we shall be.

I believe in freedom—social, economic, domestic, political, mental, spiritual.

I believe in every man minding his own business.

I believe that men are inspired today as much as men ever were.

I believe in sunshine, fresh air, friendship, calm sleep, beautiful thoughts.

I believe in the paradox of success through failure.

I believe in the purifying process of sorrow, and I believe that death is a manifestation of life.

I believe that there is no better preparation for a life to come than this: Do your work as well as you can, and be kind.

I believe the Universe is planned for good.

I believe it is possible that I will make other creeds, and change this one, or add to it, from time to time, as new light may come to me.

> *Fra Albertus [Elbert Hubbard]*
> A Message to Garcia and Thirteen Other Things
> (*East Aurora: Roycrofters, 1901*)

JOHN WOODEN—THIS I BELIEVE

My father tried to teach that although we should study and learn from others, you should never try to be better than another and never cease to be the best of which you are capable.

When I graduated from a small country grade school, he gave me a card with a verse on one side and a seven point creed on the other side. He said very simply, "Think on these, son, and try to live up to them." The verse went like this: Four things a man must learn to do if he would make his life more true. To think without confusion, clearly. To love his fellow man sincerely. To act from honest motives purely. To trust in God in heaven securely.

And these were the seven points of the creed: Number one was be true to yourself. Number two was make each day your masterpiece—just do the best you can in whatever you're doing. Number three was help others and, oh my, the help we get when we help others. Number four was drink deeply from good books. And of course, there's no book like the Bible. Number five was make friendship a fine art—don't take it for granted any more than you take marriage for granted; both sides have to work at it. The sixth was build a shelter against a rainy day, an everlasting shelter, not just a temporal shelter. And the seventh was pray for guidance and give thanks for our blessing everyday.

* * *

The program *This I Believe* was revived in 1995 by the Voice of America and broadcast nationwide over the Disney Channel. The five-minute segments have also been translated into many languages and broadcast all over the world, to a very enthusiastic response. Wooden's statement is from one of the pilot episodes of the show.

OATHS, VOWS, AND PLEDGES

Oath of Supremacy of Elizabeth I (1558)
Oath of a Free Man—Massachusetts Bay Colony (1634)
Continental Army Loyalty Oath (1778)
Oath of the President of the United States
Oath Taken by Supreme Court Justices
Civil Service Oath (1861)
Ironclad Test Oath of Loyalty (1862)
Lincoln's Amnesty Oath (1863)
The Levering Oath (1950)
Loyalty Oath for U.S. Government Employees
Oath Taken by Naturalized Citizens of the United States
Oaths of the Masonic Orders of the York Rite (1879)
The Olympic Oath
The Athenian Oath of Citizenship (The Ephebic Oath)
The Boy Scout Oath
The Girl Scout Promise
Temperance Pledge (1789)
Pledge of the American Temperance Society
Pledge of the Blue Ribbon Gospel Army
Woman's Christian Temperance Union Pledge
Antecedents of the Familiar Wedding Vows
Form of Solemnization of Matrimony—from the Sarum Missal (1526)

OATH OF SUPREMACY OF ELIZABETH I (1558)

I, A.B., do utterly testify and declare in my Conscience, that the Queen's Highness is the only supreme Governor of this Realm and of all other of her Highness's Dominions and Countries, as well as in all Spiritual or Ecclesiastical Things or Causes as Temporal; and that no foreign Prince, Person, Prelate, State or Potentate hath or ought to have any Jurisdiction, Power, Superiority, Preeminence or Authority, Ecclesiastical or Spiritual, within this Realm, and therefore I do utterly renounce and forsake all foreign Jurisdictions, Powers, Superiorities and Authorities, and do promise that from henceforth I shall bear Faith and true Allegiance to the Queen's Highness, her Heirs and lawful Successors, and to my power shall assist and defend all Jurisdictions, Preeminences, Privileges and Authorities granted or belonging to the Queen's Highness, her Heirs and Successors, or united or annexed to the Imperial Crown of this Realm: So help me God and by the Contents of this Book.

This oath, from a statute of the first year of the queen's reign (designated 1 Eliz c. 1 in *The Statutes of the Realm*), replaced all prior oaths instituted by Henry VIII, Elizabeth's father, and came to be called the Oath of Supremacy.

OATH OF A FREE-MAN—MASSACHUSETTS BAY COLONY (1634)

I, ———, being by God's providence an Inhabitant, and Freeman, within the Jurisdiction of this Commonwealth; do freely acknowledge my self to be subject to the Government thereof: And therefore do here swear by the great and dreadful Name of the Ever-living God, that I will be true and faithfull to the same, and will accordingly yield assistance & support thereunto, with my person and estate, as in equity I am bound; and will also truly endeavor to maintain and preserve all the liberties and priviledges thereof, submitting my self to the wholesome Lawes & Orders made and established by the same. And further that I will not plot or practice any evil against it, or consent to any that shall do so; but will timely discover and reveal the same to lawful Authority now here established, for the speedy preventing thereof. Moreover, I do solemnly bind my self in the sight of God, that when I shall be called to give my voice touching any such matter of this State, in which Freemen are to deal, I will give my vote and suffrage as I shall judge in mine own conscience may best conduce and tend to the publick weal of the body, without respect of persons, or favor of any man. So help me God in the Lord Jesus Christ.

This was a loyalty test for all residents, Puritan and non-Puritan, of the Massachusetts Bay Colony in 1634. It is the text of the first sheet of printed matter from an American press. None of the original copies has survived. This text is preserved in Governor John Winthrop's handwritten draft. It can be found in *Records of the Governor and Company of the Massachusetts Bay in New England* (Boston, 1853).

CONTINENTAL ARMY LOYALTY OATH (1778)

I, ———, do acknowledge the UNITED STATES of AMERICA, to be Free, Independent and Sovereign States, and declare the people thereof owe no allegiance or obedience to George the Third, King of Great Britain; and I renounce, refute and abjure any allegiance or obedience to him; and I do (swear or affirm) that I will to the utmost of my power, support, maintain and defend the said United States, against the said King George the Third, his heirs and successors and his or their abettors, assistants and adherents, and will serve the United States in the office of ——— — which I now hold, with fidelity, according to the best of my skill and understanding.

A copy of this oath, signed on the 14th of May, 1778, by Nicholas Fish, Major in the Second New York Regiment, is preserved in the National Archives.

OATH OF THE PRESIDENT OF THE UNITED STATES

I do solemnly swear (or affirm) that I will faithfully execute the Office of President of the United States, and will, to the best of my ability, preserve, protect and defend the Constitution of the United States.

This oath is contained in the Constitution of the United States (1787), article II, section 1. George Washington first swore it on the balcony of Federal Hall in New York City on April 30, 1789.

OATH TAKEN BY SUPREME COURT JUSTICES

I do solemnly swear that I will administer justice without respect to persons, and do equal right to the poor and to the rich; and that I will faithfully discharge all the duties incumbent on me as Judge, according to the best of my abilities and understanding, agreeably to the Constitution and laws of the United States.

CIVIL SERVICE OATH (AUGUST 6, 1861)

I do solemnly swear (or affirm, as the case may be) that I will support, protect and defend the Constitution and Government of the United States against all enemies, whether domestic or foreign, and that I will bear true faith, allegiance, and loyalty to the same, any ordinance, resolution, or law of any State Convention or Legislature to the contrary notwithstanding; and further, that I do this with a full determination, pledge, and purpose, without any mental reservation or evasion whatsoever; and further, that I will well and faithfully perform all the duties which may be required of me by law. So help me God.

An act of Congress first mandated an oath of allegiance for employees of the United States Government in 1861. This oath was also used as an amnesty oath for political prisoners released by the Union during the Civil War.

IRONCLAD TEST OATH OF LOYALTY—FOR EMPLOYMENT IN THE UNITED STATES GOVERNMENT (JULY 2, 1862)

I, A.B., do solemnly swear (or affirm) [that I have never voluntarily borne arms against the United States since I have been a citizen thereof: that I have voluntarily given no aid, countenance, counsel or encouragement to persons engaged in armed hostility thereto; that I have neither sought nor accepted nor attempted to exercise the functions of any office whatever, under any authority or pretended authority in hostility to the United States; that I have not yielded a voluntary support to any pretended government, authority, power or constitution within the United States, hostile or inimical thereto. And I do further swear (or affirm) that, to the best of my knowledge and ability,] I will support and defend the Constitution of the United States, against all enemies, foreign and domestic: that I will bear true faith and allegiance to the same: that I take this obligation freely, without any mental reservation or purpose of evasion, and that I will well and faithfully discharge the duties of the office on which I am about to enter, so help me God.

This oath, first passed by Congress on July 2, 1862, as the "ironclad test oath of loyalty" for all Federal officers, was extended on January 24, 1865, to include attorneys practicing in U.S. courts. Although reaffirmed as a test oath for those in government service by the Reconstruction Act of 1867, it was ruled unconstitutional by the Supreme Court in 1867 as being a requirement *ex post facto*—that is, one imposing a penalty for an act which was not punishable when it was done. With the test clause (within brackets) removed (by a general bill of July 11, 1868), this is the oath now sworn by members of Congress. The presiding officer of a new Congress administers it in the form of a question to which new members reply: I do. Each member then receives two copies of the oath, one of which he or she signs and returns. The revised oath is also used by the Defense Department as their "Officer's Oath of Office."

LINCOLN'S AMNESTY OATH (DECEMBER 8, 1863)

Whereas it is now desired by some persons heretofore engaged in said rebellion to resume their allegiance to the United States, and to reinaugurate loyal State governments within and for their respective States; therefore,

I, Abraham Lincoln, President of the United States, do proclaim, declare, and make known to all persons who have, directly or by implication, participated in the existing rebellion, except as hereinafter excepted, that a full pardon is hereby granted to them and each of them, with restoration of all rights of property, except as to slaves, and in property cases where rights of third parties shall have intervened, and upon the condition that every such person shall take and subscribe an oath, and thenceforward keep and maintain said oath inviolate; and which oath shall be registered for permanent preservation, and shall be of the tenor and effect of the following, to wit:

"I, ———, do solemnly swear, in the presence of Almighty God, that I will henceforth faithfully support, protect and defend the Constitution of the United States, and the union of the States thereunder; and that I will, in like manner, abide by and faithfully support all acts of Congress passed during the existing rebellion with references to slaves, so long and so far as not repealed, modified or held void by Congress, or by decision of the

Supreme Court; and that I will, in like manner, abide by and faithfully support all proclamations of the President made during the existing rebellion having reference to slaves, so long and so far as not modified or declared void by decision of the Supreme Court. So help me God."

This oath, part of Lincoln's plan for reconstruction (the "ten percent" plan), is Lincoln's alternative to the ironclad oath. In it he refers expressly to his Emancipation Proclamation of July 1862. Congress rejected both this and an alternative later proposed by Andrew Johnson. See Roy P. Basler, ed., *The Collected Works of Abraham Lincoln* VII (New Brunswick, 1953).

THE LEVERING OATH (OCTOBER 1950)

I, ———, do solemnly swear (or affirm) that I will support and defend the Constitution of the United States and Constitution of the State of California against all enemies, foreign and domestic; that I will bear true faith and allegiance to the Constitution of the United States and Constitution of the State of California; that I take this obligation freely, without any mental reservation or purpose of evasion; and that I will well and faithfully discharge the duties upon which I am about to enter. And I do further swear (or affirm) that I do not advocate, nor am I a member of any party or organization, political or otherwise, that now advocates the overthrow of the Government of the United States or of the State of California by force or violence or other unlawful means; that within the five years immediately preceding the taking of this oath (or affirmation) I have not been a member of any party or organization, political or otherwise, that advocated the overthrow of the Government of the United States or of the State of California by force or violence or other unlawful means except as follows: — ——— (If no affiliations, write in the words "No Exceptions") and that during such time as I am a member or employee of the ——— (Name of public agency) I will not advocate or become a member of any party or organization, political or otherwise, that advocates the overthrow of the Government of the United States or of the State of California by force or violence or other unlawful means.

The swearing of this oath, as part of the Levering Act passed by the California Legislature, was required of all public employees. It was ruled unconstitutional by the 3rd District Court of Appeals in California in April 1951 (a decision which was appealed), and was finally ruled invalid by the California Supreme Court in 1967.

LOYALTY OATH FOR U.S. GOVERNMENT EMPLOYEES

I am not a Communist or a Fascist. I do not advocate nor am I knowingly a member of any organization that advocates the overthrow of the constitutional form of the government of the United States or which seeks by force or violence to deny other persons their rights under the Constitution of the United States. I do further swear or affirm that I will not so advocate nor will I knowingly become a member of such an organization during the period that I am an employee of the Federal government or any agency thereof.

Until it was declared unconstitutional by the Supreme Court in 1969, the signing of this oath was required for federal employment. It was replaced by a standard oath of office (much like the Congressional oath) which contained a no-strike clause. It was this clause that served as the basis of Ronald Reagan's decision to fire striking air traffic controllers in 1981.

OATH TAKEN BY NATURALIZED CITIZENS OF THE UNITED STATES.

I hereby declare, on oath, that I absolutely and entirely renounce and abjure all allegiance and fidelity to any foreign prince, potentate, state, or sovereignty of whom or which I have heretofore been a subject or citizen; that I will support and defend the Constitution and laws of the United States of America against all enemies, foreign and domestic; that I will bear true faith and allegiance to the same; [that I will bear arms on behalf of the United States or perform non-combatant service in the Armed Forces of the United States when required by law;] and that I take this obligation freely without any mental reservation or purpose of evasion: So help me God. In acknowledgement whereof I have hereunto affixed my signature.

The clause in brackets is not required. Also, upon swearing this oath, anyone who has a hereditary title of nobility or privilege must renounce that title in court. The oath is contained in the Internal Security Act of September 22, 1950 (section 29).

OATHS OF THE MASONIC ORDERS OF THE YORK RITE (1879)

KNIGHT TEMPLAR OBLIGATION (1879)

I, ———, of my own free will and accord in the presence of the Sovereign Architect of the Universe and this Commandery of Knights Templar, do hereby and hereon most solemnly and sincerely promise and vow that I will ever keep and conceal the secrets of this order of knighthood, and never reveal the same except it be to a true and lawful Sir Knight of the order, or within the body of a regular and duly constituted Commandery of the same, until after due trial, strict examination, or lawful information I find him or them justly entitled to receive the same. . . .

I furthermore promise and vow that I will go the distance of forty miles barefooted and on frozen ground to save the life or relieve the distress of a worthy Sir Knight, should his necessities require and my circumstances permit. . . .

I furthermore promise and vow that I will wield my sword in the defense of innocent maidens, destitute widows, helpless orphans and the Christian religion.

All this I most solemnly and sincerely promise and vow, with a firm and steadfast resolution to keep and perform the same, binding myself under no less penalty than that of having my head smote off and placed on the highest spire in Christiandom, should I ever willfully or knowingly violate any part of this solemn obligation of a Knight Templar, so help me God and keep me steadfast to keep and perform the same.

KNIGHT OF THE RED CROSS

All this I promise and vow, binding myself under no less penalty than that of having my house torn down, the timbers thereof set up and I hung thereon, and when the last trump shall sound I be forever excluded from the society of all true and courteous knights, should I ever willfully or knowingly violate any part of this solemn obligation of Knights of the Red Cross; so help me God and keep me steadfast to keep and perform the same.

SELECT MASTER

All this I promise and swear, with a firm and steadfast resolution to perform the same, without any hesitation, mental reservation, or secret evasion of mind, whatever; binding myself under no less penalty than that of having my eyes torn from my sockets, my hands chopped off and my body quartered, and then thrown among the rubbish of the Temple, should I in the least violate this my Select Master's obligation. So help me God, and keep me steadfast in the due performance of the same.

ROYAL MASTER

All this I promise and swear with a firm and steadfast resolution to perform the same, binding myself under no less a penalty than that of being burned alive.

From Ezra A. Cook, Revised Knight Templarism Illustrated *(Ezra A. Cook: Chicago, 1879).*

THE OLYMPIC OATH

In the name of all competitors I promise that we will take part in these Olympic Games, respecting and abiding by the rules that govern them, in the spirit of sportsmanship for the glory of sport and the honor of our teams.

or,

We swear that we will take part in the Olympic Games in loyal competition, respecting the regulations which govern them and desirous of participating in them in the true spirit of sportsmanship for the honor of our country and for the glory of sport.

Written by Pierre de Coubertin (1862–1937), founder of the modern Olympic Games. The oath is read by a host country athlete.

THE ATHENIAN OATH OF CITIZENSHIP (THE TRADITIONAL OATH OF THE EPHEBI WHICH THEY ARE REQUIRED TO SWEAR)

I will not disgrace my sacred arms
Nor desert my comrade, wherever
I am stationed.
I will fight for things sacred
   and things profane.
And both alone and with all to help me.
I will transmit my fatherland not diminished
But greater and better than before.
I will obey the ruling magistrates
Who rule reasonably
And I will observe the established laws
And whatever laws in the future
May be reasonably established.
If any person seeks to overturn the laws,
Both alone and with all to help me,
I will oppose him.
I will honor the religion of my fathers.
I call to witness the Gods: Aglauros, Hestia, Enyo, Enyalios, Ares and
   Athena Areia, Zeus, Thallo, Auxo, Hegemone, Heracles,
The borders of my fatherland,
The wheat, the barley, the vines,
And the trees of the olive and the fig.

Also known as the Athenian Ephebic Oath, this was the oath sworn by young men who enrolled in the Ephebic College (circa 335 B.C.), a college of citizenship and military training. In various adaptations it has been used by many American colleges and universities. This is a translation of the oath inscribed on an ancient stele discovered at Acharnae in 1934.

THE BOY SCOUT OATH

On my honor I will do my best:
1. To do my duty to God and my country, and to obey the Scout Law;
2. To help other people at all times;
3. To keep myself physically strong, mentally awake, and morally straight.

THE GIRL SCOUT PROMISE

On my honor I will try
to serve God and my country,
to help people at all times,
and to live by the Girl Scout Law.

TEMPERANCE PLEDGE (1789)

We do hereby associate and mutually agree that hereafter we will carry on our business without the use of distilled spirits, as an article of refreshment, either for ourselves, or for those whom we employ; and that instead thereof we will serve our workmen with wholesome food and the common simple drinks of our production.

"Signed by Ephraim Kirby, Timothy Skinner, David Bush and nearly 200 of the most respectable farmers in Litchfield Co., Conn." This pledge is contained in the *White Ribbon Temperance Scrap Book* (Chicago: The Women's Temperance Publication Association, n.d.), which ascribes it to the first temperance association in the United States. The *Scrap Book* can be found in the Library of the Museum of Our National Heritage, Lexington, MA.

PLEDGE OF THE AMERICAN TEMPERANCE SOCIETY

We, whose names are hereunto annexed, believing that the use of ardent spirits as a drink is not only needless, but harmful to the social, civil, and religious interests of men; that it tends to form intemperate appetites and habits, and that while it is continued the evils of intemperance can never be done away with; do, therefore, agree that we will not use or traffic in it; that we will not provide it as articles of entertainment, or for persons in our employment, and that in all suitable ways we will discountenance the use of it in the community.

One of the first total abstinence pledges, this pledge of the American Temperance Society dates from 1826.

PLEDGE OF THE BLUE RIBBON GOSPEL ARMY

With charity to all and malice to none, I promise by divine help, to abstain from all intoxicating liquors and beverages and to discountenance their use by others.

This was the pledge administered in the "pledge booths" of American temperance crusader Richard Booth. The pledge usually ended with: "The Lord help me to keep this pledge, for Jesus' sake."

WOMAN'S CHRISTIAN TEMPERANCE UNION PLEDGE

I hereby solemnly promise, God helping me, to abstain from all distilled, fermented and malt liquors, including wine, beer and cider, and to employ all proper means to discourage the use and traffic in the same.

From the "Declaration of Principles" of the WCTU, written in 1874 by the organization's president, Frances E. Willard.

ENGLISH AND FRENCH ANTECEDENTS OF THE FAMILIAR WEDDING VOWS (QUOTED FROM HUGH STEVENSON, *NUPTIAL BLESSING*)

"N. do you want this woman," and if he answers yes, "do you wish to serve her in the faith of God as your own, in health and infirmity, as a Christian should serve his wife?"

Magdalen Pontifical, an English rite of the twelfth century

Do you really want this woman as your wife, to guard her in health and sickness, as long as she lives, as a good man should keep his wife, and to join her faithfully with your body, and all your possessions?

Roman rite, second quarter of the thirteenth century

Do you promise before God that you will have N. as your wife, and that you will keep faith and fidelity with her, and that you will protect her in health and sickness and all other circumstances; and that you will not change her or dismiss her, for better or for worse?

St Maur-des-Fosses, a French rite of the second half of the thirteenth century

FORM OF SOLEMNIZATION OF MATRIMONY—FROM THE SARUM MISSAL (1526)

Brethren, we are gathered together here, in the sight of God, and his angels, and all the saints, and in the face of the Church, to join together two bodies, to wit, those of this man and this woman, that henceforth they may be one body; and that they may be two souls in the faith and law of God, to the end they may earn together eternal life; and whatsoever they may have done before this, I charge you all by the Father, and the Son, and the Holy Ghost, that if any of you know any cause why these persons may not be lawfully joined together in matrimony, he do now confess it.

. . . After this, the priest shall say to the man, in the audience of all, in the vulgar tongue,

N. wilt thou have this woman to thy wedded wife, wilt thou love her, and honor her, keep her and guard her, in health and in sickness, as a husband should a wife, and forsaking all others on account of her, keep thee only unto her, so long as ye both shall live?

The man shall answer, I will.

N. wilt thou take this man to thy wedded husband, wilt thou obey him, and serve him, love, honor, and keep him, in health and sickness, as a wife should a husband, and forsaking all others on account of him, keep thee only unto him, so long as ye both shall live?

The woman will answer, I will.

Then let the woman be given by her father or a friend; if she be a maid, let her have her hand uncovered; if she be a widow, covered; and let the man receive her, to be kept in God's faith and his own, as he hath vowed in the presence of the priest; and let him hold her by her right hand in his right hand. And so let the man give his troth to the woman, by word of mouth, presently, after the priest, saying thus:

I N. take thee N. to my wedded wife, to have and to hold from this day, for better, for worse, for richer, for poorer, in sickness and in health, till death us depart, if Holy Church will it ordain. And thereto I plight thee my troth.

Then shall the woman say, after the priest:

I N. take thee N. to my wedded husband, to have and to hold from this day, for better, for worse, for richer, for poorer, in sickness and in health, to be bonowre and buxom, in bed and at board, till death us depart, if Holy Church will it ordain. And thereto I plight thee my troth.

Then shall the man lay gold, or silver, and a ring upon a dish or book; [if not previously blessed, the priest blesses the ring] . . . the priest shall take up the ring, and deliver it to the man. The man shall take it in his right hand with his three principal fingers, holding the right hand of the bride with his left hand, and shall say, after the priest,

With this ring I thee wed and this gold and silver I thee give: and with my body I thee worship, and with all my worldly chattel I thee honor.

Then shall the bridegroom place the ring upon the thumb of the bride, saying, In the name of the Father; then upon the second finger, saying, and of the Son; then upon the third finger, saying, and of the Holy Ghost; then upon the fourth finger, saying, Amen, and there let him leave it . . . because in that finger there is a certain vein, which runs from thence as far as the heart; and inward affection, which ought always to be fresh between them, is signified by the true ring of the silver. Then, while they bow their heads, the priest shall pronounce a blessing upon them.

Be ye blessed of the Lord, who hath made the world out of nothing.

From *The Sarum Missal in English*, a translation of the folio of 1526 by Frederick E. Warren (London: De La Mare Press, 1911)—with the spelling and punctuation modernized. The Sarum rite of marriage was retained by the Catholic Church in England after the Reformation. It is also the rite adapted by Thomas Cranmer for the English Prayer Book.

CODES OF ETHICS AND CONDUCT

PERCIVAL'S *MEDICAL ETHICS* (1801)—EXCERPTS

OF PROFESSIONAL CONDUCT RELATIVE TO HOSPITALS OR OTHER MEDICAL CHARITIES

Hospital physicians and surgeons should minister to the sick, with due impressions of the importance of their office, reflecting that the ease, the health, and the lives of those committed to their charge depend on their skill, attention and fidelity. They should study also, in their deportment, so as to unite *tenderness* with *steadiness*, and *condescension* with *authority*, as to inspire the minds of their patients with gratitude, respect and confidence. . . .

OF PROFESSIONAL CONDUCT IN PRIVATE OR GENERAL PRACTICE

The *moral rules of conduct*, prescribed towards hospital patients, should be fully adopted in private or general practice. Every case, committed to the charge of a physician or surgeon, should be treated with attention, steadiness and humanity. . . . Secrecy and delicacy, when required by peculiar circumstances, should be strictly observed. And the familiar and confidential intercourse, to which the faculty are admitted in their professional visits, should be used with discretion and with the most scrupulous regard to fidelity and honour.

THE HIPPOCRATIC OATH

I swear by Apollo, the Physician, and Aesculapius and Hygieia and Panacea and all the Gods and Goddesses that, according to my ability and judgment, I will keep this oath and covenant.

To hold him who taught me this art equally dear to me as my parents, to share my substance with him and relieve his necessities if required: to regard his offspring as on the same footing with my own brothers, and to teach them this art if they should wish to learn it, without fee and covenant, and that by precept, lecture and every other mode of instruction, I will impart a knowledge of the art to my own sons and to those of my teachers, and to disciples bound by a covenant and oath, according to the law of medicine, but to no one else.

I will follow that method of treatment which, according to my ability and judgment, I consider for the benefit of my patients, and abstain from whatever is deleterious and mischievous. I will give no deadly medicine to anyone if asked, nor suggest any such council; furthermore, I will not give to a woman an instrument to produce abortion.

With Purity and Holiness I will pass my life and practice my art. I will not cut a person who is suffering with a stone, but will leave this to be done by practitioners of this work. Into whatever houses I enter I will go into them for the benefit of the sick and will abstain from every voluntary act of mischief and corruption; and further from the seduction of females or males, bond or free.

Whatever, in connection with my professional practice, or not in connection with it, I may see or hear in the lives of men which ought not to be spoken abroad I will not divulge, as reckoning that all such should be kept secret.

While I continue to keep this oath unviolated, may it be granted to me to enjoy life and the practice of the art, respected by all men at all times, but should I trespass and violate this oath, may the reverse be my lot.

The Declaration of Geneva

At the Time of Being Admitted as a Member
of the Medical Profession:

I solemnly pledge myself to consecrate my life to the service of humanity.

I will give my teachers the respect and gratitude which is their due;

I will practice my profession with conscience and dignity;

The health of my patient will be my first consideration;

I will respect the secrets which are confided in me;

I will maintain by all the means in my power the honor and noble traditions of the medical profession;

My colleagues will be my brothers;

I will not permit considerations of religion, nationality, race, party politics or social standing to intervene between my duty and my patient.

I will maintain the utmost respect for human life, from the time of conception; even under threat, I will not use my medical knowledge contrary to the laws of humanity.

I make these promises solemnly, freely and upon my honor.

This pledge was drafted in 1948 (and amended in 1968) by the World Medical Association as a modern restatement of the Hippocratic Oath. It is taken upon graduation from medical school or, in some countries, upon being licensed as a physician.

THE PRAYER OF MAIMONIDES

The eternal providence has appointed me to watch over the life and health of Thy creatures. May the love for my art actuate me at all times; may neither avarice nor miserliness, not thirst for glory or for a great reputation engage my mind; for the enemies of truth and philanthropy could easily deceive me and make me forgetful of my lofty aim of doing good to Thy children.

May I never see in the patient anything but a fellow creature in pain. Grant me strength, time and opportunity always to correct what I have acquired, always to extend its domain; for knowledge is immense and the spirit of man can extend indefinitely to enrich itself daily with new requirements.

Today he can discover his errors of yesterday and tomorrow he may obtain a new light on what he thinks himself sure of today. Oh, God, Thou hast appointed me to watch over the life and death of Thy creatures; here am I ready for my vocation, and now I turn unto my calling.

This code is contained in a prayer ascribed to the Jewish philosopher Moses Maimonides (1135–1204), but was actually written in 1783 by Markus Herz, a German physician. Although a prayer and not properly an oath, it has been adapted to serve in place of the Hippocratic Oath by many medical schools. It also serves as a pledge for pharmacists.

A MODERN HIPPOCRATIC OATH

I swear to fulfill, to the best of my ability and judgment, this covenant:

I will respect the hard-won scientific gains of those physicians in whose steps I walk, and gladly share such knowledge as is mine with those who are to follow.

I will apply, for the benefit of the sick, all measures which are required; avoiding those twin traps of overtreatment and therapeutic nihilism.

I will remember that there is art to medicine as well as science, and that warmth, sympathy and understanding may outweigh the surgeon's knife or the chemist's drug.

I will not be ashamed to say "I know not," nor will I fail to call in my colleague when the skills of another are needed for the patient's recovery.

I will respect the privacy of my patients, for their problems are not disclosed to me that the world may know. Most especially must I tread with care in matters of life and death. If it is given me to save a life, all thanks.

But it may also be within my power to take a life; this awesome responsibility must be faced with great humbleness and awareness of my own frailty. Above all, I must not play at God.

I will remember that I do not treat a fever chart, or a cancerous growth, but a sick human being, whose illness may affect his family and his economic stability. My responsibility includes these related problems, if I am to care adequately for the sick.

I will prevent disease whenever I can, for prevention is preferable to cure.

I will remember that I remain a member of society, with special obligations to all my fellow human beings, those sound of mind and body, as well as the infirm.

If I do not violate this oath, may I enjoy life and art, respected while I live and remembered with affection thereafter. May I always act so as to preserve the finest traditions of my calling and may I long experience the joy of healing those who seek my help.

Louis Lasagna, "Would Hippocrates Rewrite His Oath?"
New York Times Magazine, *June 28, 1964*

A MID-WIFE'S OATH (FROM THE BOOK OF OATHS, 1649)

1. YOU SHALL SWEAR, first, that you shall be diligent and faithful, and ready to help every woman labouring of child, as well as the poor as the rich; and that in time of necessity, you shall not forsake, or leave the poor woman to go to the rich.

2. ITEM, Ye shall neither cause nor suffer any woman to name, or put any other father to the child, but only him which is the very true father thereof indeed.

3. ITEM, You shall not suffer any woman to pretend, feign, or surmize herself to be delivered of a child, who is not indeed; neither to claim any other woman's child for her own.

4. ITEM, You shall not suffer any woman's child to be murdered, maimed, or otherwise hurt, as much as you may; and so often as you shall perceive any peril or jeopardy, either in the woman, or in the child, in any such wise, as you shall be in doubt what shall chance thereof, you shall thenceforth in due time send for other midwifes, and expert women in that faculty, and use their advice and counsel on that behalf.

5. ITEM, That you shall not in any wise use or exercise any manner of witchcraft, charm, or sorcery, invocation, or other prayers than may stand with God's Laws and the King's.
6. ITEM, You shall not give any counsel, or minister any herb, medicine, or potion, or any other thing, to any woman being with child whereby she should destroy or cast out that she goeth withal before her time.
7. ITEM, You shall not enforce any woman being with child by any pain, or by any ungodly ways or means, to give you any more for your pains and labour in bringing her a bed than they would otherwise do.
8. ITEM, You shall not consent, agree, give, or keep counsel, that any woman be delivered secretly of that which she goeth with, but in the presence of two or three lights ready.
9. ITEM, You shall be secret, and not open any matter appertaining to your office in the presence of any man, unless necessity or great urgent cause do constrain you so to do.
10. ITEM, If any child be born dead, yourself shall see it buried in such secret place as neither hog, nor dog, nor any other beast may come unto it, and in such sort done, as it be not found nor perceived, as much as you may; and that you shall not suffer any such child to be cast into the Jacques, or any other inconvenient place.
11. ITEM, If you shall know any midwife using or doing any thing contrary to any of the premises, or in any other wise than shall be seemly or convenient, you shall forthwith detect, open, and show the same to me or my Chancellor for the time being.
12. ITEM, You shall use yourself in honest behavior unto the woman being lawfully admitted to the room and office of a midwife in all things accordingly.
13. ITEM, That you shall truly present to myself, or my Chancellor, all such women as you know from time to time to occupy and exercise the room of a midwife . . . without my license and admission.
14. ITEM, You shall not make or assign any deputy or deputies to exercise or occupy under you or in your absence the office or room of a midwife, but such as you shall perfectly know to be of right honest and discreet behavior, as also apt, able, and having sufficient knowledge and experience to exercise the said room and office.

15. ITEM, You shall not be privy, or consent, that any priest, or other party, shall in your absence, or in your company, or of your knowledge or sufferance, baptise any child, by any mass, Latin-service, or prayers, than such as are appointed by the laws of the Church of England; neither shall you consent that any child, born by any woman, who shall be delivered by you, shall be carried away without being baptised in the parish by the ordinary minister, where the said child is born, unless it be in case of necessity, baptised privately, according to the Book of Common Prayer: But you shall forthwith upon understanding thereof, either give knowledge to me the said bishop, or my chancellor for the time being. All which articles and charges you shall faithfully observe and keep. So help you God and by the contents of this Book.

QUALIFICATION OF A MEMBER—NATIONAL AUTOMOBILE DEALERS ASSOCIATION (1922)

He is a business man.

He reflects his personal integrity in every transaction.

He has capacity, credit, and financial standing.

He is one with whom you enjoy dealing because his methods inspire confidence.

He handles only approved merchandise of merit which he has bought at a price that will return to him a legitimate profit.

He is courteous and demands courtesy of his employees for his customers.

He does not disparage his competitor.

He advertises truthfully. He is building his business for permanence.

He departmentizes his business. He specializes for his own benefit and economizes for your benefit.

He is a clear thinking, aggressive business man who knows how to conduct his business and does it. He believes in the Golden Rule for himself and insists on it for his customers. . . .

According to Edgar Heermance, candidates for the Association had to have two years experience in the business and a credit rating of $10,000.

ANTIOCH BUSINESS CODE (1925)

Sound business is service which benefits all the parties concerned. To take profit without contribution to essential welfare; to take excessive profit; to cater to ignorance, credulity, or human frailty; to debase taste or standards for profit; to use methods not inspired by goodwill and fair dealing—this is dishonor. Whenever I make or sell a product or render a business service, it must be my best possible contribution to human well-being.

The Antioch code was written by Arthur E. Morgan, president of Antioch College, and appeared in *The Nation's Business* (June 1925, pp. 34–35) under the title: "This College Has a Business Code." In proposing this code for his students, who alternated study with internships, Morgan declared a desire to free Americans from "the heavy bond of tradition" (meaning "the standards of Greece and Rome") and to let them "state for themselves new standards of what is fine."

A DECLARATION OF PRINCIPLES—PACIFIC ICE CREAM MANUFACTURERS' ASSOCIATION (1922)

We Believe in ice cream, and in the great future that lies before the industry, because ice cream is the one product which contains all of the life giving, body building properties peculiar to milk, combined with a variety and palatability found in no other milk product.

We Believe that all legitimate business must rest upon the secure foundation of a fair reward for honest service;

That a condition precedent to the right to engage in business is the assumption of this obligation of service to society;

That this obligation may be fully discharged only through the fullest measure of progress in industry;

That such progress may best be achieved through the intelligent co-operation of those identified with any given line of human endeavor;

And that unrestrained competition, with the destructive practices which attend it, defeats progress and becomes a burden upon society.

We Recognize, as included among such destructive practices:

The use of adulturants, or of any ingredients other than those known to be wholesome and meritorious, or the sale of any article as a food

product or as an ingredient in a food product which, because of its
own nature or method of manufacture, or for any other reason, is in
violation of local, state, or federal food laws;

The misrepresentation, by word of mouth or in writing, of the products,
processes, service or business methods of either ourselves or our
competitors;

The use of any advertising copy which is not constructive in its nature,
or which might tend to destroy public confidence in ice cream as a
wholesome food;

Price discrimination between different purchasers or different localities,
which is not based on legitimate cost or service considerations;

Selling or offering to sell at cost or at less than a fair profit,—or offering
or rendering secret rebates or unusual and discriminatory service or
inducements,—for the purpose of injuring a competitor;

We pledge ourselves: To conduct our businesses upon the basis of service and square dealing to the public, and to the industry of which we are
a part;

To promote, in our relations with our competitors, a spirit of fairness
and tolerance;

To ourselves refrain, and to discourage others, from any and all practices which would be detrimental to the interest of the public, or of the
industry;

And to co-operate in every practicable way toward a fuller appreciation
of ice cream as a wholesome, all-year-round food.

This code incorporates the elements of a creed and an oath. It was adopted
by the Pacific Ice Cream Manufacturers' Association on November 15, 1922.

THE 4-WAY TEST (OF THE THINGS WE THINK, SAY OR DO)— ROTARY INTERNATIONAL

1. Is it the TRUTH?
2. Is it FAIR to all concerned?
3. Will it build GOODWILL and BETTER FRIENDSHIPS?
4. Will it be BENEFICIAL to all concerned?

Written in 1932 by Chicago Rotarian Herbert J. Taylor as "a simple mea-
suring stick of ethics which everyone . . . could quickly memorize." Rotary

International also maintains a statement of principles and a statement of object and purpose.

CODE OF DECENCY—THE MARION STAR (C. 1920)

Remember there are two sides to every question. Get them both.

Be truthful.

Get the facts. Mistakes are inevitable, but strive for accuracy. I would rather have one story exactly right than a hundred half wrong.

Be decent. Be fair. Be generous.

Boost—don't knock. There's good in everybody. Bring out the good and never needlessly hurt the feelings of anybody.

In reporting a political gathering, get the facts: Tell the story as it is, not as you would like to have it.

Treat all parties alike. If there is any politics to be played, we will play them in our editorial columns.

Treat all religious matters reverently.

If it can possibly be avoided, never bring ignominy on an innocent man or child, in telling of the misdeeds or misfortunes of a relative.

Don't wait to be asked, but do it without the asking.

And, above all, be clean. Never let a dirty word or suggestive story get into type.

I want this paper to be so conducted that it can go into any home without destroying the innocence of any child.

Written by President Warren G. Harding when he was the editor of the Star

CODE OF CONDUCT FOR MEMBERS OF THE ARMED FORCES OF THE UNITED STATES—"U.S. FIGHTING MAN'S CODE"

I. I am an American fighting man. I serve in the forces which guard my country and our way of life. I am prepared to give my life in their defense.

II. I will never surrender of my own free will. If in command I will never surrender my men while they still have the means to resist.

III. If I am captured I will continue to resist by all means available. I will make every effort to escape and aid others to escape. I will accept neither parole nor special favors from the enemy.

IV. If I become a prisoner of war, I will keep faith with my fellow prisoners. I will give no information or take part in any action which might be harmful to my comrades. If I am senior, I will take command. If not, I will obey the lawful orders of those appointed over me and will back them up in every way.

V. When questioned, should I become a prisoner of war, I am bound to give only name, rank, service number, and date of birth. I will evade answering further questions to the utmost of my ability. I will make no oral or written statements disloyal to my country and its allies or harmful to their cause.

VI. I will never forget that I am an American fighting man, responsible for my actions, and dedicated to the principles which made my country free. I will trust in my God and in the United States of America.

The code governs all members of the U.S. Armed Forces. It was drafted at the request of President Eisenhower, who wanted to establish guidelines for the professional conduct of U.S. servicemen. The code became official on August 17, 1955, as President's Executive Order 10631.

THE BOY SCOUT LAWS

A Scout is TRUSTWORTHY. A Scout tells the truth. He keeps his promises. Honesty is part of his code of conduct. People can always depend on him.

A Scout is LOYAL. A Scout is true to his family, friends, Scout leaders, school, nation, and world community.

A Scout is HELPFUL. A Scout is concerned about other people. He willingly volunteers to help others without expecting payment or reward.

A Scout is FRIENDLY. A Scout is a friend to all. He is a brother to other Scouts. He seeks to understand others. He respects those with ideas and customs that are different from his own.

A Scout is COURTEOUS. A Scout is polite to everyone regardless of age or position. He knows that good manners make it easier for people to get along together.

A Scout is KIND. A Scout understands there is strength in being gentle. He treats others as he wants to be treated. He does not harm or kill anything without reason.

A Scout is OBEDIENT. A Scout follows the rules of his family, school, and troop. He obeys the laws of his community and country. If he thinks these rules and laws are unfair, he tries to have them changed in an orderly manner rather than disobey them.

A Scout is CHEERFUL. A Scout looks for the bright side of life. He cheerfully does tasks that come his way. He tries to make others happy.

A Scout is THRIFTY. A Scout works to pay his way and to help others. He saves for the future. He protects and conserves natural resources. He carefully uses time and property.

A Scout is BRAVE. A Scout can face danger even if he is afraid. He has the courage to stand for what he thinks is right even if others laugh at him or threaten him.

A Scout is CLEAN. A Scout keeps his body and mind fit and clean. He goes around with those who believe in living by these same ideas. He helps keep his home and community clean.

A Scout is REVERENT. A Scout is reverent toward God. He is faithful in his religious duties. He respects the beliefs of others.

First formulated in 1908 by founder Sir Robert Baden-Powell, the Scout Oath and Laws have undergone many revisions over the years. This is the most recent version of the Law, as administered by the Boy Scouts of America.

THE TWELVE STEPS OF ALCOHOLICS ANONYMOUS

Step One: We admitted that we were powerless over alcohol—that our lives had become unmanageable.

Step Two: Came to believe that a Power greater than ourselves could restore us to sanity.

Step Three: Made a decision to turn our will and our lives over to the care of God as *we understood Him.*

Step Four: Made a searching and fearless moral inventory of ourselves.

Step Five: Admitted to God, to ourselves and to another human being the exact nature of our wrongs.

Step Six: Were entirely ready to have God remove all these defects of character.

Step Seven: Humbly asked Him to remove our shortcomings.

Step Eight: Made a list of all persons we had harmed, and became willing to make amends to them all.

Step Nine: Made direct amends to such people whenever possible, except when to do so would injure them or others.

Step Ten: Continued to take personal inventory and when we were wrong promptly admitted it.

Step Eleven: Sought through prayer and meditation to improve our conscious contact with God *as we understood Him,* praying only for knowledge of His will for us and the power to carry that out.

Step Twelve: Having had a spiritual awakening as a result of these steps, we tried to carry this message to alcoholics, and to practice these principles in all our affairs.

Written by Bill W., one of the founding influences of AA, in December 1938. The Twelve Steps were conceived as an expansion of six basic steps that Bill W. attributed to the Oxford Group Movement, to Dr. William Silkworth, and to William James's *The Varieties of Religious Experience.* These steps are the model for most recovery programs, which are generally referred to as "twelve-step" programs.

OFFICIAL CREED—E[LVIS] P[RESLEY] IMPERSONATORS INTERNATIONAL ASSOCIATION

I have an obligation to all associations, groups, and businesses who purchase my entertainment services to provide those services in a professional and ethical manner.

I have an obligation as an Elvis performer, through all my personal, business, and social contacts, to be conscious of my image and what I represent and to conduct myself accordingly.

I will provide leadership and direction in continuing the music and style of Elvis, while lending strength and direction to the growth of the activity as a great world-class entertainment medium.

Harper's Magazine, *September 1991, p. 26*

MY SYMPHONY

My scheme of life is so simple that it needs still sunshine, like a harvest field. To be a workingman, poor, humble; to perform without show or shunning menial services; to live content with small means; to seek elegance rather than luxury, and refinement rather than fashion; to be worthy, not respectable; and wealthy, not rich; to study hard, think quietly, talk gently, act frankly; to have an oratory with my own heart, and present spotless sacrifices of dignified kindness in the temple of humanity; to spread no opinions glaringly out like show-plants, and yet leave the garden gate ever open for the chosen friend and the chance acquaintance; to make no pretense to greatness; to seek no notoriety; to attempt no wide influence; to have no ambitious projects; to let my writings be the daily bubbling spring flowing through constancy, swelled by experiences, into the full, deep river of wisdom; to listen to stars and buds, to babes and sages, with open heart; to bear all cheerfully, do all bravely, await occasions, hurry never; . . . in a word, to let the spiritual, unbidden and unconscious, grow up through the common. This is to be my symphony.

> William Henry Channing (1810–1884)
> From a letter to Margaret Fuller, dated Cincinnati,
> April 15, 1841. See Octavius Brooks Frothingham,
> Memoir of William Henry Channing
> (Boston: 1886), p. 166.

FOUNDATIONS OF FAITH (1895)

To love justice, to long for the right, to love mercy, to pity the suffering, to assist the weak, to forget wrongs and remember benefits—to love the truth, to be sincere, to utter honest words, to love liberty, to wage relentless war against slavery in all its forms, to love wife and child and friend, to make a happy home, to love the beautiful in art, in nature, to cultivate the mind, to be familiar with the mighty thoughts that genius has expressed, the noble deeds of all the world, to cultivate courage and cheerfulness, to make others happy, to fill life with the splendor of generous acts, the warmth of loving words, to discard error, to destroy prejudice, to receive new truths with gladness, to cultivate hope, to see the calm beyond the storm, the dawn beyond the night, to do the best that can be done and then be resigned. This is the religion of reason, the creed of science. This satisfies the brain and heart.

> Robert G. Ingersoll (1833–1899) Works (New York:
> The Ingersoll League, 1933), Volume IV, p. 290

TESTAMENT OF A CRITIC

My code of life and conduct is simply this: work hard, play to the allowable limit, disregard equally the good and the bad opinion of others, never do a friend a dirty trick, eat and drink what you feel like when you feel like, never grow indignant over anything, trust to tobacco for calm and serenity, bathe twice a day, modify the aesthetic philosophy of Croce but slightly with that of Santanaya and achieve for one's self a pragmatic sufficiency in the beauty of the aesthetic surface of life, learn to play at least one musical instrument and then play it only in private, never allow one's self even a passing thought of death, never contradict anyone or seek to prove anything to anyone else unless one gets paid for it in cold, hard coin, live the moment to the utmost of its possibilities, treat one's enemy with polite inconsideration, avoid persons who are chronically in need, and be satisfied with life always but never with one's self. An infinite belief in the possibilities of one's self with a coincidental critical assessment and derogation of one's achievements, self-respect combined with a measure of self-surgery, aristocracy of mind combined with democracy of heart, forthrightness with modesty or at least good manners, dignity with a quiet laugh, honor and honesty and decency: these are the greatest qualities that a man can hope to attain. And as one man, my hope is to attain them.

> George Jean Nathan (1882–1958)
> Testament of a Critic (1931), p. 14

JACK LONDON'S CODE

I would rather be ashes than dust! I would rather that my spark should burn out in a brilliant blaze than it should be stifled by dry-rot. I would rather be a superb meteor, every atom of me in magnificent glow, than a sleepy and permanent planet. The proper function of man is to live, not to exist. I shall not waste my days in trying to prolong them. I shall use up my time.

Quoted in Irving Shepard, ed., *Jack London's Tales of Adventure* (1956), p. vii, this is known as London's credo. He spoke the words to his friends two months before he died, at the age of 39.

A STICK-UP MAN'S CODE

1. I will not kill anyone unless I have to.
2. I will take cash and food stamps—no checks.
3. I will rob only at night.
4. I will not wear a mask.
5. I will not rob minimarts or 7-Eleven stores.
6. If chased by cops on foot I will get away. If chased by a vehicle I will not put the lives of innocent civilians on the line.
7. I will rob only seven months out of the year.
8. I will enjoy robbing from the poor to give to the poor.

From a list of personal rules that Dennis Lee Curtis, an armed robber in Rapid City, South Dakota, was carrying in his wallet when he was arrested. [*Harper's Magazine*, January 1992, p. 24.]

CHICAGO CUBS—TEAM RULES (1913)

1. The use of intoxicating drinks of any kind is absolutely prohibited.
2. When the team is at home every player must report at the field, in uniform, not later than 10:30 A.M. each day, and must be on the field at least one hour before game time, at home or abroad.
3. All players must be in their rooms for the night not later than midnight, and should arise not later than 8 A.M.
4. The smoking of cigarettes is absolutely prohibited.

The penalty for the violation of any of the foregoing rules will be a fine, a suspension, or both according to the offense.

Charles Murphy, team president

MARQUESS OF QUEENSBERRY RULES (BOXING)

Rule 1. To be a fair stand-up boxing match in a 24-foot ring, or as near that size as practicable.

Rule 2. No wrestling or hugging allowed.

Rule 3. The rounds to be of three minutes' duration, and one minute's time between rounds.

Rule 4. If either man falls through weakness or otherwise, he must get up unassisted, 10 seconds to be allowed him to do so, the other man meanwhile to return to his corner, and when the fallen man is on his legs the round is to be resumed and continued until the three minutes have expired. If one man fails to come to the scratch in the 10 seconds allowed, it shall be in the power of the referee to give his award in the favor of the other man.

Rule 5. A man hanging on the ropes in a helpless state, with his toes off the ground, shall be considered down.

Rule 6. No seconds or any other person to be allowed in the ring during the rounds.

Rule 7. Should the contest be stopped by any unavoidable interference, the referee to name the time and place as soon as possible for finishing the contest; so that the match must be won and lost, unless the backers of both men agree to draw the stakes.

Rule 8. The gloves to be fair-sized boxing gloves of the best quality and new.

Rule 9. Should a glove burst, or come off, it must be replaced to the referee's satisfaction.

Rule 10. A man on one knee is considered down and if struck is entitled to the stakes.

Rule 11. No shoes or boots with springs allowed.

Rule 12. The contest in all other respects to be governed by revised rules of the London Prize Ring.

These are the first rules of modern boxing. They were written by John Graham Chambers, a member of the British Amateur Athletic Club, and published in 1867 with the sponsorship of John Sholto Douglas, ninth marquess of Queensberry.

BARNSTABLE (MA) BABE RUTH LEAGUE (C. 1964)— STATEMENT OF PURPOSE

A charitable, non-profit organization for encouragement and assistance of young boys in developing:

1. A strong, clean, healthy body, mind, and soul.
2. A strong urge for sportsmanlike conduct.
3. Understanding of and respect for rules, and courage in defeat, tolerance and modesty in victory, control over emotions and speech.
4. Spirit of cooperation and team play and developing into real true Americans.
5. And advancement of young boys through scholarship of merit to various schools of higher education.

ADVICE AND RULES OF LIFE

The Art of Worldly Wisdom (Baltasar Gracian)
The Ten Commandments of Success (Charles M. Schwab)
William Cecil's Ten Precepts
Sir Walter Raleigh's Instructions to His Son
The Earl of Chesterfield's Letters to His Son
George Washington—Advice to His Nephew
Ann Wright—To Her Son Frank Lloyd Wright
Occam's Razor
Parkinson's Law
Parkinson's Law of Triviality
Parkinson's Law (Culinary Version)
The Peter Principle
Peter's Corollary
Peter's Rule
Gracian's Laws
Gresham's Law
Advice from Benjamin Franklin's *Poor Richard's Almanac*
Benjamin Franklin's Thirteen Virtues
Thomas Jefferson's Decalogue of Canons for Observation in Practical Life
Make No Little Plans (Daniel H. Burnham)
Miscellaneous Advice

THE ART OF WORLDLY WISDOM

Never, out of obstinacy, champion the worse cause, because your opponent has forestalled you and taken the better one.

OR,

Don't take the wrong side of an argument just because your opponent has taken the right side.

> *Baltasar Gracian (1601–1658)*
> The Art of Worldly Wisdom, *or* The Oraculo
> Manual *(1647), Aphorism 142*

The man who does a foolish thing is not a fool; rather is he a fool who, having done it, is incapable of concealing it. You should keep your emotions under the seal of secrecy, still more your failings. All men make mistakes, but with this distinction, that the wise conceal the blunders they have made while fools proclaim those which they are about to make. . . . Do not confide your failings even to your friends, nor, if that be possible, admit them even to yourself: but here you can abide by another rule of life, namely: know how to forget.

> *Baltasar Gracian (1601–1658)*
> The Art of Worldly Wisdom, *or* The Oraculo
> Manual *(1647), Aphorism 126*

The wise man . . . knows that the first rule of prudence demands that he should behave as the occasion demands.

> *Baltasar Gracian (1601–1658)*
> The Art of Worldly Wisdom, *or* The Oraculo
> Manual *(1647), Aphorism 288*

THE TEN COMMANDMENTS OF SUCCESS

1. Work Hard. Hard work is the best investment a man can make.
2. Study Hard. Knowledge enables a man to work more intelligently and effectively.
3. Have Initiative. Ruts often deepen into graves.
4. Love Your Work. Then you will find pleasure in mastering it.
5. Be Exact. Slipshod methods bring slipshod results.

6. Have the Spirit of Conquest. Thus you can successfully battle and overcome difficulties.

7. Cultivate Personality. Personality is to the man what perfume is to the flower.

8. Help and Share with Others. The real test of business greatness lies in giving opportunity to others.

9. Be Democratic. Unless you feel right towards your fellowmen you can never be a successful leader of men.

10. In All Things Do Your Best. The man who has done his best has done everything. The man who has done less than his best has done nothing.

Charles M. Schwab (1862–1938)

WILLIAM CECIL'S TEN PRECEPTS

1. When it shall please God to bring thee to man's estate, use great providence and circumspection in the choice of thy wife, for from thence may spring all the future good or evil; and it is an action of life like unto a stratagem of war, wherein a man can err but once . . .

2. Bring thy children up in learning and obedience, yet without austerity. Praise them openly, reprehend them secretly. Give them good countenance and convenient maintenance according to thy ability . . .

3. Live not in the country without corn and cattle about thee; for he that putteth his hand to the purse for every expense of household is like him that keepeth water in a sieve . . .

4. Let thy kindred and allies be welcome to thy table. . . . But shake off those glowworms, I mean parasites and sycophants who will feed and fawn upon thee in thy prosperous hours, but in adverse storms they will shelter thee no more than an arbor in winter.

5. Beware of suretyship for thy best friends. He that payeth another man's debts seeketh his own decay. But if thou canst not otherwise choose, rather lend thy money thyself upon good bonds, although thou borrow it; so shalt thou secure thyself and pleasure thy friend. Neither borrow money of a neighbor or a friend, but of a mere stranger, where paying for it thou mayest hear no more of it . . .

6. Undertake no suit against a poor man without receiving much wrong; for besides that thou maketh him thy compeer, it is a base conquest to triumph where there is small resistance. Neither attempt law against any man before thou be fully resolved that thou hast right on thy side, and then spare not for either money or pains; for a cause or two so followed and obtained will free thee from suits a great part of thy life.

7. Be sure ever to keep some great man thy friend, but trouble him not for trifles. Compliment him often with many, yet small gifts, and of little charge.

8. Towards thy superiors, be humble, yet generous, with thine equals familiar, yet respective. Towards thine inferiors show much humanity, and some familiarity. . . . Yet I advise thee not to affect or neglect popularity too much.

9. Trust not any man with thy life, credit, or estate; for it is a mere folly for a man to enthrall himself to a friend as though, occasion being offered, he should not dare to become thine enemy.

10. Be not scurrilous in conversation nor satirical in thy jests; the one may make thee unwelcome to all companies, the other pulls on quarrels, and gets the hatred of thy best friends. . . .

> William Cecil, Lord Burghley (1520–1598)
> Certain Precepts for the Well Ordering of a Man's
> Life (1618) *as reprinted in* The Young Gentleman's
> Parental Monitor (London, 1792)

SIR WALTER RALEIGH'S INSTRUCTIONS TO HIS SON (C. 1616)

1. There is nothing more becoming a wise man than to make choice of friends, for by them thou shalt be judged what thou are.

2. The next and greatest care ought to be in the choice of a wife, and the only danger therein is beauty, by which all men in all ages, wise and foolish, have been betrayed.

3. Take care thou be not made a fool by flatterers, for even the wisest men are abused by these.

4. Be careful to avoid public disputations at feasts or at tables amongst choleric or quarrelsome persons. . . .

5. Amongst all other things of the world take care of thy estate, which thou shalt ever preserve if thou observe three things. First,

that thou know what thou hast, what everything is worth that thou hast, and to see that thou are not wasted by thy servants and officers. The second is that thou never spend anything before you have it, for borrowing is the canker and death of every man's estate. The third is that thou suffer not thyself to be wounded for other men's faults and scourged for other men's offenses, which is to be surety for another. . . .

6. Let thy servants be such as thou mayest command, and entertain none about thee but yeomen to whom thou givest wages, for those that will serve thee without thy hire will cost thee treble as much as they that know their fare.

7. Exceed not in humor of rags and bravery, for these will soon wear out of fashion, but money in thy purse will ever be in fashion, and no man is esteemed for gay garments but by fools and women.

8. On the other side, take heed that thou seek not riches basely nor attain them by evil means; destroy no man for his wealth nor take anything from the poor, for the cry and complaint thereof will pierce the heavens.

9. Take especial care that thou delight not in wine, for there never was any man that came into honor or preferment that loved it; for it transformeth a man into a beast, decayeth health, poisoneth the breath, destroyeth natural heat, brings a man's stomach to an artificial heat, deformeth the face, rotteth the teeth, and, to conclude, maketh a man contemptible. . . .

10. . . . Resolve that no man is wise or safe but that he is honest. Serve God; let Him be the author of all thy actions; commend all thy endeavors to Him that must either wither or prosper them; please Him with prayer lest if He frown He confound all thy fortunes and labors like drops of rain on the sandy ground.

Sir Walter Raleigh (c. *1552–1618*)
Instructions to His Son and to Posterity
(*first published in 1632*)

THE EARL OF CHESTERFIELD'S LETTERS TO HIS SON

[10 March 1746] There is no surer sign in the world of a little, weak mind, than inattention. Whatever is worth doing at all, is worth doing well; and nothing can be done well without attention.

[9 October 1747] People will, in a great degree, and not without reason, form their opinion of you, upon that which they have of your friends; and there is a Spanish proverb, which says very justly, *Tell me whom you live with, and I will tell you who you are.*

[6 November 1747] I knew, once, a very covetous sordid fellow, who used frequently to say, "Take care of the pence, for the pounds will take care of themselves." This was a just and sensible reflection in a miser. I recommend to you to take care of minutes, for hours will take care of themselves. I am very sure that many people lose two or three hours every day by not taking care of the minutes. Never think any portion of time, whatsoever, too short to be employed; something or other may always be done in it.

[22 February 1748] Speak the language of the company you are in; speak it purely, and unlarded with any other. Never seem wiser nor more learned than the people you are with. Wear your learning, like your watch, in a private pocket; and do not pull it out and strike it merely to show you have one. If you are asked what o'clock it is, tell it; but do not proclaim it hourly and unasked like a watchman.

[28 February 1749] You have the means, you have the opportunities. Employ them for God's sake, while you may, and make yourself that all-accomplished man that I wish to have you.

> From The Letters of Philip Dormer Stanhope, 4th
> Earl of Chesterfield, *Bonamy Dobrée, ed.*
> (*The King's Printers, 1932*)

GEORGE WASHINGTON—ADVICE TO HIS NEPHEW (1783)

Be courteous to all, but intimate with few; and let those few be well tried before you give them your confidence. True friendship is a plant of slow growth, and must undergo and withstand the shocks of adversity before it is entitled to the appellation. Let your heart feel for the afflictions and distress of every one, and let your hand give in proportion to your purse; remembering always the estimation of the widow's mite, that it is not everyone that asketh that deserveth charity; all, however, are worthy of the inquiry, or the deserving may suffer.

Do not conceive that fine clothes make fine men, any more than fine feathers make fine birds. A plain, genteel dress is more admired, obtains more credit, than lace and embroidery, in the eyes of the judicious and sensible.

ANN WRIGHT—TO HER SON

I would have you a man of sense as well as sensibility. You will find Goodness and Truth everywhere you go. If you have to choose, choose Truth. For that is closest to Earth. Keep close to the Earth, my boy: in that lies strength. Simplicity of heart is just as necessary to an architect as for a farmer or a minister if the architect is going to build great buildings.

Frank Lloyd Wright, An Autobiography
(New York: Duell, Sloan and Pearce, 1943), p. 71

OCCAM'S RAZOR

In the interpretation of natural phenomena or scientific data, the simplest and least cumbersome assumption is preferred.

William of Occam (c. 1300–1348)
The rule is informally known as Occam's Razor.

PARKINSON'S LAW

Work expands so as to fill the time available for its completion. General recognition of this fact is shown in the proverbial phrase, "It is the busiest man who has time to spare."

C. Northcote Parkinson (1909–1993)
Parkinson's Law (1957), p. 287

PARKINSON'S LAW OF TRIVIALITY
The time spent on any item of an agenda will be in inverse proportion to its importance

Parkinson's Law (1957), p. 24

PARKINSON'S LAW (CULINARY VERSION)
Appetite rises to meet food supply.

THE PETER PRINCIPLE

In a hierarchy every employee tends to rise to his level of incompetence.

PETER'S COROLLARY
In time, every post tends to be occupied by an employee who is incompetent to carry out its duties.

Work is done by those employees who have not yet reached their level of incompetence.

> Laurence J. Peter
> The Peter Principle (New York: Wm. Morrow, 1969),
> pp. 7–10

GRACIAN'S LAWS

In every profession, if a man knows very little he should stick to what he knows best, for if you may not be considered as acute, you will be considered sound.

Your natural endowments should be superior to the demands of your office, and not the other way around.

> Baltasar Gracian (1601–1658)
> The Art of Worldly Wisdom, or The Oraculo
> Manual (1647), Aphorisms 271 and 292

GRESHAM'S LAW

When two coins are equal in debt-paying value but unequal in intrinsic value, the one having the lesser intrinsic value tends to remain in circulation and the other to be hoarded or exported. [This is frequently cited as: Bad money drives out the good.]

> Sir Thomas Gresham (1518–1579)

ADVICE FROM BENJAMIN FRANKLIN'S POOR RICHARD'S ALMANAC

Early to bed and early to rise, makes a man healthy, wealthy, and wise.
[October 1735]

God helps them that help themselves. [June 1736]

Keep your eyes wide open before marriage, half shut afterwards. [June 1738]

Eat to please thyself, but dress to please others. [1738]

Work as if you were to live a hundred years, Pray as if you were to die tomorrow. [May 1757]

BENJAMIN FRANKLIN'S THIRTEEN VIRTUES
(FROM THE *AUTOBIOGRAPHY*)

1. Eat not to dullness; drink not to elevation.
2. Speak not but what may benefit others or yourself; avoid trifling conversation.
3. Let all your things have their places; let each part of your business have its time.
4. Resolve to perform what you ought; perform without fail what you resolve.
5. Make no expense but to do good to others or yourself; that is, waste nothing.
6. Lose no time; be always employed in something useful; cut off all unnecessary actions.
7. Use no hurtful deceit; think innocently and justly; speak accordingly.
8. Wrong none by doing injuries; or omitting the benefits that are your duty.
9. Avoid extremes; forbear resenting injuries so much as you think they deserve.
10. Tolerate no uncleanliness in body, clothes, or habitation.
11. Be not disturbed at trifles or at accidents common or unavoidable.
12. Rarely use venery but for health or offspring, never to dullness, weakness, or the injury of your own or another's peace or reputation.
13. Imitate Jesus and Socrates.

THOMAS JEFFERSON'S DECALOGUE OF CANONS
FOR OBSERVATION IN PRACTICAL LIFE

1. Never put off till to-morrow what you can do to-day.
2. Never trouble another for what you can do yourself.
3. Never spend your money before you have it.
4. Never buy what you do not want because it is cheap; it will be dear to you.
5. Pride costs us more than hunger, thirst and cold.
6. We never repent of having eaten too little.
7. Nothing is troublesome that we do willingly.
8. How much pain have cost us the evils which have never happened.
9. Take things always by their smooth handle.
10. When angry, count ten before you speak; if very angry, an hundred.

Letter to Thomas Jefferson Smith written at Monticello,
February 21, 1825
Writings of Thomas Jefferson [1899], Paul L. Ford,
ed., p. 341

MAKE NO LITTLE PLANS

Make no little plans; they have no magic to stir men's blood and probably in themselves will not be realized.

Make big plans; aim high in hope and work, remembering that a noble, logical diagram once recorded will never die, but long after we are gone will be a living thing, asserting itself with ever-growing insistency. Remember that our sons and grandsons are going to do things that would stagger us. Let your watchword be order and your beacon beauty.

Daniel H. Burnham (1846–1912), attributed

This quotation appears in Charles Moore's *Daniel Burnham* (Boston, 1921), v. 2, p. 147. Burnham himself did not write these exact words. They were cobbled together from a paper he read to the London City Planning Conference of 1910 by his associate Willis Polk. Most of the second paragraph comes from Burnham's text. The first and last sentences do not. See Henry H. Saylor, "Make No Little Plans: Daniel Burnham Thought It But Did He Say It?" *Journal of the American Institute of Architects* (March 1957), pp. 95–99.

Miscellaneous Advice

In every enterprise consider where you would come out.

> *Publilius Syrus (1st century B.C.)*
> Sententiae, maxim 777

In every affair, consider what precedes and what follows and then undertake it.

> *Epictetus (c. 50–120)*
> Discourses, Book III, Chapter 15, Section 1

Buy cheap, sell dear.

> *Thomas Lodge (c. 1558–1625)*
> A Fig for Momus (1595)

Marry the boss's daughter.

> *Robert Emmons Rogers (1888–1941)*
> To the class of 1929 at M.I.T.

On a good bargain think twice.

> *George Herbert (1593–1633)*
> Outlandish Proverbs (1640), #529

First secure an independent income; and then practice virtue.

> *Greek saying quoted by George Bernard Shaw in the preface*
> to Androcles and the Lion (1912)

Resolve not to be poor: whatever you have, spend less. Poverty is a great enemy to human happiness; it certainly destroys liberty, and it makes some virtues impracticable and others extremely difficult.

> *Samuel Johnson (1709–1784)*
> Letter to Boswell, September 7, 1782, from Boswell's
> Life of Johnson (Oxford: Clarendon Press, 1934),
> vol. IV, p. 157

Draw your salary before spending it.

> George Ade (1866–1944)
> "The Fable of the People's Choice Who Answered the Call of
> Duty & Took Selzer," Forty Modern Fables (New York:
> R. H. Russell, 1902)

Make yourself necessary to somebody.

> Ralph Waldo Emerson (1803–1882)
> The Conduct of Life [1860], chapter VII,
> "Considerations by the Way" (Boston: Houghton Mifflin,
> 1904), p. 275

Follow the money.

> Advice given to Bob Woodward by the informant known as
> Deep Throat in All the President's Men (1974)

MOTTOES, MAXIMS, AND SLOGANS

The National Mottoes
Mottoes of the States
Miscellaneous Mottoes
Newspaper Mottoes and Slogans
The Mottoes of the Seven Wise Men of Greece

THE NATIONAL MOTTOES

In God We Trust (the official national motto)
E Pluribus Unum (One, from many)
Annuit Coeptus ([He] favors our undertaking)
Novus Ordo Seclorum (A New Order of the Ages)

MOTTOES OF THE STATES

Alabama—Audemus Jura Nostra Defendere (We Dare Maintain Our Rights)
Alaska—North to the Future
Arizona—Ditat Deus (God Enriches)
Arkansas—Regnat Populas (The People Rule)
California—Eureka (I Have Found It)
Colorado—Nil Sine Numine (Nothing without Providence)
Connecticut—Qui Transtulit Sustinet (He Who Transplanted, Still Sustains)
Delaware—Liberty and Independence
Florida—In God We Trust
Georgia—Wisdom, Justice, and Moderation
Hawaii—Ua Mau Ke Ea O Ka Aina I Ka Pono (The Life of the Land Is Perpetuated in Righteousness)
Idaho—Esto Perpetua (It Is Forever)
Illinois—State Sovereignty, National Union
Indiana—The Crossroads of America
Iowa—Our Liberties We Prize and Our Rights We Will Maintain
Kansas—Ad Astra Per Aspera (To the Stars Through Difficulties)
Kentucky—United We Stand, Divided We Fall
Louisiana—Union, Justice, and Confidence
Maine—Dirigo (I Direct)
Maryland—Fatti Maschii, Parole Femine (Manly Deeds, Womanly Words)
Massachusetts—Ense Petit Placidam Sub Libertate Quietem (By the Sword We Seek Peace, but Peace Only under Liberty)
Michigan—Si Quaeris Peninsulam Amoenam Circumspice (If You Seek a Pleasant Peninsula, Look Around You)
Minnesota—Etoile du Nord (Star of The North)
Mississippi—Virtute et Armis (By Valor and Arms)
Missouri—Salus Populi Suprema Lex Esto (Let the Welfare of the People Be the Supreme Law)

Montana—Oro y Plata (Gold and Silver)
Nebraska—Equality Before the Law
Nevada—All for Our Country
New Hampshire—Live Free or Die
New Jersey—Liberty and Prosperity
New Mexico—Crescit Eundo (It Grows As It Goes)
New York—Excelsior (Ever Upward)
North Carolina—Esse Quam Videri (To Be Rather Than to Seem)
North Dakota—Liberty and Union, Now and Forever: One and Inseparable [From a speech by Daniel Webster]
Ohio—With God, All Things Are Possible
Oklahoma—Labor Omnia Vincit (Labor Conquers All Things)
Oregon—Alis Volat Propriis (She Flies with Her Own Wings)
Pennsylvania—Virtue, Liberty, and Independence
Rhode Island—Hope
South Carolina—Animis Opibusque Parati (Ready in Souls and Resource)
South Dakota—Under God the People Rule
Tennessee—Agriculture and Commerce
Texas—Friendship
Utah—Industry
Vermont—Vermont, Freedom and Unity
Virginia—Sic Semper Tyrannis (Thus Ever to Tyrants)
Washington—Al-Ki (Indian word meaning "By and By")
West Virginia—Montani Semper Liberi (Mountaineers Are Always Freemen)
Wisconsin—Forward
Wyoming—Cedant Arma Togae (Let Arms Yield to the Gown)

MISCELLANEOUS MOTTOES

Liberty and Property

Slogan of the Sons of Liberty

Omnia relinquit servare rem publicam (He gave up all to serve the public weal)

Motto of the Order of the Cincinnati

Victory or Death

Slogan of Andrew Jackson's soldiers at the Battle of New Orleans, January 8, 1815

Look up and not down;
Look forward and not back;
Look out and not in;
Lend a Hand.

> *Motto of the Lend a Hand Society, written by Edward
> Everett Hale, who founded the first Lend a Hand Club
> in Boston in 1871*

Don't lie, cheat, or steal.

> *The code of West Point, as propounded by Sylvanus
> Thayer (1785–1872), superintendent of the U.S. Military
> Academy, 1817–1833*

Be sure you're right, then go ahead.

> *Motto of David Crockett, U.S. Congressman from Tennessee*

When in doubt, fight.

> *Motto of Ulysses S. Grant*

For God and Home and Humanity

> *Motto of the World's Woman's Christian Temperance Union*

A Square Deal All Around

> *Bull Moose (Progressive) Party campaign slogan for
> candidate Theodore Roosevelt, 1912*

Do Right

> *Motto of the Sunbeams*

Soul, Mind, Body, Others

> *Motto of the Girl Guards*

Independence, Pride, Dignity

> *Motto of the American Association of Retired Persons*

Blood and Fire

Motto of the Salvation Army

We shall overcome.

Slogan of the American civil rights movement during the 1960s

First Things First
Easy Does It
Live and Let Live
One Day at a Time
But for the Grace of God

Slogans of Alcoholics Anonymous

Spirit Mind Body

YMCA Motto

If it moves, salute it.
If it doesn't move, pick it up.
If you can't pick it up, paint it.

U.S. Armed Forces Slogan—World War II

Keep 'Em Flying!

Slogan of the U.S. Air Force—World War II

It is better to light one candle than to curse the darkness.

Motto of the Christophers

To serve, to strive, and not to yield.

Motto of Outward Bound

Faster, Higher, Stronger

Motto of the Olympic Games

Labor Omnia Vincit (Labor Conquers All)

American Federation of Labor

Deo Vindice (God Maintains)

> *From the Great Seal of the Confederate States*

He profits most who serves best.

> *Rotary International*

We Build

> *Kiwanis International*

Keep America Singing

> *Society for the Preservation and Encouragement of Barbershop Quartet Singing in America*

Ad Majorem Dei Gloriam (To the Greater Glory of God—often abbreviated as AMDG)

> *Motto of the Society of Jesus (the Jesuit Order)*

Be prepared.

> *Boy Scouts*

Do a good turn daily.

> *Girl Scouts*

Aut Veniam Viam, Aut Feciam (I shall either find a way or make one.)

> *The soldier's motto*

One Riot, One Ranger

> *Motto of the Texas Rangers*

And ye shall know the truth, and the truth shall make you free. (John 8:32)

> *Motto of the C.I.A. Inscribed on the headquarters building in Langley, Virginia*

Newspaper Mottoes and Slogans

Ashtabula (OH) Star-Beacon—To Dispense Truth Is To Defend Freedom

Atlanta Journal—Covers Dixie Like the Dew

Baltimore Sun—Light for All

The Capital Reporter (Jackson, MI)—Once a week but never weakly

Chester River Press (Chestertown, Kent City, MD)—Truth Is Your Right and Our Obligation

Crisfield (MD) Times—This Be Our Motto: In God Is Our Trust

Geneva (OH) Free-Press—A Free Press Inspires a Free People

Indiana Herald—The Sound of Truth Is Eternally Sharp

Johnson City (TN) Press-Chronicle—What the People Don't Know WILL Hurt Them

Los Angeles Times—Equal Rights, Liberty Under the Laws, True Industrial Freedom

Manchester (NH) Union Leader—There Is Nothing So Powerful as Truth

Milwaukee Sentinel—Dedicated to Truth, Justice and Public Service

The Mountain Eagle (Whitesburg, KY)—It Screams

New Haven (CT) Journal-Courier—If It's News and True It's Here

New York Times—All the News That's Fit to Print

Newsday—Where There Is No Vision the People Perish

Pawtucket (RI) Times—Be Silent, or Say Something Better than Silence

Rochester (NY) Democrat-Chronicle—Without or with offense to friends or foes I sketch the world exactly as it goes. (Byron)

Scripps-Howard Newspapers—Give Light and the People Will Find Their Own Way

New York Sun—The Sun, It Shines for All

Hubbard (Texas) City News—We will do our best to be right, let him find fault who may.

(Note: Several of these newspapers no longer exist.)

The Mottoes of the Seven Wise Men of Greece

Bias of Priene in Sonia: Most men are bad.

Chilo of Sparta: Consider the end.

Cleobolus of Lindos in Rhodes: The Golden Mean, or Avoid extremes.

Periander of Corinth: Nothing is impossible to industry.

Solon of Athens: Know thyself.

Pittacus of Mitylene in Lesbos: Know thy opportunity (Take time by the forelock).

Thales of Miletus: Suretyship is the predecessor of ruin.

Also known as the Seven Sages, these men lived during the sixth century B.C.

INSCRIPTIONS

Post Office, Washington, D.C.
Union Station, Washington, D.C.
Watergate of the Chicago World's Columbian Exposition
Library of Congress
Boston Public Library
New York Public Library
Los Angeles Public Library
San Francisco Public Library
National Archives Building
Department of Justice Building, Washington, D.C.
Nebraska State Capitol
St. Louis County Court House
Orleans Parish Criminal Court House
Woodbury County Court House, Iowa
The Statue of Liberty
The Minute Man, Concord, Massachusetts
Statue of Lincoln, Chicago
Robert Gould Shaw Monument, Boston Common
Washington Arch, Washington Square, New York City
Kansas City Liberty Memorial
Indiana World War Memorial Hall, Indianapolis
Arlington Memorial Amphitheater, Arlington National Cemetery
Tomb of the Unknown Soldier, Arlington National Cemetery
United States Marine Corps War Memorial (Iwo Jima Monument)
Vietnam Veterans Memorial, Washington, D.C.
Robert A. Taft Memorial, Washington, D.C.
John F. Kennedy Gravesite, Arlington National Cemetery
Mary McLeod Bethune Memorial, Washington, D.C.

POST OFFICE, WASHINGTON, D.C.

(Daniel Burnham & Co., architects, 1912)
Inscriptions by Dr. Charles W. Eliot.

EAST PAVILION

CARRIER OF NEWS AND KNOWLEDGE
INSTRUMENT OF TRADE AND INDUSTRY
PROMOTER OF MUTUAL ACQUAINTANCE
OF PEACE AND OF GOODWILL
AMONG MEN AND NATIONS

WEST PAVILION

MESSENGER OF SYMPATHY AND LOVE
SERVANT OF PARTED FRIENDS
CONSOLER OF THE LONELY
BOND OF THE SCATTERED FAMILY
ENLARGER OF THE COMMON LIFE

This is only instance in which Charles Eliot was edited by a client—in this case by President Woodrow Wilson (himself the former president of Princeton University). This is the final, edited version.

UNION STATION, WASHINGTON, D.C.

(Daniel Burnham, architect, 1908)
Inscriptions chosen by Dr. Charles W. Eliot.

ATTIC PANEL, EAST PAVILION

WELCOME THE COMING
SPEED THE PARTING GUEST
VIRTUE ALONE IS SWEET SOCIETY
IT KEEPS THE KEY TO ALL
HEROIC HEARTS AND OPENS YOU
A WELCOME IN THEM ALL

The first two lines are from Alexander Pope's translation of Homer's *Odyssey*, the last four from Ralph Waldo Emerson's poem "Written at Rome, 1883." There are five other inscribed panels on the station, which was built as part of Burnham's master plan for Washington.

WATERGATE OF THE WORLD'S COLUMBIAN EXPOSITION, CHICAGO

Charles Atwood, architect, 1892). Texts selected and composed by Dr. Charles W. Eliot.

TOWARD THE LAKE

A FEW	OF MANY RACES
DARED TOILED	TONGUES CREEDS
AND SUFFERED	AND AIMS
MYRIADS ENJOY	BUT ALL HEROES
THE FRUITS	OF DISCOVERY

TO THE BOLD MEN
THEIR NAMES REMEMBERED OR FORGOTTEN
WHO FIRST EXPLORED THROUGH PERILS MANIFOLD
THE SHORES LAKES RIVERS MOUNTAINS VALLEYS AND PLAINS
OF THIS NEW WORLD
THE WILDERNESS AND THE SOLITARY
PLACE SHALL BE GLAD FOR THEM

TO THE	TO THE
BRAVE SETTLERS	BRAVE WOMEN
WHO LEVELED	WHO IN
FORESTS	SOLITUDES
CLEARED FIELDS	AMID STRANGE
MADE PATHS BY	DANGERS AND
LAND AND WATER	HEAVY TOIL
AND PLANTED	REARED FAMILIES
COMMONWEALTHS	AND MADE HOMES

TOWARD THE COURT OF HONOR

CIVIL LIBERTY	TOLERATION
THE MEANS	IN RELIGION
OF BUILDING UP	THE BEST FRUIT
PERSONAL AND	OF THE LAST
NATIONAL CHARACTER	FOUR CENTURIES

TO THE PIONEERS OF CIVIL AND RELIGIOUS LIBERTY
BUT BOLDER THEY WHO FIRST OFF-CAST
THEIR MOORINGS FROM THE HABITABLE PAST
AND VENTURED CHARTLESS ON THE SEA

OF STORM-ENGENDERING LIBERTY

YE SHALL KNOW THE TRUTH AND THE TRUTH SHALL MAKE YOU

FREE

I FREEDOM DWELL	WE HERE
WITH KNOWLEDGE:	HIGHLY RESOLVE
I ABIDE	THAT GOVERNMENT
WITH MEN BY	OF THE PEOPLE
CULTURE TRAINED	BY THE PEOPLE
AND FORTIFIED	FOR THE
CONSCIENCE	PEOPLE
MY SCEPTER IS	SHALL NOT PERISH
AND LAW MY SWORD	FROM THE EARTH

The size and shapes of the panels had been determined in advance, so that Eliot had to work within spatial limitations. "My plan," he wrote, "was to commemorate on the side toward the lake the explorers and pioneers in the literal sense, and on the side toward the Court of Honor the pioneers of civil and religious liberty. The inscription beginning 'to the bold men,' on the side toward the lake, prepared the way for Lowell's splendid verse on the other side, 'But bolder they,' etc. That verse, the two Bible texts, Lowell's lines on the left panel toward the Court of Honor, and Lincoln's sentence on the right lower panel I selected; the rest I wrote."

LIBRARY OF CONGRESS, WASHINGTON, D.C.

(Smithmeyer and Pelz, architects, 1888)

Inscriptions on tablets in the rotunda accompanying eight allegorical sculptures. The texts were chosen by Dr. Charles W. Eliot.

1. *Religion*
WHAT DOTH THE LORD REQUIRE OF THEE, BUT TO DO JUSTLY, AND TO LOVE MERCY, AND TO WALK HUMBLY WITH THY GOD?—Micah 6:8.

2. *Commerce*
WE TASTE THE SPICES OF ARABIA, YET NEVER FEEL THE SCORCHING SUN WHICH BRINGS THEM FORTH—Dudley North

3. *History*
ONE GOD, ONE LAW, ONE ELEMENT, AND ONE FAR-OFF DIVINE EVENT, TO WHICH THE WHOLE CREATION MOVES—Tennyson

4. Art

AS ONE LAMP LIGHTS ANOTHER, NOR GROWS LESS, SO NOBLENESS ENKINDLETH NOBLENESS—Lowell

5. Philosophy

THE INQUIRY, KNOWLEDGE, AND BELIEF OF TRUTH IS THE SOVEREIGN GOOD OF HUMAN NATURE—Bacon

6. Poetry

HITHER, AS TO THEIR FOUNTAIN, OTHER STARS REPAIRING, IN THEIR GOLDEN URNS DRAW LIGHT—Milton

7. Law

OF LAW THERE CAN BE NO LESS ACKNOWLEDGED THAN THAT HER VOICE IS THE HARMONY OF THE WORLD—Richard Hooker

8. Science

THE HEAVENS DECLARE THE GLORY OF GOD; AND THE FIRMAMENT SHOWETH HIS HANDIWORK—Psalms 19:1.

BOSTON PUBLIC LIBRARY

(McKim, Mead & White, architects, 1898).
Text attributed to Charles W. Eliot.

ARCHITRAVE INSCRIPTION—FRONT
THE PUBLIC LIBRARY OF THE CITY OF BOSTON BUILT BY THE PEOPLE AND
DEDICATED TO THE ADVANCEMENT OF LEARNING
A.D. MDCCCLXXXVIII

ARCHITRAVE INSCRIPTION—BOYLSTON STREET SIDE
THE COMMONWEALTH REQUIRES THE EDUCATION OF
THE PEOPLE AS THE SAFEGUARD OF ORDER AND LIBERTY

NEW YORK PUBLIC LIBRARY

(Carrère and Hastings, architects, 1911)

BUT ABOVE ALL THINGS TRUTH BEARETH AWAY THE VICTORY

BEAUTY OLD YET EVER NEW, ETERNAL VOICE AND INWARD WORD

The Boston Public Library as it looked in 1901. (Courtesy Library of Congress)

These two inscriptions stand above the statues of Truth and Beauty (Frederick Macmonnies, sculptor). The first is taken from the Apocrypha, 1 Esdras: 3; the second from John Greenleaf Whittier's "The Shadow and the Light."

INSCRIPTIONS BETWEEN THE PILLARS AT THE ENTRANCE
ON THE DIFFUSION OF EDUCATION AMONG THE PEOPLE REST THE
PRESERVATION AND PERPETUATION OF OUR FREE INSTITUTIONS

THE CITY OF NEW YORK HAS ERECTED THIS BUILDING TO BE
MAINTAINED FOREVER AS A FREE LIBRARY FOR THE USE OF THE
PEOPLE

LOS ANGELES PUBLIC LIBRARY

(Bertram Grosvenor Goodhue, architect, 1921–26)

IN THE WORLD OF
AFFAIRS WE LIVE IN OUR

OWN AGE : IN BOOKS
WE LIVE IN ALL AGES

WISDOM IS THE RIPEST FRUIT OF MUCH REFLECTION

BOOKS INVITE ALL : THEY CONSTRAIN NONE

Hartley Burr Alexander assisted in the selection of these inscriptions.

SAN FRANCISCO PUBLIC LIBRARY

(McAllister and Larkin, architects, 1916)

MAY THIS STRUCTURE, THRONED ON IMPERISHABLE BOOKS, BE
MAINTAINED AND CHERISHED FROM GENERATION TO
GENERATION FOR THE IMPROVEMENT AND DELIGHT OF
MANKIND

NATIONAL ARCHIVES BUILDING

(John Russell Pope, architect, 1931–35)

ATTIC PANEL, SEVENTH STREET FACADE
THIS BUILDING HOLDS IN TRUST THE RECORDS
OF OUR NATIONAL LIFE AND SYMBOLIZES OUR FAITH IN THE
PERMANENCY OF OUR NATIONAL INSTITUTIONS

ATTIC PANEL, NINTH STREET FACADE
THE GLORY AND ROMANCE OF OUR HISTORY ARE
HERE PRESERVED IN THE CHRONICLES OF THOSE WHO CONCEIVED
AND BUILT THE STRUCTURE OF OUR NATION

ATTIC PANEL, CONSTITUTION AVENUE FACADE
THE TIES THAT BIND THE LIVES OF OUR PEOPLE IN ONE INDISSOLUBLE UNION
ARE PERPETUATED IN THE ARCHIVES OF OUR
GOVERNMENT AND TO THEIR CUSTODY THIS BUILDING IS DEDICATED

The attic inscriptions were taken from the speeches given by President
Herbert Hoover and Secretary of the Treasury Ogden Mills at the
cornerstone-laying ceremonies. The choice was made by the architects.

INSCRIPTIONS ON THE ALLEGORICAL SCULPTURES

HERITAGE

THE HERITAGE OF THE PAST
IS THAT SEED THAT BRINGS FORTH
THE HARVEST OF THE FUTURE

Composed jointly by sculptor James Earle Fraser, Charles Moore of the Commission of Fine Arts, and Dr. R. W. D. Connor, first archivist of the United States. The words are attributed to Vice President John Garner.

GUARDIANSHIP

ETERNAL VIGILANCE
IS THE PRICE OF LIBERTY

This inscription adapted by James Earle Fraser from John P. Curran, *Speech upon the Right of Election*, 1790: "The condition upon which God hath given liberty to man is eternal vigilance." The phrase as inscribed is often attributed to Jefferson, but it is not found in his writings.

DEPARTMENT OF JUSTICE BUILDING, WASHINGTON, D.C.

(Zantzinger, Borie and Medary, architects, 1931–35)
Texts chosen by Dr. Hartley Burr Alexander.

CENTRAL ENTRANCE—PENNSYLVANIA AVENUE

THE PLACE OF JUSTICE
IS A HALLOWED PLACE

PARAPET—NINTH STREET

JUSTICE IS FOUNDED IN
THE RIGHTS BESTOWED
BY NATURE UPON MAN
LIBERTY IS MAINTAINED
IN SECURITY OF JUSTICE

Sidney Waugh's sculpture of "Guardianship" at the National Archives. (Courtesy Library of Congress)

NEBRASKA STATE CAPITOL, LINCOLN, NEBRASKA

(Bertram Grosvenor Goodhue, architect, 1922–32)

WISDOM JUSTICE POWER MERCY
CONSTANT GUARDIANS OF THE LAW

THE SALVATION
OF THE STATE IS
WATCHFULNESS
IN THE CITIZEN

POLITICAL SOCIETY EXISTS FOR THE SAKE OF NOBLE LIVING

HE WHO WOULD DULY ENQUIRE ABOUT THE BEST FORM OF
THE STATE OUGHT FIRST TO DETERMINE WHICH IS THE MOST
ELIGIBLE LIFE / MEN SHOULD NOT THINK IT SLAVERY TO LIVE
ACCORDING TO THE RULE OF THE CONSTITUTION FOR IT IS
THEIR SALVATION / LAWS AND CONSTITUTIONS SPRING
FROM THE MORAL DISPOSITIONS OF THE MEMBERS OF THE
STATE / LAW AND ORDER DELIVER THE SOUL / A COMMUNITY
LIKE AN INDIVIDUAL HAS A WORK TO DO

These inscriptions, from the arch over the front portal, from the panel over the main doorway, from the south entrance, and from the rotunda frieze, were written by Hartley Burr Alexander, professor of philosophy at the University of Nebraska. Professor Alexander derived the last inscription from Aristotle's *Poetics* and Plato's *Dialogues*.

St. Louis County Court House, Duluth, Minnesota (1908)

THE PEOPLE'S LAWS DEFINE USAGES, ORDAIN RIGHTS AND
DUTIES, SECURE PUBLIC SAFETY, DEFEND LIBERTY, TEACH
REVERENCE AND OBEDIENCE, AND ESTABLISH JUSTICE

Orleans Parish Criminal Court House, New Orleans

(Diboll and Owen, architects, 1929–31)

THIS IS A GOVERNMENT OF
LAW NOT OF MEN

Woodbury County Court House, Sioux City, Iowa

(William L. Steele and Pucell & Elmslie, architects, 1918)

OUR LIBERTIES WE PRIZE
OUR RIGHTS WE WILL MAINTAIN

JUSTICE AND PEACE HAVE MET TOGETHER
TRUTH HATH SPRUNG OUT OF THE EARTH

Inscriptions from the lobby and from the frieze of the front entablature.

THE STATUE OF LIBERTY, NEW YORK HARBOR

(statue by Frédéric Auguste Bartholdi; pedestal by Richard Morris Hunt, 1886)

NOT LIKE THE BRAZEN GIANT OF GREEK FAME,
WITH CONQUERING LIMBS ASTRIDE FROM LAND TO LAND;
HERE AT OUR SEA-WASHED, SUNSET GATES SHALL STAND
A MIGHTY WOMAN WITH A TORCH, WHOSE FLAME
IS THE IMPRISONED LIGHTNING, AND HER NAME
MOTHER OF EXILES. FROM HER BEACON-HAND
GLOWS WORLD-WIDE WELCOME; HER MILD EYES COMMAND
THE AIR-BRIDGED HARBOR THAT TWIN CITIES FRAME.
"KEEP ANCIENT LANDS, YOUR STORIED POMP!" CRIES SHE
WITH SILENT LIPS. "GIVE ME YOUR TIRED, YOUR POOR,
YOUR HUDDLED MASSES YEARNING TO BREATHE FREE,
THE WRETCHED REFUSE OF YOUR TEEMING SHORE.
SEND THESE, THE HOMELESS, TEMPEST-TOST TO ME,
I LIFE MY LAMP BESIDE THE GOLDEN DOOR!"

These words are contained on a plaque mounted in the Statue of Liberty Museum, which is housed within the fort beneath the statue's pedestal. The plaque was first mounted in the entryway of the fort in 1903. The sonnet—entitled "The New Colossus"—was written by Emma Lazarus in 1883 as part of the campaign to raise funds for the building of the pedestal. (Specifically, for the *Portfolio* of the Art Loan Collection in aid of the Pedestal Fund.)

THE MINUTE MAN, CONCORD, MASSACHUSETTS

(Daniel Chester French, sculptor;
Ralph Waldo Emerson, inscription, 1875)

BY THE RUDE BRIDGE THAT ARCHED THE FLOOD
THEIR FLAG TO APRIL'S BREEZE UNFURLED
HERE ONCE THE EMBATTLED FARMERS STOOD
AND FIRED THE SHOT HEARD ROUND THE WORLD

This, the first stanza of Emerson's "Concord Hymn," was selected in the early stages of planning by a committee charged with building the monument.

Daniel Chester French's Minute Man, Concord, Massachusetts. (Courtesy Library of Congress)

STATUE OF LINCOLN, LINCOLN PARK, CHICAGO

(Augustus St. Gaudens, sculptor; pedestal by Stanford White, 1887)

WITH MALICE TOWARD NONE AND CHARITY FOR ALL, WITH
FIRMNESS IN THE RIGHT AS GOD GIVES US TO KNOW THE RIGHT,
LET US STRIVE ON

LET US HAVE FAITH THAT RIGHT MAKES MIGHT, AND IN THAT
FAITH LET US TO THE END DARE TO DO OUR DUTY AS WE UNDERSTAND IT

The text was taken from Lincoln's Cooper Union Speech of 1860.

ROBERT GOULD SHAW MONUMENT, BOSTON COMMON

(Augustus Saint-Gaudens, sculptor; Charles F. McKim, architect;
Charles W. Eliot, inscriptions, 1884–96)

TO THE FIFTY-FOURTH REGIMENT OF MASSACHUSETTS INFANTRY

THE WHITE OFFICERS TAKING LIFE AND HONOR IN THEIR HANDS
CAST IN THEIR LOT WITH MEN OF A DESPISED RACE UNPROVED IN
WAR AND RISKED DEATH AS INCITERS OF SERVILE
INSURRECTION IF TAKEN PRISONERS BESIDES ENCOUNTERING
ALL THE COMMON PERILS OF CAMP MARCH, AND BATTLE

THE BLACK RANK AND FILE VOLUNTEERED WHEN DISASTER
CLOUDED THE UNION CAUSE SERVED WITHOUT PAY FOR
EIGHTEEN MONTHS UNTIL GIVEN THAT OF WHITE TROOPS FACED
THREATENED ENSLAVEMENT IF CAPTURED WERE BRAVE IN
ACTION, PATIENT UNDER HEAVY AND DANGEROUS LABORS AND
CHEERFUL AMID HARDSHIPS AND PRIVATIONS
TOGETHER THEY GAVE TO THE NATION AND THE WORLD
UNDYING PROOF THAT AMERICANS OF AFRICAN DESCENT
POSSESS THE PRIDE COURAGE AND DEVOTION OF THE PATRIOT
SOLDIER
ONE HUNDRED AND EIGHTY THOUSAND SUCH AMERICANS
ENLISTED UNDER THE UNION FLAG IN 1863–65

At the dedication ceremony, Augustus Saint-Gaudens remarked, "It is the finest example of inscription writing I have ever read."

WASHINGTON ARCH, WASHINGTON SQUARE, NEW YORK CITY

(Stanford White, architect, 1890–92)

LET US RAISE A STANDARD TO WHICH THE WISE AND HONEST
CAN REPAIR. THE EVENT IS IN THE HANDS OF GOD.

The text of the inscription is taken from George Washington's inaugural address.

KANSAS CITY LIBERTY MEMORIAL

*(Harold Van Buren Magonigle, architect; Edmund Amateis,
sculptor, 1921; dedicated 1926)*

THESE HAVE DARED BEAR THE TORCHES OF SACRIFICE AND
SERVICE. THEIR BODIES RETURN TO DUST BUT THEIR WORK
LIVETH FOR EVERMORE. LET US STRIVE ON TO DO ALL WHICH
MAY ACHIEVE AND CHERISH A JUST AND LASTING PEACE
AMONG OURSELVES AND WITH ALL NATIONS.

This is the inscription atop the great frieze of the eastern wall.

INDIANA WORLD WAR MEMORIAL HALL, INDIANAPOLIS

(Walker and Weeks, architects, 1929)

NORTH SIDE

TO COMMEMORATE THE VALOR AND SACRIFICE OF THE LAND,
SEA, AND AIR FORCES OF THE UNITED STATES AND ALL WHO
RENDERED FAITHFUL AND LOYAL SERVICE AT HOME AND
OVERSEAS IN THE WORLD WAR. TO INCULCATE A TRUE
UNDERSTANDING AND APPRECIATION OF THE PRIVILEGES OF
AMERICAN CITIZENSHIP.
TO INSPIRE PATRIOTISM AND RESPECT FOR THE LAW TO THE
END THAT PEACE MAY PREVAIL JUSTICE LIE ADMINISTERED
PUBLIC ORDER MAINTAINED AND LIBERTY PERPETUATED.

NORTH AND SOUTH SIDES

TO VINDICATE THE PRINCIPLES OF PEACE AND JUSTICE IN THE
WORLD

EAST SIDE

TO PERPETUATE PEACE AND LIBERTY
TO COMMEMORATE THE VALOR OF ALL WHO SERVED

WEST SIDE

TO PROMOTE ORDER AND JUSTICE TO COMMEMORATE THE VALOR
AND SACRIFICE OF ALL WHO SERVED

ARLINGTON MEMORIAL AMPHITHEATER,
ARLINGTON NATIONAL CEMETERY

(Carrère and Hastings, architects, 1915)

DULCE ET DECORUM EST PRO PATRIA MORI

(It is sweet and honorable to die for one's country.)

WE HIGHLY RESOLVE THAT THESE DEAD SHALL NOT HAVE
DIED IN VAIN

WHEN WE ASSUMED THE SOLDIER WE DID NOT LAY ASIDE THE CITIZEN

TOMB OF THE UNKNOWN SOLDIER, ARLINGTON
NATIONAL CEMETERY

(Lorimer Rich, architect;
Thomas Hudson Jones, sculptor, 1931)

HERE RESTS IN HONORED GLORY AN AMERICAN
SOLDIER KNOWN BUT TO GOD

Beneath the monument lie the remains of an unidentified American soldier from World War I, who was among the American dead at Châlons-sur-Marne. Two other soldiers, one from World War II and one from the Korean war, are buried nearby.

UNITED STATES MARINE CORPS WAR MEMORIAL
(IWO JIMA MONUMENT), ARLINGTON, VIRGINIA

(Edward F. Field, architect; Felix W. deWeldon, sculptor, 1954)

IN HONOR AND IN MEMORY OF THE MEN OF THE UNITED
STATES MARINE CORPS WHO HAVE GIVEN THEIR LIVES TO
THEIR COUNTRY SINCE NOVEMBER 10, 1775

UNCOMMON VALOR WAS A COMMON VIRTUE

Inscriptions on the base. The second inscription is Fleet Admiral Chester W. Nimitz's tribute to the fighting men on Iwo Jima.

VIETNAM VETERANS MEMORIAL, WASHINGTON, D.C.

(Maya Lin, designer, 1981)

PROLOGUE

IN HONOR OF THE MEN AND WOMEN OF THE ARMED FORCES OF
THE UNITED STATES WHO SERVED IN THE VIETNAM WAR. THE
NAMES OF THOSE WHO GAVE THEIR LIVES AND THOSE WHO
REMAIN MISSING ARE INSCRIBED IN THE ORDER THEY WERE
TAKEN FROM US.

EPILOGUE

OUR NATION HONORS THE COURAGE, SACRIFICE, AND DEVOTION TO
DUTY AND COUNTRY OF ITS VIETNAM VETERANS. THIS
MEMORIAL WAS BUILT WITH PRIVATE CONTRIBUTIONS FROM
THE AMERICAN PEOPLE. NOVEMBER 11, 1982.

ROBERT A. TAFT MEMORIAL, WASHINGTON, D.C.

(Douglas W. Orr, architect; Wheeler Williams, sculptor, 1958)

NORTH SIDE

IF WE WISH TO MAKE DEMOCRACY
PERMANENT IN THIS COUNTRY
LET US ABIDE
BY THE FUNDAMENTAL PRINCIPLES
LAID DOWN IN THE CONSTITUTION
LET US SEE THAT THE
STATE IS THE SERVANT
OF ITS PEOPLE AND THAT THE
PEOPLE ARE NOT SERVANTS
OF THE STATE

SOUTH SIDE

LIBERTY HAS BEEN THE KEY TO
OUR PROGRESS IN THE PAST
AND IS THE KEY TO
OUR PROGRESS IN THE FUTURE
IF WE CAN PRESERVE LIBERTY

IN ALL ITS ESSENTIALS
THERE IS NO LIMIT TO THE FUTURE
OF THE AMERICAN PEOPLE

JOHN F. KENNEDY GRAVESITE, ARLINGTON NATIONAL CEMETERY

LET THE WORD GO FORTH
FROM THIS TIME AND PLACE
TO FRIEND AND FOE ALIKE
THAT THE TORCH HAS BEEN PASSED
TO A NEW GENERATION OF AMERICANS

LET EVERY NATION KNOW
WHETHER IT WISHES US WELL OR ILL
THAT WE SHALL PAY ANY PRICE—BEAR ANY BURDEN
MEET ANY HARDSHIP—SUPPORT ANY FRIEND
OPPOSE ANY FOE TO ASSURE THE SURVIVAL
AND THE SUCCESS OF LIBERTY

NOW THE TRUMPET SUMMONS US AGAIN
NOT AS A CALL TO BEAR ARMS—THOUGH ARMS WE NEED
NOT AS A CALL TO BATTLE—THOUGH EMBATTLED WE ARE
BUT A CALL TO BEAR THE BURDEN OF A LONG TWILIGHT
STRUGGLE
A STRUGGLE AGAINST THE COMMON ENEMIES OF MAN
TYRANNY POVERTY DISEASE AND WAR ITSELF

IN THE LONG HISTORY OF THE WORLD
ONLY A FEW GENERATIONS HAVE BEEN GRANTED
THE ROLE OF DEFENDING FREEDOM
IN ITS HOUR OF MAXIMUM DANGER
I DO NOT SHRINK FROM THIS RESPONSIBILITY
I WELCOME IT

THE ENERGY THE FAITH THE DEVOTION
WHICH WE BRING TO THIS ENDEAVOR
WILL LIGHT OUR COUNTRY
AND ALL WHO SERVE IT

AND THE GLOW FROM THAT FIRE
CAN TRULY LIGHT THE WORLD

AND SO MY FELLOW AMERICANS
ASK NOT WHAT YOUR COUNTRY CAN DO FOR YOU
ASK WHAT YOU CAN DO FOR YOUR COUNTRY
MY FELLOW CITIZENS OF THE WORLD ASK NOT
WHAT AMERICA WILL DO FOR YOU, BUT WHAT TOGETHER
WE CAN DO FOR THE FREEDOM OF MAN

WITH A GOOD CONSCIENCE OUR ONLY SURE REWARD
WITH HISTORY THE FINAL JUDGE OF OUR DEEDS
LET US GO FORTH TO LEAD THE LAND WE LOVE ASKING HIS
BLESSING
AND HIS HELP BUT KNOWING THAT HERE ON EARTH
GOD'S WORK MUST TRULY BE OUR OWN.

The text is taken from Kennedy's inaugural address of January 20, 1961.

MARY MCLEOD BETHUNE MEMORIAL, WASHINGTON, D.C.

(Robert Berks, sculptor, 1974)

I LEAVE YOU LOVE. I LEAVE YOU HOPE. I LEAVE YOU THE
CHALLENGE OF DEVELOPING CONFIDENCE IN ONE ANOTHER.
I LEAVE YOU A THIRST FOR EDUCATION. I LEAVE YOU A RESPECT
FOR THE USE OF POWER. I LEAVE YOU FAITH. I LEAVE YOU
RACIAL DIGNITY. I LEAVE YOU ALSO A DESIRE TO LIVE
HARMONIOUSLY WITH YOUR FELLOWMAN. I LEAVE YOU,
FINALLY, A RESPONSIBILITY TO OUR YOUNG PEOPLE.

This is the text of Bethune's "Last Will and Testament."

SOURCES, NOTES, AND COMMENTS

While there are no comprehensive collections of "words we live by" as they are defined in this book, there are several noteworthy individual compilations of creeds, codes, oaths, mottoes, and inscriptions.

The authority on the ancient creeds is J. N. D. Kelly, whose three volumes—*The Anthanasian Creed* (London: Adam and Charles Black, 1964), *Early Christian Creeds* (New York: David McKay, 1972), *Early Christian Doctrines* (San Francisco: Harpers, 1978)—contain detailed studies of the origins of the Athanasian, Apostles', and Nicene creeds. Another useful reference work encompassing the Christian creeds and confessions is John H. Leith's *Creeds of the Churches* (Louisville: John Knox Press, 1982).

The most complete collection of contemporary religious creeds is contained in the two volumes of *The Encyclopedia of American Religions: Religious Creeds* (Detroit: Gale Research, 1988). Attempts at ecumenical creeds and personal statements of faith can be found in Avery Dulles, "Foundation Documents of the Faith: X. Modern Creedal Affirmations," *Expository Times*, July 1980, pp. 291–96.

There is only one comprehensive collection of oaths, and it is entitled—appropriately enough—*The Book of Oaths*. It was first compiled in 1649 by Richard Garnet, a Jesuit, who preferred to remain anonymous. Garnet's book reprints coronation and loyalty oaths, oaths of the chivalric orders, civil service oaths (of every conceivable post, from beadles to bailiffs of the sewers), guild oaths, and oaths pertaining to a wide miscellany of other occupations. It bears vivid testimony to the ubiquity of oath-taking in English life in the Tudor era and afterwards. It went through two revisions, the last in 1715. The Library of Congress possesses the first and last editions.

Most dictionaries of secret societies tend to be short on dates and sources. Consequently, their reliability is suspect. John Herron Lepper's *Famous Secret Societies* (London: Low Marstow, 1932) and William Whalen's *Handbook of Secret Organizations* (Milwaukee: Bruce Publishing, 1966) are typical of this syndrome; they list a wide range of organizations, and reprint some of their oaths, but it is unclear whether the oaths are recent or historical. Ezra Cook's exposés of fraternal rites, on the other hand, are considered reliable, and they have the advantage of revealing fraternal initiation practices during the height of their popularity and influence. For the best summary of the golden age of fraternalism, see Mark Carnes's *Secret Ritual and Manhood in Victorian America* (New Haven: Yale University Press, 1989).

An extensive collection of contemporary wedding vows can be found in Abraham J. Klausner's *Weddings: A Complete Guide to All Religious and Interfaith Marriage Services* (New York: New American Library/Signet, 1986).

There is a vast literature on the topic of business and professional codes of ethics. Most of these works reprint codes or portions of codes as examples. Notable among these are Geoffrey Millerson's *The Qualifying Associations* (London: Routledge and Kegan Paul, 1964), John Kultgen, *Ethics and Professionalism* (Philadelphia: University of Pennsylvania Press, 1988), and William F. May, "Code and Covenant or Philanthropy and Contract?" *Hastings Center Report*, vol. 5 (December 1975): 29–38. Useful collections of medical codes and oaths from antiquity to the present can be found in M. B. Etziony's *The Physician's Creed: An Anthology of Medical Prayers, Oaths and Codes of Ethics* (Springfield: Charles C. Thomas, 1973) and in Stanley Joel Reiser et al., *Ethics in Medicine: Historical Perspectives and Contemporary Concerns* (Cambridge: M.I.T. Press, 1977). Business codes of ethics from the 1920s are collected in Edgar Laing Heermance's *Codes of Ethics: A Handbook* (Burlington, VT: Free Press Printing, 1924). A more comprehensive collection can be found in *Professional Ethics and Insignia* (Metuchen, NJ: Scarecrow Press, 1974) by Jane Clapp. The most current source book on professional and business ethics is Rena Gorlin's *Codes of Professional Responsibility* (Washington, DC: Bureau of National Affairs, 1994).

Of the few volumes that contain letters from parents to children, the best is Alan Valentine's *Fathers to Sons: Advice Without Consent* (Norman: University of Oklahoma Press, 1963). For the full texts of the most famous Elizabethan era parental advice books, see Louis B. Wright's *Advice to a Son: Precepts of Lord Burghley, Sir Walter Raleigh, and Francis Osborne* (Ithaca: Cornell University Press, 1962).

There are many collections of mottoes, each with its own particular angle. L. G. Pine's *A Dictionary of Mottoes* (London: Routledge and Kegan Paul, 1983) gives an alphabetical listing. Charles Norton Elvin's *Elvin's Handbook of Mottoes* (revised and with a supplement and index by R. Pinches, London, 1971) lists mottoes by type. The title of R. T. Wyckoff's *Latin Mottoes of Universities, Colleges, Technical Schools, Academies, Theological Seminaries, Normal Schools, Individuals, Companies, Societies, Countries, States, Towns, etc.* is self-explanatory. Unfortunately it does not provide translations. Two books devoted to British mottoes are Douglas Taylor's *Discovering Mottoes, Slogans, and War-Cries* (Shire Publications, 1973) and *The Book of Mottoes Borne by Nobility and Gentry, Public Companies, Cities, &c.* (London: Henry Washburne, 1851).

Although there are no general collections of architectural inscriptions, there are a few specialized ones. Three of these focus on federal buildings and memorials in Washington. They are John L. Andriot's *Guide to the Building Inscriptions of the Nation's Capital* (Arlington: Joy-Way Press, 1955), Clint W. Ensign's *Inscriptions of a Nation: Collected Quotations from Washington Monuments* (Washington, DC: Congressional Quarterly, 1994), and John Young Cole's *On These Walls: Inscriptions and Quotations in the Buildings of the Library of Congress* (Washington, DC: Library of Congress, 1995).

In addition, Charles W. Eliot's granddaughter, Grace Eliot Dudley, put together as many of Eliot's inscriptions as she could find in *The Inscriptions of Charles W. Eliot* (Cambridge: Harvard University Press, 1934).

INTRODUCTION

1   The text of the Miranda statement was adapted from Chief Justice Earl Warren's decision in *Miranda v. Arizona* (384 U.S. 439, 1996), which says, in part, "The warning of the right to remain silent must be accompanied by the explanation that anything said can and will be used against the individual in court. . . . [A]n individual held for interrogation must be clearly informed that he has the right to consult with a lawyer and to have the lawyer with him during interrogation. . . ."

The comment on how the Miranda warning has lost its urgency through repetition was made by former judge Sol Wachtler in "Crime and Punishment," *New Yorker*, July 15, 1996, pp. 72–78.

4   Tocqueville's analysis of ready-made opinions and their role in American culture is laid out in Volume II of *Democracy in America*, principally in the first three chapters of Book One. Although he does not give any specific examples, and may have had a more general idea in mind than such formal statements as the Pledge of Allegiance, the Boy Scout Oath, and "In God We Trust" (none of which, of course, existed in Tocqueville's time), he convincingly explains how Americans have come to embrace such formulas.

7   "It is the peculiar fate of Americans . . ." The Samuel P. Huntington quote is from *American Politics: The Promise of Disharmony* (Cambridge: Belknap Press, 1981), p. 39.

CHAPTER 1. DO UNTO OTHERS: THE EVOLUTION OF THE GOLDEN RULE

17   The so-called Stoic maxim in the original Latin reads: *Quod tibi fieri non vis, altera ne feceris* (what you do not wish to be done to you, do not to others). According to the *Augustan History*, in which most of the biographical details of the emperors' lives cannot be considered reliable, this maxim was chosen by the Roman emperor Alexander Severus to be inscribed over the entrance to his palace as well as on other public buildings. John Wesley refers to this story in his "Tenth Discourse on the Sermon on the Mount," when he mentions "that royal law . . . which even the heathen emperor caused to be written over the gate of his palace." The story, of course, like those concerning the inscriptions over the palaces of Ozymandias and the Assyrian ruler Sardanapalus, is pure fiction, albeit, as Wesley's use of it attests, a particularly influential fiction.

18   The term "golden rule" first appears in a textbook of 1575 called *The Ground of Arts*, in which an English mathematician named Robert Recorde refers to a "rule of proportions, which for his excellency is called the Golden rule." Within a century it had acquired its present sense, but exactly how, where, or when is not known. In a letter dated 1668, Peleg Sanford, a merchant of Newport, Rhode Island and onetime governor of the colony, invoked it as a common figure of speech.

> Sir, I have herewith sent you a copy of a letter sent unto you per Captain Pearse desiring you to consider thereof and not to forget the Golden Rule but do as you would be done unto. [*The Letter Book of Peleg Sanford* (Providence: Rhode Island Historical Society, 1928), letter 53 (22 December 1668), p. 47]

In 1698, Gersham Bulkeley elaborated on the same idea:

> The measure that you mete should be measured to you again. Tis a golden Rule, that which you would that others should do to you, do the same to them; and do not recompense evil for good. [*The People's Right to Election* (Philadelphia: William Bradford, 1689), p. 70]

20   Thoreau's objections to the Golden Rule can be found in *A Week on the Concord and Merrimack Rivers*, "Sunday." He concludes the quoted passage by observing, "There are various tough problems yet to solve, and we must make shift to live, betwixt spirit and matter, such a human life as we can."

20   A useful survey of the history of moral philosophy can be pieced together by following the trajectory of the Golden Rule after Confucius, as it left its mark on the major religions, on the great philosophers of antiquity, on the Church fathers, the Scholastic philosophers, and finally on Enlightenment thinkers.

There are interesting discussions of the rule in Tertullian (*Adversus Marcionem*, IV, 16) and Augustine's "Our Lord's Sermon on the Mount" (see *Works*, edited by Marcus Dods [1873], Book I, Chapter XVII, p. 122). Thomas Aquinas places it in the framework of his theory of law in the *Summa Theologica* (Q 99, article 1).

Diogenes Laertes credits Aristotle with the saying in *The Lives and Opinions of the Eminent Philosophers*, bk. V, xi. Isocrates echoes the Confucian maxim, notably in *To Nicocles* 61 (also 14 and 24).

A useful summary of the development of the law of forgiveness as a corrective to the law of resentment is provided by Edward Westermarck in *The Origin and Development of the Moral Ideas* (London: Macmillan and Co., 1906), Chapters III and IV. The discussion begins with Confucius and ends with Westermarck's contemporaries, and presents Golden Rule arguments put forth at each stage in the development of moral philosophy.

So-called "modern" discussions of the principle begin with Hobbes, for whom the Golden Rule is nothing more than a convenient rule of thumb that citizens can easily use as a moral yardstick. See *Leviathan* (1650), Part I, Chapter 14. John Locke, Jean-Jacques Rousseau, and such writers as Samuel Clarke, Henry More, and Thomas Reid weigh in on the matter, mostly on the side of the divine inspiration of the rule. See More's *Encheiridion Ethicum*, noemas 24 through 26 in Book 1, Chapter IV; Locke's *Essay Concerning Human Understanding*, Book I, chapter iii, paragraph 4; Clarke's *Evidences of Natural and Revealed Religion*, p. 86; and Reid's *Essays on the Active Powers of the Human Mind*, Essay V, chapter 1, "Of the First Principles of Morals."

The basis of moral duty in a sense of "feeling" begins with David Hume's well-known remark upon the ease with which so many ethical systems slide from "is" into "ought" (see *A Treatise on Human Nature*, Book III, part 1, section 1, i). Unable to bridge this gap himself, Hume resorts to a justification of virtue based on a feeling of satisfaction (see section II of the *Treatise*). This anticipates Jean-Jacques Rousseau's justification of moral rules based on sentiment. Rousseau's "less perfect . . . but perhaps more useful" rule is contained in *The Origins of Inequality*, I. See also *Emile*, Book IV.

Baruch Spinoza was the first to suggest that moral duty is an end in itself, although it was not until Kant that this idea was fully developed. Spinoza's *Ethics* should be consulted, particularly Part IV, prop. xvii and Part V, prop. x, for his rational (as opposed to religious) approach to ethics. Kant developed this approach more fully in the second section of his *Groundword of the Metaphysics of Morals* (1785), in which he introduces the Categorical Imperative and the Practical Imperative.

In the twentieth century Alan Gewirth's Principle of Generic Consistency has emerged as a generic alternative to the Golden Rule and the Categorical Imperative. It states: "Act in accord with the generic rights of your recipients as well as yourself." By way of explanation, Gewirth says that this principle "combines the formal consideration of consistency with the material consideration of rights to the generic features of goods of action." (*Reason and Morality*, p. 135.) It is unfair to isolate this maxim from its context, but hard to resist. It clearly was not intended to serve as a popular aphorism.

22   John Stuart Mill's hyperbolic assessment of the Golden Rule as the "ideal perfection of utilitarian morality" can be found in *Utilitarianism*, chapter 2. Prince Kropotkin's endorsement of the rule is contained in his pamphlet "Anarchist Morality." Nietzsche's most disparaging Golden Rule comments can be found in *The Will to Power* (#925, #926) and *The Antichrist* (#11, #57).

25   In the Mishnah, the oral history of the Jewish law, the story is told of an acolyte who derisively challenges Hillel, the spiritual leader of the Pharisees, to teach him the entire Jewish law while he stands on one foot. The young man cannot penetrate the wall of the rabbi's great patience. Hillel meets the challenge by saying, "What is hateful to you, do not to your fellow man. That is the entire Law: all the rest is commentary. Go and learn it."

It is hardly unusual that the Golden Rule was attributed to Hillel, since his role in Pharisaic literature is similar to that of Confucius in Confucian literature. Hillel was a near contemporary of Jesus, having lived during the first century B.C. Many of his teachings find their parallel in of those of Jesus—if not always in wording, at least in spirit. As Jacob Neusner notes in *Judaism in the Beginning of Christianity*, "That saying [the Golden Rule] went from country to country and from culture to culture, always being attributed to the leading sage or wise man of the place . . . and its attribution to Hillel tells us that he was regarded as the supreme authority within the Pharisaic movement."

25   Several versions of the Golden Rule can be found in works attributed to Confucius. Some anticipate the impossibility of reciprocal actions between social unequals, and therefore stress reciprocity in kind. These include passages from the *Shu King* (or Book of Historical Documents) IV, II, 3 and the *Li Ki* (or Book of Rites) XXVII, 1, 32 and XXXIX, 10, 2. More familiar versions of the maxim can be found in the *Analects*, 6, 28; 5, 11; 12, 2; and 15, 23.

25   The passage from Seneca is contained in his *Letters to Lucilius*, one of the earliest and most popular advice books, volume I, letter xlvii, 11.

26   The Confucian ideal of reciprocity is summed up in two Chinese characters—*shu* and *chung*. A discussion of their meaning is contained in Philip J. Ivanhoe, "Reweaving the 'One Thread' of the Analects," *Philosophy East and West* 40:1
(January 1990): pp. 17–33, which examines the "one thread" that runs through the
Confucian "way," as seen by four scholars. One of them sees *chung* as the positive
sense of reciprocity and *shu* as the negative rule of restraint. A second see *shu* as a
method of drawing an analogy between oneself and others, and *chung* as the idea
of doing one's best. A third equates *shu* with Jesus' commandment to "love thy
neighbor as thyself," and *chung* with "a kind of interpersonal good faith and loyalty." A fourth interprets *chung* as a guide for conduct among one's peers or superiors, and thus as a code of loyalty, while *shu* is a feeling of benevolence towards
equals and inferiors—a way of being considerate.

Taken together, these four views cover the spectrum of interpretations and
variations of the Golden Rule discussed in this chapter. Yet Ivanhoe adds a crucial
point regarding the maxim: "It does not provide us with actions to perform, and it
does not work unless it is embedded in a surrounding ethic."

26   Discussions of the ethical superiority of particular versions of the Golden
Rule—positive versus negative, Christian versus non-Christian—can be found in
a variety of sources, most of which have a definite bias. The *Catholic Encyclopedia*,
the *Dictionary of Christ and the Gospels*, the *Jewish Encyclopedia*, and the *Encyclopaedia of
Religion and Ethics* contain such arguments under the heading "Golden Rule." Each
unconsciously displays a clarity of vision and certainty of judgment typically
afforded by hindsight.

CHAPTER 2. WE HOLD THESE TRUTHS: CREEDS AND
OTHER PROFESSIONS OF FAITH

29   The quotes from and about *This I Believe* are taken from the two printed volumes of essays of the same title published in 1952 and 1954. The first volume contains a foreword by Murrow that is herein quoted from.

30–31 Thomas Jefferson's credo comes from "A Letter to Jared Sparks "(November
4, 1820); Benjamin Franklin's from "A Letter to Ezra Stiles" (1789). The Ingersoll
Creed can be found in Ingersoll's *Works* (New York: The Ingersoll League, 1933),
Volume V, p. 20. The Huxley quote is from "A Letter to Charles Kingsley" (1860).

32   For Thomas Paine's credo, see *The Age of Reason* (1794) Part I, chapter 1,
"The Author's Profession of Faith."

35   It is most likely that the earliest creeds—the Old Roman Creed of A.D. 190,
for example, or an interrogatory creed mentioned by Hippolytus in the early third
century—were inspired by scriptural passages that showed the confession of faith

as a prelude to baptism. The Acts of the Apostles (8:36–38), for example, contains a description of such a confession:

> . . . and the eunuch said, See, here is water; what doth hinder me to be baptized? And Philip said, If thou believest with all thine heart, thou mayest. And he answered and said, I believe that Jesus Christ is the Son of God . . . and they went down both into the water, both Philip and the eunuch; and he baptized him.

35   J. N. D. Kelly believes that the *Quicunque* was most likely written in the south of France in the late fourth century, possibly as a response to Nestorianism and Eutychianism (*Athanasian Creed*, pp. 91–108).

37   The Nicene controversy turned upon the "full deity of the Son," as Kelly puts it (*Early Christian Doctrines*, pp. 252–53), and hardly at all upon the nature of the Holy Spirit. As to how well the language of the creeds was understood, Kelly notes how astonishing it is that "theological divisions . . . were created and kept alive by the use of different and mutually confusing theological terms. At the council [of Alexandria in A.D. 362] it was formally recognized that what mattered was not the language used but the meaning underlying it." This observation is consistent with the paradoxical role of creeds, oaths, and codes as tests of blind loyalty.

38   In his journal (Vol. I, September 3, 1838), Henry David Thoreau notes, "The only faith that men recognize is a creed. But the true creed which we unconsciously live by, and which rather adopts us than we it, is quite different from the written or preached one. Men anxiously hold fast to their creed, as to a straw, thinking this does them good service because their sheet anchor does not drag."

41   Harry S. Truman summarized the American creed when he said, "You know that being an American is more than a matter of where your parents came from. It is a belief that all men are created equal and that everyone deserves an even break. It is respect for the dignity of men and women without regard to race, creed, or color. That is our creed." (Informal remarks, October 26, 1948.)

Insightful analyses of the idea of an American creed can be found, among other places, in Samuel P. Huntington, *American Politics: The Promise of Disharmony* (Cambridge: Belknap Press, 1981) and Garry Wills, *Inventing America: Jefferson's Declaration of Independence* (Garden City: Doubleday, 1978), p. xxii.

43   "An American Creed," Francis Cardinal Spellman (1889–1967), *Prayers and Poems* (New York: Charles Scribner's Sons, 1946).

46   "These little journeys into philosophy . . ." Roland Sawyer, *Christian Science Monitor*, December 31, 1952, p. 9.

CHAPTER 3. SO HELP ME GOD: LOYALTY OATHS AND
PLEDGES OF ALLEGIANCE

53   For an in-depth discussion of conflicts of loyalty, see George Fletcher, *Loyalty: An Essay on the Morality of Relationships* (New York: Oxford University Press, 1993). Striking parallels between the ancient and modern uses of oaths are explored in Joseph Plescia, *The Oath and Perjury in Ancient Greece* (Tallahassee: Florida State University Press, 1970). A brief survey of test oaths is contained in Samuel M. Koenigsberg and Morton Stavis, "Test Oaths: Henry VIII to the ABA," *Lawyers Guild Review* 11 (1951), pp. 111–127.

55   The Act of Succession and the accompanying oaths can be found in *Statutes of the Realm*—26 Hen VIII c. 2 (1534): "An Acte ratifying the oath that every of the King's Subjects hath taken and shall hereafter be bound to take for due observation of the act made for the surety of the succession of the King's Highness in the Crown of the Realm." The oath contained therein refers to 26 Hen VIII c. 1, which declares the King to be "supreme head of the Church of England," and 25 Hen VIII c. 22, the first Act of Succession, which voids Henry's marriage to Catherine of Aragon, and validates his marriage to Anne Boleyn. The second of these acts also mandates one oath for nobles and another for all subjects, by which both swear to "defend and keep . . . the effects and contents [of] this act."

55   In 1880 Charles Bradlaugh, newly elected to the English Parliament, unintentionally triggered a national controversy because of his atheism. Bradlaugh at first requested the right to affirm the oath of office, although this option was legally available only to those whose religion forbade them from swearing. Being denied this option, Bradlaugh agreed to swear the oath instead, going on record as saying that he would not feel as bound by an oath as he would by an affirmation. But he was caught in a Catch-22. Barred from swearing the oath because his initial demurral was held to disqualify him from the right to it, he also was not allowed to affirm, a privilege to which he was not entitled. Bradlaugh's dilemma stirred much debate in the House and focused the attention of the entire country. He was eventually allowed to affirm, and in 1888 the Oaths Act was qualified with an addendum to eliminate the test requirement that implicitly barred atheists from serving in Parliament. See Walter L. Arnstein, *The Bradlaugh Case* (Oxford: Clarendon Press, 1965).

56   In a letter of 5 February 1864, Lincoln wrote to Secretary of War Edwin M. Stanton of his reaction to the ironclad oath, saying, "On principle I dislike an oath which requires a man to swear he *has* done no wrong. It rejects the Christian principle of forgiveness on terms of repentance. I think it enough if a man does no wrong *hereafter*." [Roy P. Basler, ed., *Works* VII, p. 169.]

56   A good illustration of how the idea of swearing loyalty has come to be regarded as an American preoccupation was provided by the British writer G. K. Chesterton, who came to the United States in 1921 as a visiting lecturer. Having survived the entry process, Chesterton was inspired to write, "I have stood on the other side of Jordan, in the land ruled by a rude Arab chief, where the police looked so like brigands that one wondered what the brigands looked like. But they did not ask me whether I had come to subvert the power of the Shereef; and they did not exhibit the faintest curiosity about my personal views on the ethical basis of civil authority."

58   For an outline of the NDEA oath controversy and other oath controversies of the 1950s and '60s, see Tom Kaser, "The Loyalty Oath: 1964–65," *Saturday Review*, November 21, 1964.

60   The California test oath controversies are the basis of Frank Rowe's *The Enemy Among Us* (Sacramento: Cougar Books, 1980) and George R. Stewart's *The Year of the Oath* (New York: Doubleday, 1950).

60   During the University of California oath controversy, according to the Interim Report of the Committee on Academic Freedom to the Academic Senate (February 1, 1951), "more than a hundred scholars have been lost by ejection, resignation, or refusal of reappointment, among them some of the illustrious minds of our generation. A great university, famous for its sacrifice in war, for its scientific and humane accomplishments, for its devoted service to the State, and for the prideful regard in which it was held by the citizens has in the space of about six months been reduced to the point where it is condemned by leading scholars and learned societies as a place unfit for scholars to inhabit." University faculty committees tend to overreact with histrionic prose when defending their academic freedoms, but this is one case where they were justified. The committee's assessment may be somewhat exaggerated, but the administration did seriously compromise the institution's integrity and research capability.

64   The Russo case is reported in detail in Daniel Lange, "Reporter at Large: Love of Country," *New Yorker*, July 30, 1973, pp. 35–48.

65   The original Pledge of Allegiance was published in the *Youth's Companion*, September 8, 1892, p. 446.

67   A joint resolution adding the words "under God" to the Pledge was submitted in 1954 by Louis C. Rabaut, a Democratic congressman from Michigan. It was co-authored by Senator Homer Ferguson, a Republican from the same state, whose name was not attached to the bill. However, they did share the honor of being the first to recite the revised pledge before Congress.

A group of Washington, D.C., schoolchildren give the original palm-down salute in this Frances Benjamin Johnston photograph of 1899. (Courtesy Library of Congress)

Although written in 1892 by Francis Bellamy, the Pledge was not officially adopted by Congress until 1945, by which time it had undergone several revisions. A sober assessment of the religious righteousness that led to the inclusion of God in the Pledge is made by Robert M. Senkewicz in "Twenty-Five Years 'Under God,'" *America*, June 9, 1979, pp. 469–70. There he quotes Eisenhower's pastor—Dr. George M. Docherty—defending the revision by saying: "The American way of life is more than the material total of baseball games, hot dogs, Coca-Cola, television, deep freezes and other gadgets. It is a way of life that sees man as a sentient being created by God and seeking to know his will. . . ." But Senkewicz believes that the meaning of the Pledge has become inverted for most Americans—that it is now God who serves the state, that he is under us. This development, the idea that God would be co-opted by a national symbol, is precisely what opponents of the revision feared.

67   "Our form of government has no sense. . . ." The Eisenhower quote is from a speech given to the Freedoms Foundation in New York (see the *New York Times*, December 23, 1952, p. 16). It is an interesting illustration of how a public figure's words can and will be used against him in the court of public opinion. The quote would have gone unnoticed had not Will Herberg used it in an essay on religion

in America (see *Protestant—Catholic—Jew: Essays in American Religious Sociology*, p. 351). In his speech Eisenhower was trying to explain the idea of an American creed, and of how difficult it would be, theoretically, to explain to Soviet officials. Placed under a magnifying glass, and with its final phrase highlighted by italics, the quote has served the purposes of many chroniclers of American culture—notably John Brooks (*The Great Leap*, 1966), Douglas Miller and Marion Nowack (*The Fifties*, 1977), and Alan Ehrenhalt (*The Lost City*, 1995)—in whose works it takes on a comical absurdity lacking in its original context. Taken out of context (as it always is), it seems to be a perfect illustration of the hollow posturing of religious righteousness in the 1950s. What Eisenhower went on to say, however, is that American society is essentially Judeo-Christian, although whatever its religion might be, it would have to be one that acknowledges the idea that all men are created equal. In other words, there is an American creed that acknowledges God, and its humanistic tenets stand above those of any one church. Eisenhower would never have said as much, but he implies that the Declaration of Independence takes precedence over the Nicene Creed, or any other creed.

70   A synopsis of the Bush–Dukakis campaign brouhaha can be found in David Whitman, "George Bush's Pledge of Allegiance Problem," *U.S. News and World Report*, September 12, 1988, p. 16. Theologian Martin Marty weighs in on the same issue in *The Christian Century* ("Original Intent," September 28, 1988), where he reviews the history of the Pledge and gives Colonel Balch's less than rousing original version. He adds this interesting fact: "A Jeffersonian, [Francis] Bellamy wanted the words 'equality' and 'fraternity' mentioned with 'liberty' and 'justice.' But he was a realist, who said that including these words would not work. . . ."

CHAPTER 4. 'TIL DEATH DO US PART: OATHS OF CITIZENSHIP, RITES OF SECRET INITIATION, TEMPERANCE PLEDGES, AND WEDDING VOWS

74   The Mafia oath is taken from the transcript of an induction ceremony taped by the FBI in Medford, Massachusetts on October 29, 1989. See Efrain Hernandez, Jr., "Tapes Reveal 'Family' Secrets," Boston *Globe*, July 4, 1991, p. 13; and Andrew Blake, "Mafia Power Shifts with 5 Guilty Pleas," Boston *Globe*, January 23, 1992.

76   A scholarly account of the use of the Ephebic Oath in academia is contained in Fletcher Harper Swift, *The Athenian Ephebic Oath of Allegiance in American Schools and Colleges*, University of California Publications in Education, vol. 11, no. 1 (1947). Swift gives the texts of several variations of the oath as it is used in academic settings. He also reprints a translation of the oath discovered at Acharnae.

79   If there is a supreme architect of the Masonic rite it would have to be Albert Pike, a lawyer, a Confederate brigadier general, and (some would say) a grand

mountebank, who rose to the position of Sovereign Grand Commander of the Ancient and Accepted Scottish Rite. Pike drew upon his vast knowledge of classical literature, ancient history, sacred books of the East, and Romantic poetry to cobble together his 861-page masterwork, *The Morals and Dogma of Freemasonry*—a complete revision of all Masonic rituals and an explication of its signs and symbols. Mark Carnes gives a summary of Pike's colorful life in *Ritual and Manhood*, pp. 131–149.

CHAPTER 5. ON MY HONOR I WILL DO MY BEST: CODES OF ETHICS AND CONDUCT

93   The Electrical Supply Jobbers' Association has undergone two name changes and is now the National Association of Electrical Distributors. They have replaced the code of 1923 with a more suitable modern code.

95   "We will face reality and embrace change . . ." The vision statement is that of HarperCollins.

100   In the 1952 film, *The Quiet Man*, John Wayne reluctantly agrees to fight Victor McGlaglen in what turns out to be a cross-country donnybrook. Wayne initiates the proceedings by asking McGlaglen whether they will be observing Queensberry Rules.

101   Percival not only pioneered the use of professional codes of ethics, but he also produced a book of fatherly advice: *A Father's Instructions*, which he followed up with a sequel entitled *Moral and Literary Dissertations*.

107   Unlike most business and professional associations, the A.M.A. has provisions for enforcing its code, principally through its control over licensing. However, as John Kultgen notes, associations with the clout to enforce their codes are quicker to wield it over economic issues than over ethical ones. "The ostensible function of codes," Kultgen writes, is moral in that they "employ the language of morality." But when the social function of a code is antithetical to the moral one, he adds, that fact is disguised by moral language. Consequently, "codes, particularly that of the A.M.A., have been used with great ruthlessness to punish dissidents who have taken the public's side on issues such as group medicine."

108   As a ready-made opinion, *primum non nocere* (above all else do no harm) is hardly uncontroversial as a maxim of medical ethics, even though it at first seems fairly obvious. Yet some writers see the maxim as worthless, as Thurston Brewin notes in the November 26, 1994, issue of the medical journal *The Lancet*. When the word *primum* is removed, however, most of these critics are placated. *Non nocere*— or simply, do no harm—is generally considered a viable principle. Yet Brewin finds

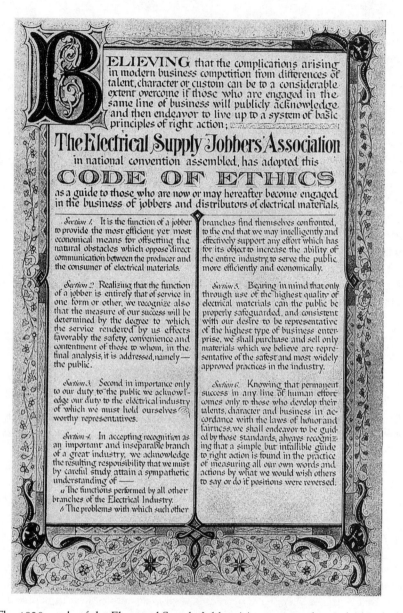

The 1920s code of the Electrical Supply Jobbers' Association shows the level of artistry once employed to convey lofty business principles.

even this to be inadequate, indefensible, or possibly unethical in the face of the decisions with which physicians are faced. Sometimes, he argues, it is necessary to risk doing harm in order to prevent death, or to risk a potentially deadly treatment in order to attack an illness. Drugs, radiation, and surgical intervention have their side effects, many of which are harmful. Thus the famous Hippocratic principle, in Brewin's estimation, can cause harm by discouraging firm action.

Brewin's point sounds sensible—he believes that a more useful maxim would be: Never forget the possibility that you may do more harm than good. It could be translated into Latin to satisfy those who prefer an antique tone, he adds. Yet Brewin is being too literal. A motto such as *primum non nocere* is sustained by a consensus of opinions that does not hang upon a literal interpretation. Brewin, commendably, adds to the ongoing discussion, but his suggestion is unrealistic. The marketplace of ideas rarely operates so efficiently.

109   College of Philadelphia commencement program is quoted in Francis R. Packard, *History of Medicine in the United States* (New York: Paul B. Hoeber, 1931), p. 368.

111   "It was, for me, a thrilling experience . . ." Louis Lasagna describes his rationale for a New Hippocratic Oath in "Would Hippocrates Rewrite His Oath?" *New York Times Magazine*, June 28, 1964, pp. 11ff.

114   Department store owner Edward A. Filene wrote a short personal business code of ethics, which was published in a special issue of the *Annals* of the American Academy of Political and Social Science (May, 1922) under the title: "A Simple Code of Business Ethics." It reads:

1. A business, in order to have the right to succeed, must be of real service to the community.
2. Real service in business consists in making or selling merchandise of reliable quality for the lowest practically possible price, provided that merchandise is made and sold under just conditions.

116   Discussions of the usefulness of written codes of ethics have been published in every generation since the 1920s. The best of the early studies, aside from Heermance's *The Ethics of Business*, is John Maurice Clark's *Social Control of Business* (Chicago, 1926). Clark has many useful things to say about the codes of his era, and many of these observations are no less true today. On pages 233–237 he explores what he calls the "unwritten code of business," which he attempts to express in written form. Its tenets are: (1) Thou shalt boost thy town. (2) Thou shalt pay thy debts, fulfill thy contracts, and give full measure. (3) Thou shalt believe in thy business and thy goods (it pays). (4) Thou shalt compete (thou shalt not compete unfairly). (5) Thou shalt not support radicalism, pacifism, nor any other "ism" which attacks the fundamentals of things as they are. (6) Thou shalt not give aid and comfort to the aims and ambitions of labor so far as these are inconsistent with the continued successful conduct of private business.

"Such," he concludes, "is the code of business: a most curious mixture of the more presentable phases of intelligent private interest, class interest, community obligation, and natural human sympathy, wherein altruism is upheld one moment and apologized for the next, and virtue and expediency are inextricably interwoven."

117   The peculiar history of "Desiderata" owes partly to mass delusion and perhaps equally to the power of copyright law. Max Ehrmann, at one time an assistant attorney general for Indiana, dabbled at poetry. He wrote "Desiderata" in
1927 in a fit of despair to help offset his melancholy, and yet it remained relatively
obscure during his lifetime. Apparently it circulated widely enough that by the
1950s it came to the attention of an Anglican priest in Baltimore, who copied
down the poem and left it lying around. It was then found by a man who affixed
to it the date 1692, which was the year in which the church was founded. Because
it was thought to be in the public domain, the poem was soon reprinted widely,
accompanied by the apocryphal story of its antiquity. Adlai Stevenson was about
to send it out as his Christmas card at the time of his death. Warner Brothers released a recorded version, and the poem was frequently read on television and
radio shows, all to the frustration of Ehrmann's heirs (he died in 1954) and the
man who purchased the copyright. In the early 1970s, *The National Lampoon* published a wicked parody of the poem (featuring such pearls as: "Strive at all times to
bend, fold, spindle, and mutilate," "Consider that two wrongs never make a right,
but that three do," and "Let not the sands of time get in your lunch.") That seemed
to be about the end of it.

120   "The great multitude of men . . ." Walter Lippmann, *Essays in the Public
Philosophy* (Boston: Little, Brown, 1955), p. 149.

120   "One CEO commented . . ." Ronald Berenbeim, *Corporate Ethics* (New York:
The Conference Board, 1987), p. 14.

CHAPTER 6. TO THINE OWN SELF BE TRUE: THE SECRETS OF
SUCCESS, ADVICE FROM PARENTS, AND THE LAW ACCORDING
TO MURPHY AND PARKINSON

125   P. T. Barnum is not on record as ever having said, "There's a sucker born
every minute," but he did say this: "I am not in show business alone to make
money. I feel it my mission, as long as I live, to provide clean, moral, and health-
ful recreation for the public to which I have so long catered." This sentiment, of
course, is not what Barnum is remembered for.
    Vince Lombardi was also misquoted—possibly. His credo was: "Winning
isn't everything. The desire to win is everything. In fact, it's the only thing." The
middle sentence, of course, makes quite a difference. While Lombardi may have
wanted to be remembered for this interpretation, Bob Rubin (in *Green Bay's Packers*,
1973) insists that Lombardi recited the received version during a training camp
talk in 1959. If true, then Lombardi would simply have been quoting someone
else, since "Wining isn't everything; it's the only thing" was first uttered, and made
at least locally famous, by Vanderbilt University football coach Red Sanders in the
late 1940s. See Leo Green, *Sportswit* (1984), p. 57.

135   The Oliver Wendell Holmes quote is taken from Alan Valentine, *Fathers to Sons: Advice Without Consent* (Norman: University of Oklahoma Press, 1963), p. xix. The letter is dated 1908.

144   Sinclair Lewis's caustic assessment of Dale Carnegie is from *Newsweek*, November 15, 1937, p. 31.

146   Capt. Murphy's identity was brought to light by *People Weekly*, January 31, 1983, p. 82.

149   Parkinson's Law first appeared in *The Economist*, November 19, 1995, pp. 635–37. For a single listing of all of Peter's laws and corollaries, see Laurence J. Peter, "Peter's People," *Human Behavior*, February 1979, pp. 68–69.

154   The Empire Diner, an art deco blue-plate classic, is at the corner of 22nd Street and Eighth Avenue in New York City. For years it has featured quotations and advice on the menu. The current menu homily is longer than the one my father copied down in the 1960s, and is worth a look if you happen to be in town.

CHAPTER 7. SEMPER FI: MOTTOES, MAXIMS, AND SLOGANS

157   Marguerite Del Guidice, "Washington Post Finds Itself on the Front Page," *Boston Globe*, November 30, 1981, p. 10.

158   "Change in the Canadian Coat of Arms Touches a Raw Nerve," *New York Times*, December 11, 1995, p. A8; and "All in a Seal: Canada's New Great Debate," *Boston Globe*, December 8, 1995, p. 2.

160   The motto of the Order of the Garter shows Edward III's flair for the romantic, at least in one plausible explanation of its origin. According to Sir Nicholas Harris Nicolas in his *History of the Orders of Knighthood of the British Empire* (London: John Hunter, 1842): "A great variety of devices and mottos were used by Edward the Third: they were chosen from the most trivial causes, and were of an amorous rather than a military character. Nothing is more likely than that, in a crowded assembly, a lady should accidentally have dropped her garter; that the circumstance should have caused a smile in the bystanders; and that on its being taken up by Edward, he should have reproved the levity of his courtiers by so happy and chivalrous an exclamation, placing the garter at the same time on his own knee, as 'Dishonoured be he who thinks ill of it.' Such a circumstance occurring at a time of general festivity, when devices, mottoes, and conceits of all kinds were adopted as ornaments or Badges of the Habits worn at Jousts and Tournaments, would naturally have been commemorated as other royal expressions seem

to have been, by its conversion into a Device and Motto for the dresses at an approaching hastilude [tilting]." (Volume I, p. lxxxiii)

161   William Jennings Bryan originated the slogan "Every Man a King" in a campaign speech in 1900.

163   Rousing battle orders such as "Don't fire 'til you see the whites of their eyes" almost qualify as a category of ready-made opinions in their own right. The common expressions they have inspired ("Damn the torpedoes, full speed ahead") pervade the language. Yet there have been no memorable battle orders issued since the end of Word War II. It could easily be argued that media coverage of wars has robbed commanders of their ability to inspire myths.

165   The evolution of "fraternity" is discussed at length in David Thomson's "The Ideal of Fraternité (1789–1849)," Fortnightly 177 (May 1952): 321–26 and (June 1952): 415–21. The discussion presented here draws mostly from that article.

165   It has been suggested that Benjamin Franklin was responsible for the French national motto—Liberty, Equality, Fraternity—having submitted it for consideration when he served as ambassador to France.

167   Churchill Williams, "Something to Go By," Lippincott's 88 (November 1971): 749–51.

171   The observation on the change in the motto that "put Dr. Coué over" with the American public is from an unsigned editorial in The Nation, 116: 3001 (January 10, 1923): 32.

172   For a detailed look at Wright's Emersonian sympathies, see Jack Quinan, Frank Lloyd Wright's Larkin Building: Myth and Fact (Cambridge: M.I.T. Press, 1987). The quote on Wright's idealism is taken from this book.

174   The story of the THINK motto is told in William Rogers, Think: A Biography of the Watsons and IBM (New York: Stein and Day, 1969).

177   Fred Gymer made enough of a splash in the 1950s to merit a rash of magazine profiles and filler pieces. Fortune dubbed him the "zany-motto man" in a June 1953 article. The American Mercury gave him a lengthy write-up in their September 1958 issue.

179   L. W. Michaelson, "Nebbish: Cynic in Low Key," Catholic World, 189: 1131 (June 1959): 214–16.

CHAPTER 8. IN GOD WE TRUST. THE NATIONAL MOTTOES

182   The most complete account of the genesis of the national mottoes is contained in Richard S. Patterson and Richardson Dougall, *The Eagle and the Shield: A History of the Great Seal of the United States* (Washington, DC: Department of State, 1976). Thus my comment that the story has been left untold is not entirely true. There are a few readily available accounts of the origins of the Great Seal and the national mottoes, but unfortunately they omit key details and perpetuate some myths. *The Eagle and the Shield* sets the record straight (in meticulous detail), but it is not easy to find because it is out of print. In that sense, the real story goes unnoticed, although not exactly untold.

187   *The Gentleman's Magazine* debuted in 1731. The original title page featured an emblem and the now-famous motto.

193   In 1959 the Judicial Conference of the State of New York recommended that the words "In God We Trust" be displayed in every courtroom of the state. The idea was proposed by Judge James McNally, who reasoned that if Congress saw fit to adopt it as the national motto, it was only proper to display it in the courts.

In the wake of the controversial school prayer decision in June 1962, the House of Representatives placed the motto on the wall of its chambers, and one representative went so far as to introduce a bill requiring the words to be displayed in the Supreme Court chamber, which was interpreted as a way to humiliate the Court for the school prayer decision. After this controversy died down, the motto went up in many federal courthouses across the country.

CHAPTER 9. NEITHER SNOW NOR RAIN NOR HEAT NOR GLOOM OF NIGHT: ARCHITECTURAL INSCRIPTIONS OF THE AMERICAN RENAISSANCE

202   The Nicolete Gray quote is from *Lettering on Buildings* (New York: Reinhold, 1960), p. 62.

In *Lettering on Architecture* (New York: Whitney Library of Design, 1976), Alan Bartram points out that the Romans were the first to use lettering in a truly architectural, as opposed to an ad hoc way. "The Egyptians carved hieroglyphs into their buildings; the Assyrians cut cuneiform script across the monumental sculptures decorating their buildings; but the Romans were the first people to

The pencil sketch of Du Simitière's first design for the obverse of the seal, found in Thomas Jefferson's papers. (Courtesy National Archives)

devise monumental inscriptions as we know them" (p. 10). Yet he adds, "the reasons for the inscriptions are not always especially admirable. Personal vainglory and propaganda; a desire for immortality, an instrument, almost, of oppression; the sheer abundance of it must have been overwhelming."

Bartram goes on to trace the use of lettering on buildings down through the Renaissance to British neoclassicism, noting that the English, for a time, fancied themselves as the successors of the Romans. He neglects, however, to make any mention of the much more successful use of inscriptions (in English) on American classical architecture.

203   The Parthenon's thematic program is discussed in Donald Kagan, *Pericles of Athens and the Birth of Democracy* (New York: Free Press, 1991), p. 169.

207   Henry Adams, who knew many of the men who staged the Chicago Exposition, wrote, "Chicago asked in 1893 for the first time the question whether the American people knew where they were driving. . . . [it] was the first expression of American thought as a unity." (*Education of Henry Adams,* p. 343.)

213   Grace Eliot Dudley compiled a book of her grandfather's inscriptions in 1934. In her introduction, Mrs. Dudley recounts the story of the Washington Post Office inscription:

In 1911, at the close of a long day's work at Northeast Harbor, Maine, Mr. Eliot went out on his boat in the company of two or three friends. Presently he produced a scrap of paper and an infinitesimal pencil and began to write. When he had finished, he read aloud the original draft of the two inscrip-

William Barton's second design. The reverse in the upper right features Barton's original mottoes. (Courtesy National Archives)

tions. . . . Possibly he had meditated these inscriptions for some time, but it appeared to those present like an inspiration of the moment. In time they came, unsigned, to the notice of President Wilson, who made a few alterations and consigned the inscriptions to the stonecutters. Only later did he learn the name of the author.

The edited inscription was known for a time as the Creed of the Postal Service until it was replaced by William Kendall's adaptation of Herodotus for the New York Post Office.

214   One of Eliot's best inscriptions looks down from atop the archway of Harvard College's Dexter Memorial Gate (1899). The student who bothers to look up on his way in will find the message ENTER TO GROW IN WISDOM; and on the way out, DEPART TO BETTER SERVE THY COUNTRY AND THY KIND. The beleaguered Harvard administration, beset with charges of political incorrectness in recent years, is undoubtedly relieved about the inscription's inconspicuousness, if they are aware of it at all. Still, anyone who studies Eliot's

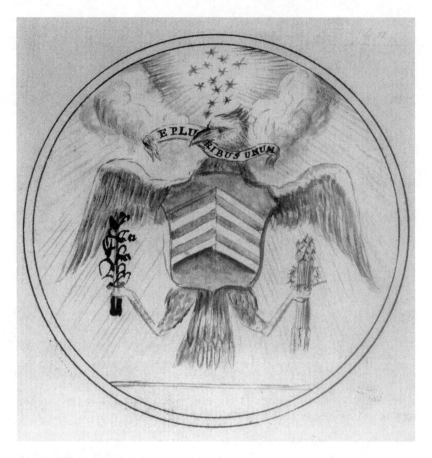

Charles Thomson's familiar design for the obverse, as traced from the original.
(Courtesy National Archives)

record and notes his generosity of mind would not be inclined to read anything sinister or exclusionary into the words "thy kind."

215   The story of the choice of inscription for the entrance to the RCA Building is told by Alan Balfour in *Rockefeller Center: Architecture as Theater* (New York: McGraw-Hill, 1978), pp. 143–45. Lifting the image of Wisdom from a drawing by William Blake was H. B. Alexander's idea. Many texts for inscriptions were submitted to John D. Rockefeller, Jr., who insisted that if he had to walk by it every day on the way to his office, it had better have some meaning for him. The last recorded proposal was: "Day unto day uttereth speech and night unto night sheweth knowledge," which is from Psalms 19:2. It is left unexplained who came up with the final inscription, or how it came to be approved.

Franklin Delano Roosevelt's corrections for the design of the silver certificate of 1935. (Courtesy Bureau of Engraving and Printing)

218   The opinion that many inscriptions constitute "a painful insult to the intelligence of the public reading it" comes from the *Federal Architect* (October 1933): 4–5.

219   The story of Cortissoz's and Bacon's struggle to preserve the integrity of their vision for the Lincoln Memorial is told by H. Wayne Morgan in "An Epitaph for Mr. Lincoln," *American Heritage* (February/March 1987): 58–63.

220   The original passage which inspired Kendall's Post Office inscription is from Herodotus, vol. 4, book 8, verse 98. As translated by A. D. Godley, it reads: "It is said that as many days as there are in the whole journey, so many are the men and horses that stand along the road, each horse and man at the interval of a day's journey; and these are stayed neither by snow nor rain nor heat nor darkness from accomplishing their appointed course with due speed."

Kendall's letter to Charles Eliot of Harvard (who had been a classmate of Kendall's father) asking him to provide the inscription for the frieze of the post office, says in part: "The long inscription for the frieze over the colonnade we thought might be some general statement about the importance of the postal service in the progress of civilization. . . . I take the success of this building much to heart and appeal to you to assist me in this important matter of a fitting idea couched in dignified language." (William Kendall to Charles Eliot, August 18, 1911, courtesy of Harvard University Archives, UA I.5.150, box 349B[2]). He also sought some help with the other inscriptions and decorative sculpture. Eliot declined the offer, citing other obligations and by pointing out that he had just completed the inscriptions for the Washington, D.C., Post Office.

The Court of Honor at the 1892 Chicago World's Columbian Exposition, as photographed by Frances Benjamin Johnston. The Watergate looms behind Daniel Chester French's colossal statue, "The Republic." (Courtesy Library of Congress)

221   The Ozymandias legend did not spring fully formed from Shelley's imagination. His poem is certainly the most memorable evocation of the tale, but it was merely the last in a long line of references which begin with the Greek epigrammists, who invented it. Which is to say that no such inscription graced the tomb of Rameses or anyone else. Instead it was attached to it in hindsight, much as similar legends have been ascribed to the tombs of other great empire builders. Because of the effect it had on the Romantic imagination, the genesis of the legend is worth a brief summary.

To begin, here is the text of Shelley's poem of the year 1818 in full, with the original punctuation and spelling:

I met a traveller from an antique land
Who said: Two vast and trunkless legs of stone
Stand in the desert. Near them, on the sand,
Half sunk, a shattered visage lies, whose frown,
And wrinkled lip, and sneer of cold command,

Tell that its sculptor well those passions read
Which yet survive, stamped on these lifeless things,
The hand that mocked them and the heart that fed;
And on the pedestal these words appear:
"My name is Ozymandias, king of kings:
Look on my works, ye Mighty, and despair!"
Nothing beside remains. Round the decay
Of that colossal wreck, boundless and bare,
The lone and level stands stretch far away.

Shelley wrote the poem as part of a contest with a friend, and both used as their point of departure a text of Diodorus of Sicily, a not entirely reliable Greek writer, who lived in the Nile Valley from 60 to 57 B.C., and explored and described many of the Egyptian temples that continue to inspire wonder to this day. On the floodplane of Thebes, among the ruins of the court of Memnon, he claimed to have come upon an inscription on a colossal seated statue. The lines read:

Ozymandias am I, king of kings.
If anyone would know how great I am and where I lie,
let him surpass one of my works" (Book I. 47).

Ozymandias was the Greek name for User-ma'et-Re, the real name of the pharaoh Rameses II. As H. R. Hall comments in *The Ancient History of the Near East* (London, 1916), pp. 317–18, "such an inscription, typical of those put into the mouths of Egyptian kings by the informants of the Greek writers, is perhaps possible under Senusert III, but never appeared on any Egyptian monument of the Rameside period." Yet another reason to doubt Diodorus is the prevalence of the same motif in ancient literature. The idea that time ultimately obliterates all evidence of man's greatness is an old one. Which is to say that "Ozymandias" is not the sole evocation of an empire builder's crumbling legacy.

The most famous parallel to Ozymandias is Sardanapalus, the mythical last king of the ancient Assyrian empire. Although not a historical person, he is thought to represent an amalgamation of the tragic fates of the last three Assyrian rulers (the most famous of whom was Assurbanipal). Like Ozymandias, Sardanapalus was a favorite subject of Romantic artists. Delacroix painted *The Death of Sardanapalus*, one of his most celebrated canvases, partly to illustrate the theme of arrogance and lasciviousness leading inevitably and spectacularly to ruin. The painting was most directly inspired by Shelley's friend Byron, who wrote a historical drama about Sardanapalus in 1821. Its subject is a debauched king who surrounds himself with wealth and women, and who sets his palace on fire when his kingdom is besieged and about to be overrun.

The legend of Sardanapalus, like that of Ozymandias, was invented by the Greek epigrammists. In the *Greek Anthology*, a collection of about four thousand poems and epigrams assembled in the tenth century by a Byzantine scholar, there are hundreds of epitaphs—some real, but many that are purely imaginary, including one attributed to Sardanapalus, which reads: "I have all I ate and drank and the delightful things I learnt with the loves, but all my many and rich possessions I left behind." Other sources for the story include (not coincidentally) Diodorus of Sicily (Book II.22.23) and Athanaeus (Book III, c. 14).

During the Renaissance this legend was taken up by the Italian architect Leon Batista Alberti (1404–1472), who wrote of it in his influential *Ten Books on Architecture*, and made it into something much more Ozymandian:

> On the tomb of Sardanapalus, King of the Assyrians, was a statue which seemed to clap its hands together by way of applause, with an epitaph to this effect: In one single day I built Tarsus and Archileum; but do you, Friend, eat, drink and be merry; for there is nothing else among men that is worthy of this applause. (Book VIII, Chapter IV)

Horatio Greenough's statue of George Washington, after its banishment to the Capitol grounds. (Courtesy Library of Congress)

Alberti also recounted a similar story told of Cyrus, the founder of the Persian Empire, who, according to Plutarch, had the following epitaph inscribed on his sepulcher:

> O man, whosoever thou art and whencesoever thou comest (for I know thou wilt come), I am Cyrus, the founder of the Persian Empire; do not therefore begrudge me this little earth which covers my body.

In Plutarch's version of events, Alexander the Great came upon Cyrus's desecrated tomb, and was so moved by it that he had the epitaph translated into Greek and inscribed below the original. "The reading of this sensibly touched Alexander," the historian writes, "filling him with the thought of the uncertainty and mutability of human affairs." (See Parallel Lives, "Alexander," 69.) Alberti gives a more detailed description of the tomb, and reproduces a similar epitaph (Book VIII, Chapter III).

The one other noteworthy example of a mythical inscription involves the Roman emperor Alexander Severus, who is said to have so highly valued the Golden Rule (or, more precisely, the stoic maxim) that he had it inscribed on his palace and on other public buildings. The source of this story is the *Augustan History*, a collection of biographies of the emperors in which most of the personal details are considered fictitious. It is about as reliable as the *Greek Anthology*. Both works, however, created folklores that enjoyed wide circulation in later generations.

222   One Chicago Exposition building—its only fireproof structure—did survive the fire which consumed the rest of the White City. Charles Atwood's Palace of Fine Arts, built to house the magnificent art collection, became the Field Museum of Natural History. During the 1930s it was rebuilt out of permanent materials. It is now the Museum of Science and Industry.

222   See "Federal Courthouses," *Architecture* (January 1996), for an overview of the GSA program.

223   Moynihan's foreword is from Ada Louise Huxtable's *Will They Ever Finish Bruckner Boulevard?* (New York: Macmillan, 1970).

225   "The translation of rhetoric into stone . . ." Horatio Greenough, *The Travels, Observations, and Experience of a Yankee Stonecutter* (1852), p. 30. The sculptor is not referring here to his statue of Washington or even to architectural inscriptions. He may have had both of these things in mind, but the comment is directed at some of the sculptural reliefs on the U.S. Capitol.

228   Lewis Mumford, *The Culture of Cities* (New York: Harcourt, Brace, and Co., 1938), p. 432.

230   Maya Lin's comments on her memorial are from Jim Sexton's "Beyond the Wall," *USA Weekend*, November 1–3, 1996, pp. 4–5.

ACKNOWLEDGMENTS

As the Preface makes clear, the idea for this book and its title come from my father, Robert J. Burrell, who has never stopped trying to understand what prompts people to say what they say, or to figure out what in the world they mean by it. He passed some of this curiosity on to me, along with his scrapbook of "Words People Live By."

Frederick C. Mish generously took the time to read through a very early and quite lengthy draft of the manuscript. It was he who convinced me to press on, for which I am ever grateful. Many of the ideas, asides, and comments in the book grew out of conversations I had with my father and with Fred.

A few special people also deserve mention. My thanks to Jim Shields, Jonathan Walters, Peter Bloom, Ed Tornick, Janice Gatty, Sean Sutton, Jim McNamara, Shana Deane, and Anne Louise Kerr for their support, suggestions, patience, and understanding. Thanks also to John Thornton of the Spieler Agency and David Bernstein of The Free Press for ushering the manuscript from proposal to production.

Finally, I cannot adequately express my appreciation of the Forbes Library of Northampton, Massachusetts and the library facilities at Smith College, and my best wishes go out to the dedicated people who staff them.

INDEX

CREDITS